To Russ Eshleman,
my cousin from the
old country!

Victory Denied

Everything You Know About Iraq Is Wrong!

Roger T. Aeschliman

by

Roger T. Aeschliman

authorHOUSE®

AuthorHouse™
1663 Liberty Drive, Suite 200
Bloomington, IN 47403
www.authorhouse.com
Phone: 1-800-839-8640

First published by AuthorHouse 12/12/2007

ISBN: 978-1-4343-4894-4 (sc)
ISBN: 978-1-4343-4895-1 (hc)

Library of Congress Control Number: 2007909280

Printed in the United States of America
Bloomington, Indiana

This book is printed on acid-free paper.

DEDICATION

This book is dedicated to Robyn, Ryan and Regan - my family -
And to yours.
They are worth fighting for.
And to the United States Soldier, Sailor, Marine and Airman
Who are doing the fighting.

FORWARD

Even before leaving Iraq for home in November 2006 I had several invitations (or demands in some cases) to speak before civic, church, school and military organizations. My initial presentation was the first week back; 169 slides and a little discussion about my work there, taking about 25 minutes. Thirty-plus speeches later (with more yet scheduled), I am still showing my slides and explaining what things were like in Iraq my 366 days in theater.

When I wrote these weekly reports, personal cards and notes to family, friends and interested folk around the world it was just my way of trying to stay in touch. Really it was more for my own mental health than anything else. Just telling what actually happened, day-after-day, from the unique perspective of chief of the Joint Visitors' Bureau; a macro-view, one shared by only a handful of the highest ranking authorities in the country.

But as time passed I encountered other audiences. Can you imagine my confusion and sadness to face repeated questioning, time after time, speech after speech from people who insisted the war was lost and I was either wrong, misguided or just lying? "Iraq is a quagmire!" "We shouldn't be there." "What about all the massacres and torture by American soldiers?"

Most people are thrilled to hear that things are going well there and continue to improve despite the negative barrage from the national media. Hundreds have thanked me for my remarks and asked me (World War II and Vietnam veterans often with tears in their eyes) how come our own media aren't telling the whole story? Are they lazy? Opinionated? Desperate to be famous and to become the next nightly news anchor? Left-wing freaks who want to bring down President Bush no matter what it takes? Or just on the low IQ end of the food chain?

When I compiled this book and reread what I'd written over the 16-month tour, the totality of the message shook me. What I experienced in Iraq was nothing like what the people of the United States of America were hearing day after day. No one was telling the whole story of Iraq. In my speeches I often spread my arms far apart to demonstrate the ENTIRE story of the war and the country. This spread reflects the creation of governmental systems and processes at the local, provincial and national levels, the development of a robust and effective Iraqi military, the expansion of education and medical care nationwide, the infrastructure improvements of all types, and incredible economic growth. At the far tip of my right hand I hold my thumb and index finger about one inch apart.

That one inch reflects actual combat, insurgency and terrorist violence. Is that one inch real? Yes, and war is an ugly, terrible thing. Does that one inch accurately represent everything that the American soldier is doing in Iraq? HELL NO!

Your national media and the anti-war/peace-at-all-costs/can't we all just get along/America sucks claque are in an alliance to deny this American victory in Iraq, both rejecting its reality and working to keep it from coming about. It is time to change the debate and start talking about the war we have already won, the insurgency we are winning and the political future of the Mideast that we must win.

I never intended to write a book, but in this past year at home have come to believe the story must be told.

To all the readers of all those weekly reports I want to apologize and warn you that this book contains many personal letters and notes to many friends and associates you have not seen. There is some coarse language and I express many more opinions in them than I expressed in the weekly reports. I hope you won't think less of me for having actual feelings and passionate beliefs.

Finally, there are those so devoted to their ill-formed opinions that facts mean nothing to them and they will defend their ideology through any means possible. After one speech an irate audience member went so far as to write to the Adjutant General of the State of Kansas accusing me of abusing my military position and seeking to have me fired from the Army. This was at a civilian event, on my own time, I was wearing a suit and tie and in my actual remarks I made it clear I was acting as a civilian, not a soldier. So, in an effort to protect myself and both my civilian and military careers I offer the following disclaimer:

I am not writing or speaking on behalf of the United States Army, Government or the President of the United States, nor am I representing the Kansas Army National Guard, the State of Kansas or the Governor of our great state. My name is Roger and I'm a trust officer at a great bank in Topeka and everything that follows is my own civilian opinion.

Roger T. Aeschliman
October 2007

DEPARTMENTS OF THE ARMY AND THE AIR FORCE
LAND COMPONENT, JOINT FORCES HEADQUARTERS KANSAS
2800 SOUTHWEST TOPEKA BOULEVARD
TOPEKA, KANSAS 66611-1287

ORDERS 217-032 05 August 2005

AESCHLIMAN ROGER T MAJ 137 IN BN 02 HHC FWD2
(PWHT3-17F) 100 S 20TH ST KANSAS CITY KS 66102

You are ordered to active duty as a member of your Reserve Component Unit for the period indicated unless sooner released or unless extended. Proceed from
your current location in sufficient time to report by the date specified. You enter active duty upon reporting to unit home station.

REPORT TO HOME STATION: 15 August 2005 , 0137 IN BN 02 HHC M113 FWD 2, 5A, KANSAS CITY, KS
REPORT TO MOB STATION: 18 August 2005 , FORT SILL, OK
Period of active duty: Not to exceed 562 days
Purpose: OPERATION IRAQI FREEDOM (DEPLOY)
Mobilization Category Code: G
Additional instructions:

(a) Permanent Orders 164-28 HQ, Fifth U.S. Army, Fort Sam Houston, TX 78234-7000 dated 13 June 2005.
(b) Travel will be paid for one time travel from home duty station to MOB station and back and includes travel and per diem from home station/MOB station or duty location/ and return to home station as well as non-temp storage.
(c) Individual soldiers whose duty station is different from the MOB station will receive funding for one time travel and return from MOB station to the duty station using the above fund citation.
(d) Multiple trips such as soldiers who will visit installations across the country conducting inspections will be funded by the MACOMS'mission funding unless specific funding from ERF, has been provided by the Army Budget Office for the mission.
(e) Army One Source is available to assist Soldiers & family members to seek solutions in dealing with life's issues and questions during deployments.Contact by phone at (US 1-800-464-8107 or outside the US 1-484-530-5889). Call 1-800-336-4590 or check www.esgr.org for questions regarding your employment and re-employment rights.
(f) Government quarters and mess will be utilized. Government transportation is directed.
(g) Family members may be eligible for TRICARE(military health care)benefits. For details call 1-888-363-2273 or go to www. tricare.osd.mil/reserve/ or email TRICARE help@amedd.army.mil
(h) ARNG soldiers are authorized temp storage of household goods and special storage under Joint Federal Travel Regulation(JFTR) para U4770b.3. They are authorized storage of privately owned vehicles at government expense per JFTR, para U6566A2.The state or an Installation Transportation Office mustapprove all actions prior to anyone entering into a contract. Commanders & 1SG's must monitor closely to preclude costly mistakes by soldiers.

Additional instructions (cont):

(i) Bring copies of rental or mortgage agreement, marriage certificate, birth certificate, birth certificate of natural children, or documentation of dependency or child support. Bring copies of family care plans, wills, powers of attorney and any other documentation affecting the soldier's pay or status IAW FORSCOM Reg 500-3-3 (RCUCH)

(j) Pursuant to Presidential Executive Order 13223 of 14 Sep 2001, you are relieved from your present RC status and ordered to report for a period of active duty not to exceed 25 days for mobilization processing. Proceed from your present location in sufficient time to report by the date specified. If upon reporting for AD you fail to meet deployment medical standards (whether temp or perm med condition), then you may be released

(k) from active duty, returned to your prior reserve status and returned to your home address, subject to a subsequent order to AD upon resolution of the disqualifying medical condition. If, upon reporting for AD, you are found to satisfy medical deployment standards then you are further ordered to active duty for a period not to exceed (562) days, such period to include the period (NTE 25 days) required for mobilization processing.

(l) Unit is ordered to active duty on the effective date as indicated below. Unit strengths will not exceed the authorized level. Unit is mobilizing in support of current operations. Unit commander is authorized to appoint rear detachment personnel (1 soldier per company-80 or more personnel and 2 per BN HQ) for unit(s) deploying overseas or out of state only if the deploying unit meets all theater-directed personnel strength requirements, (m) exclusive of rear det personnel-unit is not authorized add'l personnel above the HQDA-directed mobilization requirement. Rear det pers will go to the mob station & complete mob processing & training. Upon validation of a unit, the mob station will cut TCS orders attaching selected rear det pers to the Mob station's U.S. Army Garrison with duty at home station. TCS order will state that the JFHQ-ST or RRC in the State/Region of their duty

(n) station maintains daily operational control and supervisory responsibility over rear det pers and are responsible for providing admin and logistical support requirements without CONUSA, FORSCOM and DA reimbursement. The TCS orders for the rear det pers will include the following: Soldiers are attached to the mob station's U.S. Army Garrison for the general admin of military justice, including legal asst, claims svcs, and TDS support.

(o) EXCESS BAGGAGE AUTHORIZED.

(p) Meals and lodging will be provided at no cost to the Soldier. Claims for reimbursement require a statement of non-availability control number.

(q) For unresolved pay issues, contact the ARNG Pay Ombudsman at toll-free1-877-ARNGPAY or by email at ARNG-MILPAY@ARNG-FSC.NGB.ARMY.MIL

(r) TRAVEL ADVANCE IS NOT AUTHORIZED. INDIVIDUAL'S GOVERNMENT TRAVEL CARD HAS BEEN CLOSED OR CANCELLED. INDIVIDUAL IS EXEMPT FROM MANDATORY SPLIT DISBURSEMENT. INDIVIDUAL MUST BE WILLING AND ABLE TO FUND THE TRAVEL EXPENSES INCURRED TO PERFORM THIS

DUTY OUT OF THEIR OWN PERSONAL FUNDS PENDING REIMBURSEMENT. IF UNWILLING OR UNABLE TO DO SO, CONTACT THE SUPERVISOR IMMEDIATELY TO HAVE THIS ORDER REVOKED.
ORDERS 217-032 HQ KS NG, OTAG, 05 August 2005

FOR ARMY USE
Auth:TITLE 10 USC, SECTION 12302/HQDA MSG 130523Z JUN 05 DAMO-ODM/:ORDTYP/ MOBORD/HQDA No. 872-05 ONE/OEF/OIF
Acct clas:
Off pay/alw: 2152010.0000 01-1100 P1X1A00 11**/12** VIRQ F9203 5570 S12120
Off tvl/pd: 2152020.0000 01-0000 P135198 21**/22**/25*** VIRQ F9203 5570
S12120
Off pay/alw: 2162010.0000 01-1100 P1X1A00 11**/12** VIRQ F9203 5570 S12120
Off tvl/pd: 2162020.0000 01-0000 P135198 21**/22**/25*** VIRQ F9203 5570
S12120
Sex: M
MDC: PM
PMOS/AOS/ASI/LIC: 19B , 3X , YY
HOR: TOPEKA KS66609
DOR: 28-APR-00
PEBD: 03-DEC-86
Security Clearance: S
Comp: ARNGUS
Format: 165

FOR THE ADJUTANT GENERAL:

\\\\\\\\\\\\\\\\\\\\\\\\///////////
\\\\ HQ, KSARNG //
\\\\ OFFICIAL //
\\\\\\\\\\\\\\\\\\\\\\\\///////////

WALTER H. FREDERICK, III
COL, GS, KSARNG
Deputy Chief of Staff for Personnel

DISTRIBUTION:
1-AGKS-DOP 1-USPFO-ARC-A
1-AGKS-DPOT 1-Each HQ
1-UNIT 1-Individual
1-NGB-ARO-D 1-Cdr, Mob Site

Dear (INSERT CUSTOMER NAME) July 13, 2005

It is with both regret and excitement that I tell you I have been called to active duty in the United States Army for service in Iraq. I want to make sure you are among the first to know. While I have been expecting this for some time, it has finally arrived with short notice.

My last working day here at Commerce Bank & Trust will be Friday, August 5. My infantry unit will train in the United States for several months and then deploy to Iraq with a tentative December date. This is estimated to be a year tour in Iraq and - including training time – I do not anticipate returning to work here until early 2007.

I have enjoyed working with you and want you to know that you remain in great hands. Kirk Johnson, Senior Vice President of the Investment Management Group, has personally selected (NAME) to fill-in for me while I am deployed. (NAME) has years of experience in the Trust and Investment Management Group and you can be highly confident they will serve you well. Please find their card attached for your convenience.

In addition, (NAME) will remain engaged as your primary contact for all critical matters of your account. You should contact her at any time with questions or if you need help of any kind. Her card is also attached and she can still be reached at 267-????.

Again, I appreciate having had the chance to serve as your Trust Officer and I look forward to resuming our relationship upon my return.

My Most Sincere Best Wishes,

Roger T. Aeschliman
Trust Officer

14 July 2005

Hello everyone,

Just wanted to advise everyone (feel free to spread the word) that I will mobilize on August 15, spend a few months at Fort Sill, OK, and then ship to Iraq in November/December timeframe for about a year in the country. Looking forward to seeing as many of you as possible before then. Best wishes, rog

Roger T. Aeschliman
Trust Officer
Investment Management Group
Commerce Bank and Trust
3035 S. Topeka Blvd.
Topeka, KS 66611
**

From: Michael Ryan
Sent: Friday, July 15, 2005 11:27 AM

So does this rule out the promotion possibility? I hope to see you before you leave.
**

Mike, The command selection board DID NOT consider for the Armor battalion after all so I am out the door. This will be a great chance for you to come visit in Baghdad. You could do the Ernie Pyle thing and write some really stirring works. rog
**

From: Michael Ryan
Sent: Friday, July 15, 2005 11:56 AM

I won't pester you any more today, but how's Robyn with this? And I do think I'd rather see you in Kansas, but thanks for the offer.
**

Mike, Robyn is the best woman in the world and maybe the best person overall. She is incredibly strong and determined. We have been talking and planning on this kind of thing since before we were married so she is generally ready (details of course but big picture fine). She also understands the reality of the threat level over there and how tiny of war this really is. If the USA were not there at all but the same things were happening it would barely make the newspapers (just another Podunk country in the middle of an annoying and failing rebellion). So, she is not terribly concerned about me, more about just being away for a year.

Robyn has a great network of friends and people to help. She will be fine. Ryan will be fine. Regan will be moopy for a while...Love to you and yours, rog

From: Tim A Dreiling
Sent: Thursday, August 04, 2005 2:51 PM
To: Roger T Aeschliman
Subject: with my gratitude...
Roger-

I haven't any blinders on when I view the world around me. I recognize that there exists on this planet fools who wish me dead because I don't follow their sort of paganism or thoughtlessly submit to their particular brand of mysticism. My destruction is their explicit and outspoken goal. That you are leaving your home, family and friends for such a long time prepared to kill fools who are bent on blindly following their "leadership"-- whose philosophy is based in anti-reason and anti-logic--in their mission to destroy us, is impossible to repay.

Because he said it so eloquently, I borrow from General John A. Logan in his General Orders No. 11: *"Let no vandalism of averice[sic], or neglect, no ravages of time, testify to the present, or to the coming generations, that we have forgotten, as a people the cost of a free and undivided Republic."* I, for one, will not.

Thank you for your, and your family's, sacrifice in the coming months.

Be safe,

Tim

05 SEPT 2005

What a whirlwind! I've been on Title 10 (Army active duty compared to Title 32, Army National Guard) for almost a month now. In that time I've been on duty in Kansas City, Topeka, Fort Sill, Kansas City, Fort Riley and Kansas City. I have completed administrative processing including medical, vision and dental screening and approval, financial preparation (turning on all the Army rules and benefits), and changing hats from civilian-citizen-soldier to full-time soldier.

The only major issue has been shifting the family from private health care to the military's contracted Tricare program. Robyn has become an Internet research wizard able to find clear answers otherwise not available through a living, breathing human being.

Until now about 50 of the leadership have been on Title 10 while the remainder of the deploying 450 soldiers in the 2-137th Infantry Battalion have been traditional Guardsmen. All 500 have continued to train and in the past ten days of "normal" annual training we all fired M-16 rifles, M-9 pistols, the M-249 SAW (Squad Automatic Weapon - a small machine gun), the M-60 machine gun (a workhorse dating back to Vietnam), the MK-19 a fully automatic grenade launcher that can throw 10 grenades in 10 seconds up to 4,000 meters (accurately), and the 100-year-old yet still incredible M-2 .50 caliber Browning Machine Gun. All of that training is "normal." We also did two 100 percent equipment show downs and were issued many new items for desert use, packed up and stored all equipment that is not going to go with us to Iraq (and that's a lot including all our Bradley fighting vehicles, desks, office supplies, etc.), filled out forms for security clearances, took formal military photos for use on missing in action forms, press releases for awards and home town news, and one nice color one for our families, and then finally shipped all our personal equipment and vehicles and weapons to Fort Sill. All of that is decidedly not normal for annual training.

We had a very nice formal going away ceremony at K-State in Bramlage. I was the primary planning officer and master of ceremonies. The Governor and the Adjutant General both attended and made very nice remarks. About 5000 family and friends were there including my wife and children, Robyn, Ryan, 13 and Regan 11. My mother and father and older brother and youngest sister also attended. A lot of tears in a lot of eyes. Although there is a small chance we will get a weekend pass to return home prior to actually shipping to Iraq it is remote so most of us considered this the last goodbye. (By the way at one point I introduced General Bunting as Colonel Bunting and was promptly "demoted" to sergeant by my commander. This demotion was very amusing to all and added a bit of needed levity at my expense. For the next few days every private walking by enjoyed saluting and sounding off: "Good morning SERGEANT…Sir!"

It has been very hard to be both citizen, soldier, part-time and full-time, reporting to the Kansas Army National Guard, the National Guard Bureau, Fort Sill, 5th Army, and FORSCOM (Forces Command). Too many bosses. Thank goodness that changes now. We will arrive at Sill Tuesday evening and just get on with it. In the next few months we will qualify on many weapons systems, train on medical care, learn hand-to-hand combatives, work on convoy operations, base camp security, entry point control, recognizing and reacting to IEDs (improvised explosive devices - whatever happened to mines and booby traps? Same thing…), and many other operational skills. Additionally I have been teaching myself Arabic. Very hard language. Nothing in common with English. Very difficult verb conjugation and the verb To Be is implied.

Well, tomorrow morning we all get on buses to Sill. It is probable that I will not return home for six to ten months depending on when my 2-week mid-tour leave is scheduled. In the big picture I expect to be a civilian again in early 2007.

I'll update you all about weekly and share some of my philosophy as time goes by. I'll only begin by saying that I believe this whole thing is a continuation of the global struggle for individual liberty and freedom that began with the reformation, led to the Magna Charta, the US Revolution, and all the changes from kings and dictators to democracies all over the world in the past 200 years. (The opinions expressed here are not official US policy).

Thank you all for your support and interest. Feel free to ask questions and suggest topics for weekly updates. Also, find attached two mug shots for your dart boards.

Major Roger T. Aeschliman
Armor, United States Army

Hello everyone. 10 SEPT 2005

We are wrapping up the first week of active duty training at Fort Sill, just outside of Lawton, Oklahoma. It has been – frankly – terribly boring. The first few days of any in-processing at any Fort are slow, tedious and require endless standing in line. In the past five days we have done complete and final medical, dental, audiology, and optometry for 500 plus soldiers, gotten additional shots and blood draws, and reviewed all our finances.

We've stood in line for three meals a day; we've moved into very old, worn out barracks and spent endless hours just cleaning the place up to a respectable Kansas standard. There is air conditioning and hot water but barely.

Joe (that's the affectionate name for the typical young private who is always central to the thoughts and plans of any good officer) has truly been bored senseless. All of these administrative hurdles must be cleared before any real training is allowed. When the Army mobilizes National Guardsmen into federal service it aggressively screens out soldiers who are either currently "broken" or who are likely to become so. If you can't do the mission you are sent back home off of active duty. This sounds harsh but it is not unlike the private sector: pre-existing conditions are not covered. The United States Government doesn't want to pay huge medical bills for people who were already hurt or sick prior to starting Army work.

So Joe has been bored. I, however, and the other leadership have been busting our tails planning training for the next two months, executing plans each day, and resolving problems that still exist between Kansas, Fort Sill, National Guard Bureau, and the 5th Army. A good day so far means a 0500 wakeup and a 2400 rack time into a warmish room and a coolish shower.

I have quietly ignored the physical training moratorium and have enjoyed quiet early morning or late evening (in the dark) runs and trips to the nearby base weight room. Other than peaceful encounters with the local skunk population (and they are the vermin de jour in the dry, hot low desert environment) the exercise has been good for the body and soul.

Yesterday all 500 Joes received their desert colored uniforms and that more than anything has increased the sense of reality for all this. The plan right now is to spend another 19 days here and then go to the National Training Center (NTC) in California (desert) for another month. When we land at the NTC we will have sent the Army forest green camouflage uniforms home to Kansas and will wear the desert tans. More on the NTC in future notes.

We were issued the newest ballistic protective vests (flak jackets). They are a remarkable protective system and are saving lives every day. More later. But that issue too has made people begin to think more intensely about the seriousness of the missions ahead.

Today is Sunday and the end of the first week. Our soldiers are getting their first time off with an on-post pass for four hours this afternoon to go bowling, or the movies, library, museum, PX, or gym. As we speak my boss, THE commander, (I'm number 2) and other subordinate leaders have headed out the door to the NTC for a recon and planning session for our upcoming training . . . so, I'm in charge right now and for the next week. If anyone returns drunk, leaves the base and is caught, or worst of all winds up DUI or injured, it's my head on the block. Say a special prayer for me tonight when we do our post-pass roll call.

Best wishes to all.

Roger T. Aeschliman
MAJOR, Armor

Hello everyone, 18 SEPT 2005

Well, they all arrived back at the barracks mostly sober and without incident. Whew. And the Chiefs looked good (and the Jets looked bad). The bad news is that we are letting Joe go on pass again as I write, to watch the Chiefs 7:30 p.m. kickoff on ESPN. We have a lot of Raider Haters as half of this battalion live in Kansas City or Lawrence.

Before I tell you about this past week let me give you a brief history. This battalion was essentially a walking infantry unit throughout its history. About two years ago it was selected to receive the Bradley Fighting Vehicle, the troop carrier that looks like a tank. As an experienced senior tank officer I was asked (ordered) to the Infantry to help them learn to become armored vehicle soldiers. Over the next year we trained up and became Bradley qualified. Then the Army – seeing a bunch of brand new Bradley's with a strong motivated unit – decided to send us to Iraq as part of the 1st Infantry Division (Big Red One) to be part of combat operations. We prepared to execute this in June, then were remissioned and told we would not take Bradley's and instead of heavy combat ops would instead do force protection missions – guarding other Americans as they rebuild and fix Iraq. Ok? Ok.

I can't tell you the specifics of our missions (and there are at least five now) but we will be doing all the things you see on TV: Gate guards, watchtower guards, convoy security, escorting VIPs and work parties.

This week, in the absence of most of the rest of the senior staff (remember them? At the National Training Center in California desert?) I was tasked to figure out two NEW missions on top of the ones we already knew about. So, I spent all week asking for official orders, calling all over the US to speak to mission planners, and making email contacts with the troops in Iraq currently doing these new missions. We NEED to be clear on what we are going to be doing OVER THERE so we can plan and implement our training over HERE. We also need to order any required equipment and tools (not everyone gets the same equipment – the Army is just like the private sector: you get the tools you need to do the job you're assigned). Now, with the whole team back at Fort Sill, I've handed it all over to the other planners and the balls are rolling.

In the meantime Joe and all his buddies went through range week. This means firing all our weapons and qualifying as skilled operators. M16 rifles (480 Joes), M9 9mm pistols, (50 Joes), and then M-203 grenade launchers (80 Joes). I qualified expert with my pistol (see photos) and fired the M-16 rifle (a shortened, modified version called the M4) for familiarization, not qualification, and hit targets. I also was able to fire the M203 grenade launcher (due to weight of rank and general nice guyishness) for a few practice rounds. The troops love it when an officer comes up to them and says "hey soldier, you are the expert, teach me how to use this weapon," and then they laugh at you when you miss everything. On this weapon the practice rounds shoot giant paintballs that look like orange fluorescent field chalk when they hit. The real ammo can accurately shoot out to 400 meters and when it explodes it will cause 100% deaths within 5 meters and 100% injuries within 10 meters. It is a dynamic resource to the men and they are good with them. (I hit two out of five walls at 100 meters; they hit 9 out of 9 from 100 to 400 meters. Feel good about your Army. They deserve it).

At night each 203 shooter was authorized 5 LIVE high explosive rounds. And when you see those blowing up 200 meters away and going BOOOOOOMMMM! It is dramatic. At the end of most Army shooting events there is a Mad Minute in which uncrated ammo is expended. It is controlled, aimed and good training – probably the closest we will come to battle short of it. You have to load, aim, shoot, continuously to the limits of your ability. Last night we had a 100 round mad minute with 10 shooters and as those rounds exploded all over the old hulk targets out in the impact area it makes you very glad you are an American, and not some Hajji trying to sneak in. (Hajji is a not affectionate nickname for the enemy in Iraq; not all Iraqis and not all Arabs, just the bad dudes). I was able to shoot three hot rounds and hit the target square on twice. HOOAH!!!

Well, it was a good week. We are much trained and are exceeding the post expectations for skill levels (down here they are used to mobilizing support units that don't typically fire weapons and do all the soldiers tasks we do – on a drill weekend they were driving trucks, hauling passengers, doing medical drills, fixing things like ash and trash units do).

That's enough for now, but here's a joke:

When the second graders came in from recess the teacher asked them each what they played and asked them to spell a word. If they spelled the word, they got a cookie.
"I was in the sandbox with Billy," said Joey.
"Good, spell sand," said the teacher.
"S-A-N-D," said Joey.
"Great, here's your cookie."

Billy said: "I played in the sandbox with Joey."
"Spell box."
"B-O-X."
"Good, here's your cookie. . . and Hajji, what did you do?" asked the teacher.
"Well, am wanting to be play wiff Beely and Jooey in de sandbuux, but they are being mean to me and are hitting me wiff rox and they spit on me."
"Oh Hajji, that sounds like blatant discrimination to me," said the teacher, "and if you can spell blatant discrimination . . . you can have a cookie."

Major Roger T. Aeschliman
Armor, United States Army

"Greetings All,

"Here's the latest from Fort Sill. I'm not too happy about the broken nose.

"Robyn"
**

Hello everyone, 25 SEPT 2005

Fort Sill is hot, dry and deserty, except for the tremendous thunderstorms that roll through; we got seven inches of rain one recent evening. As a desert it has all the desert things: tarantulas, scorpions, rattlesnakes, cactus. We have found scorpions and BIG tarantulas in the barracks and soldiers have nearly stepped on rattlesnakes out in the training areas. We will feel much safer in Iraq and are eager to be moving from here to the NTC for our collective (groups, teams) training rather than the individual soldier skills we have trained here.

This past week offered the chance to become crippled in several interesting ways. First we began training on "combatives," the Army's specific method of unarmed hand-to-hand fighting. The first, most important lesson is "DON'T!" Given any other alternative (shoot, grenade, run over them with a tank. . .), don't engage in hand-to-hand. Sounds pretty reasonable. The second lesson is that if you practice your skills you can protect yourself and harm your opponent with minimal effort. That sounds nice but I am crippled up from these two days. I was unfortunate enough to draw a former Marine Corps champion wrestler as my training partner. My 25-year-old high school wrestling skills and 44-year-old shoulders just couldn't stand up to his 25-year old shoulders and current skills. I was notionally killed three times in nine minutes. Humbling and eye-opening. In the attached photos you will see me getting my nose broken (again, what? for the 19th time?), me getting strangled, and then the smile of relief that I am finished with only a couple of pulled rib muscles, two achy rotator cuffs, and a mousy right eye.

A number of the troops trained on the MK-19, a rapid firing, grenade shooting machine gun. It will hit targets accurately out to 4,000 meters, heaving about 10 rounds in 10 seconds. Those explosions will injure everyone within ten meters (at least ruptured eardrums and concussion shock). We qualified nearly 50 of our 500 soldiers with this weapon and it will be mounted in the guard towers of the Baghdad area base we will be guarding. (No one was crippled – especially not me – during this training)

It was also a pleasure to receive a final round of inoculations. Shots for smallpox, anthrax and influenza. Even though they are important and even though the docs all swear they are inert, invariably everyone gets sick after a few days. It's just too much drag on your system and everyone gets susceptible to the common cold, so we all are slumping around sniffling and draining. YUCK! Only historically (because it is important) Benjamin Franklin wrote in his diary about how torn he was about the "new" treatment for smallpox in the 1750s. He knew that back then the pox killed 7 of 10 infected. He also knew the new "vaccination" (consisting of dragging a string through the nearly healed pus wound of a smallpox victim and then dragging it through a small incision in an otherwise healthy person) would cause illness in 2 of 3 inoculated, and death in 2 of 5 thus sickened. He finally decided to inoculate his young children and was relieved when they all survived. Smallpox is the only disease erased from earth (paid for by the USA mostly) (and Rotary is very close to eliminating Polio!) and none of *our* children have been inoculated against this disease. The remaining sources of the smallpox virus are supposed to be tightly controlled (CDC in USA and some spook place in Russia) but our own CDC website declares there is credible concern that it has been weaponized and that terrorists have obtained it. So, if you want *another* reason why I am honored to go do this mission it's because I love *my* children and like *most other* children as a general rule and I would do anything to ensure smallpox never ever emerges again. Speech over.

Fort Sill is an historic place, created as an early outpost against the Indians shortly after the Civil War. Phil Sheridan founded the place. There are early concrete guard towers still atop the nearby small mountain range. Geronimo surrendered here and spent his final years living in the prairie nearby. He is buried here with a very modest monument in a simple cemetery surrounded by wives, children and grandchildren. Many of them died from smallpox.

Major Roger T. Aeschliman
Armor, United States Army

"Greetings All,

"Roger's weekly update is posted below. I had several people who were unable to open the attachment so his update will appear in the body of the email message. The kids and I enjoyed spending some time with Roger over the weekend. Two days of leave isn't much but we were happy to take what we could get.

"Robyn"
**

Hello everyone, 02 OCT 2005

Another busy, sweaty week at Fort Sill beginning with grenade throwing, rocket shooting, and claymore mine exploding, mid-pointing with our formal departure ceremony from Fort Sill and culminating with a two-day pass back home, and then concluding with our return to Fort Sill today.

The troops trained hard this week with all soldiers getting final training. Because we are infantry and because we are pushy we requested a lot of additional training and with some surprise received it. Thus a number of our soldiers were able to train with real grenades, real AT-4 anti-tank rockets, and real claymore anti-personnel mines (which are truly cool and send several thousand buckshot sized steel balls out in an arc against the enemy foot soldier). About 125 soldiers were able to become combat-lifesavers - typical Joes given additional medical skills. This is about 25% of our unit, more than twice the Army standard of 10%.

We did a prevalidation meeting reviewing our overall status with the Fort Sill leadership and received their initial blessing that we have done what we were supposed to do here. So, on Thursday we participated in the formal departure ceremony from Fort Sill. Our commander was on emergency leave due to the death of his mother-in-law and I was asked to give the remarks to the unit. They follow at the end.

After the brief ceremony we all caught contracted school buses for home for a two-day pass. It was painfully short and this goodbye was even harder than the first one knowing now that it will be five weeks in the California desert and then 6-8 months more in Iraq before seeing Robyn and my children again. Robyn had a list of honey-do's for me, we went to the Tecumseh South Elementary School Carnival, and I was able to see the

Wildcats lose on TV. I wouldn't have traded it for anything. It was so nice to just be NORMAL and do NOTHING but sit around with my wife, kids and parents!

The school bus ride back was interminable and hard on butts and now we are back at Sill on Sunday night. There will be no sleep at all tonight as more than half of the unit concludes packing, empty their rooms and get on airplanes at 0300 Monday heading to the National Training Center at Fort Irwin, California. I'll be up seeing them off and then moving straight into Monday's training events for our remainder 1/2 personnel. Early Wednesday the rest of us leave this place for good and hit the ground in the CA desert. Right now it is cooler there than here. My departure ceremony remarks follow:

"Thank you COLONEL McDonald. On behalf of Lt Col. Jim Trafton I want you to know we appreciate your kind remarks. As infantrymen we are not used to hearing nice things said about us . . . and while we have been known to fall short on the social graces from time to time I assure you these men regularly overachieve in training . . . performance . . . esprit de corps . . . and mission accomplishment. "Thanks to the efforts of the entire Fort Sill and 5th Army teams we are leaving here today a better unit than when we arrived and we are teed up high for our collective training at the NTC . . . We ARE eager to move out into theater . . . I know I speak for every man here when I say the First Kansas Volunteers are ready to GET 'ER DONE! "We ARE ready for these missions . . .we are HONORED to be soldiers in the United States Army . . . we are GRATEFUL to be Kansans . . . and we THANK GOD we are Americans. "Do you know why we go to war? I'll show you. Soldiers, if you are a brother please raise your hands. If you're an uncle? Fathers? Grandfathers? "In my opinion we are engaged in a continuing epic struggle: the 500-year-old global battle for democracy and free enterprise, and individual freedom and liberty, over the forces of totalitarianism and dictatorship . . . This Global War on Terror is about more than Osama . . . Saddam . . . or Al Qaeda. It is about what kind of world our children, our grandchildren and all of their children will live in. Because WE go to fight now, I am confident our children will see a freer, more peaceful world. "Men, I can't tell you exactly what the next year holds, only that I know each and every one of you will do his duty with dignity, and will bring honor and glory to his family, city, state and nation . . . . I can tell you one thing . . . When our time comes and we get in line before St. Peter at the pearly gates and he announces "Oh Dear Lord, it's another one of those damn First Kansas Volunteers," the Great Lord God Almighty himself will leap from his golden throne and shout: "Throw the gates open wide . . . and all you REMFs step aside – THERE'S AN INFANTRY MAN COMING THROUGH."

Major Roger T. Aeschliman
Armor, United States Army

P.S. REMF is an acronym for Rear Echelon Mother - F-----! I was going to say P------, but there were too many General's wives attending...

Hello everyone, 09 OCT 2005

As I write this Sunday afternoon I am sitting in a connex (the ubiquitous cargo container seen on semis, trains, ships and ports all around the world) inside a two square mile fenced-in cantonment area at the National Training Center, Fort Irwin, CA, unaffectionately and accurately known as the "Dustbowl."

This area is the staging facility for all units arriving here to train. As a result of decades of traffic on this plot the dirt is finely ground red sandstone (a remarkable shade of pinkish-tan) that is fine enough to sift through solid glass. We are dirty and there's no getting around it. The Army has issued us all several pairs of sunglasses, goggles and ballistic eyewear and we are using it all to keep our eyes protected.

My connex is air-conditioned, has lights and electrical outlets, doors and windows. I can't complain, except that I'm sleeping on a standard Army cot which my wife will tell you means I'm not sleeping. Given a few more days I'll wear out and begin to sleep well. Joe is sleeping in one of two dozen circus tents that really are pretty nice, with a carpeted floor, lights and electrical drops. Behind the tents are the 200 vehicles we just drew today from the central motor pool here to train on. There are 500 of us. This area can hold 4,000 and several other units are on the way.

Most of the Joe's arrived at Irwin last Monday morning. I was awake all Sunday night seeing them off on the airplanes from Fort Sill. Later Monday I jogged out (six-miles round trip) with the Chaplain to see Geronimo's grave. This is a rite of passage at Fort Sill that typically means busing out there then running back three miles. Few people run the whole six miles. While everyone in the unit talked about doing it I think the Padre and I were the only ones who actually did. It was hot and windy. After we cleaned up and offered prayers of gratitude for our survival we drove back out to take the photo you see attached.

The rest of us left Sill early Wednesday arriving at Irwin with most of the day ahead of us. I promptly had a relapse, suffered terribly for two days and now am on antibiotics for what my good Dr. Doug Iliff will recognize as my semi-annual, incapacitating sinus infection. As of now I am much improved and can speak a language other than frog. The miracle of the Z-pack. (By the way, if you need a wonderful personal physician in the Topeka area, Doug Iliff is erudite, conservative, Christian and a fun guy. I commend him to you.)

Since arriving here we have prepared to move further out into the desert to begin the training required for Iraq: convoy operations, recognizing and reacting to improvised explosive devices, raids, search, entry control point security, watch tower duty, and more. Vehicles today, MILES equipment (the Army's laser tag system for individuals and vehicles) tomorrow, formal in-briefing and training schedules the next day and then we get to the real work. About two weeks out in "the box", as the remote desert training areas are known. (And not to be confused with Iraq which is called the "Sandbox.")

It is the real desert here, with sand, dirt, bare rocks, mountain ranges, cactus and Joshua Trees, 2 scorpions, four rattlesnakes, and a rare desert tortoise that is protected and offers the promise of $10,000 fines and imprisonment if you so much as think about one. There is a silly little one-foot high fence along both sides of the small highway leading from Barstow to the NTC. It is intended to keep the tortoise from becoming road kill. Along the same 30-mile road (that goes solely to the NTC and nowhere else) are several dozen white crosses. One for every traffic fatality – usually young soldiers returning from Barstow or Vegas too late and too drunk. But if you were stationed out here you would probably drive the two hours to Vegas as often as possible; there is simply nothing to do at this desolate and isolated post. Check out Fort Irwin on Mapquest.com to see what I mean.

My best to you all.

Roger T. Aeschliman
Major, Armor

"Greetings All,

"Here is this week's update. Photos are in a second email. Roger will be out in the desert for the next few weeks so we don't know if he will have the opportunity to do an update or not. I will keep you posted if I hear from him.

"Thanks,
"Robyn"

**

Hello everyone, 16 OCT 2005

The National Training Center (and oh by the way I am feeling great and am now getting four or five real hours of sleep a night so that's all good) is about 40 miles by 40 miles, the final remnant of the enormous desert training center created by General George S. Patton at the onset of World War II. THAT training center was centered on Indio California and covered most of southern CA, Nevada, and chunks of Utah, Arizona and even New Mexico.

He planned on training men on one quart of water a day to get them used to the North African desert invasion that happened on November 11, 1942 (Patton's birthday). Today we force drink soldiers about six liters of water a day, even though it is only in the low-mid 80s. It is simply too dry out here. Almost no one sweats (including me and I am a horrible, sweaty guy) because the water leaps from your pores and evaporates without you noticing it. Thus one can dehydrate quickly. We are happy so far that no one has suffered any heat/dehydration problems. It is a focus for us here and in Iraq (which runs a about 10-12% humidity too).

This past week we First Kansas Volunteers hung MILES on our vehicles, our weapons and on ourselves. This means when we do our real war games in the box, aim a weapon and squeeze the trigger, a laser beam (invisible and eye-safe) shoots out. If you aim accurately the beam will hit a sensor on a person or a vehicle and that person or vehicle will be injured, killed, damaged or destroyed. Then we have to exercise our medical personnel and vehicle recovery personnel to take care of the "wounded" soldier or "disabled" vehicles. This all adds additional realism and allows us to learn hard lessons the easy way. No one has to die to learn not to be stupid.

As I write this we have not begun this training. When we do we will be leaving the base before 0530 every day in order to be at the distant training sites by 0800, training through all the daylight and returning again in the dark to a late chow around 2100 (9 p.m.) or so. With the remaining hours of the day we will need to (in sequence) fuel vehicles, maintain vehicles, eat, personal hygiene, sleep, rise, prepare to move, eat, and then move out again. This will continue for 14 days.

Additionally there is no cell phone coverage out there and certainly no Internet. I've already told Robyn and the kids that I may not be in touch for a couple of weeks. And I may not be able to write…we'll see.

What follows now is not complaining or whining. It is a little bit of how the Army works and doesn't work. IF you are a normal National Guard unit and are called up to Iraq you report to one Army base and go through between 3 and 6 months of training. At that "mobilization" site you get resources thrown at you. You don't provide your own mechanics, cooks, medics, trainers, refuelers, ammo handlers, water providers. The Army takes care of you so all you have to do is train on your specific theater missions. IF you are normal.

We are a very special unit. Our battalion (and two others) were selected to do individual soldier training at Fort Sill, followed by collective (squad, platoon, company) training here at the NTC. The NTC has not done much of this theater specific training to this point, and it is my understanding they have never been a mobilization site. They are working hard to figure it out. We are fighting hard to keep from getting task after task to support our own training and be our own trainers. So far it's been a losing cause. We are doing details and support missions and are apparently going to be our own primary trainers.

There will be NTC observer-controllers with us all the time who will advise and coach. That helps. The good news is that we know how to train and we have a lot of expertise throughout the Battalion so by the end of the two weeks I am confident we will be certified as fully qualified to move into Iraq and do the missions assigned. It's just a lot more work to have to do everything yourself when you would really rather just be learning and training. Again, not complaining. The other good news is that by this method we are only preparing for about 2 ½ months rather than 4 or 5. Sooner out the door, sooner home!

American by birth; Soldier by choice; Volunteer by God!

Roger T. Aeschliman
Major, Armor

Hello everyone from the First Kansas Volunteers,

A week ago Saturday my unarmored, Hajji-style Humvee was struck by a rocket propelled grenade (RPG). I was seriously wounded and because I failed to receive treatment within twenty minutes I died from my wounds. Throughout this week I have been the victim of mortar shrapnel, IEDs (improvised explosive devices), VBIEDs (vehicle borne improvised explosive devices), sniper fire, rifle fire, and grenade attack. In all of these cases I was either killed outright or later died of untreated wounds.

These field exercises are ***THE*** critical piece of our mobilization training. We are learning to recognize threats, react to them aggressively, defend ourselves and strike back. On the very first day we learned the importance of rapid medical treatment for casualties and the barriers to gaining rapid treatment when you are 30 or 50 miles (or 200 in Iraq) away from a surgical suite. This has been another of those eye-openers for most of our soldiers.

Army training is based on classroom, crawl, walk, run. In this model so far I have trained on convoy operations, culminating in a real bullets exercise in which we drove through a town full of static "civilians" to spare and pop-up "hajjis" to kill. With seven or eight people all firing real bullets from the same truck at the same time, safety controls are critical. But it is very close to what we will do if attacked during an Iraq convoy. We also conducted Joint Visitor's Bureau (JVB) operations – the mission I will most often perform in Iraq. Our small convoy picked up and escorted a series of distinguished visitors (DVs) (including our own Kansas real Brigadier General Jon Small who was visiting his Kansas boys down here) to "meetings" with "Iraqis," sadly resulting in numerous IEDs, mortars, sniper attacks, and suicide bombers. The good news is that our DVs were never injured or killed. The more good news is that EVERYTHING about the training here at the National Training Center is harder and less pleasant than the mission we will face in Iraq. In Iraq, the bad guys simply don't have the resources to try to kill the DV and us seven times during one four-hour mission. In fact, the word from Iraq is that 99 of 100 missions are completely uneventful. Big difference! The attached photo is me with two Iraqi-Americans who are well paid by Raytheon to role-play on the NTC battlefield. In this event one was the mayor and the other was his senior aide. They laughed at my Arabic but praised me for trying and said that even the effort to speak would be appreciated and useful in Iraq.

At the same time all this training is going on our soldiers continue to be real people with real problems. Sprained knees, twisted ankles, bruised tailbones from the training, and the real world birth of children, the pending divorces, the court-ordered removal of children from the home, and most tragically, the in-Iraq combat death of one of our 45-year-old soldier's sons. With a population of more than 500 people, life and all its tragedies and joys, goes on regardless of the deployment. A key task of leadership here is to stay hard-wired to the men so we can help them through these times. One little example is my daily birthday list. I was a bit bummed out when my October birthday passed unnoticed by the entire battalion. No one deserves to be invisible on their birthday and I vowed and have kept it that I would personally wish every man here a happy birthday, shake their hand and tell them how proud I am of them and appreciate their sacrifices. This has meant staying up late, making several attempts to find people and leaving notes that "the Major" wants to see them. But you should see their faces shine and their eyes light up when it happens. One young fellow just turned 21 (he was called in to our unit as a Reservist from another state – not a volunteer – we have 30 of these) and has not yet made many friends. With tears in his eyes he told me his life story and how grateful he was that someone remembered. I called his immediate team around and broke open a box of cookies and when I left there was a small birthday party going on. It's not much but it may make a difference over the course of the year.

This week I received mail from Robyn, Rick (my brother), Kirk Johnson (my boss at Commerce Bank and Trust in Topeka – and if you don't bank with us, you should and you should see Kirk about your trusts and wills and investments too . . .) and my mother's sister, my Aunt Nancy (as opposed to my father's sister, my Aunt Nancy – who were both in my parent's wedding long, long ago, as a pair of Nancy flower girls). Thanks to you all and if I can get out of the dirt long enough to get to the PX for some stamps and stationary I'll write personal notes back. (It's about midnight as I write this and we get up again at about 0400.)

American by birth; Soldier by choice; Volunteer by God!

Roger T. Aeschliman
Major, Armor

Hello everyone (now with readers in Africa, Europe, and Central America),
30 OCT 2005

When you are in the field continuously for five, seven or ten days three things become of paramount importance (stop reading here and go on to the third paragraph if bodily functions are disturbing to you): eating, sleeping and good bowel movements. Ask anyone who has ever been through basic training. *If* you can get enough calories, and *if* you can get four *uninterrupted* hours of sleep a night, and *if* your digestive system is nice to you, you can function a long time despite discomfort.

If any of these three break down you can expect to be exhausted, dysfunctional and miserable. This week I struggled through about three days of unsatisfactory latrine usage. On the fourth morning we rose about 0300 hrs (3 a.m.), were in bouncy and rough-riding Hummers at 0400, and at 0500 (with 90 minutes of travel still to go) my system decided it was time for relief. In agony I suffered every rock, wadi (gully/wash/arroyo), every bone-jarring bounce for 90 more minutes. As a Major and the ranking official I almost ordered a stop for my own personal relief and was enormously pleased to arrive at our training site just as I opened my mouth to do so. I was also relieved of embarrassment as another 10 or 15 soldiers all sprinted for the closest wadi. The lucky ones found a smooth, flat rock to sit out over, the unlucky squatted and prayed not to soil their trousers and boots.

So, food, sleep and daily constitutionals keep an Army moving. And coffee too.

This week concluded our hard field training at Fort Irwin. I trained with one company (Bravo Company out of Wichita – the Bizerkers (I know it's not spelled right but that's how they do it)) the entire time as this is the Joint Visitors Bureau mission unit that I will most often work with in Iraq. Most of you know I was a career tanker (an officer that moves, shoots and communicates from a tank) and have been working with this Infantry Battalion almost two years now. As tanker there are a number of common skill sets with Infantry, but a great number of differences. As a tanker you are never trained to raid a town, go door-to-door, or to shoot a huge variety of weapons (just a tank and a pistol in Armor).

When I announced I intended to do all the training the Bizerkers were going to do I was highly discouraged by the other senior battalion leaders for a number of reasons. One, they thought I was too old and would get hurt (45 is pretty old to be jumping out of a 5-ton truck or raiding cave tunnels); two, they thought I would be interfering with the planning and operations of the younger Company Commander Captain, his Lieutenants and Sergeants; and third, they thought I would be more useful around the headquarters doing paperwork, planning, reports and investigations. I disagreed and had the best two weeks of training in my entire military career.

I initially met with the Company commander, the Lieutenant I would be "assigned" to, and the Staff Sergeant/Squad Leader who would be my direct "boss." I told them four things: 1 – I was to be considered the lowest ranking person in the company for training purposes; put me where you want me and assign me any duty. 2 – I would in no way interfere with or exert my authority over anyone in the Company at any time. 3 – I would hold my opinions to myself and would only make the suggestions and recommendations that a private in a similar situation would make (and that turned out to be the hardest part). And 4 – that I had three reasons for wanting to train with them the entire time: A – I needed to learn the fundamental Infantry skills to improve my chances of survival and mission success in Iraq. B – I needed to see the training the men were receiving and the difficulty of the work so I can better understand how things really are and how they will work. And C – and to me most importantly – I wanted to prove to these young men that I have what it takes. When I show up for a senior escort officer mission in Iraq, I need them to think "Great! Here's the Major. Here's another warrior to help us get the job done," not think "Oh hell, here's the Major. Now we've got to worry about taking care of him too."

So though I am exhausted this Saturday morning, October 29, having slept about 10 hours the last five days, I did complete short range rifle fire training (18 of 18 rounds in the expert zone), 4-man team live fire in urban areas, platoon (30 Joes) urban patrolling and combat, and Company (110 Joes) raids on a cave and a town. As a private I led on point several times, humped a radio around for a day, and held precarious positions for hours at a time. During one terrible battle with the Iraqi-American "insurgents" I was surrounded by dead and wounded Americans, running out of ammunition and yet required to hold the position. Because of the previous ten days of training I was able to pick up a Squad Automatic Weapon (SAW) (which I had never even seen before as a tanker) load it up and continue to protect the entire rear of the Company. The next day I was assigned as a number four person into a cave. In the smoke, dust, dark and confusion I found myself as the lead man, stepping over the wounded and dead heading into unknown tunnels. When it was all over I had survived the entire week alive and unwounded. Score: Roger about 10 – Hajji 0.
None of that is intended to be bragging. I was not trying to Rambo anything. I was just a Joe doing my job and I have a better picture of how hard Joe's job is. I was very gratified to hear from a dozen or so of the young soldiers and sergeants that they were pleased to serve with me and eager to do so in the future, and especially how thrilled they were to see a senior officer not just watching the training, but doing ALL of it with them. I met my goals and had a lot of fun. Kind of like fishing: the worst day

in the field doing real Army work is better than the best day in the command post doing paperwork.

Sorry this one's so long. Just wanted to explain the last two weeks. The next one may be in a week or not. Sometime in the next 5-6 days I move to Kuwait and may not be in Internet range for awhile. Thanks to Dad, Dr. Doug Iliff, Becky Evans (the single hot nurse), Mark Harris (who can do anything for you in the car business), and Jerry Lonergan (a great friend and co-worker over the years) for the cards, notes and articles. Always good to hear from everyone. You might was well hold off for a while now until I get set in Iraq. Anything mailed for the next two weeks or so has a high probability of getting lost.

American by birth; Soldier by choice; Volunteer by God!

Roger T. Aeschliman
Major, Armor

These gentlemen are Americans of Kurdish-Iraqi descent. They and many others role-played both civilians and terrorists during our training at Fort Irwin, CA.

"Good Morning All,

"Here is a mid-week update from Roger minus the mushy love note he sent me. ☺ As I write this he is enroute from California to Frankfurt, Germany to Kuwait then on to Baghdad. I'll keep you posted as I hear from him.

"Robyn"
**

Hello everyone, 02 NOV 2005

As I write this I am in the final packing stages and preparing for a 0330 Thursday, November 3 flight out of Victorville, CA. It has been a fast and short week. I'm writing so Robyn has something to blast out in the event our travel to Kuwait makes it impossible to be in touch on Sunday.

It has been hard training and useful. I believe we are a much better unit now than we were three months ago when this all began. That is important because we are going to a real war in a real war theater. There are people dying for freedom over there. Just a reality check for everyone: the three units that have done this mission before us (including the current one) have suffered one or two combat fatalities (out of about 500 men) and about 5% wounded rate. While that is pretty low historically compared to other wars it is our daily reminder that this is for real.

The difference between the two sides is amazing clear: We and our Iraqi allies are willing to fight and if necessary die so that their own children, even the children of terrorists, will have the chance to grow up free, exercising free will, making individual choices. The terrorists are willing to kill other people's children so they can have their way and enforce their beliefs on the entire world. What's the confusion?

What follows is a hastily written rant I sent when my dear friend Mike Ryan in Georgia asked me what it was all about. It is not literature but I think it gets to the heart of why I go to this war at this time.

Mike,

The Code of Hammurabi, written more than 4,000 years ago in Iraq, is the earliest recorded effort by man to create rules that would apply to all. Before then (and for most of recorded history since) humans have survived under the iron and usually terrible rule of "Power." One powerful person, usually a man, ruled all at his whim. If you were "in" you were going to do just fine. If you were out, you were probably going to be destitute, enslaved or dead.

Even the Greeks and Romans, long praised for their innovations in democracy, had kings, Caesars or dictators. Even in their enlightened states the man in charge had the power to throw down competitors, give away their lands and estates, enslave, exile or kill them. History is often an ugly thing.

This pattern was world-wide, across all cultures. A chief may have had counselors but the bottom-line was absolute power held in the hands of the few over the many.

While there were many wars and conflicts over the millennium they were almost never about liberty or freedom and almost always were about power – those without seeking it from those with or those with inflicting it on those without. No serious challenge to the rule of "power" was seen until the development of Christianity as a revolutionary idea of individual freedom and responsibility. Not until the Magna Charta in 1215 did the higher ranking subordinates of kings first throw off some of the shackles. Not until 1314 at Bannockburn did we see the Scots rise up in a limited sense of freedom based on nationalism (but even they were internecine squabblers based on formal clans). Not until the Reformation in 1517 did religious leaders begin a serious examination of their doctrines leading to an examined faith. Not until the English Civil War in 1642 did the ideas of real democracy begin to root in Western Civilization. That war set into motion the American Revolution, the French Revolution, and all the wars of liberation since. The US Civil War is an example of revolution against what might at least be called "perceived" tyranny.

There have been many revolutions over the past 200 years that simply exchanged one dictator for another. They are not the point.

The point is that after 5,000 years of recorded human history it is only in the last 400 years that the world began to move away from the "power" rule of the one, or the clan, or the tribe; the rule of the "them" over all the rest of "us." Only in the last 400 years have we begun to see the rule of law over the rule of caprice. It is really only in the last 50 years that we have seen true leaps of personal responsibility and liberty over the control of the "power."

I believe that history will record the time from 1700 to 2100 as the Great War for Freedom, of which this current effort against fundamentalist, Wahhabist,

Baathist, Muslim, non-state terrorists in Iraq is just another Theater of that War. We are naïve if we think the current combat is somehow individually special; The Great War, the War to End all Wars, is already forgotten and World War II is fading rapidly from human awareness and into remote history.

If this current war is only about 9/11 or Saddam or Osama, then it is only revenge and the strong subjugating the weak. Fortunately I believe this current war is important in the greater sense as a part of man's struggle for liberty.

Because men and women have fought and died for freedom, especially in the last 300 years, the world has moved systemically away from the mercurial whims of the powerful at the expense of the weak. It is still happening today, hopefully accelerated by the advance of telecommunications. The youth of the world will see life in the USA and will want our lifestyle. They will demand freedom. I believe Iran is the best example of this. That country is boiling now and the children will take it over soon from the mullahs. They already did in the late 70s by deposing the Shah.

Those who would oppose this global tide will be swept into the ash heap of history as Reagan said. Time is against them.

Finally, our opponent at this time was often in history the most powerful force on the planet – often to great good. The Sumerians, the Assyrians, the Caliphates, the Ottomans. Their developments in the arts, sciences and reason were incredible. But something happened 1,200 to 1,400 years ago and despite their military reach their culture froze in time. They have never had a renaissance or a reformation. They live an unexamined faith, an unquestioned faith, an obedient faith. Islam needs a reformation.

It took nearly 1,000 years for Western Civilization to adapt and shape into its present form, to move from being owned/controlled to being prepared for individual liberty, democracy and free enterprise. We mustn't be short-sighted as we fight now for an extension of these noble principles. It's probably the only thing worth fighting for."

Thanks to my Aunt Janie Evans and my baby sister Karen for their letters, and to Robyn for the monthly magazine bundle, and to Mom for the goodie box. Lots of happy soldiers shared those!

I'll write again about the trip if things come together. If not, I'll be in touch when I can.

American by birth; Soldier by choice; Volunteer by God!

Roger T. Aeschliman
Major, Armor

Somewhere enroute

DATE: Nov. 3, 2005 8:12 a.m.

TO:Everyone on Robyn's list

This is Michael Ryan in Augusta, Ga. I don't know if anyone else has anything like this planned, but I would like to put together a cash gift for Robyn. Roger is being pulled away from supporting his family in order to serve all of us and help freedom get established in a very uncivilized part of the world. I don't know what the military pays him, but I have to guess his considerable physical sacrifice is being joined by a considerable financial sacrifice.

If you would like to contribute to a gift for Robyn and the kids please send it my way and I will pool our cash and send it all to Robyn.

When I went to Vienna to write my book on pure speculation, and I couldn't afford it, Roger helped put together a roast of me to raise money. Payback is hell, baby. Or sometimes pure heaven. Roger is my hero, my best friend and a great leader and a great American. I'll overlook the fact that he's a lousy dancer and can't carry a tune. I never dated him anyway. But I love him with all my heart.

Here's my address. I will not only take good care to pass along your gifts, but will add to them.

Michael Ryan
Augusta GA

"Greetings All,

"I spoke with Roger a few times over the last several days as he traveled from California to Kuwait. He called from Gander, Newfoundland, then again from Kuwait when they landed there. He called early this morning and was able to talk a short time before the line was disconnected (see his message below). The good news is his calling card seems to be working and while the Internet access is available it is in heavy demand. Please feel free to send me emails and I will forward them on to him and I will let you know a mailing address as soon as he is located in Baghdad.

"Thanks to everyone who has sent him a note or email and has offered support to the kids and I over the past week. This one was rough. It's one thing to have him gone but still in the states – sort of like an extended business trip. But knowing that he is halfway around the world has been difficult for the three of us. So . . . thanks for all your words of encouragement, support and most importantly – prayers.

"Robyn"
**

Hi Darling, Hi Kids,

Sorry the phone disconnected. The service here is wireless and runs off of a big tower right outside my tent. It is very windy and everyone cut out at the same time. SO, things are fine. I tried to get back on but couldn't. I'll try again when I leave this Internet service (free, but crowded) here. See the attached newsletter; no photos yet. Please do send me email notes at any time so I have something to look forward to. Love you guys, rog/dad

Greetings from Camp Buehring, Kuwait; 05 November 2005

From the time I left my NTC hooch at 2:30 a.m. Thursday with my bags, the bus ride to the airport at Victorville, the series of six hour flights to Gander, Newfoundland, to Rhamstein, Germany, to Kuwait International Airport, Kuwait City, the bus ride to Camp Buehring through the both the urban AND trackless desert, then the hasty in-briefing, it was a full 30 hours of travel from bunk to bunk. Most of it in the dark it seemed.

So we are seriously jet-lagging today and a bit lost in this isolated desert forward operating base of the United States military. Buehring is the furthest north of the several Kuwait staging camps where those inbound and outbound Iraq stop and regroup prior to moving on. Today it is nearly 90 degrees and the wind is blowing up what we are told is a very minor dust storm. We are in a 16-man tent with wooden floors and a limited air conditioning system that is saving our lives.

This Camp appears to have everything you could want – big, plentiful mess halls, exercise and rec centers, movies round the clock, food court, hot showers in trailers. There is a limited ability to use either paid or free Internet and phones (you wait for an hour on the free stuff). Everything except the slightest sign of anything green. Flying in over the Persian Gulf it was 1000 miles of tan. Kuwait City runs for miles along the Gulf and it is all tan. Every building, dust mote, sand speck and rock is tan. Incredibly the sand is a finer texture than the dust at NTC. We have been here less than 24-hours and are already coated with dust. It is on my Ipod in a Ziploc bag, inside a computer bag, inside a closed Samsonite carry-on case. Geez. The tent is completely closed in (it has windows but the dust would be horrific) and the AC helps mitigate the airborne effects of the dust but it shuffles underfoot despite our already desperate sweeping attempts.

So, my 25 traveling companions on the advanced party and I agree: This place sucks too and we are eager to move on into Iraq. Perhaps this is the Army's way of encouraging us along, by making each place a little worse than the next. As I have said before, all reports from our station in Iraq indicate a much nicer billeting and living condition than anywhere we have been so far.

This is clearly NOT a hot zone of the war. While there is good base security with fences, guards (and the two-hour drive through the desert that concludes with a five mile drive on the worst dirt and rock road I have ever seen that can still be called a road), and armed reaction forces, we are not wearing any of our bullet and shrapnel resistant hero gear, and most soldiers walk around in their PT (physical fitness) uniform. We do carry our rifles and pistols everywhere but that's just so we don't lose them as we are not authorized ammo down here.

The in-briefings included all the normal stuff: don't look at Muslim women, don't show the bottom of your feet, don't play with the vipers, do be nice to the Kuwait people as they are our allies (which is easy as we don't see any Kuwaitis being two hours from Kuwait City and in that all the unarmed worker-bees out here appear to be contractors from Indonesia, Pakistan and India, while the armed guards are American contractors).

So, I'm here. The main body follows soon and we will all stage and train a bit more before heading north to take over from the Texas National Guard unit that has been doing the job. They are eager to get home and we are ready to start.

Everything in this note is first impressions; I'll update as things change. By the way kids, one of the in-flight movies was Napoleon Dynamite! I laughed and laughed while everyone else thought I was crazy.

My best wishes to everyone. I'll send an address along in a few weeks.

American by birth, Soldier by choice, Volunteer by God!

Roger T. Aeschliman
Major, Armor

"Greetings all,

"Attached and copy/pasted is this week's update. Roger sent a number of photos which I will forward as well. They are bunched up in groups of two. Sorry for the download time for those of you on dial-up. We spoke with Roger this morning before leaving for church and he sounded upbeat and excited about what he is doing. Communication is good by both email and phone so we've been talking regularly. I am very grateful that he is able to stay in touch with us so easily. He called and spoke with Ryan after his performance in The Music Man on Friday night and that just made Ryan's day. ☺

"His new mailing address is:

MAJ Roger Aeschliman
B Co 2-137 INF
APO AE 09342-1400

Many of you have asked for care package ideas and I will put together a list for you over the next few days.

"Thanks,
"Robyn"
**

Greetings from Baghdad! 13 NOV 2005

I could write a book about these last seven days and not scratch the surface so let's just do a travelogue of sorts.

1 – Sat around Camp Buehring Kuwait for 36 hours bored. Watched two movies, jogged around the perimeter and looked out over the berms into 50 miles of terrible wind-swept desert. Decided to leave.

2 – Set staff to work moving me and the Battalion Sergeant Major into Iraq.

3 – Minivan to Doha to try and find Battalion property and to learn how to get required items issued. Passed the info on and then rode around the desert for a while to Camp Ali Al Salem, a staging area and airport for units moving into and out of Iraq. Slept in a tent with a bunk (mattress!) for four hours then up to get on a stand-by C-130 to Baghdad International Airport.

4 – Short 90 minute flight to BIAP (as the airport and entire military area around it is known). Called number of Texas unit we are replacing and was greeted with "Yee Haas! of joy. Wonderfully received by these hard-working Combat Engineers. They are truly happy to see us because it means they are really going home soon. Until your replacements arrive and you train them there is always the chance you will be extended in country. They are lucky. They will be heading home just short of 11 months on the mission.

5 – Moved straight into another connex; napped for three hours. Ate, showered, walked around on a brief tour of the Joint Visitors Bureau in a small palace in the Baath Party Lakeland area full of palaces and villas. Again, I encourage you to search for Camp Victory and Camp Slayer on the Internet. There are unclassified satellite photos showing where all this is. The entire area around BIAP is one giant US/ Coalition base camp with tens of thousands of servicemen and women of all branches and two dozen allied nations. It is all surrounded by double or even triple walls emplaced by the Saddam regime and improved or maintained by the USA and allies. Each Camp there represents a section of the wall to be guarded and people inside to be protected. Our guys will guard Camp Slayer and will also run the Joint Visitors Bureau in Camp Victory as well as a couple of other force protection missions.

6 – Had a great night's sleep on a bunk with a mattress! Had two hot showers in two days! Had two hot meals in one day!

7 – Drove around all of Camp Victory to see the lay of the land. This is palace central and I will be working right across a lake from the palace of General Casey, the commander of the Multi National Forces – Iraq (MNF-I). We will work in his chain of command as a strategic asset moving, housing and caring for distinguished visitors to the country. More later.

8 – Slept.

9 – Moved into a villa out in the middle of a lake temporarily. Am sleeping in a room most certainly occupied by Saddam, using his shower and toilet (and the toilets here are awful-more later).

10 – Met with the Texas commander (Col Sanders ☺) and discussed transition training. We agree to begin ASAP. More training is better than the minimum.

11- Met with all the subordinate Texas commanders and reviewed their operations, their gates, towers, logistical sites, planning centers. Prepped them to receive the Kansans. Camp Slayer is at the southeast corner of the airport area and thus has major walls to guard east and south and some lesser walls north and gates onto the famed Route Irish that runs from the airport into the equally famed Green Zone downtown where all the ministries and embassies are.

12 – Went on a JVB mission to transport the Polish Minister of Defense to meet with the Iraqi Minister and later with General Casey. By Blackhawk helicopter. The minister is US educated and at a press conference in English indicated the Poles are here to stay to the end (this in response to the Ukrainians who announced the mission is complete and they are ready to head home with their 800 troops). See attached photo or photos depending on what Robyn wants to pass on.

13 – Ate hot food. Had a hot shower. Slept in a comfy room. Did laundry.

14 – Jogged twice around Camp Victory shielded by the 20-foot-walls looming in all directions, past many palaces and villas including one bombed out wreck in the middle of a lake (under very heavy guard) where legend has it that Saddam is being held for trial.

15 – Slept, ate, etc. Very happy to be here and ready to get on with it. A small number of our guys arrived yesterday and slept. The rest are now all in Kuwait and join us soon.

Commentary only: Morale here is very high everywhere. The Iraqis working here are all way up and eager to see us stay until things settle out after the vote and trial. The bad guys are not winning! The people here are running their own government, their own economy and a huge part of their own self-defense. This is a great example of things going right. I will keep telling this story in hopes that the national media reps here start to get it right. Remember in our own country we fought another war of freedom only 25 years after our Constitution was approved (1812) and another final country-defining war amongst ourselves about 50 years after that (Civil War – 1860). Important things, big things, take time.

My best to you all!

American by birth. Soldier by choice. Volunteer by God!

Roger T. Aeschliman
Major, Armor
Deputy Commander, First Kansas Volunteers

Nov. 19, 2005

Greetings All,

For those of you who have been asking for items to send Roger here is a wish list from him at long last. I have added a few items at the end but the rest is directly from him. Let me know if you have questions or concerns.

Robyn
**

Roger's Wish List

- Gatorade powder mix – original flavor
- Starbucks house blend or Classic Bean house blend
- 100 mile an hour tape (it's like duct tape kind of only more cloth-like and heavier duty). Green, one, two or three-inch-wide. We use it all the time.
- Green, tan or black parachute cord. People use this all the time.
- D, AA or AAA batteries
- Kansas Flag
- Seeds for planting: Kansas Sunflowers (not the big edible kind, but the wild kind that are the official Kansas Sunflower, also purple coneflower and brown or black-eyed Susan's. I think the weather here will very nearly support these year-round. Everything is so dirty and dusty. Planting things will help and add some color.
- Family Guy DVDs
- The movie "Wizards," a cartoon
- John Wayne movies
- AAFES gift cards. Go to www.AAFES.com and click on "gifts for troops." That is the only area of the site you will be able to access unless you have a military ID. AAFES is like a military Wal-Mart and there is one where Roger is. So rather than sending him packages of batteries, tape, etc. you can send him a gift card and he can purchase what he needs at AAFES. This will save you considerably on postage. If course, if you want to send a package please feel free to do so.
- Baked goods: cookies, brownies, etc. Chocolate chips should be ok for now as the temperature has dropped to 50/60 during the day in Baghdad.
- Junk food: cheese puffs, tortilla chips, Twinkies, etc.

"Greetings All,

"Here is this week's update. I will forward a few photos of Baghdad from the air as well. The kids and I spoke with Roger this morning via video conference for about 45 minutes. Roger purchased and set up a webcam on his end and we did the same. It took some effort on both our parts to figure it all out but it was well worth it. It was great to be able to see him and speak with him at the same time. The time delay was a bit weird but again worth it to actually see him. We are going to try that on Saturday mornings so that the kids are home to participate. He is off on two different missions over the next several days so will more than likely be out of touch. Please keep him in your prayers as he helps escort visitors on these missions.

"As an aside, if anyone sends him coffee be sure it is already ground. He found a bag of Starbucks on the supply closet that has been there for a while because it is in bean form and they don't have grinder. I was going to send ours but it's not compatible with the electric system in Baghdad. Roger said this morning that he is just about ready to put some beans in a sock and hit them with a hammer to grind them. Sounds like he is in need of a quality coffee fix. ☺

"Robyn"

**

Good afternoon from Baghdad, 20 NOV 2005

Baghdad is very much like LA right now. 70s during the day. Mild breezes to blow away some of the smog. Cool nights. There are blooming bushes and date palms. We are told this is the nicest part of the year and that it lasts a month or so. December-March brings the rainy season. Not the monsoon but cooler days with cloud cover and rains that come and go. Apparently the land turns into soupy, sandy mud as it does not soak in and there is no where for it to run off.

So right now I'm enjoying it with great jogging weather and time to do so. April starts to warm up and everyone says June-August is truly miserable, oven-like heat. We'll see. It did rain one night (I slept through it) and things were sloppy for a day. When the sun came out it dried very quickly. The palms, eucalyptus and some variety of locust – which looked so dead the day prior - were washed clean of six months of dust and sand and turned nicely green. A pleasant change from the browns of Ft. Sill, the pinks of Ft. Irwin and the raw desolation of Camp Buehring, Kuwait.

The time difference EST is 8 hours and 9 in Kansas. With the military lines and Internet resources we have here I can try to call home right before school starts as it is mid-afternoon here. I also can call right at bedtime Kansas once in a while but that means getting up at 0500 and walking in the dark to find one of those free lines so I tend toward the former now.

Here in Camp Victory we are surrounded by walls and towers but right outside starts the metroplex of Baghdad. It is a true world city of vast size. It sprawls in all directions. In camp we do hear sporadic small arms fire from celebratory Iraqis and from the even less occasional firefight. We also hear regular explosions but they are usually the nearby USA planned demolition of old Iraqi ordnance captured or turned in by the Iraqi people themselves. There have been a few IEDs or VBEIDS go off elsewhere in Baghdad – 3-10 miles away – and I have heard a few of those. But again, the ones that rattle the windows are all planned USA (as many as five or six a day – and I just heard one at this very moment: 1415 hrs, Saturday, November 19, 2005 – how about that?).

I saw a family of jackals wander across the road at night – very fat, very well fed. They looked like a cross between wiener dogs and little coyotes with pointy ears. Until hearing jackals I thought a gathering of coyotes was the weirdest sound on earth. Now I know better.

Here on Victory there is a bombed out palace in the middle of a lake with a drawbridge, brand new extra-tall guard towers, numerous guards, sand-bagged lower floor windows and signs saying "No photographs or recording devices." The urban legend is that Saddam is being held there prior to trial. The gospel is there are also giant carp-like fish that can suck the flesh off a man, and jumbo eels specially hybrid to skeletonize humans. There were also 500 bodies found at the bottom of one of the lakes we drained. How there could be bodies with giant carp and skeletonizing eels is still a mystery...

Stop reading if you don't want to learn about smelly bathrooms. Robyn asked me to explain: The workmanship of all this beautiful palace/villa area is terribly shoddy. The architecture and engineering is flawed and the actual construction was done with poor materials. All the marble is extremely thin, veneer-like and the stone work is similar, over poured concrete or fragile brick. Saddam apparently insisted on speed and appearance over quality. SO, it should be no surprise that the facilities in the palaces have no u-traps and no vapor vents. All the sinks, showers and toilets drain into the same pipes so when you flush the toilet you can hear and see the result going down the shower drain. The toilets are also all low-water usage flushers and the result of that is poor flushing with predictable residues and subsequent odors. This place stinks!

We drink only bottled water from Iraq, Kuwait or Saudi springs as it is cheaper than building pumping and water purification stations and then trucking bulk water all over the country. No one drinks from any sinks. The risk is too great. I even use bottled water to brush my teeth.

Well, this week gets more into training for the mission. I am going out for three days with a group of USA dignitaries, then one day off then back out again. All of our guests are classified and the rule of thumb is just not to talk about them at all in advance. I'll let you know next week who I was escorting around the country.

American by birth. Soldier by choice. Volunteer by God!

Roger T. Aeschliman
Major, Armor
Deputy Commander, First Kansas Volunteers

Welcome to the Victory Base Complex! This was hunting and fishing Lakeland; the palaces and villas were all for the selfish use of the Baath Party leadership. They now house the headquarters for the US and coalition forces.

"Greetings All;

"Below is a note from Roger concerning the photo he sent and his weekly update. He is attempting to compress the photos on his end but this is a bit too much compression. I will let him know for his future attempts

"Robyn"
**

The photo is a gift shop in Mosul, the actual site of Nineveh of the Bible. There is even a Mosque of Jonah in Mosul.

Hello everyone! 27 NOV 2005

Vocabulary lesson:

JVB:Joint Visitors Bureau. A nice lakeside palace where we greet, house, escort and protect official military and governmental dignitaries to Iraq. Currently run by a Texas unit.

RIP:Relief in Place. One unit moving into the area/zone/workplace/foxholes of another unit while they are still there.

TOA:Transfer of Authority. The official date the RIP is complete and the relieving unit officially takes over from the relieved and the relieved go home to Texas.

Left Seat/Right Seat Ride:Slang for the training needed before TOA. The old guys sit in the driver's seat for a period and show the new guys in the passenger seat how it is done. Then the new guys sit in the driver's seat for a period and actually do the mission with the old guys still there to advise, assist and prevent mistakes.

This past week we all left seated to prepare for TOA. Drivers learned to drive the extra heavy, armored Humvees, plated "ice cream" trucks that carry a number of guests, and 20 passenger buses. Senior NCOs learned to plan movements, place guards, track and control VIP movements and reporting. Lieutenants learned to plan missions from airplane landings to helicopter flights, to which person rides in which motorcade vehicle to sending soldiers all over Iraq in advance of the dignitary's arrival, AND how to be an escort officer, responsible for the movements, safety and well-being of the VIP throughout the trip from wheels down to wheels up.

I learned how to manage the entire operation, interface with higher commands, and to serve as a senior escort officer, traveling with the DV (distinguished visitor) and responsible for the entire mission. This week I was all over the northern half of Iraq: two days with five Congressmen and three days with the Secretary of the Army. The Congressmen visited several Baghdad areas and also several FOBs (Forward Operating Bases – the "forts" from whence units of soldiers live and operate). They observed training centers where Americans are teaching the Iraqi Army how to do everything an Army should do. The Secretary spent half his time visiting with the several Generals in command of Divisions or sectors of Iraq and half with troops. We were in Taji, Tikrit, and Mosul as well as several smaller FOBs out in the middle of the desert. All of our Bases and FOBs are very well protected and there is very little enemy activity against them. Typically only randomly fired mortar rounds or unaimed small arms fire from far away (because if they were close enough to aim they would die quickly).

I had the opportunity for six Thanksgiving meals as the Secretary met and ate with soldiers everywhere he stopped but the actual result was no turkey for me as I mostly observed and monitored throughout the day while he ate and talked. At our last stop in Mosul I was prepared for a big turkey dinner but they ran out of gobbler. There was however plenty of ham and numerous other holiday foods including yams, stuffing and pumpkin pie. Not as good as mom's or Robyn's but tasty enough and lots of it. There is way too much food for the good of a lot of the soldiers here. Mess halls seem to run pretty much all day and many offer a midnight meal for night shift workers. In the more remote and hostile areas even the small camps try to offer three hot meals a day. My concern about food is too much of it and for a lot of our soldiers not enough time to exercise. We'll see if we can stay in shape as a unit with all this food available.

Throughout these trips I flew more than 2,000 miles, mostly by helicopter but one long trip from Mosul back to Baghdad by C-130 cargo plane. My aching tush! I intend to describe some of the sights and lands of Iraq in coming letters. It is a lot of different lands and peoples, not unlike our own vast country.

Oh, Governor Sebelius came to visit for a day and met with Kansas troops in several units. I was not planning on seeing her as I was out with the Secretary but did get home on the early C-130 flight, walked around the lake and was able to chat briefly. She gave me a hug and a nice smile much to the envy of the rest of the guys on the mission. Also saw her three other Governor traveling companions including the Governor of Georgia who says hello to Mike Ryan in Augusta in hopes that Mike will say something nice about him on the editorial page.

Letters from Maria Russo Wilson and Kirk Johnson this week caught up from their NTC addressing, also a letter from Aunt Nancy in Tennessee, and a nice care package from the Topeka Bible Church where my parents attend. I have now moved out of the villa and into my new permanent connex hooch. I am home for a year, but not settled in. A full week of missions coming up too so I won't be unpacked out of the duffle bags for a while yet.

American by birth. Soldier by choice. Volunteer by God!

Roger T. Aeschliman
Major, Armor
Deputy Commander, First Kansas Volunteers

"Greetings everyone,

"Just a quick note from me to say "thanks" for the letters and packages you have sent to Roger. Whenever I speak with him he mentions what he received in the mail. This is huge for him and really makes a difference. So, a sincere thank you from me for your efforts in keeping Roger's morale high.

"Robyn"
**

Greetings from Baghdad! 04 DEC 2005

The first time I saw the Tigris (sounds just like a female tiger) River I was terribly disappointed. This is the mother of all waters, the famed east side of the Fertile Crescent, the nectar of Eden? This murky, shallow and narrow ribbon of water bisecting Baghdad? It's not even as wide as the Kaw through Topeka. The same goes for the Euphrates, 50 miles west. Two narrow streams meandering through the desert. Very unimpressive.

But this week's flights hither and yon give me a quite different perspective. These two rivers are intensely channeled, canalled, and diked for hundreds of miles, all in the name of irrigation. The Fertile Crescent *IS* fertile, only because most of the water of both rivers is siphoned off to flood thousands and thousands of square miles of otherwise barren desert. The crops I could identify (in November!) from 300 feet include wheat (cut by scythe and shocked), corn (with cattle, sheep and goats eating everything left after the harvest), numerous orchards of many different fruits and nuts, hay (a little baled but mostly stacked), and north of Baghdad all the way to Tikrit – grape vines. Spreading from horizon to horizon, east to west and north to south.

You should see the goats and sheep scatter when the helicopters zip over. The cattle are too lazy to hustle. Chicken are everywhere too and sprint away from the roar of the rotors, perhaps genetically and instinctively fleeing some giant raptor. People almost always wave and smile (yes, you can see a big white, toothy smile at 300 feet and 160 miles per hour), and the children hop around excitedly, waving with every ounce of strength and running to keep up for a few steps until we are suddenly two miles down the road and then out of sight.

There are many center-pivot, drip irrigation wells, making the same crop circles that litter the western United States. There are also archaic "L" – shaped, hand-dug wells, perhaps 20 feet wide and 30-40 feet deep, that simply ramp down so people can walk or drive into them to get at the ground water. These are everywhere and are in common use. There are tractors of various kinds but for every piece of equipment you see there are five horse, oxen or mule teams. There are also many, many farms with no animals or equipment, just people out with a hoe. There are farms with very nice three-story villas but also mud huts and stick corrals. The contrasts are remarkable. The number of farmsteads apparently abandoned is beyond number. Additionally, nomads exist and roll in caravans with yurts from one desert grazing patch to another, perhaps still beyond the reach of government.

Whether in the fertile crop lands, mid-desert or in Baghdad proper the number of satellite dishes is incredible. Those here previously have told me this is a huge difference from a year ago. EVERY house, villa and mud hut has at least one dish, and in the city most rooftops sport a half a dozen. There are places with no electricity coming in that have a dish and a generator. Places where cattle and sheep live inside with the people have dishes. If there is any one sign that this war is won, I believe the dish is it. Once freedom of thought like this is in it can only be taken away by the most draconian of action. VIVA MTV! VIVA Fox News!

This week I was the escort officer in charge for a group of Congressmen for three days and then a very senior US General for three more. All this was the final training component and "exam" for Kansas assuming the mission which we formally did yesterday. The Texans are now on the way home and by this time next week will be kissing their wives, husbands (Engineers have females, Infantry doesn't), parents and children hello and resettling into civilian life. They trained us well and we will both miss them and envy them. Several have promised to hoist a beer to me personally once they land in Germany, Ireland or Newfoundland.

So, it's now my hotel, my Joint Visitor's Bureau and my head on the block if some General or other dignitary gets lost, they are unhappy with the color of the sheets, or the hot water runs out. And God have mercy on my soul if the Internet goes down!

American by birth. Soldier by choice. Volunteer by God!

Roger T. Aeschliman
Major, Armor
Deputy Commander, First Kansas Volunteers

To:Robyn Aeschliman
From:Roger Aeschliman
Date:December 9, 2005
Subject:Draft of Aeschliman Family Christmas letter

T'was the night before Christmas
And here in Iraq
I'd only arrived
Yet wished I was back.

The stockings? Not hung.
The chimneys? Bare.
In Iraq, St. Nicholas
Doesn't enter there.

And I in my hooch
Had just settled down
To slumber between
Each incoming round,
When out in the wire
There arose such a clatter,
I sprang from my bunk
To see what was the matter.

And what to my wondering eyes should appear,
But a sleigh built by combat engineers.
With a little old driver so lively and quick,
I knew in a moment it must be St. Nick.

More rapid than Blackhawk's his coursers they came,
And he whistled and shouted, and called them by name
"Now, 3rd Division! Now, 18th Corps!
"Now, Hawaiian BCT. Now, Wisconsin, for sure.
"On, 2nd Marines! On, 10th Mountaineers!
"On, Texas Guard! On First Kansas Volunteers!
"Up over the wires, up over the wall!
"Past the gun towers!
"Dash away all!"

"Santa," I said. "What are you doing here?
"They don't have Christmas. They don't even drink beer.

"The Iraqis don't celebrate Christmas you see.
"They're a different religion than you and me."

Saint Nicholas he smiled,
And gave me a wink,
Then said something
That made me think:
"These Iraqis need help.
"Many are poor.
"To a man, woman and child
"They are sick of the war.
"It's peace they want,
"Security they need,
"And you're here to oppose those
"Who'd make them bleed.
"So I'm giving them Christmas
"Want it or not.
"I've a present for them
"They need a whole lot.
"I'm bringing them liberty
"And elections too,
"All courtesy of
"America and you.
"And one day when there's peace
"And brotherly love,
"There's another gift waiting
"From heaven above.
"A gift to accept,
"Or not, as they choose.
"They've all to gain
"And nothing to lose."

He went back to work
Spreading love and good cheer
(But he still wouldn't leave me
Just one can of cold beer!)
Then laying his finger aside of his nose,
And giving a nod, up he arose,
He sprang to his sleigh, to his team gave a whistle,
And away they all flew like the down of a thistle.
But I heard him exclaim as he drove out of sight,

"Merry Christmas to all and to all a Good Night!"

"Merry Christmas from me.
"Merry Christmas to you.
"Merry Christmas, Iraq,
"From the Red, White and Blue!"

"Greetings All,

"This week's photos include the office with the new big Kansas flag on the wall and Roger with a candy dish from the Commerce gang in the hotel sitting room surrounded by some of Saddam's extravagances. Roger's words, not mine.

"Robyn"
**

Greetings from Baghdad! 11 DEC 2007

I am now convinced more than ever that the war here is already won. The evidence is this: while preparing to run for exercise I was confronted by a First Sergeant (totally unknown to me) bicycling by, who pointedly pointed out that I was wearing an unauthorized bandanna as a sweat band. It may surprise you to know that I have been wearing apparently unauthorized sweat bands for many years with no one expressing a prior concern. It may surprise you to learn that I am glaringly ignorant of the rules about what is appropriate exercise wear. And it may surprise you to know that the ONLY authorized headwear for exercise is the Army Black Stocking Cap. So, unless I want to wear a woolen stocking cap while jogging I must go bare-headed from now on. So, when it's 120 degrees and I want to exercise I must also contend with the sun baking my head and the buckets of sweat pouring off my scalp and into my eyes. (And if you don't think this is serious then it means you have never exercised with my grotesquely perspiring self).

What does that have to do with winning the war? By the time it was all over, a complaint had moved up the chain of command all the way to the office of the most senior general in the country and then back down to my battalion commander. So, if the US can spend that much time worried about one guy wearing the bandanna his children and their friends gave him as a going away present (and good luck charm!) we have obviously won as there are no more important things to do, and can start planning the trip back home . . .

I am now settled into my living quarters. I have about a 10'x10' space with a single bunk and real mattress with sheets. I have two wall lockers, a bookshelf and a dresser with mirror. I acquired a table for my computer and my "away from the office" workspace. There is a nifty wall-mounted a/c-heater that simply switches back and forth so temperature comfort seems good to go. Dad sent a number of State Farm calendars (thanks to Gary Lucas in Topeka. See Gary for all your insurance needs), and one of them is hanging from a piece of wire taped to the wall (nails are verboten!).

Our ship finally came in and the clothing and equipment we shipped from Fort Sill in September is here. I am still short one duffle bag of gear containing gloves, goggles, protective pads and a lot of colder, wetter weather gear. It will turn up sooner or later (one would hope prior to the short, soon-to-arrive colder, wetter season).

As you have probably read or seen on the news, the number of mass killings of Iraqi civilians is daily news. The reason for this is very clear: those are the easy to hurt people and media grabbing attacks. The Anti-Iraqi-Forces (AIF: the bad guys) are killing indiscriminately without regard to Sunni or Shia, military, government or civilian. It is pure terrorism and a sign of total desperation on their part. All they want is attention and to keep the fiction alive that they have power. This Onanistic display will not bear fruit. The US forces, the coalition forces and especially the Iraqi military and police are daily capturing dozens of AIF, seizing a dozen cashes of munitions, and receiving hundreds of good intelligence reports from Iraqis all over the country. I have seen entire brigades of Iraq soldiers in good equipment, doing the job, and training bases full of privates, young officers in training, and Special Forces already out doing the same combat work the US special ops are doing. The corner has been turned. Don't let the national media tell you otherwise.

Received many letters and packages the past few days: Mom and Dad, the whole family from Thanksgiving, Benny Meyer pecking away at a MANUAL typewriter, early Christmas gifts from Brent Nichols in Arizona, and mom Mary Lou in Hays. A note and hand moisturizer from Maria Wilson (nee Russo), a nice letter and card from my boss Kirk Johnson. A card from the Adriel class at Topeka Bible Church, and a card from Sally Calamunce, a friend of my mother. AND FIVE HUGE GIFT BOXES from the gang at Commerce Bank and Trust. Thanks everyone!

American by birth. Soldier by choice. Volunteer by God!

Roger T. Aeschliman
Major, Armor
Deputy Commander, First Kansas Volunteers

15 DEC 2005

To Whom it May Concern:

I'm Major Roger Aeschliman, Deputy Commander, 2-137 INF, running the Joint Visitors' Bureau. I was recently informed in excruciating detail by some bypassing First Sergeant that my sweat band was unauthorized for PT. Now ignoring the fact that a first sergeant had enough time to both be concerned about me and further had the time to shoot the issue up the chain of command, I accept that my tie-died bandanna (a going away gift from my daughter who knew it was hot in Iraq and that I sweat a lot when exercising) is a bit flashy for the Army. OK. Fine.

But the 1SG went on and on to explain that nothing is authorized for sweat and nothing is authorized to protect your head and face from the heat. My cursory review of policy 11 whatever and AR whatever seems to suggest that while NOTHING is CURRENTLY authorized that the commander CAN clearly AUTHORIZE accessories.

I request that both sweat bands (if my bandannas are just not acceptable) in some plain Army color be authorized by policy letter and that further, that some sort of head covering be approved for the heat of the summer. Preferably white to reflect the heat with a bill to cover the face.

This is a soldier care issue. For me with a sweaty metabolism it is dangerous to run without a sweatband. I must take off my ballistic sunglasses to wipe my eyes on my sleeves or my eyes fill with sweat. And anyone living west of the Mississippi knows it is just insane to be out in the summer sun and heat without a head covering.

I'm sure you have a lot to do and that this sounds silly. It is silly to me too that some busybody NCO had nothing more important to do than explain obscure regs to me when all I'm trying to do is stay in shape now so that I can perform the mission when it's 120 degrees next summer.

How about a simple policy ASAP? Here's a draft:

"In addition black, gray or white sweat bands for the head and wrists are authorized at the soldier's discretion. When the temperature is over 80 degrees the patrol cap, the boonie hat, or a white baseball or bicyclist style cap with a bill is authorized at the soldier's discretion."

MAJ Roger T. Aeschliman

From:Roger Aeschliman
To:Robyn Aeschliman
Date:December 13, 2005
Subject:Happy Birthday darling

My bunk is not big enough for two,
Even intimately like we used to do
When we spooned and cuddled.

In the darkness huddled
Under Army blanket; sleepy brain muddled
Beside me there . . . I saw YOU.

Sheet tucked under chin.
Moonlight pours in
And sparkles on your lip.

Reaching to caress cheek and hip
Ephemerally, I find no grip.
But still . . . I SEE you.

Merry Christmas everyone! 18 DEC 2005

My pre-Christmas wish for everyone is that your lives are NORMAL (or at least as normal as things can be during the busy holiday season). Normal, ordinary, uneventful. Knowing that things in the USA, Kansas and Topeka are normal is really what this is all about for most of us here in Iraq (or Afghanistan, Kuwait, Pakistan, Kosovo or anyplace else where we are separated from family over the holidays). If your life is normal then it means the bad guys are losing. If grade school Christmas programs are not being blown up, if Christmas Carolers can still walk around with candles and sing to neighbors about their religious beliefs, if the malls are so damn crowded that shoppers start to get cranky and panicky about getting done by Christmas Eve, then everything is NORMAL, we are winning and being away from home is worthwhile and meaningful.

It hit me this instant: in my 45 years on this earth this is the very first Christmas (and was the very first Thanksgiving) that I will not be with my parents and siblings. It is the first time I have not been home for my wife's birthday, the first time I will not be home for Christmas Eve dinner out with Robyn to quietly celebrate the anniversary of the night I proposed and she accepted (December 24, 1987, 9:30 p.m. in the back corner room of the now used car lot that once was Steak and Ale – and it was terribly romantic, just ask her). It is the first time I will not be home to see the joyful rendering of presents by my children Ryan and Regan (even though they long ago left Santa behind). So, yes, all this sucks and none of us truly want to be here but we all chose this, we all volunteered and we are all honored to do this part for you and our great nation, and only ask that you please live a happy and normal life, free of fear, free of the threat of fundamentalist, wahhabist, baathist, Nazi-Islamo-terrorism worries. That's the real gift we all want from all of you. Be normal this Christmas.

In Iraq the week started with bullets falling out of the sky and ended with an incredibly successful election. Saturday night (Dec. 10) about 2230 hours, gunfire erupted. Leaping outside I saw tracers flying skyward in all directions, nearly encircling the camp. The noise and display was incredible. I raced to the command post in my Three Stooges Curly PJs, tee-shirt and flip-flops, carrying a pistol in hand. Bursting in the doors I cried out (edited for strong language) "what is going on?" To my horror, the only person there was a medic, talking to his wife on the telephone. The next few minutes of failed radio contact and cell phone dropped calls did not help. I ordered a total stand-up, posted guards, suited everyone up in armor and helmets (and if you don't think a person looks really stupid in Curly jammies and body armor your sense of fashion is sadly impaired) and generally got ready to fight hand-to-hand. Relief followed when the word came that Iraq had just defeated Syria for the soccer gold medal in the South Asian Games and that all the million rounds expended in those few minutes were simply 12 million Iraqis celebrating with their traditional gunfire (not unlike Mom ringing her bell and Pop shooting the shotgun at midnight on New Years only with automatic weapons). To my knowledge no one was injured by this display but we read in the papers once in a while that some innocent bystander is killed by stray bullets from celebratory Iraqi gunfire....geez.

During the week I was pleased to escort two missions around and am preparing for a third. Senator Inhofe of Oklahoma came expressly to learn the current successes he could pass on to the media back home – in his words, to counter those who are calling for immediate withdraw (obviously I love him and would bear his child were it possible). Senators Biden (Del.), Chambliss (Ga.), Graham (S.C.) and Cantwell (Wa.), all came together for the elections. They (I too) visited polling stations, met with the Iraqi elections commission, and they had state dinners with the Prime Minister and US Ambassador (I – not invited in - stood outside telling jokes in pidgin Spanish to the contractor security guards). All four were polite and appeared to be open-minded. All said very nice things about the mission and appeared to be supportive on TV and radio stops throughout the mission. A reporter from Gentlemen's Quarterly was on the trip too and he indicated that Biden may again be looking at the presidency but is a bit coy, and that Graham is considered a rising star in D.C. and could be presidential material. I was able to pass on greetings to Sam Brownback (perhaps our own contender), Pat Roberts and the whole Kansas gang. Both Chambliss and Graham send greetings to Mike Ryan!

While spending the night in the International Zone a single rocket did come in on election morning, about 0700 – WHHOOOOSSSH – BOOM! About 300 meters away with very minor damage and scratches to a couple of soldiers. Loud and annoying to us used to hearing it but kind of made the Senators jumpy all day. They probably followed instructions better after that . . .

The elections were a tremendous success, peaceful, massive and honest. The Iraqis I try to speak with (we babble at each other and show pictures of our families) are very proud of what they have done and where they are going. These were THEIR elections with limited US support around the country and they know it. The Sunnis came to the table because even though some of that element want the "occupiers" out and see us as the real enemy, most of the Sunnis realize that freedom, liberty and independent open elections now and in the future are here and will be a way of life. They understand deep inside that once we go, if they aren't in the political game they will be fringers with no access to revenues, health care, road and infrastructure improvements. SO, they voted. It looks like nearly 80% of voters turned out. WOW!

I'm writing on Friday, with flying missions ten of the next 14 days. Will be working on Christmas day, but then again we're working every day ;)

Received mail from Dolores Waldy, Betty Cazier and Jim Condon at TBC, from Aunt Nancy (Dad's sister), a box of goodies from one of my longest term friends Jeff Wagaman, letters from my boss Kirk Johnson, fraternity brother Troy Mcvicker in Seattle, and dear friend Susan Anderson in Topeka. Also fellow GI MAJ Joe Mcguire sent a DVD of the Governor's press conference following her trip to Iraq. She was very gracious and said nice things about all of us. Christmas presents from Mom and Dad Reimer in California. A nice note from Pop and a card from Mom, followed by their box of Christmas presents. Glad to hear everyone survived the first big storm of winter. We continue to suffer with daytime temps of 72-75 and nights in the 50s.

American by birth. Soldier by choice. Volunteer by God!

Roger T. Aeschliman
Major, Armor
Deputy Commander, First Kansas Volunteers

PS – I have sent Robyn a list of my soldiers who are not getting much support from home. If you would be willing to write to a soldier or send them a care package please call Robyn and she'll give you a name and address. I would appreciate it very much. rog

Hello gang! (Dennis, Mike, Adina, Alicia, Shawn, Nancy – and everyone else, but those were the only names on the gift card); 22 DEC 2005

Thank you so very much for the gift certificates to AAFES. What a nice surprise and how generous you all are! I will horde these jealously pondering whether to buy shaving cream in bulk (or other toiletries so I have a year's supply and never have to shop again), or whether to splurge on some music or DVDs, or buy additional underwear so I don't have to do laundry quite as often . . . But . . . if history is any pattern at some point I will run into soldiers who send every penny home to feed their families and wind up using some portion of this to help them with their needs here, and I will remember each of you and your great kindness in making it possible.

You can't imagine the tempo here. By the time you get this I will have worked with (from a tiny bit to a whole lot) the Vice President, the General of Central Command, the Secretary of Defense, the Chief of Staff of the Army, the Chairman of the Joint Chiefs and a gob of Congressmen and women. That's just about ten days!

The time flies and when we can just sleep in a bit, do laundry and write a few letters (like this) it is a nice day. I fly all over the country frequently as an escort officer (no smirky comments Hitt), putting people on helicopters and planes, getting them off (again, no comments Dennis) and pointing them in the right direction to the next person they are to meet or the next door they should enter. If it all goes well I am kind of a silent traffic signpost unobtrusively pointing the way; if it goes less well I have been seen sprinting down a runway in full battle gear to flag down an airplane trying to leave prematurely without our passengers.

We will be busy all through January with Congressional visits (until they get back into session). Perhaps will slow down a bit in February – we'll see.

Thanks again to everyone. I truly appreciate hearing from you and receiving your very useful Christmas gift.

rog

Dear Doug, 23 December 2005

Thanks for the coffee gift box! Great to get some of the good stuff from back home and your nice note too. To this point I have totally avoided the rectal-cranial inversion to which you allude...

Although I don't mind being healthy I do miss the opportunity to visit with you and perhaps quaff an ale, stout or bitter. I think you would find this experience remarkable and would greatly enjoy visiting with the locals, traveling around the country and seeing the tri-ality of this (1) modern nation trying to tear itself away from (2) millennia of history and old ways (yet still relying on a lot of those old ways to feed the nation) and (3) the similar struggle over the role of religion.

Islam is a demanding religion (if you practice it) and throughout its history of conquest and expansion has demanded that the conquered convert or die. But, once converted, it has not historically required that you practice it, only that you do NOT practice some other religion. Here in Iraq there is a broader history of tolerance and some degree of secularism. The forces calling for stronger adherence to religion are nowhere near a majority. The more powerful influences here are this goofy familial, tribal, regional HONOR code, and then really a broad stroke sort of nationalism, especially among the Kurds to the north (whom, if consolidated from Turkey, Syria, Iraq, Iran and other northern tier counties would number into the 40 or 50 millions), and to a lesser degree the Shia in the south (who I believe are using Iran to leverage themselves but really would not want to live in a theocracy like Iran).

The Iraqis range from intensely religious to not a bit – just like so many Christians who neither practice nor even really believe anything but would be terribly angered if you suggested they were not really Christians. There is open access to alcohol, porn, pork, and everything else forbidden by Islam for all comers. Prostitution is common in the city. Having said that I want to be clear that it is open access for Iraqis! Not GIs! We are sheltered, cloistered and living under general order No.1 which is clear on zero tolerance for alcohol, porn, prostitution, and even prohibits eating local foods or fraternization with the local population. The point is we live a more "Islamic" lifestyle than many Muslims who call themselves that but don't practice any of the five pillars.

Well, rambling on. Sorry. My best to you and the lovely wife. Looking forward to seeing you at whatever soonest opportunity.

Your Friend, rog

"Greetings All,

"Roger sent this yesterday so he was on time but I'm late in getting it out. So sorry. We made it through Christmas so I'm thinking we can make it through all of the rest of this deployment now. Yeah! Roger was able to call Christmas morning which helped tremendously and then again today at his parents home during our family gathering there. He sounded tired (end of the day for him) but he is keeping busy and the days are flying for him. Roger is very grateful for the support and notes and the packages are huge morale boosters. He is particularly fond of the coffee that people are sending him – he mentions it every time I speak with him. Enjoy the weekly update and photos.

"Robyn"
**

Merry Christmas Everyone! 25 DEC 2005

It is mid-afternoon on December 25 and I would be lying if I didn't admit that it is a homesick kind of day. I opened presents from Robyn and the kids, my mother and father, and mother-in-law Mary Lou that have been sitting around staring at me for a week or so. Sardines and oysters, nuts, batteries and DVDs, (and please don't send any more of either batteries or DVDs as I can't possibly use/watch what I now have on hand), and many other treats.

Let me go back a week and come forward in time:

Since last week's writing I escorted General Abizaid, the highest level of direct command in this theater. He comes frequently from the US and works an aggressive schedule so I am very busy for 3-4 days at a time with his mission. But he was small news this week as Vice President Cheney came to town. I saw the VP only briefly when he met with my general for dinner along with a host of other Generals, the Ambassador and others. Our little five vehicle security convoy was swallowed up by the 13 vehicle convoy of the VP (and my backpack I take everywhere with every possible thing necessary crammed into it was run over by an armored limo when they moved suddenly to make more room – broken cell phone and flashlight, but camera and IPOD survived undamaged).

Abizaid and the VP moved on and were replaced by the Albanian Prime Minister (my mission) and he announced that Albania was going to stay the course as an ally here until the Iraqi government asked them to leave, by the Polish Prime Minister, by Congressman Osborne (former football coach great), and big whoop…two MORE Georgia Congressmen. What's up with this Georgia travel Mike?

Suddenly it was Thursday and my mission with the Secretary of Defense began. I want to confess up front that I have been an iconoclast ever since I learned that the word means one who rejects icons. This is especially true of pop culture stars and "celebrities" of all types. So I am much unimpressed with all the stuffy VIPs who arrive here full of themselves: I am polite, official, and respectful but not much impressed.

I'm not sure what I expected Secretary Donald Rumsfeld to be like but I can tell you I have a new hero. I watched this man get mobbed by adoring soldiers, contractors and foreign nationals, over and over and over again for three days, all over the country. He shook thousands of hands, posed for many hundreds of pictures, chatted about homes and families. Not once did he complain about getting hugged, pawed over, arms thrown over his shoulders. He greeted every soldier/marine/sailor/airman within shouting distance. In the twenty-some stops/events we did he didn't quit a location until every single person had been shaken, photoed or clapped on the back. It was remarkable.

He is loved over here and it is clear to me that he loves the fighting man and woman right back. You can't fake what I saw for three days. He knows what everyone here knows: this war is won. It is just a matter of wrapping it up, putting a bow on it and keeping things moving forward until the Iraqi government tells us it is time to go. The only thing that can stop this from being the greatest success of freedom since the end of the cold war is if people at home cave-in to the caviling naysayer's and we leave too soon. (You read the papers so you know he also announced troop reductions effective ASAP – the Iraqi and International media had several huge media events and THAT was hard to control; the fledgling free Iraqi media have learned from the American free press some of the worst habits of crowding, obnoxious and aggressive posturing, and frankly inane and silly questions).

The schedule took us into the International Zone downtown and at the last minute Rumsfeld decided to RIDE back to our hotel rather than helicopter lift. Although I and my team did not go with him (we had to escort the rest of his staff and media back) he rode in an armored Humvee convoy down the notorious Route Irish in the dead of night. This was quite a statement on his part and a real spit in the eye at the anti-Iraqi forces. If the US Secretary of

Defense can ride safely down what six months ago was the most deadly stretch of road in the world then progress is being made.

Saturday we wound up in Mosul in the north where he served Christmas Eve dinner of steak, lobster tails (I snarffed down two standing in a corner) and crab legs to troops. He and his 40-person travel squad then flew out on a C-17 super cargo plane (truly incredible; more some other day) for the USA and we were left to find our way back home. The only available flight took us three hours south, all the way to Kuwait, and then back north two hours to Baghdad. In bed around 0300 this morning and up again after a restive four hours. Today has been laundry, an after-action-review of the Rumsfeld mission (we always review our work for improvement and sustainment items), and UNWRAPPING presents, which I think is where I began?

In the next few minutes I am going to eat some smoked oysters and sardines, an old Aeschliman family Christmas and holiday treat (I don't know why, ask Pop). Then we will review today's missions and we have four of them (holidays are MORE busy for us than a regular day). Tomorrow and for the next month we have many military, government and foreign leaders pouring in. The days and weeks just rip by and that is good because as Robyn and I have already shared it is pretty easy to be separated if you are busy and don't think about it but it's pretty terrible when your mind wanders and you get to feeling sorry for yourself. Christmas I think will be the worst . . .

So, a bit homesick but not terribly down because of all of you! This week cards from Aunt Janie and Uncle Bob, Helen and Chuck Worthington, Aunt Nancy and Uncle Nate, old friend Juanita Kendall of Grantville, and more notes and clippings from Pop x 2. Christmas gift certificates from Greg Nelson, and the gang at Commerce Bank & Trust: Dennis Hitt, Mike Lott, Adina Eaton, Alicia Rothe, Shawn Tipping and Nancy Goodall! And just arrived today: a Christmas box from sister Karen Orr (full of TOYS!), Mark Harris (a book and coffee), and First Baptist Church gang. Thanks everyone!

Finally, thanks to everyone for your response to my request for notes and packages to soldiers. You are great!

American by birth. Soldier by choice. Volunteer by God!

Roger T. Aeschliman
Major, Armor
Deputy Commander, First Kansas Volunteers

Secretary of Defense Don Rumsfeld was one of the most popular people in Iraq and took endless photos with US troops. Here he is with "Flat Matt," a school geography project of the Wichita Marine Mom's Association.

28 DEC 2005

Dear LTC Trafton,

I am writing to offer my most sincere apology for my recent unprofessional correspondence. In a misguided effort to use sarcastic humor to draw attention to a minor policy recommendation I now recognize that it interfered with our Battalion's missions, came to the attention of senior leaders in the theater wasting their time, and cast unintended aspersions on the NCO Corps.

None of this was deliberate and I regret it terribly.

I am most embarrassed and saddened that this incident has lowered your opinion of me. I want you to know that I will do everything possible to regain your confidence and to perform the mission in an exemplary manner.

I do not know who the original NCO was and have had no communication with him. Nor do I know by name whom I sent the e-mail to. I simply responded to the POC at the bottom of the policy letter directing concerns about the policy to that office. If there is anyone to whom I owe a personal apology I will certainly make one when you advise me of the offended party.

MAJ Roger T. Aeschliman

"Happy New Year everyone,

"I just got off the web cam with Roger and he looks healthy and happy. We were able to video conference for about an hour this morning and it was really great to see and hear him. We don't get to do that very often so it is a special treat when all the technology works and we can see each other. Too Cool!

"Robyn"
**

HAPPY NEW YEAR! 01 JAN 2006

Please vote for the best beginning to this week's report:

a. Winter tore into Iraq: highs of only 50, lows near freezing!

b. On Monday I kissed the President of the Ukraine.

c. The palace attic full of pigeon poop and bat guano caught fire Wednesday.

The weather quickly: it got cold (relatively so anyway). The highs aren't getting to 60 right now and at night you need the entire sleeping bag set or to turn the window heaters all the way up. Rains are expected and it poured up north in Mosul and south in Kuwait (our all-night flight last week landed during a toad-strangler in Kuwait). This cycle is expected off and on through March. (I am still missing my last bag with the water-proof desert boots, gloves and various goggles, pads and cold weather clothing). My early Friday morning, wind-chilled flight at 160 MPH to the snow-covered mountains north of Mosul was cold, cold, cold!

After finishing the Rumsfeld mission and my quiet Christmas Day I had two "pop-up" missions (they are not scheduled in advance-they just pop-up). Monday was the President of the Ukraine, Victor Yuschenko (remember? The guy poisoned by the opposition with dioxin?). He brought about 50 support personnel to "officially" close out the Ukrainian mission here. Big dog and pony show in Al Kut and then final meeting with the Iraqi Prime Minister. I asked the Ukrainian support team for a formal goodbye or a patriotic phrase in Ukrainian and was told that "Surpa OO-Crania" meant sort of Viva Ukraine. I was a tiny bit skeptical (if you've ever seen the movie "My Big Fat Greek Wedding" you understand that I did not want to say "your mother smells of goat urine" or something worse). But late at night on the tarmac I officially said goodbye and thanked him for the Ukrainian role in the war effort, then saluted and bellowed "Surpa OO-Crania". He perked up, grinned, gave me a bear-hug (he's a big guy) and a three-cheek kiss so it must have been the correct phrase after all.

The next day was Senator Arlen Specter from Pennsylvania. This was a unique trip in that Specter is the Senate Judiciary Chairman and his visit was all about the law. He was the first American to visit the courtroom where Saddam is on trial (it is small and his "cage" (see photo-I'm leaning on it) is strictly symbolic as anyone could just about step over it), and he was the first to meet with a group of the Saddam trial judges. Specter asked a lot of questions but an interesting one was "how come you aren't controlling Saddam's outbursts?" The answer was that when it is all said and done no will be able to say that he was prevented from defending himself in any manner he wished. Further, they said that the more he talks the more public opinion turns against him as he convicts himself by word and deed. A very interesting meeting.

Wednesday the palace "attic" crawlspace caught on fire as decades of pigeon and bat dung ignited from some electrical short. You don't know what stink is until you smell burning guano and bird carcasses. The contractor fire department arrived, handled things promptly and there was negligible damage. We stood outside for two hours then resumed the mission with only minor difficulties. It had been a point of argument about how to afford dung removal (estimated $25,000 hazmat clean-up) to improve the air quality in the hotel and command post. Now it may be moot and may have to be done as fire risk mitigation. I hope. The air quality in here is poor with airborne, particulate bird crap...

Spent New Years Eve Day flying all over northern Iraq with General Abizaid (mostly in very cold helicopters), huddled in the Embassy for a while as Abizaid and the Ambassador visited during a small mortar attack, and arrived back at the office late to find a contingent of Australians having a party in our hotel conference room. Worried that the Iraqis might indulge in celebratory gunfire all night but it passed quietly and I slept in. I may or may not stay up to watch the Chiefs probable final game tonight.

Letters and cards from Dad x 3, (and yes, our Chaplain and my Fort Sill and NTC roommate Father Pete Jaramillo is the nephew of the Chavez patriarch and you have met him), sister Ronna with questions about chow and the mail system, dear Kansas City adopted grandmother and night owl Dorothy Hamler, flower seeds from my growing up next door neighbor Tam Engler nee Beeler, Mom x 3, long-unseen friends Curt Rees in Yellowstone, Judy Wood in Topeka, and Kay Scheneman, CA (who must be ecstatic over the NU last second, goofy play, bowl victory over Michigan), Topeka Rotary friends and bankers Andy Chandler and Jack Dicus, former co-worker Connie Hammond, Christmas card (and grandchildren photo) from dearest friends Jack and Marilyn Rees, and a snack box from Charlene Patton and the Grantville United Methodist Church youth group (all of the same last names there as when I was as a child...made me smile).

American by birth. Soldier by choice. Volunteer by God!

Roger T. Aeschliman
Major, Armor
Deputy Commander, First Kansas Volunteers

PS – Hey Pop, as of today I have flown 4,495 miles over Iraq and jogged 125.

Subject:letter from Roger
Date:Jan. 2, 2006

"Greetings All,

"You get two notes in one week. Below is a letter that Roger wrote his sisters in response to questions they had asked. It's all pretty interesting and I thought you would enjoy the information as well – it's mostly everyday living types of questions.

"Robyn"
**

My dear sisters;

It was so very nice to get your letters and to hear all the news from home. I'm not going to repeat back all your questions, I'll just answer them.

Mail to and from here is very good, run by a teamwork of the Army, contractors and the US Postal Service. I have gotten letters and packages in as short as five days and as long as 20. All the letters I send are free and there are tons of donated stationary around so I am not missing anything there. Mailing a package is a little harder but there is a post office that has boxes and tape and they work with you to get it all organized and packed. I have sent one package home that hasn't arrived yet with souvenirs type things, a palm leaf, desert sand and rocks, cans of pop in Arabic, etc. Kids should find it interesting.

I am going to have to confess sooner or later in my report that I have been unable to keep up with the birthday greetings. Once we got here my work schedule and the location of most of the troops makes it time wise impossible. I am traveling about fours days a week on average - if not overnight then at least late into the night. Also, most of the soldiers live between one and three miles away from me, and then they are working on different shifts. So it is frankly impossible to find them at any given time when I would have the free time to go look for them (which isn't any...). I really can't even call them for the same reasons. They are out doing Army work with out easy access to a telephone. So, I have failed on this one. A great idea that I just can't humanly do in this environment. Not like at Ft. Sill and Fort Irwin where everyone lived within 200 meters and I'd walk around and see them around bed time...

As escort officers we are "ON" mission all the time and really have an informal rule to keep out of the faces of our VIPs. So I do not ask for autographs or ask for photos with them and neither do the rest of the men. In some cases it is even part of our job to keep other autograph seekers away for security reasons. I will return with an official record of visitors and a few keepsake items that they may choose to give us as a thank you for our work but not a big pile of autographs or photos.

Have not eaten anything Iraqi; it is in fact prohibited by General Order No. 1 as a health and safety issue. Hygiene is part of the concern but actually being out in the economy to eat at a restaurant is a bigger safety risk. While 99 times out of 100 any of us could walk around downtown Baghdad for a couple hours to shop and eat, the other time we would all be blown up or kidnapped. So there really isn't any tourism yet and I don't anticipate any for the reminder of our tour. I did eat one Turkish meal up in Mosul at the Army Base airport where there is a contractor-run mini-bazaar. It was chicken in sauce and was tasty. I understand from visiting with Iraqis they eat lots of breads, rice, fruits and veggies, as well as mutton and chicken. Less beef and no pork.

I don't miss foods so far. I have had steak, lobster, corned beef, prime rib, Mediterranean, stir fry, fast food, Cajun, etc, etc. The Mexican night entrees are not as good as any Topeka tex-mex place and disappointing, but the fact that we have a Mexican night is amazing. There is Baskin-Robbins at lunch and supper nearly everywhere I go and for all the food you have to ask for specific small amounts or they just heap it on the plate in incredible amounts. Two or three t-bones, two cheeseburgers, three giant scoops of ice cream...it's wild. I always do portion control. I eat mostly here at our own hotel dining hall. We have rations laid on to feed 150 every breakfast and supper. This can feed the entire hotel guest list and most of the working people (us) on duty. I usually eat breakfast and supper but often limit it to just one or the other as my metabolism just doesn't burn off energy like it used to. If I ate three meals I would swell up even though I try to do some sort of exercise every day.

The big main mess halls are very democratic. Everyone waits in line (except for us at the JVB WHEN we have a VIP on a tight schedule), even generals. The lines move quickly though as people split off to get the main hot chow, or the fast food line, or the salad bar, potato bar, taco bar, ice cream bar, the carving station or other special lines. (I'm not kidding about this. These big places can feed thousands of people an hour). There is no reserved seating for officers and people tend to sit with their co-workers, just like in the real world, regardless of rank. In many mess halls there are a few private rooms that anyone can reserve for special events. When we take a visitor in to one of these it is about half the time in a special room for working lunch meetings and about half in the main areas where they visit with soldiers from their home states or old units.

Back in our own JVB mess hall the selection is more like school lunch style, two or three hot choices, a salad bar and some sort of dessert. It is exactly the same food from the big halls just a reduced selection. We have a daily meeting at 5 p.m. in my office so I usually walk down the hall to the mess to eat right after that. It just makes no sense to go 500 yards to the main chow hall. But then I live right outside the office. Most of the JVB soldiers live right beside the main hall so it is very convenient for them to eat there most of the time. I usually exercise over the lunch period so I am not tempted to eat food I don't need. I've probably only eaten at the big places four or five times and most of those have been during missions after we escorted a VIP in, sat them down for their meeting/visit and then had an hour to sit around. When I am traveling/working I may eat more often as I am burning more energy, but even then really try to limit myself. We all know what our family genetics are like. I think most of us Aeschliman's and Brunson's tend to the bowling ball shape by nature. We are fortunate that dad and mom have set us the example for exercising and eating wisely all these years. I know that if I were not in the Army and required to be in shape I would be very round.

The Army has extensive abilities to purify and move water. So in the early part of the war that is what they did. But that takes a lot of people and more trucks and tankers so it is easier just to buy it locally and it is good for the local economy too. Yes, we did have an awful lot of shots. Sometimes over and over if the record-keeping is poor. Some soldiers so dislike shots that they carry their life-time shot records with them just to prove they don't need it again. I don't much care although I did get sick after the smallpox, anthrax, flu, and TB skin test all at one time.

I was thrilled to get Ryan's Music Man DVD in the mail yesterday and just finished watching it on the computer. He did a great job. The whole cast did. The blocking was good and most of them projected out pretty well. I giggled throughout but was very proud of him, especially on the dance scenes where it was clear he had little enthusiasm for it.

I'm so pleased to hear Simon is back on his feet and feeling better. I'm glad he enjoys the school routine and that it gives you some valuable time with the babies. Mom sent a photo of Palin and now I think of her (and you) each time I watch a Monty Python episode. Glasses for Simon too. Give me feedback about how that goes. I expect he will love them and it will broaden his world.

I remember seeing Ferris too, especially how you wanted to leave when it was over but I wanted to stay and see the credits and then we saw all the extra ending stuff including the very final "what, are you still here? It's over. Go Home!"

Thanks for all the videos. Will last all year as I really don't have much downtime. On days with no missions I am go go prepping for the next one, doing laundry, working email and orders. So when I am free, I exercise and then go to bed. Am now trying to watch something every day at least for a little while just for the relaxation so thanks. The guys are loving all the toys. They are scattered all over the HQ and they are always throwing something around. We have one very talented artist and you wouldn't believe the wonderful things he draws on the etch-a-sketch. Amazing.

We regularly have USO show types coming in and some minor celebrities. We usually do not support them or escort them in any way except to house them in the hotel and will perhaps see them at breakfast. The TV anchor on ABC 20-20 (I forget her name) was here. Several cheerleaders from several football teams, and some C team country groups so far. The biggest name so far is Al Franken (whom I despise) so you see that we are not getting the really big stars. Will let you know when it happens.

Thanks for the air freshener. Really came in helpful with the poop fire...

Dear Keith, 03 Jan 2006

Thank you so very much for the $50 of music cards. It sure brightened my Christmas. I have already spent about $10 on one of my favorite albums and downloaded it. I'm pondering on my many other choices now... THANKS!

Things are going very well over here and I do have a very interesting assignment escorting all sorts of VIPs around Iraq. I am in western Baghdad, near the Baghdad International Airport (where we frequently pick up our visitors as they enter the country). I travel a lot and am flying by helicopter several times a week. Very busy and the time is flying by. I do very much miss my wife and kids. Robyn, Ryan and Regan are doing fine and the kids are doing well in school. They have both grown a couple of inches in the past five months (Ryan is 13 and Regan 11 so they are both in that growth spurt phase).

Was able to visit with them all via the internet/video yesterday and Ryan now towers over Robyn. He may well be taller than me by the time I get home. That will be weird . . .

Miss running with you and our good conversations. I am in pretty good shape though and run 5 miles 3-4 times a week pretty consistently (once in a while will do 6 pushing 7 but my knees don't like it). Have lost some weight (low 170s) but am also lifting some free weights once again and enjoying that. Looking forward to seeing you. It now looks like I might get home in March for a two-week leave and would very much like to run with you a couple of times then. Will be in touch as the time draws near and the schedule becomes clear.

How's the hotel business in New Orleans? Damage? Customers coming back?

Best wishes for a great new year and that 2006 is joyous and prosperous for you.

Your friend,

Roger Aeschliman

From:Roger Aeschliman
Date:Tuesday, January 3, 2006 12:17 pm
To:webmaster@chrisvanallsburg.com
Subject:A small note to forward to Mr. Van Allsburg if you would please

I don't have any other way to reach Mr. Van Allsburg from here in Iraq so I would appreciate it if you would pass this on to him. Please.

Dear Chris,

I address you informally, as a dear friend. We have never met but your stories are such a wonderful part of the rearing of my children that I consider you a friend. Thus I relate the following:

I am on duty in Baghdad, a mobilized National Guardsman. My assignment is to escort, transport and provide security for VIPs that enter the country. It has its risks but is not especially hazardous compared to those in front-line duty.

On Christmas Eve I was escorting Secretary of Defense Donald Rumsfeld as he visited troops all over Iraq. I wish I could describe the joy he brought with him to literally thousands of men and women with whom he stopped to shake hands or pose for photos. It was fabulous. During one stop at a Forward Operating Base (FOB) called Speicher (Spiker) the Secretary was visiting with soldiers and shaking hands. I was posted outside on guard duty and waiting for the next agenda move. While waiting and observing the world a twinkle caught my eye. I followed.

On the very edge of the FOB nine-tenths buried in the sand was a harness bell. I shook it clean and for a very brief moment heard it ring clearly. Then it went silent. At that very moment I could feel the presence of my children (13 and 11 whom I miss terribly) and was flooded with many memories of reading the Polar Express over and over and over to my little ones (read it again daddy, read it again.)

I phoned my family as quickly as possible (a day or two later) and shared it with them. My daughter, the 11-year-old, thought she could hear the bell ring just a little bit. The rest of us could not.

I know it is a silly story. But I just want you to know that you helped bring Christmas to me, here in Iraq, in a very special and real way. And I will always, always be very grateful.

Your friend and devoted reader,

MAJ Roger T. Aeschliman
Deputy Commander 2-137 INF
APO AE 09342-1400

Helen Chanay
Shaffer Circle
First Baptist Church
3033 MacVicar
Topeka KS 66614

Dear Helen and friends; 03 JAN 2006

I want to apologize if I have already sent a thank you note to forgive me for my absent mindedness; if I have not, forgive me for my tardiness. Either way thank you so very much for the care package of treats and hygiene products (we're so far away that I'm really not going to assume any offense intended about body odor). It is wonderful to get mail from home and it really is just like in the movies: a mob gathers around and you lay out every item for display. There are "oohs" and "aahs" just like watching fireworks on Independence Day. Then you hear "are you going to use that?" and "hey I am out of that," and "oh man, I haven't had one of those in three months." After a few moments the swarm moves on and everything is gone to good use.

As an example, I run the Baghdad Joint Visitors Bureau, receiving, escorting and protecting US and foreign dignitaries as they come to see the truth of what's happing in Iraq. One part of that is that we also run a hotel to house them in the Baghdad area. While I don't eat much hard candy, there is an unending demand for them at the reception desk at the hotel. Your candy is now in a beautiful wicker basket greeting VIPS to Iraq. Over the course of the year it will have been consumed by US Congressmen, Prime Ministers of foreign nations, General Officers and the highest levels of US statesmen and women. The toothpaste, socks, a camera, etc., went to several younger soldiers I know that send all of their money home to support their families. On the other hand, I am jealously, selfishly hoarding all the Pop Tarts for myself. I know that's not very Christian, but perhaps I get bonus points for honesty.

Things are going tremendously well over here. Iraqis are running their own government at all levels. They are rebuilding all types of infrastructure and running it well. Commerce is growing with passenger and freight flights out of Baghdad. They are running more and more of their own police security and daily assume more control over the entire military activities. The people are very friendly and eager to see us here yet at the same time eager to see us go (probably just like you would feel if strangers were in your city but you knew your own people would kill you if they left). The bad guys are losing day by day. Their most common tactic now is to hire some under educated and under or unemployed person to make a vehicle delivery of a package of some kind, or just to take a car to a "friend" and it just happens to blow up with the innocent driver in it. So when you hear about suicide bombers you are really most often hearing about a double murder: They kill the driver and the nearby innocent civilians. That is not the way to make friends. They are losing.

I have written to other friends my own opinion of what this war is all about. In short, I believe this is part of the change from the rule of kings, dictators, and tyrants that began 2000 years ago with the ministry of Jesus Christ who spoke of a new type of freedom and personal responsibility and new rules for living. This war of change accelerated about 200 years ago with our own war of revolution and continues today. I believe this is all about what kind of world we will all live in 20, 50 and 100 years from now.

Having said all that, I am in a very safe environment here, with a room of my own, a shower trailer very close at hand and all the food a hungry soldier can eat so other than being away from family and friends this is not especially burdensome for me. I have the greatest respect for all the combat soldiers out there who are facing the terrorists directly, daily and I commend them to you all for your prayers.

My thanks again.

Major Roger T. Aeschliman
B Co, 2-137 INF
APO AE 09342-1400

Hi everyone! 08 January 2006

This week in Al Hillah (Babylon area) at the Embassy a deputy ambassador named Gary looked at my name tape and asked me: "Are you ROGER Aeschliman and you must know my brother-in-law Mr. Cornelius in Iowa?" Well, I admitted to being Roger but confessed I did not know Mr. Cornelius in Iowa (and I may have the name and relationship wrong as we were prepping to board the helicopters to leave). It turns out the deputy ambassador is now reading this weekly report sent to him by his relation in Iowa, who is getting it from someone else. So that makes it official: readers on five continents. (If anyone is reading in Australia or Antarctica please let me know). Small world these days...

I had a nice visit in Al Hillah with a local Iraqi Embassy employee. He talked about the ancient Hanging Gardens of Babylon (which evidence suggests was really a giant air cooling system capable of keeping ice frozen in the summer); about the legendary nearby location of the Garden of Eden; about the very real and historical but long-crumbled Tower of Babylon (the site temporarily closed to tourism for historical research). As we left we flew over all of these and while the future tourism is going to be important to Iraq right now all there is to see are mounds and rubble. The interpretation of the sites will be critical to visitors in the future. All of these places were made of mud/straw bricks that tend to crumble over time, especially in the winter rains and the annual floods that eroded the bases.

Flanking all these sites are two recent additions – giant mounds thrown up by Saddam, one with his palace on top and one with the abandoned foundations of Uday and Qusay's uncompleted palace. The area is lush and productive farm land and the region is currently very stable with only random and occasional terrorist acts against local Iraqis. It is also very flat between the Euphrates and the Tigris Rivers, much flatter than any part of Kansas. So any mound you see is almost certain to be man-made and most often an historical site.

Up north in the wheat and barley region there are miles of crop lands void of buildings as all the farmers cluster in villages. Every village appears to be built on a central hillock amid the otherwise flat plains. My hypothesis is that the hills are the trash piles of thousands of years that people just kept building on, layer after layer. Even here in our own Victory Base Complex the only terrain features are man-made: Saddam dug lakes and had all the dirt piled up into three hills. Otherwise flat, flat, flat.

The trip to Al Hillah was to escort Senator Reed from Rhode Island. He is on both military and economic development related committees in the Senate so his interests took us to new places (like Al Hillah) to visit and learn about the economic progress in the country. Iraqis have a long history of mercantilism and industry. They aren't afraid of hard work and like to be in charge of things. I see one incredible example of this every time I fly. All over the country people are building their own houses. You never see them there (as they work all day on some career path) but each time I fly by there are two or three more layers of cinder blocks up on the walls. The infrastructure growth is incredible and most visitors to the country hear long and detailed reports about how many schools, roads, bridges, electrical sub-stations, sewer lines, etc, have been completed. Daily progress on all these fronts. There is even a military acronym: SWEAT-M, that means Sewer, Water, Electricity, Academic, Trash and Medical. Every general and congressman wants to compare old SWEAT-M to the current SWEAT-M and it always looks great, all over the country.

Finally, as the Hajj nears completion, here's a comment on the five-times-a day call to prayer that issues from mosques. Not unlike church bells pealing, some call five times every day, others only once in a while. Friday is the especially holy day here and all the mid-morning calls issue forth all at once. Hundreds of dueling mosques with hundreds of loudspeakers. It is an amazing din. It sounds like swarms of very loud, very angry bees surrounding you. Perhaps Iraqis can distinguish one voice and call from another but for the untrained American ear it's just noise. Once the call is over the prayers begin. Most mosques don't broadcast services but a few of the big ones do from external loud speakers and the tone sounds much like an American preacher. Gentle, then stern, then railing, then forgiving; building to some sort of enthusiastic climax and settling down for probably a final blessing. Then quiet. The first time I heard this was on a Friday jog. All the calls belted out all at once. I was so startled I nearly wet myself...

Letters and cards from Shawn Tipping, investment wizard at Commerce Bank and Trust, Mom and Dad enclosing a couple of Christmas newsletters from family friends and a note about deer hunting, long letter from little sis Karen, card, letter, photos and CD of western tunes from Jackson County Commissioner, gunslinger reenactor and dear friend Brad Hamilton, candy box from bestest family friends the Heryfords, and nice coffee package from Dave and Joyce Phillippi, my parents' college friends. Also, Mrs.

Wenzel's 4th Grade class at Sunflower Elementary in Lawrence sent notes and candy for a group of soldiers. Thanks to everyone!

American by birth. Soldier by choice. Volunteer by God!

Roger T. Aeschliman
Major, Armor
Deputy Commander, First Kansas Volunteers

MEMORANDUM FOR:S-4, 2-137 Infantry Battalion, Camp Slayer, Iraq

DATE:11 January 2006

SUBJECT:Recovered duffle bag and cut lock

1.Approximately November 27, 2005 I was informed in passing that my final duffle bag of RFI and CIF gear had been located in Camp Slayer. Subsequent phone calls and requests for delivery and two visits by SSG Bruner failed to recover the bag. Continued inquiries did not produce the bag.

2.Upon reading an e-mail that all remaining unclaimed bags were to be centralized I went to Camp Slayer and made a circuit of connexes and in the connex storage yard found my bag. The lock was missing and the bag was half full. My name and location were clearly marked in indelible ink on the bottom of the bag. From memory I believe the bag was tightly packed and that the following items are missing from the bag: old style Kevlar helmet and cover, RFI ballistic glasses of the Oakley style, heavy winter-weight gloves, two sets of polypro underwear, four RFI wicking t-shirts, a set of gortex jacket and trousers, a camelback, and a wet weather suit. There may be other items as well. It is possible some or all of these items are in my Kansas bags but I believe they were packed in this bag.

3.Please let me know what if any action is required at this time.

Roger T. Aeschliman
MAJOR, AR
Deputy Commander

From: Pat VanHooser
Date: Saturday, January 14, 2006 8:58 pm
Subject: settle the argument

Hi Roger...hope the New Year is going well for you.

Mike and I had lunch yesterday and it turned into a 2-hour "discussion" about women in the military. I don't think women should be in the same units with men. I think they are a distraction, get pregnant way more often than is reported, disrupt the mission...which is to protect America, and add a lot of drama to a situation where there is already plenty of drama. My thinking is the military should not be subject to some social experiment.

Mike says I want to punish women for getting pregnant when it takes 2...and besides, women have a positive effect on morale and contribute in ways that overshadow my concerns. Also, it just isn't fair to exclude women from jobs they can do. That's not the American way. Then he made some crack about a slippery slope to Taliban thinking. Oh boy.

I agree it's unfair but the fact is, it is women who get pregnant not men. We are going to try to research this and find out how many actually do get pregnant... maybe it doesn't happen as much as I think. And he really is fun to debate on this kind of stuff...a real mental exercise for me that helps clarify what I think and why.

He knows I'm very conservative and politically incorrect about everything but I think even he was surprised about my take on this. So we agreed to ask you what you think. And, has your opinion evolved over the years....did you have one opinion when you started out and now see it differently? Inquiring minds want to know. I'm going to copy this to him so he will know exactly what I told you and can add anything I might have left out...which I don't think I did. Take care and stay in touch when you can. I'll keep you informed on how the "debate" is going.

Your pal, Pat
**

Dear Pat;

WOW! WOW! Asking me to step right into the fire . . . geez.

Well, I have lots of dislocated thoughts on this subject. Let's sort them out if we can. The Greeks were very clear on this 3,000 years ago: Agape versus Philia versus Eros. Spiritual love versus Fraternal love versus Erotic (romantic or lustful) love. They were completely clear: no Eros on the battlefield. Brotherly love, friendship and the bonds of affection were the primary tool to victory. In the end you fight and die for the man next to you based on spiritual kinship, a combination of agape and philia. When Eros entered the mix there were always problems. Suddenly your attentions were on that one person and not your mission. Historically very dangerous on the battlefield. Even when the Greeks (and other warrior groups) were engaged in pre-battle man on man sex it was JUST sex with no attachments, not Eros. Letting your mind wander into romantic love is dangerous . . .

Yet there are many historical events of woman on the battlefield performing heroic deeds: 1 - Mary Pitcher; 2 - the Crimean "doctor" in charge of all the theater medical issues (who threw out Florence Nightingale and her nurses for being a prostitutes) and who upon autopsy turned out to be a woman (I forget her name); 3 - the legendary Amazons; 4 - many Civil War women posed as men to fight and got away with it; 5 - All the Russian pilots of WWII yadda, yadda. It's clear that women who choose to serve CAN do the job.

Today the question is nearly moot. At 20% or so of the total manpower, all of the Armed Services currently depend on women to fill the ranks. There may be a cause and effect question of whether women in the military causes men to stay out or attracts men, but the bottom-line is it would be nearly impossible to fill the services without women today.

Should they be in combat units with men? The question of "with men" is nearly moot. They serve with men in all services and types of units now. They share floors and hallways in barracks (and informally and illegally rooms from time to time). They have the same missions, same training, and same work in general. In theory they have the same standards but this is probably the area of greatest concern to the most men . . . that the standards are not the same. So, should they be in combat units with men, in the most primitive conditions and most stressful, violent situations?

I wrote in a professional journal a couple years ago a real but slightly tongue-in-cheek article about fitness standards. The gist was that the standard should be different for different military jobs. We have different academic standards for different military jobs, and we already have different fitness standards for the Special Forces, green berets, etc. (they have a higher level of fitness because of a higher level fitness required). So if a person can do a military job pushing buttons on a computer need they have the same level of fitness of a combat infantryman?

I concluded this article with the thought that different fitness standards for different jobs could include women in the combat units. IF they could meet the fitness and mental standard for the unit and the job then they could serve. At least there would be a rationale for keeping them out or letting them in, not just based on emotional energy about wombs and nurturing.

Recently I saw the Army uniform catalogue and it included the ARMY COMBAT UNIFORM FOR PREGNANT SOLDIERS!!!!AAARGH!!!! That has to be a total sanity disconnect. Anyway, there is much sex over here. From previous reports from deployed friends there was a lot of tent-hopping during Desert Storm and all actions since. A senior general recently got canned for an affair (in the USA) and the "understood" standard over here is that sex with another soldier is ok as long as it is not chain of command, or position of influence/power over another, or as long as you don't cohabitate to the to detriment of other roommates. Also, there is a government report of some kind showing what would correlate to a deliberate increase in pregnancies among deployed women in order to go home early.

So, all that brings us back to "what was the question again?" Oh, yes. The question of same units is moot. The question of combat units: I would oppose it until such a time that everyone must meet the exact same standards. Same strength, same speed, same endurance, same hair length, same ability to lift a .50 cal machine gun and run 100 meters with it, same ability to drag a 250 pound combat loaded wounded comrade 50 meters, etc. etc. Real standards that had real meaning. If that all happened then I would further bar romantic and sexual relationships within a small unit, punishable by transfer to some other distant unit. Back to the beginning: When Eros is on the battlefield there is a loss of focus and people die.

Once again a rambling letter. Is there a pony in here anywhere? rog

Hi everyone! 15 January 2006

The good news is that I found my last duffle bag. I went to look for it myself as everyone swore there was no bag anywhere with my name on it. At one point between looking in various connexes and supply rooms one supply sergeant told me there was no point to what I was doing as every bag was positively identified as belonging to someone else. I insisted and was given that "you are a dumbass but because you are a Major we'll do it your way" look. When found, my bag was in plain sight and clearly marked with my name. The lock had been cut and there are a few items missing. The appropriate paperwork has begun.

The bad news is that the winter rains are now falling in Iraq so I was especially fortunate to get the water-proof boots. The silty sand that passes for soil here creates a soupy mud that balls up and tracks in everywhere. A quarter inch of rain pools and makes a three day mess. As I have flown over Iraq this past week the normal winter flooding is evident everywhere. Fields are soaked, canals are overflowing and water is standing throughout the river plains.

Seeing what one inch of rain can do here has led me to ponder biblical history and the story of the great flood. While flood stories are common across most cultures it is not a great leap to see how the Noah story could have played out in flat Mesopotamia: Five or ten thousand years ago as the exceptionally heavy snow pack in the mountains of Turkey and Iran began to melt, a low pressure system stalled over the Tigris and Euphrates Rivers. For forty days this stationary front rained off and on (not unlike our own American floods of 1993 when it rained off and on for four months), and both rivers overflowed. This great flat plain saw the water rise one foot then two then ten. At ten feet deep and 50 miles wide this flood would have knocked down every tree, every mud brick building, every mud brick ziggurat. As far as the eye could see, nothing but water. A survivor on a barge with his family and livestock would have floated down river into the Persian Gulf, and out into the Indian Ocean. Nothing but water . . . until they landed on some strange shore looming from the ocean.

Well, my hooch does not leak, it just requires daily sweeping.

This past week or so I escorted a number of Congressmen and women, most notably Senator Obama from Illinois (recognized for his speech at the Democratic National Convention a couple years ago). Also Senators Bond (Missouri and we chatted extensively about his work with Pat Roberts on the Intelligence Committee), Bayh, and House member Ford (running for Senate in Tennessee). We stayed the night at the Embassy (and when we do that it is behind the embassy in a tiny but dry and warm trailer with a bunk) and I got up at 4 a.m. to watch the NCAA National Championship in the mess hall. At 0430 it was just me and two other Texas fans. By the final gun it was about 500 excited Texas fans and two dejected USC rooters. A great game and perhaps the greatest single individual performance ever on a football field. Very tired the rest of the day but a good memory.

Several missions suffered rain delays and on Bond/Obama we were fortunate to get the last flight out of Kirkuk between storms and fog. That was the same day that the Blackhawk went down and Robyn was pleased to hear my voice when I called. Had a mission with six Congressmen after that including Jeb Bradley, perhaps the only Republican in New Hampshire. I asked him on a long shot if he knew my New Hampshire friend and college buddy Pete Eckhoff and the answer was Yes, Of Course, and that he had coached Pete's kids, and how was Pete anyway? Small world or else New Hampshire is even smaller than it looks on the map...

Finished off this week with another group of six House members, especially Congressman Jerry Moran of Western Kansas, a friend since 1988 when he first ran for the Kansas Senate and won. Also Virginia, Oklahoma, Ohio, South Dakota and oh, yes, another Georgian – what a surprise...

The hotel is chockablock full as Generals and Colonels from units trading places (RIP and TOA, remember?) stay here temporarily while they prepare to leave the country, and we are full-up on missions with all our teams, escort officers and vehicles assigned out. Crazy like this at least another week until Congress goes back into session and the RIP/TOA process is completed for the big divisions and corps.

Letters and cards from Pop x 2, package from Mom and Pop, card from Adriel Class at TBC, and nice letter from little sis Karen with photos of my niece Abby serving as Santa for her three little siblings. Very precious. Thanks everyone!

American by birth. Soldier by choice. Volunteer by God!

Roger T. Aeschliman
Major, Armor
Deputy Commander, First Kansas Volunteers

Dear Ryan and Regan, 15 JAN 2006

This is the letter that every soldier/father knows they should write but they almost never do write. The reason most never do write is because they are afraid that they will scare their children and they don't want the kids to worry about them while they are deployed. I believe you are old enough and mature enough to separate the real level of risk here from the excessive fearfulness that so many people seem to have about this war so I going to risk you being a little scared because it is important to tell you a few things.

But let me begin by reminding you once again that the risk here is very low. I live in the middle of a very large base completely surrounded by walls with guard towers and check points. Lots of heavily armed soldiers are on duty every night and day to make sure no one gets in without permission and clearances. The only real risks are the occasional mortar round or rocket that the bad guys shoot into the area at random. They don't aim; they just launch one and run away so they don't get killed. This risk is a lot less than getting into a car accident at home. It could happen but it is very rare. Not one of the 30,000 people here has been injured in the past year by a random mortar or rocket. The other risk I face is helicopter flights. This is a big part of my work so there is no way around it. But there are about 500 helicopter flights a day in Iraq and in the past year only four helicopters have crashed so the odds are about 182,500 to 4 against anything happening to me. That's pretty good, much better than driving around Topeka. So, weigh the risks in your mind and you'll come to the same conclusions I have. Something could happen, but it probably won't happen. Don't let worry get in way of having a great, happy 8th and 6th grade year, a wonderful summer and good start to high and middle school in the fall.

So, with that preface, I want you to know I'm not worried about getting injured or killed. It's so unlikely to happen and I'm so busy I just don't have time to waste thinking about it. That's a key lesson for you: Don't fret and worry about things. It is usually a waste of time. There was a cute little song 15 years ago called "Don't worry, be happy." One line of that song says: "In every life we face some trouble, when you worry you make it double, so don't worry, be happy." That is so very true. If something is going wrong and it's causing concern, I always ask myself the question: OK, what is the very worst thing that could possibly happen? If you can figure out what that worst thing is, it almost always turns out to be not worth worrying about. If something *is* important enough to worry about then it is important enough to fix, improve, hustle, work, resolve. Do something to make it better, don't just *worry* about it.

Hard work, knowledge and persistence are perhaps the three most important things to an economically successful life. And they are of equal value. They go together. There are some very smart people who know an awful lot but are just hopeless because they never learned how to work or they get discouraged and give up. There are a lot of people who work hard but lack the education and information required to do things smarter, better and more efficiently. There are many people who try over and over and over but never learn from their mistakes or they are working on the wrong things. Hard work is good whether it is mental work or physical work. Hard work makes the time pass quickly, makes your earnings more precious, makes food taste better and helps you to sleep at night. At day spent at hard work is a day spent well.

Education and knowledge are vital to a good life. Dr. Seuss said: "The more that you read, the more that you'll know, the more that you'll learn, the more places you'll go." When you read and learn you are nourishing the brain just like eating nourishes the body. When you put lots of disparate information into the brain you have more tools with which to make the best decision. Learning is like building a house. If you only have a pile of sticks and some rope you *can* sort of make a place to live in but it won't be much. But if you have hammers, nails, drills, saws, screws and other tools as well as lumber, shingles, bricks, plumbing, wiring, paint and carpet you can build a lot better place. It's the same in the brain. If all you know is football or math or flower trimming it is possible you can earn some sort of living, but if you know history, mythology, science, mathematics, languages, human relations, emotional psychology, art, music and bits and pieces of hundreds of other disciplines you can start to see connections and can make linkages to resolve problems before other people can even see the problem. A brain full of knowledge is the result of reading, paying attention to others' words and deeds, and from personal experience of trying new things. You will be offered knowledge and education your whole life from many sources. Only a fool chooses to stop learning.

Persistence cannot be overrated. It is just as important as the first two. Calvin Coolidge said: "Nothing in this world can take the place of persistence. Talent will not; nothing is more common than unsuccessful men with talent. Genius will not; unrewarded genius is almost a proverb. Education will not; the world is full of educated derelicts. Persistence and determination alone are omnipotent. The slogan 'press on' has solved and always will solve the problems of the human race. When troubles attempt to beset you, when it seems your struggles for success have all been in vain, remember to hold on to the slogan: Nothing can take the place of persistence." The history of mankind of full of examples of people who gave up then someone else came along, picked up the pieces, carried on and got it done. There are many stories of survivors of disasters who just refused to give up hope, gritted their teeth and were determined to live. They survived when others gave up hope and died.

Altogether, hard work, education and persistence are undefeatable. There may be unrewarded geniuses, educated derelicts, and talented buffoons in the world, but there are no failures among those who work hard, learn hard and keep trying.

The world is full of people who know the entire world is against them. They whine and complain. This is too hard or that is impossible or it's never been done. The truth kids is that the world does not care about you at all, one way or another. Not for you, not against you. There are two sayings: "When I was 20 I worried what everyone was thinking about me. When I was 40 I decided I did not care what people thought about me. By the time I was 60 I realized no one was ever thinking about me at all." And: "Given a choice between conspiracy and incompetence go with incompetence every time." The second one means that as much as we would like our misfortunes and accidents to be caused by someone, to be the result of others trying to make us look bad or our lives miserable, it is almost never true. Everyone is much too busy to worry about you and to take active measures to thwart you. The truth is that most of the time what happens to us is caused by us, or if not by our own choices then by sheer coincidence or more commonly the mistakes, errors and incompetence of others. People are not trying to get us; they wind up getting us because they messed up and it affects us in unexpected ways. All of that leads to this: "Stop whining and get on with it." – Roger Aeschliman, 2006

Whining may make you feel good for a while but it never gets the job done, never pays a bill, and only makes people think you are a whining dork. Getting on with it is what has to be done eventually so you are better off gritting your teeth again and charging ahead now - despite the pain or worry - than you are sitting around moping, whining and feeling sorry for yourself and then after all that you still have to get on with it sooner or later.

This next piece I'm not a good example for you but I believe it nonetheless. It's this: You can never have too many friends or too many people who love you. I confess I am a bit of a loner and a bit of an introvert. I don't really like big crowds or mingling at parties. I have many, many friendly acquaintances but I have very few deep, close friends. I wish I had the ability to open up more and to have more people I cared about deeply, but I really don't. Those I love I love totally, deeply and eternally. For everyone else, there are a lot of people I like but am not deeply attached to, and an awful lot of people I just don't care about at all. So, I confess again: I'm not your best example. But this is a good time to be a typical parent and say: "Do as I say, not as I do." A wide and deep network of friends, close and loving relationships with an extended family, and giving your heart to those who can use some affection is the recipe for good emotional health and a long life of happiness and joy shared with others. Ty Cobb, a great baseball player from long ago was a notorious loner and kind of a jerk to people. In his old age some reporter asked him what he would have done differently with his life if he could do it again. "I would have more friends," Cobb said.

Save 10% of everything you earn and invest it. I have no confidence that government will help me in any financial way. Those who count on government or charity to survive may *survive* but that's all they'll do. They will be poor and miserable survivors. Count on yourself for your financial well-being. Save 10% of everything you earn and you will be well off when you get older. This requires discipline. Too many people think they can get rich quick. The truth is you cannot. Only a few random, lucky ones do. But everyone can get rich slow. Save 10% of every paycheck, every earning, every gift and it will grow and compound over time. You will have money when you need it and will be independent and self-sufficient all your lives. Start now. Save 10% in the bank for now. Mother and I have not enforced this enough with you but we do try to practice it ourselves. Other than the time I was unemployed we have saved – sometimes more than 10% sometimes less. But we keep trying. The trick is to save before you spend. Put the money in the bank and get it away from your wanting eyes and spending hands.

Additionally, give 10% to charity. This will seem even harder to do than saving 10%. But we do this and have for many years. Even when I was unemployed we still gave to charity because it was the right thing to do. I believe that you almost always get back more than you give, if not financially at least emotionally, psychologically and in civic standing. In the bottom-line 10% to charity is the right thing to do. Again, don't count on government to take care of the needs of others. It's our job, one person at a time.

Help others. Not just giving them money or things, give time. Karl Menninger the famous Topeka psychiatrist was once asked what he would do if he were feeling depressed. He answered he would get out of this chair, walk to the wrong side of the tracks and find someone to help. Helping others is a powerful antidote to the blues and again, it pays you back in unexpected ways. Volunteering to help others is always time well spent.

I think mom and I have tried to both teach you and demonstrate in our lives all these lessons and behaviors. I think you already know these things and I believe you will apply them all your lives. You also see these things in Grandma and Grandpa and in many other of our family friends. What that means is that you already know most of the critical things necessary for a happy, healthy life. You have a lot of knowledge yet to learn and many hard lessons yet from growing up but the basic building blocks of growing up a good human being are already there.

That's why I'm not worrying about you two. I know you will make good decisions about friends, about drugs, alcohol, tobacco and sex. I also know you don't want to hear about these subjects anymore and are a bit embarrassed but I am so proud of you both for what you know and believe in that it's worth repeating. You are entering the most dangerous time of your lives. At your ages there *are* already some children drinking, taking drugs, having sex and smoking. You probably know a kid that smokes or drinks, and you probably have heard about someone in your school taking drugs or having sex. All of these things can kill you and I'm not exaggerating. Drinking at 11 or 13 or 18 can result in alcohol poisoning and drunk driving. Having sex or oral sex can result in diseases that last a lifetime, like herpes, or fatal, like AIDS. Drugs melt your brain. There is nothing more clear than that. And even cigarette smoking is proven to cause many fatal diseases as well as costing thousands of dollars a year. Take this test. Write down the names of every adult you really like, admire and respect. Overwhelmingly the list will not include heavy drinkers, smokers, and drug users. The smokers and drinkers that do show up on the list will be like Nana: sick and illnesses that are not going to ever get better. Some other smokers and drinkers on the list will have made poor decisions about drugs and alcohol and sex and as a result will be living in conditions that are of a poorer quality than if they had avoided these things, stayed in college and gotten better jobs before they had children.

You are reaching the age where members of the opposite sex are going to become very interesting to you. That is normal and a critical part of growing up. You are going to begin dating and will have boyfriends or girlfriends. You will probably fall in love pretty soon. I can only tell you to remember what you have been taught by us and have learned in church. Sex before marriage is not the right answer for boys or girls. No matter what you hear from "friends" or the media, most kids are NOT having sex or oral sex. Most kids are letting themselves be kids and grow in maturity before making this important decision. The possibility of sex is exciting and your bodies and hormones are going to be urging you to go ahead. It is critical that you resist and let your intellect and morals guide you. It is important to say NO until you are fully prepared for the emotional pain that comes from sexual relationships that then breakup, and especially for the lifetime commitment of raising a child. And with AIDS you will not have a second chance. It means sick forever, until you die young. It will be hard to tell boys and girls who are interested in you NO but it is the right thing to tell them. This is especially true for you Regan. I know it is unfair because you are a female but you are the one that can get pregnant so you have to be the one to say no. Older boys especially will say and do almost anything to have sex and they will lie to you. You will be better off dating boys your own age and both of you remember that <u>someone who really cares about you will not pressure you to drink, take drugs or have sex</u>.

Lastly, for this letter, is to remember that you are unique. No matter how much mother and I may want something for you or hope that you grow up to be astronauts or concert musicians or cowboys, you are going to grow up to be your own person. You'll start learning who you are now and it will continue for 20 more years. You are going to do things your own way not the way we expect. You will learn to meet your own goals and expectations, not ours. What you will need to remember is that the world is full of 6 billion people, all of them meeting their own goals and expectations, living their own lives their own way. If you think that people will always be the way *you* want them to be or that they will always live up to *your* expectations you will be disappointed over and over and over. Everyone is wired differently, thinks differently, and has a slightly different set of values and principles. You need to trust people, love people, respect people but remember that they live things their way, not your way. Sometimes these differences will be so clear cut that it will be uncomfortable or painful to even be near them. When you meet these people just stay away. For everyone else, enjoy the differences that make us all unique, but don't expect them to change for you. When it is all said and done, the only person you can change is you.

I love you very dearly my darling children. I hope I haven't embarrassed you much. This letter is for you. If you want to share it with mother or others you certainly can but it is specifically for you.

I'm looking forward to getting home on leave within a few months and seeing you. If you want to discuss any of this we can then, or on the phone before then (or never if it's too sensitive). I'm sending you each your own copy of this and they are identical. They may arrive on the same day or may not, so you can choose to visit with each other about these things if you wish or no one. It's up to you.

Love,

Dad

"Greetings All,

"The kids and I webcammed with Roger after church today and he looks and sounds great. He does have this funky haircut though. I told him he looks like Mr. T. He assured me it was just the webcam image and that it really doesn't look like a Mohawk. I can only hope that is true because it looks really ugly from where I'm sitting.

"Robyn"
**

Hi everyone! 22 January 2006

We just finished the busiest week so far at the Joint Visitors Bureau. The hotel was completely full for three days; every escort team, every escort officer, every vehicle was in use all week. We pushed back to our higher headquarters when they tried to give us even more missions – sorry sirs, we are maxed out!

Within the hotel the hierarchy is clear: if a more senior general or government leader comes in needing a room you may be asked to leave. That happened a few times this week as unexpected visitors joined us and bumped out others. If you don't think it's hard to tell a two-star general he has to leave his king sized bed and private bath inside, and instead sleep in a trailer and walk to a port-a-potty in the dark then you haven't experienced the stress that some of our lieutenants and sergeants do every day.

Probably the most interesting thing this week was an off-season dust-storm. It was not a major storm for Iraq but it was quite an event for us. When we went to bed Friday night the wind was blowing briskly; it smelled and felt a lot like a Halloween night in Kansas. By morning the sky was hazy; by noon the visibility was down to 200 meters and by dusk it was 50 meters. Again, this was not a major storm. It did not blow up like a thunderstorm or roll in like a wall from the movies. It just kind of sneaked up on us until all our missions were shut down. At this writing we still have missions grounded in other parts of the country, unable to fly due to both the wind speed and the visibility. It is, however, clearing here in Baghdad this Sunday morning, and you can see the sun again. We expect everyone back home safely by evening, but expect some dissatisfied customers who did not complete their agenda to somehow blame us for the storm.

The attached photos show our area: the JVB is the long, flat building just right/above center on the isthmus. This old photo shows the area when it was originally under construction 20 years ago. You can see how close the JVB is to the main palace, just left/above the JVB. This is reference for the dust storm photo. It shows the effect of the storm. You can barely see the palace less than 150 meters away!

Major General Todd Bunting, the adjutant general of Kansas, stayed with us for four days this week. He visited with nearly every soldier in the battalion and spent most of his time in Camp Slayer with LTC Trafton (the boss) and touring our towers and entry control points down there. He also flew down into the International Zone and visited with soldiers in the 127th Field Artillery, another Kansas unit on duty here. General Bunting is an old friend of mine back to the days when I (as a First Lieutenant) trained him (a Lieutenant Colonel) on total quality management as the Air Force was learning that system of skills and tools. We had no time to visit during his trip as I was on missions most of the time but I was very pleased to see him and extra pleased to see him put in the time with all our soldiers. He knows where the rubber meets the road. My extra old buddy Command Sergeant Major Steve Rodina was also on the visit and it was great to see him. Steve and I go all the way back to the days when he was on the Governor's personal security team and I was a young pup working for the Speaker of the House. Steve looks and sounds a lot like Sam Elliot . . .

Towards the end of the week I spent another two days with General Abizaid on his semi-regular monthlyish visits. I was in Al Ramadi for the first time, where the Marines, Army and Iraqi Army are all working together to pacify the Anbar Province where the main Sunni resistance remains. I wish every reporter in the USA could spend a week with General Abizaid hearing all the briefings and seeing all the progress. In Anbar the general saw maps comparing enemy "safe" territory a year ago to today. What was all "red" and friendly to the terrorists then is now nearly all clear and occupied by US and Iraqi soldiers. Where US forces once would clear the bad guys out and then leave – allowing the bad guys to return – they now leave enough combat punch and especially Iraqi soldiers in place to maintain the hard-earned peace. Enemy forces are increasingly encircled into constricted areas. (I nearly jumped out of my skin when US cannons about 200 meters away fired a series of OUT-going rounds; it shook the dust down from the ceilings. The loudest thing I have heard here yet. Would not want to be on the receiving end because *our* guys *aim*...). Another very interesting thing: Abizaid met with this dynamite Brigadier General, Rebecca Halstead, the commander of an enormous logistical system at Balad.

She talked about how close they are to turning on local water purification and bottling systems that will provide for all the US military water needs in country. This, she said, will take 700 trucks a day off the highways from Kuwait AND provide enough excess water capacity to take care of most of the Iraqi military needs too. And when the USA goes home all that capacity will be available for the Iraqi economy. Boy, the Kuwaitis are going to be torqued off to lose all that water business.

Letters and cards from Kirk Johnson, the boss at Commerce Bank & Trust, mom and pop X 3, sister Karen, John and Joan Crouse, Jeff Wagaman, Co-worker and friend Joyce Merryman at CBTKS, book about the Irish rebellion of 1916 from the kilt-wearing Irish Lonergan's of Topeka, and goodie box from Robyn with *MY* soothing aftershave and magazines. Thanks everyone!

American by birth. Soldier by choice. Volunteer by God!

Roger T. Aeschliman
Major, Armor
Deputy Commander, First Kansas Volunteers

Hi everyone! 29 January 2006

Thanks to everyone who has written and told me about your "normal" days. I share your comments at the evening BUB (battle update brief). Often the letter-writers ask me: "What is a normal day for you?" The easy out is to say there are NO "normal" days and that would be true but lazy so I'll try to describe a *typical* day instead.

On a mission day, when I am actively engaged with dignitaries, I begin at 0430 or so. I shave and dress then walk 100 meters in the dark to the "office" in the Joint Visitors' Bureau palace. There I check the military's secret internet system for last minute updates to the schedule and agenda and make last minute coordination with anyone so affected by those last minute changes. This can be anywhere in the country and you would probably be surprised at how many people are already up and on the job at 0530 or 0630. I drink a couple cups of coffee (thanks to all of you it's good coffee!), then get breakfast in our hotel dining facility (DFAC). I eat a hearty breakfast of eggs, meats, biscuits and gravy, grits, cold cereal, Pop Tarts, juice and milk. Then I check all my hero gear a final time, check my small backpack (overnight gear), hook up the portable radio with the wires down my back, the microphone on my collar and the speaker/plug in my left ear, and do a radio check with the team.

We get into armored but comfortable Chevy Suburbans (like the one that ran over my backpack), add an unarmored 20 passenger bus to the line and then convoy with 3-6 vehicles about 10 miles to the Baghdad International Airport (BIAP). It takes about 30 minutes to get there as we wend through several base camps, several checkpoints, over badly potholed, narrow roads and generally heavy traffic. We go to a VIP landing area we call the "Glass House," due to its domed roof that is lined with overhead mirrors (it has an odd acoustic effect: if you are under the dome you can hear others under the dome whispering, but if you are outside of the dome you can not hear someone inside speaking...interesting). The Air Force runs the reception center there and processes people in and out all day and night so we become good friends with them even though they rotate home every four months (unlike the Army's year-long tours).

Our VIPs usually arrive on 40-year-old C-130 cargo planes but sometimes the larger jet C-17s, or occasionally a small executive jet or a larger commercial-style passenger plane. Most often they fly in from Kuwait but sometimes from Turkey, Qatar or Jordan. I and the Air Force folks (and sometimes higher ranking Generals or Embassy staff if the VIP is VIPish enough) meet the distinguished visitors (DVs) at the plane, shout greetings over the propeller noise, walk a few steps to the Suburbans, then drive a short way to a quieter spot where we give them a safety briefing (trying to scare the hell out of them so they pay attention and follow directions for a few days – and most of them are used to giving directions so that *can* be a big challenge), suit them up in ballistic vests, Kevlar helmets and ear plugs, let them use the latrine, then drive them or walk them (depending on the weather and their physical condition) 100 or 200 meters to the helicopters taking them all over Iraq.

We put the DVs mostly on the first helicopter, with aides and assistants (strap-hangers) in the second or third. Our medic and I are always on the second bird so we can try to exercise some sort of control and recovery in the event of a disaster with the DVs helicopter. I always check with the pilots before takeoff to ensure they are going where we want to go . . . you never know where you might end up otherwise. You learn not to assume anything over here. Our most frequent stop is the International Zone (IZ) in downtown Baghdad; it is also the closest, about 5-10 minutes depending on how evasive of route the pilots take. In the IZ we are received by either a team of our own JVB Suburbans or a team from the Embassy's staff of agents, ride a short but bumpy block through all kinds of guards and barricades then enter the Embassy proper. Usually a DV group will spend most of a day in the IZ, with numerous one hour to 90 minute meetings in the Embassy, or at one of the dozen Iraqi Ministries within the IZ. The Prime Minister, the President, the Minister of the Defense (Army) and the Ministry of the Interior (police) are the most frequent stops but the Elections Commission was the most popular of all up to and through the December 15 vote.

I am a fly on the wall in these meetings and briefings and hear all of the good news on what is happening here. If I'm not in a meeting I am either on guard (depending what the security is like where we are) or on one of the four radios or phones I carry to guarantee communications. I report our location and status throughout the day so if General Casey asks where "his" guests are and how they are doing the JVB battle captain and staff will always be able to answer. I also spend a lot of time every mission ensuring the next location is prepared to receive us, the next helicopters are ready to go and that next meal will be on-site, on-time. Most trips include several DV meals each day with soldiers from the DVs' home states. Once the DVs are seated I will usually eat as well, tactically so I can be at the right place instantly if needed. So on missions I will eat two or three times a day and burn it all up. I drink coffee, water and Gatorade all day, wherever I can get it (and will even more so when it starts to heat back up – by the way we had pea-sized hail in a humdinger thunderstorm last night). Occasionally DVs will rest over night (RON) somewhere in the country but most often we fly back to either the JVB hotel (and I sleep in my own hooch for a few hours) or fly down to the Embassy where the DVs sleep in a nice pool-side villa and we peons sleep in closet-sized rooms with a cot and a light bulb. (Side note, the Embassy has a 20-seat movie theater in the basement and I watched "Chisholm" with John Wayne earlier this week – free popcorn too…).

This is getting way too long so I'll stop by saying that second, third and fourth days are identical to the first, with lots of helicopter trips ranging from 10 minutes to two hours, meeting with generals and directors and ministers and soldiers all over Iraq to learn about their missions, programs and results. Eventually we wind up back at the Glass House, put the DVs on an airplane, wave goodbye and drive back to the JVB for a good night's sleep. During missions I stand almost all day, usually get to sleep after 11 p.m. with early wake-ups so it is great to sleep-in and I always look forward to recovering on a non-mission day or two (which I'll describe shorter in some future report).

This week I had Governors from Texas, Arkansas, Wyoming and Wisconsin, followed by Congressman Hunter, the Chairman of the House Armed Services Committee. Uneventful all, except for rained out flights hither and yon. We just worked around it. Everyone seemed happy when they left.

Letters and cards from Mom and Pop x 2 (and a magazine/snack box), Melba Waggoner, the Waldy's, and the Adriel Class at TBC, sister Karen Sue and college roommate and neighbor Kent Townsend. Thanks everyone!

American by birth. Soldier by choice. Volunteer by God!

Roger T. Aeschliman
Major, Armor
Deputy Commander, First Kansas Volunteers

From: Pat VanHooser
Date: Thursday, February 2, 2006 6:24 pm
Subject: Happy Groundhog Day

Hi Roger,
It is February already! That means it's just about dust bowl time for you, doesn't it? I love the pictures you send. It gives a sense of what being Saddam must have been like. Wow!

Can you tell me if John Murtha has been over to visit? He is making a big deal out of how Iraq is a losing proposition. If he has been there and seen what is really going on then I can only conclude his agenda is one of self interest. Mike says he has heard that Pelosi has promised him a chairmanship if the Dems can get the house back. If true, and he knows better, that spells treason to me.

I may have a clue about my dating life I'll share with you. There is an entomologist in Oklahoma (Oklahoma!) who kind of has a thing for me. He is coming out to do some work with my company in March. He called and asked if I'd like for him to collect some live Brown Recluse spiders and bring them along. I SAID YES! See, that's a clue. Remember when a guy would bring you flowers? They bring me poisonous spiders and I'm happy about it. Actually, lately a lot of interest has been shown on the part of some eligible Augusta gentlemen so I'm having some fun. Don't know where they've been up until now. Not much else happening around here that's worth reporting. You, on the other hand, have a fascinating life right now. Just stay safe, my friend. Oh yeah, and I hope you get to enjoy the Super Bowl!

All my best, Pat
**

Hey Pat! Great to hear from you. Brightened my day as always. That's a big NO on Murtha. There is no way he could reconcile his beliefs with what's going on over here. It would take the most devoted of ideologues to refuse to see the facts (but on the other hand, Biden was here and he saw and heard what he wanted to see and hear). It is a big country and the whole situation is sloppy enough that one CAN probably validate themselves . . . I just realized that. I guess it's like any other hot political issue. One can find and cherry pick the facts required to support what you believe.

I have made a similar argument about voting in the past. Mike may remember. People vote almost entirely for the person that makes them feel the best about themselves. We will find "opinions" "positions" and "voting records" to validate that good feeling, but that is just cover for the deep-rooted good feeling. That explains a country that can vote overwhelmingly for Ronald Reagan and then follow up with Bill Clinton. Two people who could not be further apart but both of whom exuded good feeling (in very different ways but they both made people feel good around them).

So, Murtha and the others all suck but in 12 hours of meetings over two short days they can find "proof" over here that it is not working and will not work. Sad...

Spiders huh? Well the male of most species is typically a provider . . .

I intend to stay up all night for the 2 a.m. Superbowl kickoff! Aretha Franklin AND Rolling Stones! WOW! Who cares about the game? Best to you, rog

From: Robyn Aeschliman
Date: Thursday, February 2, 2006 6:08 pm
Subject: hey from home

Hi Babe,

Wanted to let you know that we will be going to the Harris's for the Superbowl. Ryan was quite adamant that we attend that party. He really didn't want to consider doing the ABY party. I guess the big screen TV, food, and company won out for him. I haven't said anything to them that you might call so they aren't disappointed if you are unable to do so.

I dealt with plumbing issues yesterday. Oh, joy. The kids shower was clogged and not draining well so I poured some drain stuff in and that appears to have fixed that problem. The other issue is the toilets. None of them are flushing very well and the kids assure me that they are not using large amounts of tp. I tend to believe them since my toilet is not flushing well even without tp. I had the plumber out about a month ago to look at my toilet and he made a few adjustments but it doesn't appear to have made a difference. I'm now wondering if we might have some sort of clog in the main system that is impeding the smooth flow of a flush. So I dumped a box of rid-x or something like that that is suppose to break down stuff in the system. It was the only thing at the store that you could use in the toilet - everything else was just for drains. We're going to watch this for the next few weeks and see if there is any improvement. If not, then I'll call a different plumber in to assess the situation. It's times like these that I really wish you were home. I'm really tired of plunging toilets!

Another problem is the darn computer mouse. It stopped moving around last night and I have no idea what the problem is. It appears to be "on" but the curser won't move. I'm going to have to find the owner's manual and see if there is any trouble shooting listed. And no, it doesn't need a battery. The red light is still on so it's getting power. In the mean time, I'm using the built in mouse and you know how that bugs me. Every time I type I end up moving the page up and down because I accidentally touch the mouse pad. Very frustrating.

I sub for Emily this afternoon. Hopefully, the kids will be great. They usually are since they know me and I'm in there enough that they don't try stupid "sub" stuff with me.

This coming weekend is full of activities - especially for Ryan. He has a merit badge conference all day on Saturday at WU. He needs to be there at 7:30. UGH! On Sunday he has Scout Sunday at the UM church and needs to take a dessert. UGH! Then on Sunday night we will be at the Harris's for the Superbowl. Regan needs to work on making some swaps for Midnight at the Mall which is the following weekend. I need to take her at 9:30 on Saturday night and pick her up at 7:20 on Sunday morning. I foresee little sleeping in and leisurely reading the paper over the next few weekends. Oh well, at least it's not 5:00 AM.

I'm getting ready to send you a magazine box. Is there anything you want me to include in it that you need from home? I'm thinking I'll make cookies for Scout Sunday so may put a few in your box. How about choc. chip? I think they will travel ok right now since it's not too hot.

Hope all is well with you and am looking forward to talking soon.

Love you.
Robyn
XXXOOO
**

Good morning darling,

Sorry about all the ordeals. Everyone will be worn out by Monday morning! I will call Harris's around halftime or so. Thanks for the phone number. Mike will probably call too...

No clue on the plumbing. The last time that happened we replaced the entire guts on all the toilets and they worked fine. How long ago was that? Computer mouse: There may be a little tiny synchronization button on the bottom of the mouse or on the little hook shaped thing attached to the computer. There also may be an icon on the bottom right of the screen for the mouse that will let you click and troubleshoot. I don't remember if we had to install software . . . if we did you can reinstall. Good luck. Don't agonize though. Just go buy another one.

And yes, your wonderful chocolate chip cookies would be great! YUM!!! I could also use a bottle of Refresh Tears, the 1/2 ounce size. Everything else is fine. I miss you totally and terribly most days but am busy and just keep going. Today it is cool, windy and rainy. Power is out sporadically. It is gloomy and dreary. I have no mission and I can't even go run to take my mind off of things so it is a bad day so far.

Only knowing that you and the kids are safe at home worrying about plumbing and getting the kids places on time (NORMAL!!!!) make days like this one bearable. Thanks for being such an incredible person and thank you for loving me. Your most devoted husband, friend and admirer, rog

02 FEB 07
Robyn, also please send 2 Oral B Ultra Flosses. Can't get those here either and I'm about out. Two should last all year. Love you for taking care of me, rog

ALSO ALSO:

Please pass on to Ronna:

Hi sis!
Thanks for the nice letter mailed on Jan. 20. I received it on 2 Feb. Usually USA letters arrive in about a week. Packages take just a few days more. Thanks again for sending me the nice gift certificate. I have a pretty nice pile of them and am thinking of buying a small TV/DVD player for about $150. We'll see. It would be quite a splurge but I'm not spending money on anything else except hygiene products and haircuts (and a new holster I truly needed and Valentine's Day gifts for the wife and kids)...

I did mail you a thank you note. Sorry it didn't arrive . . . I also made sure YOUR soldier has your email address and mailing address. I even reminded his officers that all soldiers should write thank you notes for things but I can't MAKE them do it. Just like children except you CAN make your children (or beat them). Perhaps one of the reasons they don't get much mail is because they lack social skills . . .

Well, nevertheless thanks for writing to me and to these young men.

I am missing protective eyewear for sure, and a wet weather suit for sure. I may be missing a number of other items like long underwear, gloves and a helmet but they may be in bags stored in Kansas. So I'll need to get home to reconcile all the supplies I'm issued.

Morale is pretty good overall. There is enough going on that soldiers are staying busy and are happy to have a down day when they get one. There are always issues back home. Babies are being born, parents and grand parents are dying, family members have cancer. We've now got over 600 people assigned to us so in that number of people you just have to expect these things to happen. We are now starting to send people home on emergency leave for these things and also home on the normal 2 weeks vacation leave. I hope to be home in late March. I DO NOT expect to be home for the Anniversary party. I do not control the process and will be coming home when assigned leave. We have rightly given the most junior members of the unit first choice on when to go home and those of us old guys with rank will just be filled in the blank spots. So most of the young folks are taking all the mid-year summer time slots leaving me and others the times early in the year or very late. We will still have people going on leave in August and September even though we hope to be home in November or December. That's because we can only allow a maximum of 10% of the team to be gone at one time. We just can't get the work done otherwise as we run out of troops to fill the towers and gates and mission.

Have a nice trip to Panama; enjoy your "winter". We expect another month (February) of cool and wet then only random springtime thunderstorms in March and April but warmer. By May it should be hot and getting hotter and dryer. We'll see. Today is rainy, windy and dreary. Many FALL days in Kansas just like this.

Thanks again for writing. The mail is nice. You can also send email through Robyn. It is more reliable than the Costa Rican postal service!

My love to you and Ken, rog

Last thoughts and wishes (not demands, not instructions, not legally binding in any sense) of

Roger Timothy Aeschliman
03 FEBRUARY 2006

Hello Robyn, Ryan, Regan, Mom, Pop, and Rob initially, then anyone else that you all wish to share this with later,

If you are reading this then I am dead. Sorry about that.

Please know that I believe in what we are doing here. I believe the Wahhabists when they tell us their goal is to rule the world in an Islamist fascist state and that everyone will live their way or die. They have said it. Why do we refuse to believe them? I died for individual liberty and freedom, for our great nation, for Kansas, Topeka, my wife and children and the grandchildren and great-grandchildren not yet born (and who had better not be born for at least another 15 years or so – are you listening Ryan and Regan?).

I've had a wonderful life, filled with love and joy – family and friends. I have had challenges and successes and setbacks. I have seen and done things most people never dream of. I am fortunate to have made it out of high school and college alive and could recite any number of near death experiences from hanging by fingertips from the top of a silo, to being knocked out and 9/10ths buried in sand at a construction site, to passing madly on a highway, facing a head on crash with no where to go, to careening out of control into trees while skiing. So, every day since has been a good one . . .

My life was fine until I met Robyn and then it became perfect. Every day, perfect. I can only wish that my children will be patient and thoughtful as they begin selecting life partners. While the first loves are passionate, and painful when they end, they are seldom the right loves. Grow up before you choose a husband or wife. Let your brains work with your hearts and then if you are lucky you will find someone to love you and to love like your mother and I love each other. I was a very thoughtless and shallow young man when we met and over the years she turned me into a man. Perhaps I had a similar influence upon her. Ask her. All I know is that my life would have been meaningless without Robyn and then later, you two children.

I've already written to you two, Ryan and Regan, discussing a few things. I believe you are on your way. Oh the Places You'll Go! As you grow older and move through Middle School and High School you will be faced with infinite choices. The most important ones will revolve around friends. As crazy as it sounds not everyone who is nice to you is your friend and not everyone who harms you is your enemy. I guess I'd just say hang out with people who make you feel good, who help make you a better person and who help you grow. Don't hang out with people who make you feel bad. That should seem obvious but too many people never seem to get it.

So everyone, go ahead and feel sad. There's no way around it, but do remember that I lived a wonderful life, did most of what I wanted to do and I think I made a difference in a few lives. That's pretty good.

Rob and Robyn, please enlist Kirk Johnson and Mike Lott to help out if you need any assistance in tracking things down. As a starter, the file cabinet in the basement has everything. It may not be as organized as it could be but it's all there in the second drawer. Other documents are in the downtown bank safe deposit box. I believe at a minimum there is:

1-$800,000 from the Army and Air Force Mutual Aid Association, www.aafmaa.com

2-$400,000 from SGLI, call the Adjutant General's Office

3-$200,000 or so from the State of Kansas for a death benefit, call Adjutant General

4-$30,000 from SSLI, that should come within a couple days; call the National Guard Association of Kansas, or the Adjutant General

5-$100,000 from State Farm for whole life. There may be a war clause and we might only get back the cash value. Call Gary Lucas.

6-There may be something through Commerce Bank & Trust but I don't think so. Call Kirk Johnson.

7-There may be a death benefit through KPERS, retirement system, or there is a payout of contributions, or you may be able to receive my retirement payments. Work through this carefully to make the right choice.

8-Something from Social Security and something from Army Retirement too. No clue but something.

So I think you and the kids are going to be in good shape. I would suggest you pay off the house, just to be done with it. It is not the best investment but it is a decent one and would relieve a lot of worry. You do what you want to do.

I would encourage you to continue your normal gifting until the kids are grown. It would be generous to give sums away now but you and the kids ARE the critical need right now and all of our parents may become critical needs later so I'd resist any new or special gifting until the kids are grown. You do what you want to do.

Long in the future when your time comes and the children are successful adults I'd suggest some significant gift to the Boy Scouts, the Girl Scouts, to Topeka Rotary or Washburn. In my perfect world I would create a trust for 100 years and leave it all sit to grow. At the end of that time create a foundation for the conservative support and defense of the US Constitution from the judiciary, the protection of both individual and state's rights, and the thought that the best government is the least government at the lowest possible governmental level. You do what you want to do.

Right now, my body is somewhere. If there remains any possibility of transplant or donation for the benefit of a living person please see that it happens. If that is not possible then please offer my corpse for any research up to and including dissection and weapons testing in the US military. You do what you want to do.

Ultimately I would ask to be cremated and either scattered in some Grantville cornfield or mixed into concrete for some new downtown Topeka construction – either is a nice sign of hope for the future. I have no feelings about a physical memorial of any kind. If one is desired I leave it to you but would suggest that it be interesting and serve some kind of public good – an arboretum, a park bench, or something to attract tourists to Topeka like the Hiawatha memorial or the Garden of Eden at Lucas. You do what you want to do.

Immediately I would hope you all will have a big party. I mean big! Roll out some kegs of Blind Tiger, rent a big hall, hire a karaoke system with lots of microphones and an enormous inventory of music across all genres, and everybody drink and sing. Ask the Topeka rugby team to come in and lead some obscene rugby party songs. If people would like to tell Roger stories that would be great. I always like being the center of attention. You do what you want to do.

As far as funeral services, I kind of like the military stuff: folded flag, rifle salute, Taps. It's all so dramatic and makes for great photos. So much more interesting long term and for memory making than formal church/chapel services. As far as those go, you guys do what you want. Services are always for the living anyway.

Finally, I give you all permission to be sad now and happy soon. Go ahead and be sad as long as you need to be, but please don't dwell and linger there. Move on with your lives. There is so much out there in the world yet to see and do. Don't get locked up in sorrow for too long. I want you to be happy and joyous. Robyn especially. You are so beautiful and such an incredible human being. Every man in America would be lucky to have you in their lives. You have my permission to meet someone and to love again. And there is no timetable. It will happen when it happens and no one will think poorly of you (not parents, not siblings, and especially not my children – Mom deserves all the love and happiness she can find. Never, ever make her feel bad about living her life as an individual person).

Well, I love you all. I wish I weren't dead but apparently that's no longer an option. So go ahead and be sad as long as you need to, but then remember: Sooner or later you'll need to stop whining and get on with it!

rog/daddy/Ash/MAJ A/Lucky

"Greetings All,

"For those of you who want to see Roger I will ask him to send a photo of himself next week. I know several of you have asked for a recent photo of him after my comment concerning his haircut.

"Robyn"
**

Hi everyone! 05 February 2006

A continuation of last week: "what is a typical non-mission day like?"

On the first day after a mission I almost never set the alarm clock and just sleep in. On second days (common) or third days (rare) I may or may not set the alarm for 6 or 6:30, depends how much catch-up work and how much next mission preparation I have to do. Shave and dress, (usually do NOT eat breakfast) walk to the office, read the e-mail on the secret net, read the e-mail on the non-secret Army net, and read e-mail on the non-military commercial net, then do any work generated or tasked from all those contacts.

I will usually write letters or memos for a couple of hours, have a couple of cups of coffee, make a number of phone calls and respond to requests for JVB support. Once a month or so I just walk around and inspect the hotel and the command areas directing improvements or repairs. Once a week I do laundry in the nearby self-service machines. Twice a month or so I have to walk the ½ mile to the barber shop for a haircut ($3 from Indian barbers). I usually will walk over to the Water Palace (the big one in previous photos) and meet with my "informal" commander, not my real Lieutenant Colonel but another one who works directly for General Casey (the general who runs the whole war in Iraq). This Lt. Col. runs the planning operation for all the visitors missions and once they are planned turns them over to us to implement. We do additional planning in order to implement every mission, thus work very closely with him and his team. So, he's not officially my boss but he gives us work to do that we have to do and he can make my life miserable so it sure sounds like a boss doesn't it?

Anyway, around noon or so I will change into the Army Physical Fitness Uniform – shorts, t-shirt, sweat suit (but absolutely never, under no circumstances whatsoever, a sweatband) – and run 5-6 miles around the lakes and palaces here. I ran seven miles once but my old football and rugby knees just can't handle the pounding. I do push-ups and sit-ups too, or lift some weights (we have a small set on the back deck overlooking the lake for the benefit of hotel guests). I try to run every day I'm not on a mission (189 miles as of Superbowl Sunday!). I never, ever eat lunch except on missions.

Mid-afternoon shower, back to the office, drink Gatorade (thanks to you all!) read e-mail again, do required paperwork, then attend the daily 1700 briefing about our missions, JVB status reports and the upcoming calendar. Supper at the JVB hotel chow hall for my daily calories, a final paperwork review and e-mail check, then around 1900 (7 p.m.) wind down, personal hygiene, write cards or letters (and weekly reports), maybe watch 30 minutes of a DVD movie or TV show, then read for an hour, then lights out 2200 (10 p.m.). Just not very interesting . . .

This week I had the assistant secretary of state for Iraq reconstruction, and then Congressman Shays (very bright from Connecticut-big in Homeland Security), Doolittle (second cousin of the famed Jimmy Doolittle of WWII heroics) from Northern California, including Tahoe where Robyn and I honeymooned 17½ blink-of-an-eye years ago, Congresswomen Brown-Waite of Florida, and perhaps most interestingly, Katherine Harris of Florida/ Bush/election fame. She is considering a run for the US Senate and is an itty-bitty speck of a thing. Made all of them promise to say hello to the Kansas delegation for me. We were all the way up on the Syrian and Turkish borders on this trip but other than saying we were there, nothing special to see and nothing special happened.

I am writing this at 2100 hours (9 p.m.) Sunday of that all-weekend mission and intend to stay up to watch the Superbowl (0200 Monday kickoff in Iraq). Silly I suppose but it just wouldn't be right with the world were I to miss this. Even during basic training 1987 we were allowed to watch the Superbowl...not going to miss one now.

Letters and cards from Pop x 2 (describing perfectly wonderful, NORMAL days), and sister Ronna in Costa Rica, coffee and a nice note from Rick and Sarah Beyer (former boss and dear friends), Valentine's day card and candy bars from my adopted Bible study group at TBC, and a snack box from my sixth grade pen pal Hannah Holden from Valley Center Middle School. Thanks everyone!

American by birth. Soldier by choice. Volunteer by God!

Roger T. Aeschliman
Major, Armor
Deputy Commander, First Kansas Volunteers

Hey Pop! 06 FEB 06

Just got your letter of 1/28. I had just been thinking about you and our adventures during your heart attack; I was thinking it must have been around about the end of January . . .

I remember thinking what a tough cookie you must be to suffer through a heart attack for 24 hours (or longer probably), but what a dumb-ass you must be to suffer through a heart attack for 24 hours. Anyway, sure glad you called that morning. In far hindsight now it is clear you did have a significant attack but also that we could have avoided that whole week of crisis caused by the dye.

Around here we are in Kansas October kind of weather = cool then nearly freezing at night followed by two days of drizzle, followed by a thunderstorm, then beautiful pleasant days of sunshine and 60 degrees. It does dry out pretty quickly. A few nights ago it thundered and poured, then cleared. I stepped out to use the Porto potty before sleeping and stepped into shin-deep water over the walkway. By morning it was gone.

I remember the Challenger clearly. Was in the newsroom and was one of two people who saw it actually blow up the first time. I remember the NASA announcer saying "Clearly some sort of major malfunction..." and I shouted back at the TV "malfunction my ass! It blew up!" I was then surrounded by everyone in the whole place and we watched it blow up over and over and over. I also remember being pretty upset and remember you offering some kind and wise words that helped but I forget what they were☺

You wouldn't find my basic training ship date on the 1986 calendar. You would have to look at early January 1987, the second or third or fourth. You dropped me at the old bus terminal (now a bank) and that was my first and only US bus trip (to Kansas City). Waved goodbye to someone but don't remember who dropped me off. I wasn't too sad then; you can handle anything for four months. Also remember you three coming to get me at Knox. Remember sleeping most of the way home...

It appears that I will be coming home on leave in late March. I have asked to be shifted up to be home in time for your 50th anniversary but right now it doesn't look like it will happen. Will certainly let you know if it is going to come about. I won't surprise you either way. You can tell Mom if you wish but tell her NOT to plan in it for now. Even if I get shifted forward, delays and air problems can still leave me stuck in Kuwait, Germany or Ireland.

Got back in late last night (Sunday), slept for three hours then got up and watched the first half of the Superbowl and the halftime show. I was just too wiped out and too not interested in either team to stay awake for the second half. Back at work now today and back on a mission tomorrow. Busy.

Thanks for the letters dad. I sure do appreciate it. Love, rog

From: Michael Ryan
Date: Tuesday, February 7, 2006 8:36 pm

How about those damn Muslims and the cartoon thing? They want everyone to follow the dictates of Islamic law. Kind of like Pat Robertson and Christianity... :)
**

Mike,

Muslims. Can't live with 'em, can't nuke Mecca. The hypocrisy is the worst part, followed by their weakness of faith. Are they really so shallow and tepid in faith that they fear seeing a picture of Muhammad? So unselfcontrolled they fear their own primal selves will be released by simply seeing woman's ankle? So unable to think and study on their own they can only do what they are told to do and believe what they are told to believe by the Imams and Ayatollahs? Not unlike the 1600s in the pre-USA and the Spanish Inquisition (no one expects the Spanish Inquisition!)

By the way, many if not most male Arab Iraqis practice sex with boys and oral sex on each other. They regularly proposition our soldiers...our guys are so disgusted. This more than anything else is making it hard for our guys to see them as people worth saving...interesting.

Dear Mom and Pop, 11 FEB 06

As of right now it looks like I should be home on Friday, March 10 for two weeks leave. I will leave Iraq on the 8th and then after that am at the mercy of the military and civilian airlift system. So plan on seeing me Saturday at the party . . . but, be prepared for me to be stuck in Kuwait, or Frankfort, or Ireland, or Newfoundland or wherever, waiting on a flight. I will be in touch with Robyn during that movement so she can keep you informed. I really want to make sure there is no surprise either way as not to steal any attention from you two on this wonderful milestone day.

Thanks for all the mail, notes, cards, clippings. It does really brighten up the day and the wall where I tape all the cards and pictures. I get e-mail from Robyn and talk to her and the kids four-five times a week. I also call Mike Ryan once in a while, and you guys too.

In your recent letters you both expressed some concern. I'm really not in harm's way much. The biggest risks I face are vehicle accidents on these narrow roads and the normal risk that comes from riding in helicopters. There is more danger of falling down on the typically gravelly and rocky landing pads than there is of getting shot down or crashing from mechanical failure. The proof of this is that anytime a helicopter goes down for any reason it is page 1 news. Anything that happens that infrequently isn't a big deal. I always wear seatbelts ☺

I wrote home to the kids talking candidly about the risks here and reassuring them. It is not impossible I could be injured or killed but the odds are really against it. We just are not out running the roads where the IEDs and bombers try to work . . .

I did send a "to be opened in case of death" letter to our friend and attorney Rob Telthorst. You two along with Robyn and the kids are on the initial "read to" list. When I get back home for good we'll open it up and read it over a beer and see what I wrote as I've pretty much forgotten.

Changing gears back to you two: Thanks for being such good parents and for providing such a good example for me. I learned much of my behavior from you both and find myself modeling you more and more as the years go by. I know neither of you are perfect and that you had troubles over the years but always pulled it back together. I believe Robyn and I are of the same mettle and we continue to profit from your example. Robyn, perhaps even more than me, loves you as the stable, nurturing family she did not have...

50 years is a remarkable length of time...

You also are surrounded by friends who share the same philosophy and commitment. This makes a difference and is one of the things I told the kids in my letter to them: Surround yourself and associate with people who make you feel good about yourself and by people you want to be like and it will tell in the end. You have done that to good result over the years.

Ty Cobb (a notorious loner and tough guy) in his last years was asked what he would do if he could do it all over. He answered that he would have more friends. And Ira Price said: I don't want a million dollars but I do want a million friends. Clearly you two are wealthy beyond measure and have set this example for us kids throughout your lives.

Well, I just wanted to calm your nerves and to wish you a wonderful anniversary celebration just in case I'm sitting in some foreign airport while you all are celebrating.

Love and thanks for the letters,

rog

"Hey All,

"Roger included a photo of himself this week....looks a bit like Rambo meets the Terminator with his big gun....and the haircut, well, you be the judge. This week's update should provide some good giggles.

"Enjoy, Robyn"
**

Hi everyone! 12 February 2006

There are a lot of small things that happen (occasionally surreal) that make life here interesting. In no particular order:

- On a mission this week I spent an interesting hour outside of a meeting talking to a Master Sergeant who trains Iraqis. He is the guy who told the wounded TV anchorman (who's name escapes me and I don't care enough to look it up) not to go on the mission, not to ride in the Iraqi vehicle, and not to stick his head out of the hatch. He was ignored. He was also the first person to get to the wounded crew and said he was sure the anchorman was dead and was a lot more concerned about his own soldiers, the Iraqis, than he was about a "pretty-boy dumbass that won't listen to someone who knows better."
- I met LTC Randy Lane at a briefing. LTC Lane was an instructor of mine at the Fort Knox Armor Officer Advanced Course in the mid-90s. He didn't remember me but did comment that "it's good to see I didn't ruin everyone."
- After writing to you all last Sunday I slept three hours then got up at 2 a.m. to watch the Superbowl in our command post. Ate sardines and oysters, pistachios, cookies, drank one near beer, pretty much dozed throughout the unexciting first half, watched the old geezers prance around at half-time, called my family and wonderful friends the Harris's and the Towle's at the annual multi-family Superbowl party, and then called it quits. Will remember it as the most interesting locale for watching the big game but one of the least interestingly played games.
- The hotel staff has learned not to bother me with names of celebrity guests as I just don't care about that ilk. So I was totally pissed off when they did not tell me that Nick Lowery (KC Chief kicking great) had come and went. He is a huge hero of mine for both on-field and off-field performance. I went on my next mission and by luck ran into

Nick at the VIP holding pen at the airport. We had a nice visit. He belongs in the Hall of Fame but kickers never get in. Nick has radio programs and runs charities in Arizona for the benefit of American Indians. He used to date State Senator Barbara Allen, a friend of mine from my days working in the Legislature. Got an autograph for dad and mailed it home to Robyn for delivery as I can never remember Mom and Pop's address since it was changed from Rural Route 3 to some street whatever.

- While jogging I heard the discordant (but to me delightful) tune of a bagpiper. Changed my route and followed to the source. Admired his playing for a bit and then asked him "where you from Mate?" assuming he was a Brit or an Aussie. His response: "Laredo. How aw-bout c'hew," in the drawliest Texas accent I ever heard.
- I was suddenly and loudly attacked by a colorful male goose of some sort whilst jogging by his harem on a lake. I survived but had to change my shorts...
- Another goose – looks like a normal Kansas snow goose to me – is nesting right in the middle of a street, right in front of the big HQ palace. Traffic zinging by and hundreds of pedestrians within inches daily. Reminded me of reading my children the classic "Make Way For Ducklings."
- Some more military vocabulary:
- "POO" – the Point Of Origin of incoming fire, as in "Do you know where the POO is?" No, and I'm not sure I want to.
- "MAM" – Military Age Male, an Iraqi suspect of fighting age. In this culture MAMs would be terribly offended to be called a ma'am in their own language.
- "FOBBIT" – A person who never leaves the Forward Operating Base (FOB) but thinks they know what is going on outside the wire. We see FOBBITS regularly as the people who tell us to unload our weapons while we are actively on guard duty for a VIP.
- Who says the Army doesn't have a sense of humor?

This week General Wallace (commanding general during the initial attack into Baghdad three years ago and now Training Commander for the Army) was here. Other than arriving late, helicopter breakdowns and every meeting running long it was uneventful. That pretty much describes a normal mission. Also my favorite General Abizaid returned to review progress and set direction for the overall campaign. When he got off the plane he slapped my on the back and greeted me as "Ash." That was very nice to be remembered.

E-mail from Cameron Rees and work pal Joyce Merryman, letters and cards from Pop and Mom x 3, sis Karen, boss Kirk Johnson, Topeka friend Susan Anderson, big Valentine's's Day box of candy, tollhouse cookies, and flower seeds from the whole gang at the Commerce Bank & Trust Investment Management Group, and coffee beans, nuts and John Wayne DVDs from my lawyer and dear friends Rob and Margaret Telthorst, and younguns Mike and Anna. Thanks everyone!

American by birth. Soldier by choice. Volunteer by God!

Roger T. Aeschliman
Major, Armor
Deputy Commander, First Kansas Volunteers

KANSAS STATE UNIVERSITY COLLEGIAN PROFILE – 14 FEB 2007

NameROGER T. AESCHLIMAN
RankMajor
Age45
Years in the Military/National Guard 19
HometownTopeka
Active student or AlumniAlumni
If active/year in school
If alumni/year graduatedDecember 1981
EmploymentTrust Officer, Commerce Bank &Trust

1. What is your duty position? Deputy Commander of the 2nd Battalion, 137th Infantry Regiment, Kansas Army National Guard. Number 2 guy responsible for 700 soldiers and 200 combat vehicles.

2. What do you do over here? What is your job? Chief of the Joint Visitors Bureau for the Multi-National Force – Iraq. We work directly for General Casey, theater commander, handling, moving, housing and protecting his strategic visitors into the theater. This includes military, civilian and government VIPs from news reporters up the Vice-President.

3. What did you think about when you found out your unit was being deployed to Iraq? 1 – This is the right enemy in the right place at the right time. 2 - Because we are going over there we are keeping them from doing evil over here. 3 – We, America's soldiers, are willing to fight and die in order that their (even the terrorist's) children will have a chance to grow up and live in freedom and liberty. They (the terrorists) are willing to kill our children and anyone else in order to force the world to be the way they want it to be (dictatorial, repressed, stagnant). There is no moral confusion or equivalency here.

4. Besides your family what do you miss the most from back home and why? Having a day off, really truly off with no requirements of any kind, not shaving once in a while, the chance to just be a slacker for a few hours. I also miss fresh bread, soft and fluffy.

5. How is your family coping with the situation of you being deployed? I am fortunate that my wife and I are and always have been true partners. She is the most remarkable person I know and is running our affairs entirely. She has a great support system of friends and family. She stays very busy working on

her master's degree and volunteering all over Topeka. My children are both pubescent and miss me terribly but are also glad I'm not around to probe into their personal lives and embarrass them in front of their friends. They are old enough to understand how important this is. We all agree it would be better if I were home but understand when the time comes and your nation calls that you have to grit your teeth, stop whining and get on with it. We all agree that staying busy helps. It is only bad when you sit around moping and give into to homesickness (like Christmas morning...)

6. What do you do to pass the time or unwind to keep your mind off of duty in a War Zone? My job involves traveling all over Iraq for several days at a time. I escort very senior dignitaries on a daily basis. When I'm not on a mission I have just enough free time to exercise, do laundry and catch up on all my other military work (paperwork). I try to read for an hour or so every night. I miss reading a lot (No. 4).

7. What has been your most memorable moment here? I escorted Secretary of Defense Donald Rumsfeld for four days including Christmas. I watched this remarkable man let himself be pawed over and hugged, stand for thousands of photos, sign hundreds of autographs, shake every hand offered, for four days, with a smile on his face and joy in his heart. This man loves the American serviceman and woman and truly appreciates what we are doing here. He never left a place until every soldier was satisfied. Incredible devotion to duty.

8. Has your opinion about Iraq changed since you've been here? Yes! I believe more than ever that this will be a great nation in only a few short years. The people here work hard, have an entrepreneurial spirit, and want their lives to be better. They know they have a chance never before given to an Arab-region peoples: to live in freedom and democracy for the first time in 10,000 years. There are lots of problems here but this is an ancient region, the cradle of civilization, and they have the pride to make a better future happen.

9. Do you think the news coverage presents an accurate account of the Iraqi conflict? Are you kidding me? The national media outlets are so far out of touch with the real story here they might as well be making it up. All they care about is getting video of blood. Death sells and brings in viewers. The real story is in the daily SWEAT-M analysis that is going on all over the country: Sewer, Water, Electricity, Academics, Trash and Medical improvements and development. All more and better every day. Also improvements in the training and deployment of the Iraqi Army and Police forces, and in the development,

spread and adoption of the rule of law after 10,000 years of the rule of the tyrant.

10. Do you think the news coverage in Iraq is beneficial to the support of the war in Iraq? No. In fact I believe the current media is directly responsible for undercutting the president's conduct of the war and is harming the American soldier over here. This war is already won. What remains is managing the peaceful transition from us to them. Spastic terrorism is big news but it is the worst kind of Onanism. The only way the bad guys can win is if we lose our national will, quit and go home too soon. If today's media had been at work on December 7, 1941 the headlines would have read: "US imperialism forces humble Japanese to defend themselves," "WE DESERVED IT," and "US to surrender and apologize."

11. Do you think the election process will work for Iraq and the Iraqi people and do you think Iraq will ever achieve some democratic form of government? The process has already worked three times! As I write this the Prime Minister has been selected and other ministers are being negotiated. It is important to note they have chosen a parliamentary type system, not an American system of government. It will take a little patience to work out how many ministers and how many/who will be delegates to the national assembly. Each election participation has increased and the buy-in improves. I'm no Pollyanna. I recognize the difficulties ahead, especially in keeping the various factions from going their own ways as independent mini-states. But I believe they are all wise enough to see that five or six mini-states can not stand against the Iranians, the Syrians, the Turks. Only a united Iraq can be strong enough to maintain itself in this hostile region.

12. What are your personal experiences with the Iraqi people and how do you think they perceived you? The Iraqis I have met (a lot, all over the country) are friendly, social and eager to be appreciated. There is a lot of poverty still, as there was under Saddam. But as the economy improves more people get work and provide for their families. This is a requirement for the men over here. Regardless of whether we like it or not, this culture values men over women and a man who cannot care for their family suffers shame. Shame is very, very bad here. Sorry, I'm kind of rambling. I have tried to learn a little Arabic and they really appreciate the attempt to be polite and greet them in their own language. Also, I give away buffalo nickels to everyone I meet and through pictures and bad Arabic explain I'm from Kansas where the buffalo roam. Also, I show pictures of my children and wife. This is a powerful tool to connect as family is SO important over here. Family and honor are what is place is all about.

13. Do you agree with all of the decisions made by President Bush? Concerning the situations in Iraq? Why or why not? It is so easy to second guess one year or three years later. Anyone can Monday Morning Quarterback. It's the man in the arena that matters. Yes, had we realized the entire national police and all local governments were going to collapse along with the military victory then another approach would have been a good idea. But no one saw that coming. Had we seen the development of Iraq as THE theater of combat for the current (and next 40 years) global war on terror then different steps could have been taken to prepare for the IEDs and suicide bombers. But no one saw that coming. Not even the left-wingers who now profess to have all the answers. So, no, our president is not perfect or omniscient. But he is pretty damn good and I'm proud to have him as my Commander in Chief.

14. Do you believe the pressure put on President Bush by the American people is fair, now that you are serving in Iraq? Why and Why not? I don't think the American people are putting pressure on the President. It is the national level media doing what it did during Vietnam – presenting its liberal view as fact. Presidents get selected to take pressure and this current situation is not nearly as bad as other presidents historically have faced. Look at the President's reception at KSU recently. Did he look pressured to you or did he look respected and appreciated?

15. What is the morale of your troops and peers and if low, why? Contrary to popular opinion morale is not about the president, our national agenda or media, or the big picture mission. Morale is ALWAYS. ALWAYS, ALWAYS about the front-line leadership of the troops. If that Sergeant, that Lieutenant, that First Sergeant and Company Commander are squared away, look out for their troops and prove day in and day out that they really care about their men, the troops could be burning feces every day and morale would be high. Contrarily, soldiers could be on a high-speed mission and having tactical successes, but if their front-line leaders are dirt-bags looking out for themselves first, the morale will be low. Our morale is generally high. The soldiers understand their mission and its importance, where they fit in and they have leaders looking out for them. It goes up and down. That's normal.

16. How do you feel about the drawdown of troops in Iraq? It is appropriate and proof of progress. Daily additional Iraqi Army units and policemen are standing up and taking over chunks of the country. As of today nearly 70% of Iraq is under the control of the Iraqi Army, the police and local governments. You don't hear about that do you? Our forces here are at a tipping point where as one combat soldier leaves the front-line two support soldiers can fall

back as well. I personally believe that by the end of this year our forces will be significantly withdrawn and mostly in support of the Iraqi government and military. I'm sorry to say that I cynically believe the anti-war goobers are postured to take credit for this. They will claim it only happened at their insistence when it was the plan all along.

17. How much longer do you think we will be in Iraq? I personally believe (not as a soldier or spokesman for the US government- only as Rog, the guy who reads a lot of history and pays attention to world news and patterns and trends) that our forces will drop from 160,000 to fewer than 80,000 by the end of the year and will be down to 40,000 the year after that. I believe, like in Japan, Germany and Korea (where we still have troops 60-years later) that some American forces will remain for an extended period – at the invitation and insistence of the Iraq people and government – as a buffer against the aggression of Iran and Syria.

18. When the US finally pulls out of Iraq, do you think Iraq will remain an ally of the US? Why? Yes, because people and nations almost always act in what they believe are their own best interests. In this world if you are a democracy with a vested interest in freedom, your self-interests will lead you to formal or informal alliances with nations that will support you. Additionally, today, the USA is the only military superpower. Only our country has the ability to throw its military weight over the seas. That is a significant deterrent to the evil intent of neighbors. Finally, the dollars that come into a country from USA bases and structures AND tourism, will be welcome here. The typical Iraqi is not an American-hating, Wahhabist, baathist, fundamentalist, Islamist, Nazi who believes Americans are an abomination on sacred ground. The typical Iraqi wants a job, wants to feed their kids, wants to be able to worship as they please, and wants some of the luxuries they see on the American TV shows they receive through the satellite dishes seen on every roof in the country.

19. How has being deployed changed your outlook on the future? It has reinforced my opinion that the United States of America is a force of good in the world. And that the continued advance of freedom and individual liberty over dictatorship and totalitarianism is a requirement for long-term world security and peace. I know it's a contradiction that we must fight to have peace, but the history of the world shows this is true. Those who will not fight for their freedoms are doomed to disappear from the Earth.

20. When this is over, do you think it was worth it? I recently wrote to my children explaining I am here today for them, their children and their

grandchildren. Our president has finally drawn a line in the sand and said that this non-state terrorism must stop and he has distinguished between the methods and targets of terrorism versus the methods and targets of those seeking freedom under oppressive dictators. Advancing freedom, individual liberty and the rule of law over the rule of whim and caprice of the dictator, king, or tyrant is always worth it. It is probably the only thing truly worth fighting for.

From: Pat VanHooser
Date: Wednesday, February 15, 2006 4:01 pm
Subject: Feb.15

Good Morning Rog,

It is 7:30 and I've already been to the local TV station to do a live segment for the morning news about my Smart Girls reading program I started here in Augusta. The great thing about being in business is you get to know everyone and they let you use them for something worthwhile. I took one of the Smart Girls with me, a twelve year old who has been in foster care since she was 5. How does that happen? She is pretty, smart, articulate and can be anything she wants to be...and her own family just threw her away.

Turns out a lot of these girls have those kinds of problems. It was naive of me to not expect that. Their relatives call me and ask for advice...which is funny since I don't have any kids and never wanted any! But I try to remember what it was like to be that age and apply a little common sense. Maybe just the fact that some other adults care will be enough to make a difference. I hope so.

So do you get any time off? Like a vacation? It seems like a funny question but are you allowed to go on leave? If so, where would you go? Just curious. Hope all is well with you. I appreciate the time you take to answer my mail. It really is a treat to know you. I'm going to work now; have a great rest of the day. Pat
**

My dear friend Pat,

I've done that early local TV show circuit several times over the years. They have so many zombies on that someone with personality blows them away. You'll be invited back!

Be careful falling in love with the customers. You'll be adopting one soon and then your life will REALLY change. You can't save them all and even Jesus said the poor will always be with us. But it does tug your heart when you see people that are either a long way down the hill or starting down. Short of taking over their lives and making all their decisions for them they are going to live short, nasty and brutish lives. Too many people (who FEEL too much and THINK too little) can't live with the pain they feel from seeing other people suffer so they think they should spend other people's money in order to relieve the pain. I think this is at the root of modern liberal activism (and my mother, for example). This will always fail as the basic laws of economics rule like physics: when you subsidize something you get more of it; when you tax something you get less of it; expectations drive to and yield the expected result. Taken all together, in poverty and low-socioeconomic class terms it means no matter how much you spend on poor people they will still make bad decisions and will remain poor and will produce more poor. Cynical sounding but proven true by the terribly flawed policies of the Great Society.

Also, people ask for advice but they almost never take it because good advice almost always means doing difficult/less fun things. The easy way is always too attractive.

I do get two weeks leave and my block is coming up soon. I will go home and spend serious family time including my parents' 50th anniversary and my kids' spring break. All soldiers are authorized these two weeks with travel at Army expense. There is also a Pass policy that allows soldiers to take 3-4 days off (not using their leave time) in Qatar where they have beer and prostitutes and beaches. We will not be using this very much as we just don't have the manpower to spare on a daily basis. We can barely fill all the guard towers, all the entry control points and man all the vehicles on patrols as it is and if we start sending more people away it just becomes impossible. Please recognize this is not complaining. No one wants to have more people over here than are absolutely necessary to get the job done. So everyone here is running lean. This may feed a bit into the Murtha "the Army is broken" crap and a little bit of whining from Joe back home to Mamma: "I never get any time off." But Joe and mamma have never read anything. Everyone in the US should read Audie Murphy's BOOK (not movie) "To Hell and Back." THAT describes WWII from the dogface perspective and the misery of 400 days of front-line action, sleeping in the mud, the cold, the rain, no food, no socks, not cleaning up for a month...This one year tour is hard, it's awful, it's boring, it's dangerous, but it's also NOTHING compared to the misery of combat troops throughout history. We don't read anymore therefore we don't know our own history or the lessons there.

So, yes, I'm going on leave SOON!!!! HOME!!! Others without wives or kids may go to Europe or someplace else for fun, but I believe most will go home to see friends and family.

Thanks for continuing to write to me and allowing me to vent back. Best to you and keep me up to date on the Smart Girls. rog

"Greetings All,

"We were able to webcam with Roger yesterday morning and it was good to see him on the screen. It will be even better to see him in person when he comes home on leave soon! All is well with him but I think he's ready for a break. He keeps complaining about visitors who don't follow directions but fall into line when they hear their first explosion. Sounds like my life as a sub-teacher. Maybe I should take a recording of the principal's voice into the classroom with me and play it occasionally to keep everyone on track.

"Robyn"
**

Hi everyone! 19 February 2006

Here's another "typical" mission from this week:

Up at 0500, reviewed all the e-mail, ate breakfast, suited up in all 60 pounds of gear, turned on the radio and caught a 0700 helicopter flight with my medic and two riflemen. This initial flight was to link up with our distinguished visitors (DVs) who were flying in directly by airplane. We flew about 40 minutes (pretty chilly at 40 degrees), and landed at Forward Operating Base Al Taqqadum (TQ for short). TQ has two runways and several more helio landing pads. We were dropped off at the wrong one and spent the next hour trying to get movement priority over the 300 soldiers who were trying to go on leave.

Made phone calls and were eventually picked up by confused young marines who were going to take us to the Military Police so someone could figure out who we were and what we wanted. As we started to roll out I saw OUR DVs (a group of congressional Armed Services Committee staffers) rolling in the opposite direction and after much teeth gnashing and rank-pulling finally convinced the young driver to take us to them.

Quick introductions, head-counting and then continued briefings and meetings. TQ is a huge logistics base moving materials all over western Iraq and there is also a contractor group there that adds armor to big trucks – we frequently take visitors there. Squabbled with the Marine tour guide a little bit about where the next helicopters were going to be and when, and then set the drop dead time for all the meetings and to get flying again. All of our schedules have "soft times" and "hard times." A soft time means the next event is less important than the current event so the deadline for moving is not firm. A hard time means that the next person to be visited outranks the current person, or more often means that a scheduled flight cannot be changed or delayed so we must be onboard, on time. Half of the work on a mission is constantly adjusting schedules, events, movements and flights in order to keep the DVs happy, but to hit all the hard times. At DV request we try to make changes, back up plans and contingency movement plans, only to stick with the original plan in the end.

So, next flight was across the western Iraq desert for nearly two hours. We stopped mid-way at Al Asad (in the middle of the desert and a major US Air Force fighter plane base and training center for the Iraqi Air Force) to refuel. Then on to the end of the earth, Al Qaim about 20 miles from Syria. The flight was cold and I told all the DVs to bundle up. When we arrived they all pointed out that it wasn't that bad and they weren't that cold. OK…

We visited with the Marines out there for nine hours, talking about maintenance and equipment and resupply. This really is the furthest point of American soldiers so the supply chain is at its maximum stress. Still, they had hot water, trailers and heaters, and Baskin Robbins in the mess hall. Tried to reschedule flights to leave earlier but could not get anyone out 300 miles on short notice ☺

Finally flew out at 2200 hours (10 p.m.). I reminded everyone it would be cold. Told them to wear everything they had. They collectively pooh-poohed me, reminding me I had told them the same thing during the day and they had been fine. So, I internally laughed when two hours later, at midnight, after 160 MPH in 30 degrees, they all were shivering and whining.

Finally in a bunk at Balad (FOB Anaconda) about 0100 after THEY were all settled in. Alarm rang at 0500 and up again for another full day of meetings, briefings, equipment displays. Finally flew back to Baghdad and then waited at the main airport four hours (due to a flight freeze from incoming rockets). Finally, finally they flew away at 2350 hours and back in my trailer at 0030. Made sure my alarm clock was turned OFF and went to sleep. And, because I am stupid, I was terribly startled and disappointed when my alarm rang at 0500 having turned it on rather than off…

In review, 600 miles and six hours in the air, 43 ½ hours total on the job, four hours sleep and 38 hours in full 60 pounds of gear. Four DVs and two strap-hangers alive and pleased. No lost equipment, no injuries. Perfect mission.

Finally spent some of my Christmas gift certificate money from so many of you good friends. Bought a mop and bucket, Pine sol, laundry soap, two pair of underwear, and other such un-dramatic "presents." THANK YOU!!!

Letters and cards from Pop, Aunt Nancy AND Aunt Nancy, and Valentine's Day gift boxes from Mom and Pop, Jeff Wagaman, and from dear friends Ed and Becky Linquist and kids Ekatrina and Eduardo. Two packages from Robyn and the kids! Thanks everyone!

American by birth. Soldier by choice. Volunteer by God!

Roger T. Aeschliman
Major, Armor
Deputy Commander, First Kansas Volunteers

February 22, 2006

"Greetings All,

"I'm sure many of you have heard the news that a soldier from Roger's battalion was killed earlier this week when a bomb exploded near his vehicle. SPC Jesse Davila was with A Company. Please keep his family and the battalion in your prayers. I should stress to you that Roger is fine and the kids and I spoke with him yesterday. He wasn't at liberty to speak about what had happened but I could tell from the tone of his voice that something had occurred. Like you, I found out through the media coverage on TV and the paper. This certainly brings the danger home to all of us. The kids and I had started to think in terms of Roger being on a long business trip due in part due to the great communications we have. But, this brings home hard and fast that he's working in a war zone and people do die. When I told Ryan and Regan this morning, you could tell that it bothered them but they took deep breaths and said, "OK," and got back into their regular routine. We'll see if there's any fallout later today once it sinks in how close to home this really is for us. Thanks for your continued thoughts and prayers.

"Robyn"

"Greetings All,

"We just got off the webcam with Roger and he is doing well – folding laundry and other housekeeping chores while talking to us. The memorial service for Jesse Davila was today. Roger talks about what happened and gives us a bit more insight than what we heard and read. Be sure to grab a box of Kleenex before reading on…

"Robyn"
**

Dear Friends, 26 February 2006

What do you say on a day like today? When a warrior falls on the field far away?
What do you say?

What do you say on a day like today to a town that remembers a child at play, who laughed and grew, was happy and gay?
What do you say?

What do you say on a day like today? To a child whose memories – we pray – will be only of love. Will she be okay?
What do you say?

What do you say on a day like today to the soldiers, about their friend? Such a price to pay…
What do you say?

What do you say on a day like today? To those left behind, will they fall prey to doubt and pain, or will God, their fears he stay?
What do you say?

What do you say on a day like today, when the sun shines and the sky is blue, the birds sing and the breezes blow, yet all is gray? All is gray.
What do you say?

Jesse Davila: father, farmer, soldier. Killed in Action, 20 FEB 2006. Baghdad.

We've all known it could and now the worst has happened. Specialist Davila, 29, of Greensburg, Kansas, a young farmer in far South-central, Kansas, was killed in the line of duty. He was not in the Joint Visitor's Bureau; indeed he was new to the First Kansas Volunteers. In fact, he was not even a volunteer for this mission in the correct sense of the word. He was an artilleryman and was command directed – ordered by the state – to join us for our mobilization. Early in that process he was selected for special training and assignment as a personal security officer – one of about 80 from our Battalion. He and all these men are on security missions all across Iraq, guarding and driving officials from several US government agencies as they work in various ways to break the back of the terrorists.

It was on one of these protection missions that Specialist Davila's vehicle was slammed into by a car bomber. In addition to Davila, one of the officials was killed, one wounded and two of our soldiers also wounded. Fortunately our other two men are healing and have already returned to duty.

What do you say?

Our men are a bit shaken up and feeling some of "but for the grace of God..." It could have been almost any of us. Most accept the facts and are dealing with it. Our Chaplain, Padre Pete, is very busy. Other chaplains and counselors from higher levels are available. LTC Trafton and others have been visiting with troops extensively. But the towers still have to be guarded, the gates have to be manned and the JVB still has to transport and protect officials all over Iraq. So we're all just getting on with it. The real heroes of past wars who faced death daily will understand.

The memorial service is in a few hours, here on the back deck of the JVB, overlooking the palaces and lakes. It is a beautiful day, nearly 80 degrees, clear, sunny, breezy. These memorials are intensely moving, sad and joyous, patriotic and devotional. After the prayers, the National Anthem, TAPS, Amazing Grace on the bagpipes, a choir from the Army Band, and a 21-gun salute, we will all leave with tears in our eyes and rededicated to the great cause remaining before us. That this nation – Iraq – like our own nation, will experience a new birth of liberty and join the great nations of the free world.

Earlier this week a team of our JVB soldiers rolled up on a group of Iraqi Army soldiers who were in an ambush and getting the worst of it. Our men fought back, killed some of the enemy, drove them off, then treated the wounded Iraqis. This is the first real face-to-face combat of our nearly four months here and your Kansas soldiers performed magnificently. You should be proud of them.

Also this week you know that the Golden Mosque was bombed. According to the news media we see Iraq is now officially doomed and the country is in flames. WELL IT AINT TRUE! While there were a few "counter" attacks on mosques (rifle fire and poorly aimed rifle grenades), there have been many more PEACEFUL protests. There are no riots, there are no roaming gangs randomly killing Sunni or Shia. The number of total events is pretty much the same as it has been over the past month. There is tension and everyone is concerned, but overall the Iraqis are working very hard to calm this down and not let it escalate into "the" civil war that our own media seem so desperate to actualize. You also read about the FAILED attack on the Saudi oil refinery and how this FAILED attack also means the end of the world. Who are these insane news people and what planet are they living on?

Letters and cards from adopted grandma Dorothy Hamler, former co-worker Linda Hubbard, Pop and Mom x 3 (with cookies!), California parents Roger and Audrey, little sis Karen, Topeka buddy Maria Wilson (nee Russo), Commerce Bank and Trust Co-worker Peggy Bukovatz, thank you note from Congressman Chris Shays (the only thank you anyone has EVER sent), and clippings about the renovation of the Kansas State Capitol (which I directly caused to happen but will never get any credit for but that is a long story for another day) from Martha Ozias. Thanks everyone!

American by birth. Soldier by choice. Volunteer by God!

Roger T. Aeschliman
Major, Armor
Deputy Commander, First Kansas Volunteers

From: Robyn Aeschliman
Date: Wednesday, March 1, 2006 4:59 pm
Subject: regs

Hey Darling,

Just took Regan to the bus stop and she was talking to the birds. She kept whistling and the bird kept whistling back. At one point she goofed and the bird answered back with a different whistle as though saying, "What did you say?!" It was too funny. It made me think of you when you talk with the birds.

Love you.
XXXOOO
**

My dear Robyn,

There are so few trees over here that birds don't appear to be as numerous or varied as Kansas. There are pigeons and ring- necked doves, and a sort of sparrow commonly seen. Around the lakes I will see an occasional white heron/crane thing and a couple of shore birds. But very few song birds. I have only heard a bird singing twice this whole time...

Can't wait to get home and talk to the cardinal, bobwhite and turtle dove.

I love you my turtle dove! rog

Hi gang, 01 March 2006

This has been circulating around Iraq....I wonder who could have possibly written it?

The Fobbit's Creed

I am an American Soldier who never leaves the FOB. I watch Warriors leave the FOB every day. Gee, it must be hot in that IBA, Kevlar, and pads.
I am a member of a team that ensures warriors clear their weapons six times before getting a hot meal, and yells at them as they trudge back to their hooches without wearing reflective belts.
I serve the people of the United States and live the Army Values, (except for APFT, weight control, and military discipline and bearing, and weapons qualification, and General Order No. 1 – well screw it. I live a few of the Army values – sometimes).
I will always place the mission first, except when it means missing Salsa Night at MWR. I will never accept defeat because I can always file a discrimination lawsuit against someone. I will never quit except at 1700 hours like clockwork (and don't even think about me working on Saturday or Sunday. I will never leave a fallen comrade (hey, if I were falling down drunk and tripped on a sidewalk crack staggering back from Karaoke night I'd want someone to help me up . . .).
I am disciplined, physically and mentally tough, trained and proficient in my warrior tasks and drills (Puleeazzee). I always maintain my arms, my equipment and myself (Yeah, WHAT-ever).
I am an expert and I am a professional and when I get out of this hellhole I am going right to work for a major contractor prostituting my expertise to the highest bidder, and then sue them for discrimination.
I stand ready to deploy (back home, as soon as possible), engage (with my one clip of dirty ammo and my rusty rifle), and destroy the enemies of the United States of America in close combat (especially platoon sergeants, platoon leaders, first sergeants, and company commanders by suing them in the court room for discrimination).
I am a guardian of freedom and the American way of life here on the FOB and I will never leave the Baskin Robbins or smoothie bar unguarded.
I am an American Soldier who never leaves the FOB.

From: Lyn Smith@cargill.com
Date: Tuesday, February 28, 2006 0:03 a.m.
Subject: Duty

Roger, I was moved by your weekly update that provided your insight on the event that took SPC Jessie Davila from our ranks.

I sent LTC Trafton a personal note with my thoughts. I don't know if he shared them with you or not, but here are some additional thoughts for you and your soldiers.

Determine if proper planning took place prior to the event. If all was done according to established processes: review the processes, make changes where necessary, train the changes and drive on. Determine if mistakes were made in mission execution. If mistakes were made, correct them, modify training where needed and drive on. I get the feeling from your note that you have already done this. Remember: You don't get to pick who gets hit and who doesn't.

Don't let the event cause leaders (especially junior NCOs) to become over-cautious in mission planning and/or execution. That will be the tendency especially for those involved with that particular mission. If they get too cautious, they will cause more casualties, not fewer and probably not complete the mission.

Everyone now knows for certain that they are not invincible. It is up to Squad, Platoon, Company and Battalion Leadership to step up and carry the burden of overly-heavy green tabs. The young soldiers in the Regiment will look to their direct leadership for guidance on how to carry on and the confidence necessary to be successful in a combat zone. Soldiers will emulate their leaders. See to it that our soldiers continue to practice the calm, professional competence displayed for many generations in our Regiment.

I am confident that you and LTC Trafton will see to the needs of our soldiers while setting new standards of mission performance.

Thanks for your service to our State and Nation. God Bless!

Lyn Smith
FIRST KANSAS - Volunteers By God!
**

Sir,

Thanks for the very important comments and suggestions. I read the majority of your letter to the E-5s and up at our daily BUB. LTC Trafton used some of your comments at the memorial service as well. I appreciate your mentorship and guidance very much. It is comforting to know you and others are still looking out for us over here.

The initial discussion of our TTPs indicates the attack was a totally random target of opportunity. This area is heavily bombed compared to most and is in the hottest part of the city. Apparently the attack vehicle was staged, waiting for a soft target, and came down an on-ramp to hit them as they passed. One of the NCOs who survived (SSG Sean Resare) did an exceptional job - while wounded - securing the scene, triaging, positioning, calling for help and then making the call to self-evacuate when help did not arrive. His was the stuff of heroes. What men we breed in Kansas...

Most truly your friend,
rog

From: "Bob Caplinger"
Sent: Thursday, March 02, 2006 11:25 AM
Subject: RE: weekly report

Robyn,

As I mentioned, I am an alum of GHS in Greensburg, the same as Jessie Davila. I forwarded Roger's report to an old time friend in Greensburg. He has visited with the Minister and the Minister wants to make use of it at the Memorial Service now set for Saturday. Roger has used his talent well on this report.

Bob
**

Dear Robyn, Please forward to Bob...

Dear Bob, I appreciate the feedback and am humbled. Thank you for your kind words.

Your grandson continues to do a great job here. He is bright, works hard and has a great attitude. He is one of my favorites (I know we're not supposed to have favorites but he's such a good kid with a great smile).

Hope this finds you well and looking forward to seeing you at Rotary March 16 or 23 when I'm home on leave.

rog

From: Joyce A Merryman
Date: Wednesday, March 1, 2006 9:49 pm
Subject: Hi there!

Sorry about the loss of Specialist Davila. I also lost a friend last week who died of a heart attack or stroke while driving on I-70 near the MacVicar exit. He was able to slow down, but hit the center retaining wall. Fortunately, no other cars were involved, but he was dead by the time they got him to the hospital. He was only 56. I can relate to the pain and loss you are feeling. I hope Specialist Davila's family is doing alright.

Here's the office news: Jane had her knee replacement surgery on Monday (2/27) and all went well. They had her up and walking, with a walker, not long after she woke up. When I talked with her yesterday morning, they were going to be coming shortly to walk her to the lunch room. In the afternoon she had physical therapy, which just about did her in. They don't fool around getting you back on your feet. Haven't been able to reach her today yet.

We just finished the Project Topeka Food Drive and our team won the gold medal (it was Olympic theme). Our team consisted of the second floor of the main bank. Last night the trust department sponsored a musical presentation of "A Night at the Movies", which Nancy Goodall planned, at Aldersgate. It was a success. Nancy and I are working on a Women's Management Seminar which will be two different days (Mar. 11 & 16), so lots of planning. You know I love event planning, so I'm feeling in my element. I'm working with Bob on several upcoming events-May 17th a lunch for Topeka Bar Association Probate Division and the May Day Tea at Aldersgate on April 28. We are a busy bunch. Email went out and article in this morning's paper that $80,000.00 is missing from the bank. Haven't heard much more than that. I didn't take it! D'Ann's mom isn't doing very well, but she is still working everyday.

We had bank wide meetings last week to go over the incentive information and awards. They have changed the weighting format for the incentive, but we haven't gotten an email yet. They went over it in the meeting though.

You'll be happy to know we put your office to good use last week - goody day! Bob Franke was here and using the library, so we put all the treats in your office.

I had a phone call from a sales person for you this morning, something about a newsletter subscription. When I told him you were not here, he asked for your voice mail. Then I told him you didn't have voice mail, since you were in Iraq, he was silent and then said, "where?" It's funny the reaction you get. I told him to mail a sample to Kirk.

Sounds like you are keeping very busy, just remember to stay safe. We miss you!

Joyce
**

Dear Joyce,

Thanks for the updates! Sorry about your loss. Was this the same gentleman who was doing the redevelopment at College Hill? Please let me know if I may comfort you in any manner. You and all the gang are constantly in my thoughts and prayers. Please tell Jane and Dee I'm praying for them as well and eager to see them (and YOU silly).

I'm pretty sure I didn't leave 80K around randomly. If it turns up tell folks to feel free to put in my account with Mike!

Glad to hear about Goody Day! We have our own permanent Goody Day here at the JVB. All the yummies sent to everyone by friends goes into the table by my desk for open grazing. Too much good stuff...we're all getting fat. There is a small set of weights right out back on the deck so a group of us lifts daily (or whenever we are in from mission) to help burn off a few calories.

The Army has some incentives. Tax free war zone income is the biggest; bonuses for reenlisting, and other things for everyone except us officers. But nothing like incentives for achieving goals. Maybe we should consider that: Extra pay for killing Bin Laden, extra time off for locating bombs before they explode...) Probably not.

Looking forward to seeing you within the next two weeks now! rog

From: Michael Ryan
Date: Thursday, March 2, 2006 11:22 pm
Subject: Your call

Rog -- So sorry I missed your call. Glad to hear your voice and to know you're OK. Is it as bad as the American media are making it appear? Are they on the verge of civil war?

Wish I could see you while you're here. But I know your family comes first. If there is a way, I might want to pursue it.
**

Dear Mike,

It's kind of amazing to see the total disconnect from reality over there. All this killing is being blamed on "sectarian" violence but where are the deaths coming from? The same place they have for the last year. Big vehicle bombs! And who has the vehicle bombs? The same assholes who have always made them: The Saddamists, the Baathists, the pro-Iranian factions, Al Qaeda yadda, yadda. They are simply targeting mass civilians rather than the US forces and the Iraqi forces. Civilians are soft targets and easy to get headlines with...This is still just terror, designed to cause terror and to destroy faith in institutions so they can have things there way. Joe six-pack Iraqi can't build a truck bomb or an IED. And Joe six-pack is not going to run out the door and shoot up his neighbors with his AK because the neighbors have AKs too! If it were all blowing up we would be seeing 10,000 dead every day rifle to rifle, street by street. It AINT REAL!!!!

It's still the same people doing the same thing, using all their resources to mass fires on the most vulnerable targets. These murderers suck. But they are not momma and poppa Iraqi...Momma and Poppa want jobs and to feed their kids.

The truth is the same as it has been for six months. The war is won. We just need the time to stand up the Army and Police and all the LOGISTICS that support them. The government is still forming and is moving ahead.

I will be in Topeka through much of March. Was just curious if you were going to accompany unspecified dignitaries at unspecified times anytime soon? Cause I won't be here. No travel plans away from Topeka during March. Two weeks will pass all too quickly...

Love you. Make sure Sue sends me some photos of your family. Rog
**

From: Michael Ryan
Date: Friday, March 3, 2006 3:45 pm
Subject: Re: Your call

Thanks for the reality check. I may build an editorial off it. More and more, the American media suck. And despite alternative media and the ability to point out liberal bias, the liberal media chug on. In fact, I think they've actually gotten worse, figuring, well, the conservatives in the media are being honest, so we will too...

I'm toying with coming up to see you in Kansas. I didn't detect any red light in your response, so I will look seriously at it. First option: I'll ask the corporate pilot if there are any plans to fly to Topeka in March. But I am more than willing to fly there to see you.

About going to Baghdad: I got an offer of a free trip to Israel a couple years ago and Sue nearly had a panic attack. I couldn't put her through that, regardless of how safe it is. I hope you understand. She's pretty tender, and actually I'm pretty proud of having preserved that in her over 22 years.

Besides, it would probably involve some cost and they won't send me 60 miles away right now; the owners are panicking about budget again...
**

Hey Mike, don't spend a penny on me...Airfare would have to suck at this short notice. You are of course welcome at any time and I know there would be lots of people who'd love to see you, so, come if it works to your satisfaction. Just remember Robyn will be pretty jealous of my time (and I with hers too).

I saw Murtha again on TV just a few minutes ago and he said something to the effect of only Iran and Al Qaeda want the US in Iraq. He is now officially an ignorant buffoon who is out of touch. I gave him the benefit of doubt until he said that . . .now he's either just a Rita Cline: criminal, psycho or poor misunderstood halfwit.

Love you and your family. rog

Hello everyone, 05 March 2006

I have a number of disjointed things this week and no way to thread them together so please forgive the lack of story-telling.

First, and most importantly to me: I AM HEADING HOME FOR TWO WEEKS LEAVE!!!!!! YAHOOOOOO!! I start traveling mid-week, stop in Kuwait, then on to Europe and home. Should take 24 hours or so but people can get stuck almost anywhere in route and wind up taking 3-4 days. I am eager to be home by the end of the week in order to be there for Mom and Pop's 50th Anniversary and Regan's 12th birthday. Spring break follows and we will have lots of family time. In addition to Robyn, Ryan, Regan, family and friends I am most looking forward to a cold beer, some decent Mexican food, and not shaving for a day or two.

This is in the early part of the leave cycle. All of us senior/old guys got last choice for leave dates. Had I my druthers I'd have come home for the big family 4th of July party and our own anniversary but the young privates and officers took the summer dates. We allow a maximum of 10% of the battalion to be on leave at one time; any more would make the mission impossible. Too many holes…By the time I return we should be closing in on the halfway point☺

Second, we had scarcely finished the services for Sergeant Davila (promoted posthumously) when a second incident shook us all up. One of our young soldiers was playing with a pistol when he shot another in the leg. The wound is clean and he is back on light duty but we can only shake our heads and wonder how it can happen? With all the training and rules and leadership and oversight (and common sense) how can it happen? My son (a young hunter) already knows you never, ever point a weapon at anyone, EVER. The answer is these highly trained and skilled soldiers are YOUNG and sometimes young men will act like boys despite the training, leadership and coaching. If it ever sounds like we are being too hard on the men it is because if we weren't then this kind of ridiculous thing would happen more often. John Wayne said: "Life is hard. It's harder when you're stupid."

Third, we did a safety pause (we have too many missions to take an official stand-down) and went over all the rules and practices and policies intended to keep us all alive. We asked the young sergeants to step up once again and enforce, train, and lead. It is always in the small teams of four or five where the rubber meets the road.

Fourth, it went up 20 degrees in one week, from the high 50s to nearly 80s. Incredible! Suddenly we are all once again pushing water and eating requirements. 80 feels very hot in that short amount of time. 120 expected in two months! Egad!

Fifth, Iraq is GREEN. From the Euphrates to 25 miles past the Tigris things are growing. Will last about two months 'til the 120 degrees wave hits.

Sixth, last night a young medic, Doc Martin, and I ended our monthly mission with General Abizaid when he flew away in a C-17 (jumbo cargo plane) and we were left to find our own way home from Balad/Camp Anaconda. After checking helicopter flights and cargo planes we found an obscure place that flies C-12s (seven-seater Beechcraft-type planes) around and caught a ride back to Baghdad in the dark. Iraq by airplane at 8,000 feet looks very different than by helicopter nap of the earth. We could see for one hundred miles and the entire Tigris valley was alit. Iraq glowed like L.A. It was a spectacular view during our 80 mile, 30 minute flight. When we landed we dropped out of the sky nose down and I watched the altimeter tick off 100 feet increments about every second. The automatic system was announcing "ALTITUDE!" "ALTITUDE!" Pretty dramatic. All intentional to avoid potential enemy fires. People would pay a lot of money to simulate that at a carnival or Disneyland.

Seventh, Mike Ryan asked me about the current surge of violence over here and if this was the civil war? No. No. NO! The death toll is up because the big IEDs are targeting mass groups of civilians. The total number of incidents is about the same as it has been. The average Joe in Iraq can't build an IED. It is the just the bad guys trying to make the civil war happen. Mom and Pop Iraqi are not out killing each other. Neighbor is not killing neighbor. These attacks are (in a sick way) good for the US forces as the target de jour is to cause massive civilian casualties rather than American casualties. We expect the anti-Iraqi-forces to use up all their IEDs and ready supply of suicide volunteers then we'll see a slow-down and a quieter period while they recruit and build more bombs.

Letters and cards from Commerce Bank pal Laura Bond and her DAR group, Robbie and Linda Orr (Sis Karen's in-laws!), everyone in the Adriel Class at TBC, Martha Ozias, Cam Rees, Joyce Merryman, Rotarian buddy Bob Caplinger (whose grandson is one of my soldiers here), and gift box full of books and treats from dear friend Ed Linquist (along with the world record belated birthday and Christmas cards!). Thanks everyone!

I may report from home during my leave, or not. Depends if there's anything you all want to hear about and if Clio and Calliope return after this week's conspicuous absence.

American by birth. Soldier by choice. Volunteer by God!

Roger T. Aeschliman
Major, Armor
Deputy Commander, First Kansas Volunteers

PS – Dad, 7,865 miles by air so far and 280 exercising.

Greetings from TOPEKA!!! 13 March 2006

Home, home, home and enjoying the mostly quiet time with family. Made it in time for the folk's big 50th anniversary too-do and saw many of you there. Also sang happy birthday to Regan celebrating her 12th. Good food, good cake and punch, and much conversation. Very soft, comfy bed and have already had deep-dish Chicago style pizza and a heap of Gonzo (spicy potatoes with meats and gravy) from Larry's Shortstop (my favorite South Topeka dump with great food). Only two wonderful, ice cold beers so far, but who's counting?

I started traveling at 0430 Wednesday reporting to the Baghdad Airport R&R flight center, learned my first flight would be at 2200 hours (and it really turned out to be 2330 hours), so went back to the office and worked and exercised. At 2200 hours they told us we were free but to be standing by at 0030 (midnight 30) to board. Planning on two hours I went to get a cup of coffee and walk around the airfield. I came back at 2330 (an hour BEFORE we were told to be back) to find the waiting area deserted and the plane spinning up propellers on the runway without me on board. I scurried out, was the last in line, and was standing on the back ramp of the C-130 with all the seats filled. Looking forlorn the pilots took pity on me and put me in the cabin. I was so excited about seeing everything up there that I promptly fell asleep and woke up landing in Ali Al Saleem, Kuwait 90 minutes later.

We all processed into Kuwait for about four hours and then about sunup we were assigned tents and bunks for our wait at that R&R movement center. I dozed for a couple hours, watched a movie in morale tent, ate lunch, then got in line to continue processing out of Kuwait. We dumped all our gear for customs (I lost a very dangerous set of grooming scissors), heard all the rules and then waited until 1930 hours to get on buses to the Kuwait City International Airport. 90 minute bus ride then waited another two hours at the airport to board. Finally loaded and take off about 2330 hours Thursday night. Big cheer when the wheels went "thump-thump."

Great ride on a MD-11 jumbo, wide-body commercial carrier. Great crew, good leg room and meal after meal. I took a sleep aid and pretty much slept the eight hours to Shannon Ireland. Got off there and cleaned up. Was deeply saddened to see all the taps of Guinness and Harp at the bar and not be able to try them but we were under no alcohol orders. Navy travelers however appeared to have no restrictions and were drinking pint after pint. What's up with that?

Reboarded and slept most of the nine-hour flight to Dallas (all R&R goes through either Dallas or Atlanta per some contract or other). Were greeted by fire trucks spraying arches over the plane, and after clearing customs ran a wonderful gauntlet of local citizens and volunteers who greet every R&R flight. So many cheering people, and hands to be shaken, and hugs and kisses. It brought tears to all our eyes. Dallas knows how to treat people. On the ground there about 1000 hours Friday, my flight on to Kansas City was scheduled for 2200 Friday night. The people at American Airlines bent over backwards to get me home sooner. Paid our way to Love Field near downtown and put us in first class on a small commercial jet. Everyone on board there applauded us. Everywhere we were in the USA we were kindly greeted, had our arms pumped and backs slapped. I think the regular American clearly gets it.

Smoochy greeting from Robyn at the airport, and a nice drive home arriving about 3 p.m. Friday, Kansas time. About 72 hours total transition time but only about 24 hours of flights or buses. Enough for now except to say the air is cleaner here, the sky is bluer here, and the bathrooms don't stink.

American by birth. Soldier by choice. Volunteer by God!

Roger T. Aeschliman
Major, Armor
Deputy Commander, First Kansas Volunteers

March 27, 2007

Greetings All,

The fun had to end sometime but it sure went quickly. Ryan, Regan, and I loved having Roger home on leave for 15 days - I only wish we had 15 more. We put Roger on a plane this afternoon for the first leg of his journey back to Baghdad. I asked him to check in with me periodically and definitely when he is back at the "office". As expected, there were tears from all of us. This was by far the hardest departure. Knowing we won't see each other again until the end of the year made this really difficult - we know what it's like now. The house seemed very empty when we arrived back home from the airport. Looks like we get to start the withdrawal symptoms all over again. We have 8 months more or less - I can only hope it goes as quickly as these first 8 months have gone. Look for Roger's next update a week from today if not sooner.

Thanks to all of you for your continued support and prayers.

Robyn

Dear Walgreen's of Andover Management and Staff, 31 MAR 2006

Here's a quick yet heartfelt thank you for your generosity and kindness. The gift bags filled with your candy were greatly appreciated and brightened everyone's day around here. It was very nicely St. Patrick's Day and in the absence of beer the chocolates were the highlight of the week.

Thank you for thinking about us and for your sweet gifts. It does us all good to be remembered and appreciated.

Your Kansas Friend In Baghdad,

MAJ Roger T. Aeschliman
Deputy Commander
2-137 Infantry
Kansas Army National Guard

Dear Ralph, 03 APR 2006

Greetings from Iraq! Hope this finds you well and the Koyotes off to a good start. I have seen a couple of items about the team on the Internet and just wanted to wish you, the players and coaches well.

I will miss the entire season but will look forward to reading about the games through the Capital Journal on-line. The kids and I very much enjoyed attending most of the games of the first few seasons and I'm sure this year promises even more excitement. Sorry I won't be there to cheer you on...☹

Things are going very well over here with tremendous progress being made every day. Daily improvements in infrastructure, the development of the Iraqi Army and police forces and the civilian government at all levels. There is no civil war here and the national media just aren't telling the story like it really is.

I guess I really just want to say thank you for starting and running a great football program that adds to our quality of life in Topeka. It really means a lot to all of us over here to know that things are going on like normal in Kansas and nothing is more normal than a WINNING KOYOTE SEASON and CHAMPIONSHIP!

Will enjoy reading all about it. Thanks again and tell the team their fan club extends all the way to Baghdad.

Most Truly Your Friend,

MAJ Roger T. Aeschliman
Deputy Commander, 2-137 INF
APO AE 09342-1400

WHAT I DID DURING SPRING BREAK
By Roger Aeschliman
45th grade, School of Life
02 APRIL 2006

I already mentioned that I was home in time for Regan's birthday and Ash and Mary Jo's 50th Anniversary Saturday. I saw several hundred people there, mostly family and oldest family friends, then slept. In rough sequence I saw or did the following things (stop reading here if you get bored easily):

Saw Colonel (R) Lyn Smith, mentor to the entire Kansas Guard Infantry and Armor communities and had two wonderful Blind Tiger beers then slept. Jogged with Keith Olson and played handball with Gary Miller, then slept. Went to Commerce Bank & Trust for the morning Tuesday and saw everybody! Then slept. (some of this sleeping time was spent dozing in front of the TV watching the Simpson's, Buffy the Vampire Slayer, Charmed, and horror movies, and some was spent cuddling with wife and children, but mostly it was sleeping). Somewhere around here ate at McDonalds and Los Fuentes.

Wednesday had burgers at the PAD with folks and siblings. Thursday went to Rotary to see all the gang. Had a short notice that something special was scheduled for Robyn but was very suspicious that it was a trick to get me there. So was not surprised when the speaker went on and on about me. But then he said: "Well, enough about Roger. We're here today to talk about Robyn!" She was awarded a Paul Harris Fellowship for extraordinary public service. Roy and Gerry Browning, Topeka notables, made a contribution to Rotary in her name. She was surprised, honored and graceful. I love her.

Saw Colonel and mentor Bob Bloomquist at his home. He has only just returned from a year tour in Kosovo. His wonderful children have grown nearly as much as mine (and my two wonderful, sweet delightful little children have, since August, both grown three inches and lost the ability to speak other than monosyllabically).

Friday went to the Capper Foundation Blarney Breakfast fund-raiser and saw many friends there. Lunched with Commerce Bank & Trust broker Mike Lott and boss Kirk Johnson at the Harley Café (best ribs in Kansas). Later saw KU lose first round at friend Mark Harris's where I had one beer and couldn't finish it. Alan Towle also joined us and we all fell asleep at some point. Then woke up and went home.

Saturday played handball with the usual gang then jogged with Mark Hood, then three hours at Blind Tiger nursing two beers and visiting with Tom Rose, Vera Goodman, Joe Cutter, Terry Kimes, Kirk Johnson, Brad Hamilton, Dr. Doug and Dorothy Iliff, Mike and Maria Wilson and their two wonderful college students, Becky Evans, and Mark and Lori Harris. That evening had a game night at the Telthorst's with the Heryford's and the Linquist's. All the children grew.

Church at First Baptist Sunday followed by family lunch at Mom's with homemade ham, beans and cornbread, and also chili, neither of which can be had over here. Lot's of leftovers which I was unable to eat all of despite my best effort. Breakfast Monday with Colonel Walt Frederick, and napping. Both Ryan and Regan became ill over this time and spent many unpleasant hours puking (I don't think it was me as Robyn was fine the whole time). Sometime here we brunched at the Downtowner and I had pancakes with diced bacon inside (Mary Jo's most secret treat).

Tuesday went hunting at the Cokely Game Farm with Ryan, Regan, Benny Meyer, and Pop. Right off the bat I fell out of the truck (yes it was stupid and I knew better but my follow orders instincts overpowered my common sense instincts) and hobbled around the rest of my leave with a bruised kidney (self-diagnosis Dr. Doug; no problems evacuating, no blood, and no fever. Pain decreasing everyday but still tender after two weeks so not a normal tissue bruise. What do you think? Sorry I missed the March Hare run but was crippled…) Otherwise a great hunt with lots of Chukar partridge and a few roosters. Saw Mike Ryan Wednesday and tested the blackjack tables in Kansas City. Was up three hundred then down one, then up six hundred and finally wiped out. What fun! Mike, playing a very controlled game, went home with casino money and bought me lunch at Bryant's BBQ. Forget when exactly but visited with General Jon Small (one the key people/reason's I'm in the Army at all) and also former Adjutant General Greg Gardner.

Thursday yard work all day and was horrified to see last year's brand new pool liner was leaking. Robyn will have to deal with that. We were also graciously invited by Commerce Bank & Trust big boss Duane Fager to attend the Boy Scouts Annual distinguished citizens dinner. Was recognized by several speakers including honoree, Kansas Governor Kathleen Sebelius. Very nice and again, saw another large group of Topeka friends. Friday took kids to Kansas City to the Nelson, lunch on the Plaza, a nice visit with dear friend Dorothy Hamler, and a walk around Cabela's.

Lunch Saturday at Topeka's new On the Border with Mom and Dad and nephew Rocky, then ready to return. During this time was able to read Appaloosa by Robert Parker, also a Spenser detective novel by Parker, a book about the Yellow Fever epidemic in Philly in late 1700s, and two other books Regan recommended. On the trip back read a Grishom thriller and Dick Francis mystery. Love to read. Almost no time to do it over here.

Uneventful travel after the crying at the airport. Great support again at Dallas. Were not allowed off the plane at Budapest so can't speak to the culture there. Arrived Ali Al Saleem 0200 and up all night processing. Killed another 24-hours there dozing and watching movies before final plane ride to Baghdad where I promptly slept for 14 hours. Am still not time-synced but improving. Light schedule for a few days here then back to work with many dignitaries scheduled in April.

I know I left many, many people out and apologize; that's the risk of not taking notes and being jet lagged.

Waiting for me upon return were cards and letters from Grantville United Methodist Church, Melba Waggoner x 2, Adriel Sunday School Class at TBC, Peggy Bukovatz at Commerce Bank & Trust, Susan Anderson, Jean Crouse of Chester, Nebraska, gift bag from the Wichita Family Support Group with candy from Andover Walgreen's, goodie box from Jean Nickell (sis Ronna's mother-in-law), two boxes from Robyn full of Girl Scout Cookies!

American by birth. Soldier by choice. Volunteer by God!

Roger T. Aeschliman
Major, Armor
Deputy Commander, First Kansas Volunteers

Dear Susan and Dennis, 06 APR 06

Thank you both for the nice box of videos. I will circulate broadly and eventually get them all into the hands of our chaplain for his continuing use with our 600 plus soldiers.

It was great to see you both at the anniversary party. It was too brief . . . as these moments pass it becomes more and more likely that us cousins (and all our children and their children) will not see each other and likely that your grandchildren won't know my grandchildren at all. Gosh, our own kids will scarcely know each other. Mostly sad but mostly normal in today's world.

I have seen the photo of me tormenting the lamb but mom and pop neither had any memory of it. Thanks for telling me the history. Easter and a little lamb...appropriate☺

I'm not sure of the compliment about looking like my 45-year-old father. I guess I'll have to take your word for it. It amazes me how much your father and mine STILL look like each other. There's no question about paternity of those two. At the party I saw a recent photo of me and another old one of grandpa and was initially surprised at how much he and I looked alike. It was interesting to see him as a 40-something trim, handsome man, rather than the heavier and old man I barely knew as a child...

Well, enough history. Thanks again for the nice letters and tapes. Prayers are greatly appreciated as is good coffee like Starbucks or Millstone, and powdered Gatorade (hint, hint).

Love to you both and have a great tornado-free Spring and Summer,

rog

Dear Peggy, 07 APR 2006

Thank you for another nice note. It's interesting to learn about your country life. I grew up near a small town in Jefferson County and although my family did not farm for a living I did all the traditional farming stuff for a variety of neighbors. At home we had chickens, horses and rabbits as well as an enormous vegetable garden and grape vines resulting in endless hours of work feeding, mucking, planting, weeding and picking which is why I hate horses and gardening to this day.

Here in Iraq the country life appears to be a real mixed bag. There are farms that have modern equipment, numerous well-built out-buildings, and clean and tidy homesteads and fields. But there are many, many more that appear to be mud-brick houses surrounded by mud-brick or stick-built corrals. A variety of animals live in the corrals and wander around with the people in common spaces. Usually sheep and cattle but sometimes goats and camels. Chickens everywhere. We see herders out grazing animals. The canal system is robust and critical to the entire agricultural system. They extend a hundred miles from the Tigris and Euphrates Rivers. Many are ancient and abandoned but most are still in use. Some are huge, concrete lined and pumped by the government but most are small, hand-dug and maintained over a thousand years. Amazing. Once in a while we will see a center-pivot but not very often. Up north I have seen true nomads living in caravans and yurts, grazing flocks of sheep in the middle of desert – WITH a generator and a satellite dish! Also north there are huge grain fields that go on for several miles and no farmsteads to be seen. Up there people live in central villages and apparently go many miles to work their fields. Probably an artifact of survival from ancient times of raiders and unending wars.

Even in Baghdad and the other cities there are sheep, cattle and goats living right with people. And little food plots quickly spring up on piece of un-occupied land. I don't think Iraq has a food problem but I also don't think they are exporting much if anything...

Please tell your Roger if he wants to rebuild any old clunker convertible or a motorcycle for me I would appreciate it very much but am way too cheap to PAY for it so it would have to be a labor of love (HA!). I would like to have a big old convertible or a big highway bike of some kind but sadly I have children instead so am living the wind-through my hair dream only

airborne here in Iraq when we whistle along at 160 MPH in Blackhawk's. (When I put it that way I don't sound so deprived...)
Go with a turquoise shade on the Daimler . . . and then pimp it with wide whitewalls!

Thanks again for the nice note and your kind thoughts,
Your friend and co-worker, rog

Dear Walt, 07 APRIL 2007

Greetings from Baghdad! I can't promise you that the Leadership Topeka program will take you all over the world to exciting and intriguing places like Iraq, but I do promise that participation will open new doors and broaden your world views.

First, congratulations on being selected. As last year's Chamber of Commerce Leadership Topeka Program Chairman and a member of the 1997 Class (the greatest class ever!), I know the selection process is highly competitive. You are to be commended just for making it this far. But the real value of the program comes not from the inputs you receive during the days of training and education, but from your outputs into it. Your classmates who choose to throw themselves body and soul into the program will find themselves growing in new, unexpected ways. They will make new and dear friends. They will connect with a vibrant and charming city and find dynamic and exciting opportunities. Those who sit back, listen and only punch the ticket (or "check the block" in Army terms) will gain little for themselves and likely miss a tremendous chance to become a part of something bigger and better.

Good luck in the coming two months and best wishes in the future. I hope your leadership experience will be everything mine was to me.

MAJ Roger T. Aeschliman
Deputy Commander, 2-137 Infantry
Kansas Army National Guard
(and Trust Officer at Commerce Bank & Trust!)

"Greetings All,

"Roger is back in the saddle so to speak and busy with missions. Being busy helps the time to go quickly though, so that is all good. We were able to webcam earlier today and he mentioned his coffee supply is getting quite low. If you'd like to send a bag I'm sure he would be very grateful. He refers to the coffee in the mess hall as "sludge" and it just doesn't start the day as well as a mug of Starbucks.

"Thanks, Robyn"
**

Hi everyone, 09 APRIL 2006

Started this week with Condoleezza Rice, middled with the President of Poland and ended with Congressional delegates from Washington, Texas and Georgia (yes, Georgia, what a surprise…)

All the Joint Visitors Bureau was supposed to do for the Secretary of State was move luggage from the Baghdad International Airport to the International Zone downtown one morning and back the next. Instead what happened was a small demonstration of the eternal conflict between the Department of State and the Department of Defense with our puny little JVB and I stuck right in the middle. The story:

Rice was delayed due to thunderstorms and when she arrived (by the way, she is an ultra-petite, 5 foot nothing, twig) due to weather instead of flying by helicopter to the IZ she drove the airport road - Route Irish – in an armored motorcade of limos, Humvees and a couple of the Rhino buses. Our mission plan was to take all their luggage in our armored trucks while they flew in helicopters. By the time everyone had instead loaded into the wheeled vehicles there was no luggage left for us to haul, so no mission. All fine. We worked all day with the department of state security agents, the state trip planners, the state "luggage-master", and several department of defense people and everyone agreed that we WOULD NOT need to haul on the return trip either. All fine. So, of course, 0-dark-thirty next morning the phone rang ordering us down Route Irish to the IZ to haul baggage. Despite the fact that all the baggage was already loaded onto a helicopter, and despite the fact that our work would DELAY the arrival of the baggage at the airport, and despite our vigorous arguments against making an unnecessary trip through Hajji-land, we did the mission.

Although there has not been a major IED on Route Irish for several months annoying small arms attacks are frequent and it is an on-your-toes experience. It takes about 15 minutes on a good day and 30 minutes on a bad one. If not for all the checkpoints and heavy traffic the run from downtown Baghdad to the International Airport would only be about 10 minutes. Pretty good design and to be envied by most major metro area dwellers world-wide. Along the way you see the worst of Baghdad: garbage, rubble and mud everywhere. If the Iraqis started high loaders, bulldozers and dump trucks working today they would have years of clean-up. Anywhere there is unbuilt space there are squatter food plots. Traffic moves briskly and millions of Baghdadis go about their lives daily without real concern over violence (like Kansans don't worry about tornadoes and Californians ignore earthquake fears).

So, we arrive at the helipad, UNLOAD the loaded helicopter, drive like madmen back to the airport, run to the airplane and frantically load baggage while Rice's entourage glare at us for being two minutes late. Some self-important flunkey yelled at us.

So, why did this happen? Because the State Department thinks they should be running things in Iraq and the Defense Department thinks they should. This struggle has been ongoing since Jefferson was Secretary of State and Henry Knox was Secretary of War under George Washington. Defense thinks state has its head in the sand about realities on the ground and state thinks defense has its head somewhere else. So, the bottom-line is that somewhere in the Army/Defense/State chains of command everyone so distrusted everyone else to get the job done correctly that in order to guarantee the job correctly done, error was instead induced. This was only the first time this week that important people yelled at me.

Lech Kaczyński, President of Poland, arrived for a big rah-rah day. This was huge international news. You probably heard nothing about it in the US media. Great mission; on-time, on-schedule, well-coordinated, well-executed. So of course I got yelled at. President Kaczyński also arrived in storm conditions but we timed squalls and weather to fly into the IZ, then drove to meet with Iraq President Talabani. The South African security contractors, Peruvian gate guards, and Iraqi-Kurd personal guard of the president would not let the extra Polish vehicles or Polish security forces into the area, but I was able to prevent an international incident by giving away a pocketful of buffalo nickels to the Iraqis, talking rugby with the South Africans and telling my one dirty joke in Spanish to the Peruvians. Everyone wound up happy and left behind a good meeting. We flew on to Ad Diwaniyah (Camp Echo) where the President met with local Iraqi leaders, coalition military officials and especially with a large number of the 2,000-some Polish soldiers who run that South-Central part of Iraq. Although a smallish fellow (he looks a lot like a frumpy CPA), the President was very personable and did a lot of photo-ops and handshaking. The troops were delirious to see him, just like we are to see Bush, Rumsfeld, etc. Had a bite of REAL polish sausage…yum. In a well-controlled and planned flight we came back between storms and fronts. The final five minutes ran us into lowered visibility and a minor dust storm. Upon arrival I was yelled at by the second-highest ranking general over here for risking the president's life by flying in a dust storm. I surprised him by suggesting it would have been stupid to turn around and fly back 200 miles in the same storm the whole way. He yelled at me some more so I wisely shut-up. Anyway when President Kaczyński left I saluted and shouted "Nyeck Zhee Polska!" which (I hope) meant Long Live Poland. He grinned, shook hands heartily and flew away. The Polish Ambassador was totally pleased. Good mission.

Finally, a short Saturday mission with three US House Reps. They too arrived late, and one of them yelled at me for shortening their agenda (because THEY were late?). Otherwise uneventful flight to Tikrit and Fallujah and then helicopter back about 11 p.m.

I know I'm supposed to quake in my boots when Generals and Congressmen yell at me but I've been yelled at by Perry Middle School Principal Henry Murphy so I just don't quake much these days.

The ducks are all gone from the lakes and the swallows and bats have returned to feast on the mosquitoes. We've crept into the low 90s now and may have seen our last major rains. Iraq is green and growing with the occasional wildflower here and there.

Cards and letters from Pop x 2, co-worker Peggy Bukovatz, coffee, cookies and magazines from Robyn, and a box of movies and videos from cousins Dennis and Susan Hiatt.

American by birth. Soldier by choice. Volunteer by God!

Roger T. Aeschliman
Major, Armor
Deputy Commander, First Kansas Volunteers

Good morning daughter Regan, 15 APR 2007

It is early in Iraq; still dark at 5:30 a.m. There is a lovely vanilla moon shining over the palace waters and when I look at it I see the Shrimp in the Moon and think of you.

I hope you have a great, relaxing and fun weekend and then another great week at school with the best teacher in the whole wide world. And here's another poem for you.

Love, Dad

THE SHRIMP IN THE MOON

When Ryan looks into the night sky
There's the Moon, shining on high.
And Ryan sees the Man in the Moon:
Big round eyes, just like a cartoon.

When I look up, instead I see
The Woman in the Moon looking back at me.
Black hair pulled up in a bun
Smiling like she's having fun.

But when Regan looks (it will never fail)
That she will see a head and a tail
Of the Shrimp in the Moon, curled around,
Sometimes facing up, sometimes facing down.

Shrimp or woman, woman or man,
They're all there to see if you can.
Shrimp, woman, man – at least those three;
What else does your imagination see?
**

Dear Dad
We had a full moon too. But ours was not very bright. I hope you have a good week and call soon.

Love, Regan

"Happy Easter Everyone!

"Roger's update this week has him being yelled at ... again. Poor guy. I guess he's just too friendly for the regular Army.

"Enjoy, Robyn"
**

Hi doll,

Just finished day one of five. Here for the night then gone overnight for three days. Will be hard...Love you and already looking forward to talking. One photo of eastern Baghdad slums; yes, those are buffalo in town. Another of me during a good mission before someone yells at me. Love you, rog

Hi everyone, 16 APRIL 2006

I had two very good missions this week, most importantly with my old friend Congressman Todd Tiahrt of Wichita, Kansas USA!

Todd got off the airplane at the Baghdad International Airport, looked at me like I had tentacles coming out of my forehead, then it clicked. We last visited in Washington D.C. three or four years ago when I was number two guy at the Kansas Labor Department, so it was good to see him again. His wife Vicki, and my wife Robyn, are by far the better part of each couple. Todd and his two other Congressional peers spent most of the day in closed briefings on matters of military intelligence (and no, it's not an oxymoron). But during the drives between meetings we were able to talk old times. Todd looks great and plays basketball for exercise with other congressmen – several whom have been here to visit and previously mentioned Todd's flatfooted jump shot and his inability to leave the ground when rebounding...Tough getting old.

In Balad we visited the military hospital there; the modern US version of a MASH in inflatable, pressurized tents, all linked together. It covered a couple of acres. While there the Congressmen saw two Iraq civilians helicoptered in, victims of terrorism. The doc there said they treat more Iraqis than soldiers. If a soldier cannot be fully treated at Balad they are sent to Germany. If they are fully treated but need recovery they are sent to Kuwait. Most wounded are treated, recover for a few days and return to duty. As we were preparing to fly Todd and the others back home from Balad we looked across the runway to see if the C-130 transport plane was sitting there waiting. All we could see was a C-5 Galaxy – the enormous US cargo plane that can carry M-1 tanks and entire Chinook helicopters. As we neared we could make out the relatively dwarfish C-130 completely hidden behind the C-5. Last week's news talked about a C-5 crashing in the USA. That is really a career ender for some young Air Force pilot but it is a spectacular plane.

I said we had two good trips and we did. I wish I could say I wasn't yelled at but I was. Apparently some of Department of State officials who travel with the Congressmen here are irked that I visit with these men and women. So now the guidance for all the soldiers at the Joint Visitors Bureau is to be seen and not heard and try not to be seen very much. It kind of gets your dauber down to run into these Active Duty versus National Guard versus Department of State "cultural" differences and to learn by trial and error that they are meaningful. If there were just some kind of textbook or the "Complete Idiots Guide For Real People Going Into the Active Component in Iraq" perhaps I wouldn't be such a dirt bag over here. Well, one thing I do do well is follow orders so I reckon we'll just keep going and watch the days and weeks speed by until we are all safely back home.

Congressman Tiahrt, his fellow travelers and US Ambassador Khalilzad all posed for a photo with Flat Matt, a two-foot tall, laminated, paper Marine whom we are touring around Iraq. There is a Marine Moms' Association in Wichita, Kansas, that asked us to show him around and then send him back to Kansas. So far Flat Matt has had his picture taken with Secretary of State Rice, the President of Poland, a number of US and Iraqi soldiers in different parts of the country, and various US dignitaries and military leaders. Hope to capture some more interesting people and places before the end of April when Matt has a flight back home.

My back feels good. Only minor twinges during very long chopper flights. Thanks for asking.

And it is HOT in helicopters as the temperature is over 90 degrees as now. Returning from a mission Thursday night at 2200 (10 p.m.) it was 80 degrees outside and 110 inside while flying. I am now eating more and drinking water all day long. It is dry and doesn't feel as miserable as a 90-degree Kansas day but we are creeping towards the anticipated 110-degree AVERAGE highs of July. Yuck...

I learned three words this week from various sources. Frenum: the little membranous, connective tissue that holds your tongue to the bottom of your mouth. Filtrum: the indentation above your lip, under your nose. And Benighted: to have night fall around you, or to be completely in the dark about something, or just plain stupid as in "Roger was benighted regarding talking to Congressmen."

A hearty thank you to everyone who sent me an AAFES gift certificate. I just spent the last of this Christmas money on new running shoes and a pair of gee whiz, extra comfortable yet light-weight boots so my feet thank you too! My rule of thumb over here is don't spend ANY money but my iron-clad rule is NEVER buy anything the Army should provide. The Army boots issued are satisfactory but when you are a flat-footed, knock-kneed, 45-year-old who stands up all day something a little better really makes a difference.

Cards and letters from Commerce Bank & Trust co-worker Peggy Bukovatz and a box of goodies, coffee and Gatorade from Mom.

American by birth. Soldier by choice. Volunteer by God!

Roger T. Aeschliman
Major, Armor
Deputy Commander, First Kansas Volunteers

Dear Kirk, 20 APR 2006

Thanks as always for the newsie update. Great to hear about it all.

The continuing adventure of children. How do we all make the time to do all their things and still earn a living and have something resembling an adult life as well? There are so incredibly many things for children to do now. When I was a kid in Grantville all there was was 5-6 games of little league in the summer, a few years of swimming lessons, and random, infrequent but incredibly glorious trips to the Topeka library. Poor Robyn this week is: working full-time, preparing for her huge comprehensive master's degree final exams, working the school science fair, kids to track practice, scouting meetings (weekly), Scouting at KSU merit badge conference, two music lessons, and church multiple events. She is a Superwoman that I am lucky to have. (similar to your wife and you). We're both fortunate to have great kids too...

In comparison I work 15-20 hour days 2-5 days in a row and am physically exhausted, but it is all I have to do and pretty straight-forward. Looking forward to reestablishing my Trust Officer multi-tasking skills upon my return.

rog

April 20, 2007

Hey Darling,

Just a quick note to tell you I love you and miss you dearly. I am sooooo stressed right now and could really use a hug and some cuddle time. I was insane to say I'd take this long-term sub position and study for comps at the same time. Ugh! One or the other would be enough all by itself. I have no idea how full time teachers work on a master's degree, have a family, and do their job. Ryan and Regan have been helping me study this week. They read the question and I answer it while they look at my notes that go over the question. Hopefully, by the end of the week I will have all of the details memorized. I really wish I could just write several papers over this material rather have to do this essay test with no notes. I'm so bad with the details - but know where the answers are. Oh well, just my learning curve. At this point I just hope I pass the darn thing and don't have to rewrite anything. Thanks for letting me vent.....Love you and hope everything is going well for you.

Robyn XXXOOO
**

Hello my lovely dearest,

I am now in the final stretch of this five day mission. Very long days all over the country. Severe weather disruptions and delays. Very, very tired. First night back "home" in four days. Should get six hours sleep and then back at it. (Six hours will feel GREAT! compared to what it's been)

Sorry to have been out of touch but looking forward to calling you Wednesday morning your time to say hello. Love you and the kids.

Sorry you're so maxed out. You will drive through it though and come out even stronger. I know you are doubting yourself a bit, but remember you have doubted yourself in nearly every class so far and come out smelling like roses. All the same schmuck "classmates" that you blew out of the water by GPA will be taking the same exams so you just know they aren't going to clobber people at this point.

You are going to do fabulously! I know it even if you don't ...

Love you and YOU ROCK!
rog

Dear Pop, 22 APRIL 2006

Thanks for the nice letter. It is great to hear about everything at home, even the sad news. I'm so very sorry to hear about Dave. He has fought through in the past and I know he will make a good effort against this cancer too.

You and mom are reaching an interesting age where your older friends will begin to pass away, and the occasional unlucky same-age friends. It will be difficult and growing at the same time. I know my little old lady friend in Kansas City, when her brother died, she was saddened but pretty much said well that just leaves me. There's nothing to be done about it. For you two, in our current times and health care it is likely that both of you will live into your 90s and in pretty good shape as well.

Please wish Randy well and tell him he is in my thoughts. Same with Don. Good luck on the cattle and the wheat harvest. Over here the wheat is already browning. Short seasons.

Please tell folks hello for me and that we are winning, that there is a plan and that the Iraqis are taking more and more responsibility every day. Closing on the halfway point now and I am looking forward to heading home. I do greatly appreciate your kindness in writing so frequently. It makes things much easier over here to know people care about you.

Your loving son,

rog

"Hey All,

"He didn't get yelled at this week. Yeah!! Note the photos...the one of him all wet is after a run. That's not water, that's sweat. No wonder he prefers to run with a sweat band. Too bad he can't use one – though he did mention that he's seen Generals and Command Sergeant Majors running with hats and sweatbands. Hardly seems fair.

"Robyn"
**

Hi everyone, 23 APRIL 2006

This week included a five-day mission, dust storms, massive thunderstorms, red zone moves to interesting places, and real prime rib on Easter!

It was truly an honor for me to escort Retired General Barry McCaffrey all over Iraq for five days. He was highly decorated from Vietnam on, commanded a division during Desert Storm and concluded his governmental career as the Drug Czar under Clinton (icky-yuck!). A year ago he did a review of the Iraq situation for Congress and the public and was here again to do the same thing. It was the most aggressive schedule we've had so far. My mission folder was a full inch thick and the itinerary changed over and over and over . . .

Lowlights were the 0500 to 2200 hours schedule every day and heat into the 100s! On the third day a major dust storm blew in grounding all flights of all types. We spent the entire day with the 101st Airborne Division near Tikrit making up new meetings to productively fill the time. These included briefings from combat commanders, reviewing up-armoring facilities, secret briefings about targeting the highest ranking terrorists, and concluding with a night-time combat patrol to Forward Operating Base Remagen in the sheeting rain of a raging thunderstorm.

FOB Remagen is located just outside Tikrit. The US soldiers there mostly train the Iraqi Army. In addition they have one platoon (40+ soldiers) of the Puerto Rican National Guard, operating a small detention facility for bad guys. It was formerly a stable of Saddam's and is clean and tidy but Spartan. "Guests" stay for a maximum of 10 days before being released or forwarded elsewhere for interrogation or adjudication.

Some history as it was told to me: Saddam is from a very small town called Owja, near Tikrit. He had no tribe and when he came into power he artificially consolidated five tribes into the "Al Tikritis" and claimed it as his. His grandfather and his own two goon sons are buried in Owja. Tikrit is no longer the hotspot it once was but in the previous week a dozen IEDs were found along our route and one exploded causing no injuries or damage. Normally we Joint Visitors Bureau types would not allow a risky patrol movement like that but the instructions for General McCaffrey were to facilitate his desires and when the 101st Division Assistant Division Commander Brigadier General Oates said he was going too then it was most definitely on. With higher level approval we did it but I insisted we take the longer, safer, highway route rather than the "through the heart" of Tikrit route. It all turned out uneventful and the General had a nice review of how well US troops are training Iraqis to take care of themselves.

Earlier in the trip we had Easter lunch and while there were heaps and mounds of much good stuff for me the highlight was a scrumptious hunk of prime rib carved right off the cow. Just a tiny bit under medium and loads of fat! Better than the Topeka Steak House, about the same as Tony's, and not quite as good as the Timberline.

At the very beginning of the mission my General attended a major planning meeting of all the most senior people in Iraq. I counted 28 Generals, wearing 50 stars! The room sparkled like the Milky Way over the Flint Hills on a dark summer night.

Speaking of Generals, Division Commanders and higher are authorized an enlisted personal assistant with the primary mission of tending house and cooking. At the 101st the General and his top assistants have their own mobile homes with running water and their own private dining room. I sat outside for four hours one night, smelling the food, hearing the laughter and the clink of real metal silverware and real glass glasses, and praying for the dinner to end so I could get a couple hours sleep before the next day started.

Speaking of Generals one final time, toward the end of the mission my favorite General Abizaid and General Schoomaker – the Army Chief of Staff – were in town to meet with my General McCaffrey and with General Casey, the overall war chief in Iraq. As I was waiting for my guy to leave I noticed the hallway was full of subordinate Generals all waiting to brief one of these four. As a Major I was the least ranking person within 50 meters. We tend to lose our intimidation of Generals at the JVB as we are surrounded by them so much.

They become more like a product (we use the term "package") to be delivered; fragile, handle with care.

No one yelled at me all week.

In the shower trailer this morning I met Adolpho (a US citizen originally from Mexico City), Rami (from Andhra Pradesh in southeast India) and "Hank" (a Pilipino who wouldn't tell me his real name because "you not say it right"), all Kellogg, Brown and Root electricians working on the exhaust fans. This is a contractors' war all right. We could not do what we do here without them fixing things, pumping gas, feeding troops and rebuilding the nation's infrastructure.

Cards and letters from Pop, Mom Mary Lou, Tam Engler, Judy and Jim Wood, Linda Crandall, the Berry's, Adriel and Koinonia Class all of TBC, Peggy Bukovatz, box of cookies and coffee from Rick and Sarah Beyer, and box of books, candy and jerky from the Linquist family (please patronize Taco John's in Topeka – run by Ed and Becky Linquist – yum yum!).

American by birth. Soldier by choice. Volunteer by God!

Roger T. Aeschliman
Major, Armor
Deputy Commander, First Kansas Volunteers

Hi everyone, 30 APRIL 2006

Lots this week, but especially Secretaries Donald Rumsfeld and Condoleezza Rice in a joint pop-up visit. The pop-up part is the key for us here at the Joint Visitors Bureau. It means instead of one or two weeks of advance planning we get one or two days! We had four meetings in two days with Army planners, Air Force planners, bomb sniffer dog planners, Army helicopter planners, Iraqi government planners, Embassy planners. Late nights planning...

The result was a wonderful two days with both parties leaving the country very happy. Helicopters were never late, meetings generally were on time, and I was able to facilitate the enormous number of agenda changes that occurred on incredibly short notice. It was a miracle. The two secretaries met with all the top Generals in country, the Ambassador and especially with almost all of the out-going and newly elected Iraqi national leadership. It was a powerful message of support for the Iraqis as they develop a government. At our final meeting – a training seminar for the top leaders of the Iraqi Ministry of Interior (the national police) – the Minister made remarks to the effect that President Bush and Secretary Rumsfeld deserve the thanks of the world for removing Saddam and leading the global war on terror, and for STICKING WITH IT in the face of the naysayer's. He said Iraq is not in a civil war and is making good progress toward being able to take care of itself. He went on to thank the parents, spouses and children of all the American soldiers on duty over here for the sacrifices those families are making, and at that point we all had teary eyes, including Rumsfeld. The minister promised that Iraq was going to be a country of freedom and a strong ally of the USA in the ongoing global war on terror. I think the Iraqis get it.

Secretary Rumsfeld likes butterscotches and caffeine-free Diet Coke. I made sure our hotel staff had both in his room.

General Casey – THE general in Iraq – came by the JVB last night to thank us all for executing the dual missions on short notice and for the six months we have been in country so far. He said he has not had one complaint about the JVB the entire time and many, many compliments. He passed out a lot of his commemorative coins and as he was leaving the room he yelled "Aeschliman" and flipped a coin to me. Well, I'd been looking the other way at all my happy soldiers, snapped around to see what he wanted and took the coin right on my lower lip. (These things are the size of an Eisenhower dollar and it hurt). The coin fell to the ground and a great collective groan went up from the assembled company. I just started doing push-ups ...

No one yelled at me this week either.

Several times this week the Iraqi Army or Iraqi Police came under significant attack from Anti-Iraqi Forces (AIF). They did not hide or run. They fought back and seized the day. The Iraqi police and Army continue to grow and improve and are truly taking over from the Coalition more and more every day. When you read about group murders you are mostly reading about one bunch of bad guys taking out another bunch of bad guys – more like the Crips and Bloods in LA than civil war. (I'll write more about this and other divisions and splits in Iraq soon).

At the beginning of the week Charlie Daniels and his band were here and played to enormous crowds around Iraq. We visited briefly in the hotel, I thanking him for coming and he thanking me for being here.

I sent an e-mail to a wonderful pianist named Barbara Higbie just offering a word of praise for a delightful instrumental I enjoy called "Charlie Riley." I expected nothing back but she responded and is sending me a CD. She said she reads all her own e-mail because "while I am busy I'm not very famous." Please go listen to some Barbara Higbie music and buy some. Someone this talented and this nice deserves to be famous.

My Aunt Nancy (Tennessee) sent some Starbucks coffee and related how the shop gave it to her for free when she mentioned it was for me. I looked up the address on the Internet to send a thank you note and found a number of postings talking about how Starbucks opposes the war effort and hates soldiers. I can swear this is not true. In fact the JVB hotel received a huge pile of Starbucks coffee for free that we serve in the hotel and the restaurant 24/7. Starbucks Rocks!

One evening the sky turned green and yellow and thunderheads towered to 30,000 feet. In Kansas we would have run for the basements as a tornado or grapefruit sized hail was on the way. Here, the temperature dropped 20 degrees in five minutes (like Kansas) and then it rained mud (unlike Kansas) for twenty minutes, stopped, cleared and reheated 20 degrees in an hour. I guess I was wrong about the end of the rain. It is 100 or over every day now and last night didn't drop below 80.

One of our soldiers participated in outdoor boxing last night. It was great entertainment but of the 14 matches (limited to three one-minute rounds) only a couple were anything like real boxing. Most were just flailing about, sweating and praying for each round to end. Our soldier boxed well but lost to probably the best fighter of the night, a Brit from Belfast.

Cards and letters from Pop, newsletter reader and unmet new friend Linda Dale, Peggy Bukovatz with her super-cool handmade cards, and boxes of goodies from Mom, my darling Robyn, Flat-Matt creator Pam Crane, Unk Nate and Aunt Nancy Thomas, and Topeka super accountant Terry Kimes .

Rumsfeld took a great picture with Flat Matt and on second look Rice is probably 5' 3" but still a twig.

American by birth. Soldier by choice. Volunteer by God!

Roger T. Aeschliman
Major, Armor
Deputy Commander, First Kansas Volunteers

PS – Pop, at this end of this April 2006, 9,475 miles in the air and 392 running on the ground.

Dear Ed, 01 MAY 2006

Thanks for another great gift box. The gang loves the Giant Goldfish Grahams and I have shared books with half a dozen of the men.

Like you I greatly enjoy westerns, especially Louis Lamour. While I am still short 15 or 20 of his books, I have read most and have most of them on the shelf. About ten years ago I went to an auction that had the complete REAL leather bound (not leatherette) set of his works. I bid up to around $700 (about $7 a book) and had to give it up. Someday I'll try again to collect that set.

I love to read and try to make time every day. Mostly it is magazines but I force in a few books from time to time. I've been keeping a list of books I've read over here as something to show my dad as he likes lists and records...

As I am not much afraid of Generals and other big shots I feel free to talk with anyone. But common courtesy dictates not to interrupt conversations so I mostly stand to one side and let the Generals and other VIPs do their own thing. If they engage me I visit freely but usually don't just go start a conversation.

I keep looking on the Internet for something from McCaffrey but nothing, so I suspect he is still drafting his report. He left with huge piles of reports, slides, papers and photos so he does have a lot to work with. I'm sure it will be news when he does make his report and will testify in Congress like last time.

When you clear the property feel free to give Ryan and Regan rides. I think they would find it great fun to ride on an actual bulldozer (provided there is a safe place to stand/sit). Hell, I'd like to ride on a bulldozer and knock over trees (I have done it with a tank several times – a 70 ton tank will knock down a pretty good sized tree).

What events is Katherine doing? Field, sprints, distance? Results? Ryan is out for track in the throwing events but seems to have little chance to participate as half the school is out. I have hypothesized to Robyn that he is out mostly for the socialization and perhaps specifically a girl or two rather than the athletics...

I look forward to some Shakespeare upon my return. Steamroller is pleasant and enjoyable music but I don't think I'd pay to go see them. Is Heritage Greg

Fankhauser? He's a good guy and a seldom seen friend of mine. Hope things are going well for him and you if that's the right bank.

Yes, please call Kirk about your sister, and (not hoping to sound at all being pushy but rather your adoring friend who wants the best for you and your family) you may want to visit about whatever the results of the estate for yourself. I've never had money to worry about but I have worked with enough people now to know that planning is critical and that a good, caring and independent banker can really help you sort through what the present is and what the future may offer. Robyn and I both have trusts we created (there not much money but there's a ton of life insurance) and we are our own trustees, but if we are deceased or incapacitated then Commerce takes over so I put my limited money where my mouth is. Just a thought. Take it or leave it ☺

Robyn is overjoyed to be done with her coursework. I think she probably nailed the written exams and is done but until she hears the final word she will be edgy. She is handling a pretty difficult class (Regan's) at Tecumseh South with a few too many kids and several unpleasant ones that will wind up stoned, pregnant, dead, or in jail at a young age. Too bad. It really does interfere with other children's ability to learn. She was thrilled though when I talked to her yesterday to have gotten her first real paycheck for two weeks work. She earned it!

I appreciate you, Becky and the kids so very much and am grateful you allow me to be a part of your lives. Thanks for your great kindness toward me here in Iraq and even more for your friendship and love shown to my family. I live over here nearly worry free because Robyn and the kids are strong and wonderful, but also because I know you are there to help in any way.

Most affectionately,

rog

MAJ Roger T. Aeschliman 02 MAY 2006
B Co 2-137 INF
APO AE 09342-1400

My Dear Nearly Lifelong Friend (through your music) Bruce Springsteen,

I was terribly saddened by your uninformed opinions about the War in Iraq. But I forgave you from our past 30-years of (musical) relationship. But your recent attack on the President over the hurricane in New Orleans just makes you look ignorant. Please explain how the President caused the hurricane. Please explain how the president caused levees to break. Please explain how it is his fault that people refused to leave, that the Mayor, Governor and other local officials sat on their hands, that 500 miles of airports, highways and rail lines were flooded. Please explain how ANYONE could have responded better or faster. Bruce, you can't beat nature and blaming Bush does not help. It just makes you sound like a silly, whining, left-winger.

I have rescinded my earlier forgiveness regarding Iraq. I now consider you ill-informed and an emotive jerk rather than a thoughtful man entitled to an opinion.

Stop your whining and either come to Iraq and see for yourself or just shut up. We are at war here and you are not helping.

MAJ Roger T. Aeschliman
Baghdad, Iraq

Hi everyone, 07 May 2006

It's Spring in Iraq, albeit 100 degrees, and in Spring every young man's fancy turns to love. Because any form of physical love is prohibited by General Order No. 1 our fancies must all turn wistfully to home.

And thinking of home is especially appropriate now: No matter how you count it we are at least half done!

Army National Guard units are mobilized on 18-month orders, with the rule of thumb that one full year will be boots on the ground in the Theater of War. We stood up September 1 and arrived boots on the ground in Kuwait in early November. So no matter how you count it as of early May we're half done with 18 months and half done with one year. There is some minor hope that we'll be sent home at 11 months in country as most units recently have been. Though it's way too early to start counting days we can project hanging uniforms in the closet sometime in November or December.

The Army Guard units have the longest row to hoe over here. With the initial training, and the standing down period, we will be gone from home for very close to 18 months. The active duty Army deploys straight from their bases; they are gone from home for a year or less in most cases. The Marines (and no, none of us want to have the required lobotomy to be a Marine) deploy for about eight months and are often gone at seven. And the Air Force units deploy for four months only. We scarcely get to know them before a new crew rolls in.

Well, half done.

When I began this weekly report Robyn sent it to about 50 or 60 people. I can't even begin to guess how many readers there are now, but I get letters each week from new friends reading it third, fourth or fifth forwarding. Many of you have asked: "Who are you?" Here's the sanitized version.

I am the second child of five to Ash and Mary Jo, two hard-working school teachers who realized they couldn't feed five kids on school teacher salaries so moved to the country outside of Grantville, near Topeka, and pop became a wonderful and kind State Farm Insurance man. I attended Perry-Lecompton schools and because it was a little place was able to do everything: football, wrestling captain, couple years of track, and many acting events, especially state championships in oration and duet acting, homecoming king and student body president. Pop and Mom made sure I worked on the nearby farms and had jobs from age 12 on.

Went to Kansas State ostensibly to major in photojournalism but quickly majored in beer and girls instead. Straightened out and wound up with degrees in print journalism and political science in 3 ½ years. Played scrum half on the KSU Rugby team, and sang second tenor in Men's Glee. Wrote for the campus paper for three years and always worked 2-3 part-time jobs. Graduated on Friday in December and started work at the Topeka Capital Journal newspaper on Monday. Did general reporting, then police/fire news, then the education beat and won several state, regional and national awards for writing and reporting. During those reporting years I ran for a seat in the Kansas House of Representatives and was thumped by a long-term incumbent. Best thing that ever happened to me. It really turned me from being a self-centered jerk onto a different life path. I also enlisted in the Army National Guard. It has been a remarkable 19 years so far and has given me many looks at systems, processes, people and the world that most people never get.

During the same time I met and wooed Robyn. She turned me down for three dates before caving in and my life has been perfect ever since. Together we transitioned from reporting to public relations for the Kansas Republican Party, to becoming chief of staff for the Speaker of the Kansas House of Representatives, then eight years as the appointed chief operating officer (the number two guy) at the Kansas Department of Labor under Governor Bill Graves. After 13 years of appointed government work a new governor of the other political party asked me to move on (expected and normal with no hard feelings – although it was tough landing a position in that post-9/11 economy; six months unemployed) before being taken on by Kirk Johnson at Commerce Bank & Trust, as a trust officer.

I love Topeka, holding board positions in Rotary, the Boy Scouts, a local school district board of education, and many other organizations including four or five military groups. In the Army I am a career combat leader, a tanker by training. I was serving in the tank battalion in Kansas when my brigade commander called and asked/told me I was going to transfer to the state's infantry battalion to help/plan/train them to transition from walking infantry to Bradley Fighting Vehicle armored warriors. I did this for a year when my current commander called me aside and told me two things: One, I had made the promotion list for Lieutenant Colonel and two, the battalion was mobilizing for Iraq. Accepting the promotion would mean staying home, being a first-look, high speed promotion to LTC, and in competition for command of my own beloved tank battalion. Deferring the promotion met loss of time in rank, and pay, going to Iraq and losing the chance to command the tankers. Instead of being a LTC in four-some years by the time I get home it will be closer to seven. While I would love to be a combat battalion commander in Kansas, the only job left will be this one – the infantry battalion. And while I think I would be the best choice and do a wonderful job it will be very hard for the Kansas Infantry "community" to accept an armor officer in the top job. I hope I am wrong as that selection process is underway and the First Kansas Volunteers will change commanders promptly upon our return to the states.

Robyn and I were blessed she was able to stay at home at raise our two wonderful children. We both have our masters' degrees – mine in Public Administration and hers, just this month, in Gifted Education. She is teaching right now in our daughter Regan's classroom, filling in the remainder of this year for the regular teacher on maternity leave. Ryan and Regan are both gifted children, and are kind, witty and pleasant people. I am the luckiest man in the world.

If anyone has other questions of any kind, send them on. Future reports will answer several already received.

Cards and letters from Pop and Martha Ozias, and gift boxes from Ed Linquist full of westerns and cinnamon grahams from Taco Johns, and coffee from boss Kirk Johnson.

American by birth. Soldier by choice. Volunteer by God!

Roger T. Aeschliman
Major, Armor
Deputy Commander, First Kansas Volunteers

Dear Brad, 07 MAY 2006

Congratulations on this great news. I am thrilled for you and wish you all the best.

Here are a few lessons I have learned of 45 years of being a son and brother and 17 years of marriage:

1 - The woman is always right.

2 - Tell the woman that she is right.

3 - Tell her that you love her all the time.

4 - When the woman is wrong and being wrong poses no physical or monetary danger to anyone make sure to follow through on rules 1-3.

5 - When the woman is wrong and being wrong endangers life and limb and poses financial ruin make sure to follow through on rules 1-3 and then quietly save the day behind the scenes and never, ever tell her that you did so.

6 - Repeat after me: Yes dear. You're right dear. I love you dear.

7 - Never, ever, ever honestly answer any question about how the woman looks. Really, avoid answering at all if possible.

8 - If you must answer then just say: Your sense of taste and style is always so much better than mine. What do you think/how do you think you look?

Hope this helps in the coming few months of terribly painful and mind-numbing wedding planning.

With greatest affection, rog

From: Richard Meck
To: Roger Aeschliman
Sent: Friday, May 05, 2006 7:16 AM
Subject: Thanks

Roger I have thought about you and your family a lot the last few months and finally settled down to write. I remember you as a cub reporter and thought then there was something different about you. As a police officer I had learned not to trust anyone in the press as they would misquote and try to show you as a dirty cop no matter what you said or did. I knew right away that you were different. I learned to trust you and think I spoke to you more than about any other reporter. I grew to respect you. Now I really respect you for all your contributions to this country. I just wanted to say thanks for what you do. My family and I will continue to pray for you and all the troops world wide until you're all home safely. Take care and see ya soon at some school activity.

Dick Meck
**

Dear Richard,

Thank you for your very kind note. It is nice to be remembered over here and to hear nice things about yourself. I always tried very hard to look at every news story from every side and just let the people involved tell their own story without my interpretation. All I know is that being nice and being fair got me a lot of stories that other people didn't get. That also has helped me throughout my life in the civilian and military sectors. Hard to imagine that being nice and fair are rare traits but perhaps they are...

I also want you to know that you are one of my heroes as well, not only for your law enforcement career (which I greatly respect and appreciate) but for your willingness to step up to the plate and make the world better in a real and tangible way through the adoption of an entire family of children. Few people would do this and you have proven to be a brilliant father raising decent, pleasant and bright kids.

I admire you.

Thanks again for writing, rog

From: Robyn Aeschliman
Date: Wednesday, May 10, 2006 1:37 am
Subject: job opening?

Hey Babe,

Got home from school today and there was a message from Warren Watson about the secondary gifted position calling to see if that is something I would be interested in. Honestly, high school is not an area I had thought of pursuing but wanted to get your thoughts on this. What do you know about Watson, anything about the gifted program at the high school, etc.....

I had just told someone today that I'm actually relieved that I didn't get the other job since I'm having such a hard time working full time and doing everything else too. But...I think they are making the high school job part-time. I don't know ----what do you think?

Love you.
Robyn
**

Gosh honey,

How interesting for you. Warren was always very pleasant to me as a board member. I liked him but really didn't know him very well.

I know less than zero about the program in the high school. Sorry. The overall environment there seems pretty good.

It sure is flattering and you should be proud that you are being sought out.

Only you can answer the question of whether you really want to go back to work now or not. If it is part time it could be the final link in the chain that gets you into the grade school position later, without killing yourself full-time. You'll have to ponder whether you want to work with a whole bunch of Ryan's and Regan's and their hormones.

You know I support you no matter what you choose. Work, great, I can get a motorcycle. Don't work, great, I'll still love you without a motorcycle.

I'd suggest like me when I was looking for work that you should initially show interest and look into it. See what the position entails and how the whole team plays nice or not there. It can never hurt to meet more people and make new connections and do interviews, etc. etc. And just like me, you CAN grit your teeth and turn down offers if you get one and it's just not right.

Love you and looking forward to visiting in another day or so. rog

From: Joyce A Merryman
Date: Thursday, May 11, 2006 11:55 pm
Subject: cookies

I am sending the recipe for the no bake chocolate cookies. I can send everything but the butter & milk. Can you get those?

Here's the recipe: Unbaked chocolate cookies

Bring to a rolling boil 2 cups sugar, 1/4 c. cocoa, 1/2 c. milk, and 1/4 c. butter. Boil for 1 minute. Add 1 tsp. vanilla, pinch of salt, 1/2 c. peanut butter, and 3 cups of oatmeal. Mix together, and drop on wax paper until set.

Hope this works. I'm sure you will want to double or triple the recipe, so I'll send enough ingredients to make several batches.

Jane's second knee surgery went well. She had it on Monday, and she gets to go home this afternoon.

Sounds like you are looking forward to coming home. I can imagine that after being home on leave, it was really hard to go back. Start marking the days off on the calendar.

Joyce
**

Yahoo! I can surely do milk and butter and will enjoy goofing around in the kitchen for a while. This will really be a treat for the guys. If it goes well we'll call for a repeat.

Glad Jane is doing well. Sure she'll be wobbling around in no time.

There were a number of very hard decisions that got me over here in the first place: turning down promotion, missing out on command of the tank battalion, family agreement that it was the right thing to do. It was very hard. But coming back after leave was much worse. When you leave the first time you don't know what to expect and you are so hyped on the potential dangers and combat roles that leaving is really only painful on the family side. Everything else of the equation says GO! Once you've been here with all the knowledge of what it's like, what it will be like and how long you have left to go, and how much you are really missing back in the USA, returning here is nearly an act of lunacy. I think it is a great credit to the discipline and goodness of the typical US soldier that there are so very few AWOLs from these two-week leaves.

I said good bye at the airport and just cried for five minutes, all the time going through the drill of metal detector, emptying pockets, and even taking off my boots. One of the security ladies there patted me on the shoulder and apologized for making me take my boots off and she really meant it, but everyone had to under the rules. A number of people had seen the tearful farewell and I saw a lot of strangers with shiny eyes and several people gave me thumbs ups or "we're proud of you" in passing.

So, yeah, it was very hard. I must be fucking crazy.

Well, thanks again and looking forward to this special cookie treat. rog

From: Linda Hubbard
Sent: Thursday, May 11, 2006 4:20 PM
To: Roger Aeschliman
Subject: how are things?

Hi Roger-

I purposely waited awhile to write since someone told me you were going to be home recently. Bet you enjoyed that immensely but the return trip was hard. I didn't ask how long your tour was-will you get to come home for good in August or will be it longer than that?

I really enjoyed reading your accounts since I do believe that we never get "the real story" from the media-and I am someone who supports the media generally! But still good to hear your perspective. Now that you're not my boss anymore, I can tell you that I just can't understand and probably never will, how you (or others for that matter) can be so supportive of the military. And please, don't get me wrong, I totally support you and all those serving, but I can't see the point of being in Iraq (you know, just my old "peacenik" thoughts coming out!!). Please feel free to change my mind-even though I just turned 57, I still try to keep an open mind!

On a much different subject, I still enjoy seeing the painting (A.K. Longren) that you and I got done on the 420 Jackson building-we have that for our lasting monument at KDHR/KDOL-whatever it's called. I hope Rev. Taylor enjoys it, too. That was a good thing we did!

I like retirement and not having the everyday stress, but I am having trouble "just sitting"-I never was very good at that and am still not. So I have formed Hilltop Communications and will try to find several organizational newsletters to produce for people-it was easier at KDHR where we had all the resources, but I'm getting there and have several prospective clients I'm working with to ink a deal. I am also doing some freelance writing-nothing published yet, but first you gotta write, then try to publish!

I pray for your safe return and that of all the soldiers, sailors, etc. Write or email anytime you have time-sounds like your job is pretty demanding.

This is my new email address at home and I check it often, so feel free to use this if you want. Take care, Linda
**

Dear Linda,

Thanks for writing. It is great to hear the updates from everyone about everything normal in Kansas. I've said many times that hearing about "Normal" is what makes this all worthwhile. I was home during your retirement ceremony and had hoped to attend but it fell on my last day and I really wanted to spend my final time with family. Sorry I missed your big day. Congrats and thanks for your wonderful career serving the people of Kansas.

At the earliest I'll be home by Halloween and we would consider that fortunate. By Thanksgiving would be an expected "normal" rotation home date. If we are not home until Christmas then most of us would consider that the system is screwing us. But National Guard is on orders for 18 months start to finish and if it suits the government to keep us here until March 2007 they could. But it would piss off a lot of governors and US Senators.

I am a confessed right wing nut, but I try to be a consistent right wing nut. I am probably really more of a combination stoic/libertarian than anything else and really think people ought to leave each other alone. Internationally I think there is room for a new "Monroe Doctrine" for modern times and our current state of affairs that would go something like this:

1 - Leave us alone and we will leave you alone.

2 - We will support free trade around the world.

3 - We are going to live the lifestyle we are accustomed too and we need certain resources to enable this. See number 2.

4 - Any intentional effort to deny us resources through free trade will be considered a violation of 1, 2 and 3.

5 - We will support those who seek overthrow of tyranny in favor of individual liberty and freedom around the world. Democracy is a bonus but is not always required for individual liberty.

6 - We will not support terrorists who seek to overthrow stable, freely-elected governments.

7 - We will not support "nationalist" movements where one linguistic or ethnic group believes it is entitled to its own nation.

8 - The difference between a freedom fighter and a terrorist is determined by cause and targeting. A freedom fighter opposes unelected tyranny where people have no individual liberty or freedom of action and thought. He targets military and governmental institutions and people. Those seeking to inflict their will and their version of society upon an unwilling public and targeting non-military and non-governmental people and institutions are terrorists.

9 - Believe people when they tell you they hate you and want you to die.

10 - First strike is always reserved as an option.

Iraq is not a special place. Under my rules Saddam could have gone on torturing and killing and destabilizing this region for a long time if he had not been a primary supporter and exporter of terrorism. The media is screwing the American public on this key fact. He did support and export terrorism. There are clear links to Osama and 9-11. It matters not at all if we ever find the chemicals and biological agents he had. The fact is that he did have them and he had plans to use them. We know this because HE TOLD US SO. In my world when people say they hate me and want me to die, I believe them.

Also, it matters not to me at all why I was sent here. What matters is that I am here, that the WAR is HERE. The war is not being fought in Kansas at Little League games with bombs under the bleachers. Being here is drawing all the bad guys from all over the world here to us and to the Iraqi Army and that means we fight here, not in Topeka. This war is a 30 or 40 year war against non-state players who want to truly control the world and have told us so. They want us all to live in a fundamentalist Wahhabist Islamist state under their control. They have told us so. We have to confront them and wax their asses anywhere we can at any time. Sometimes this will be a hot war, like here, now, where a nation had to be destroyed and rebuilt into a modern form. Other times it will be very cold with our spooks out covertly killing evildoers and preventing them from harming mom and pop in Grantville. It's going to take a while. But it is very, very important. If we don't fight here, I truly believe we will fight them one bomb at a time in the United States.

Don't intend to convert you, just a little food for thought. The lynchpin is whether a person believes these people will come after us. If you do then we have to go after them first, where ever that takes us. If one believes that if we somehow change our ways to pacify them, then they will leave us alone, then nothing we do anywhere around the world will make sense or ever be justified.

I personally believe them when they say they hate America and that will intend to come get us. Rule 9.

Yes, babe, we (mostly you!) did a very nice thing with the airplane factory. No cost to taxpayers, and with just a little local push it can become a tourist walk-by point and a nifty little preservation of history. You ROCK!

I know you will be tremendously successful as a writer/publisher. Give Steve Kearney a call. Steve is a friend of mine who runs a major lobbying and association management firm in Topeka. He could very well be looking for someone to work on association newsletters and publications as part of his operation. Kearney and Associates in the phone book. Just tell him Roger said to call and thought it would be worth an hour and a cup of coffee to visit about possibilities for your mutual benefit. At the worst you meet a nice guy... I think Steve was a special work comp judge for a while before he got too busy with his own business.

Well, happy Saturday morning from Iraq and I'm wishing you and yours many very normal days. rog

P.S. you forgot to mention that I was your BEST boss ever.

Dear Pop, 13 May 2006

Just want to thank you for all the letters! You really are my letter warrior over here and I look forward to hearing from you a couple of times a week. It's so nice to hear it's normal, for better or for worse (because worse sometimes comes with normal life in the USA). So thanks for all the little updates.

I enjoy the clippings too. While I do look at the Topeka C-J on-line news every couple of days I mostly just headline scan. I do read the big national news daily but miss most of the local stuff that you send so please keep it up.

You asked what I want people to send. That's really a lot harder than it sounds. I don't *NEED* anything. I either buy or have Robyn send the hygiene things I do actually need. I have more books than I can possibly read thanks to many well-meaning friends who over estimate my free time. I enjoy the magazines from you, Robyn and Aunt Nancy (and occasionally others) and after I read them they are very popular with all the soldiers. Everything gets read to tatters as many of the troops have a lot more sitting around/waiting time than I do.

That kind of leaves food and I've said many times there is too much food over here already. Please don't hurt anyone's feelings but I give away 90% or more of all the junk food people send. Mostly because if I kept it I would eat it and then I'd blimp out.

So, perhaps Twinkies? I don't know how well a box would travel but it's worth trying once. I enjoy the cans of nuts I get from various folks. They make a nice snack. I give Robyn short lists once in a while and while I like getting packages it costs people about as much to send one as it does to fill it.

Rather than wondering what to send me it might be easier just to collaborate with Robyn and send your magazines along with the boxes she prepares. If people want to do the computer work, gift cards from AAFES or for I-Tunes are great. Robyn could help with this too.

Well, that probably didn't help much, but I don't need much and the things I want I really don't want to have around too often in too much quantity. Sorry. Send what makes you happy as there is always a soldier who will eat/consume it keeping me popular.

Things continue to improve here. There is a significant amount of thuggery on the street – gangland warfare. And the IEDs go off miles away; we still hear them and feel them. Despite all that the Iraqi Police are doing better daily and the Iraqi Army is really performing very well. Most of the violence over here now is bad guy against bad guy. Nothing to cry about.

I feel safe most of the time and when we're out flying the odds remain heavily in our favor. The only thing I really dislike is the noise. I sleep so poorly anyway that three or four uninterrupted hours of sleep is a real treat. I typically wake three-four times a night due to low-flying helicopters, generators kicking on or something blowing up miles away. I look forward to being home where it is quiet.

Still running and exercising every day I'm not on a mission. Most days I run 9 miles now in about 1:15. I stop halfway to drink water and wipe down then take off again. Hot and humid right now so it's terrible. But will dry up soon and not be so bad. At night gets back into the 70s and 80s and that feels very cool after 105 and humid.

How are the cattle?

Love you very much and looking forward to November in Topeka. rog

Happy Mother's Day to everyone, 14 May 2006

Early this week as I stepped out of a porta-potty I smelled something. After hearing me complain about how foul this place smells most of the time, I must give equal time to the overwhelmingly beautiful fragrance that washed over me here at Victory Base. There is a locust varietal that is in full bloom right now, with hand-sized, fuzzy, pale yellow flowers. Its aroma is cloyingly sweet, perhaps a cross between lilacs and honeysuckle, and powerful. And as it is a very common tree (at least here where we are) the hundreds of trees offer tens of thousands of intensely fragrant blossoms. It's like strolling through perfume and wonderful while it lasts. Not as good as being at home in April to smell the dwarf lilacs and viburnams, but a tremendous morale boost nevertheless.

Had a group of Congressmen in for one day. Visited with Jim Costa of California and he said he would look up his constituent, my sister-in-law Amy, in Bakersfield and tell her hello. Later my wife reminded me Amy lives in San Bernardino. Duh! Hopefully he won't look too hard.

At the end of this same trip one of the Congressmen grabbed me, put an arm around my shoulder and had an assistant take our picture. I caught the department of state guy giving me the evil eye and after they left I went to make sure he knew the man grabbed me for a photo and that I was not excessively "talking" to the Congressman. Didn't want to be and was not yelled at over that. On the good side, the top three generals in this theater all know me as Aeschliman, Ash or Lucky with a smile so I'm feeling not so dirt-baggy right now.

Flying over Iraq you see the wheat harvest coming in. Great swaths of countryside. Many combines but many more small plots of backbreaking scythe and sickle. As I understand it, typically they will graze sheep and goats through the stubble, then burn, then plant something else to grow and harvest when it gets cooler – October-January or so.

A tremendous dust storm blew up. I was inside about 1900 hours. The sky went rosé, then taupe, then green, then black in the space of 30 seconds. Visibility dropped to about 30 feet and the fine, silty sand blew in through every possible tiny crack. In less than one hour everything was coated with talc-like dust and we were all coughing for two days afterward. Those who saw it said it was a rolling wall of sand, much like the scene from the recent film "The Mummy." Blew through and was gone in an hour. Weird.

General Abizaid was back again this week. An uneventful two days. Perhaps interesting as an example of the kind of thing we escorts have to do:

The Chairman of Defense for the island nation of Tonga (equivalent of Secretary of Defense for us) was here in preparation for a contingent of Tonga soldiers joining the coalition forces. General Abizaid returned late from a very informal dinner with General Casey wearing his PT uniform (t-shirt and running shorts). The Tonga delegation was still up in the lounge area of the hotel. No meeting was scheduled so I warned the general he was going to walk right past them. He disliked the idea of meeting this level of VIP unprepared and underdressed, so I recommended that I transit through the hotel, past the Tongans and unlock a highly secure, seldom-used rear entrance so he could bypass an embarrassing moment. Got me a "Quick thinking, Ash," from Abizaid and that made my whole week.

Part protocol, part hotel operator, part military aide, part diplomat, part bodyguard gunslinger. There's just no good description for this work, but if we mess it up, everybody knows.

This morning in the cool of the darkness I took the official Army Physical Fitness Test (APFT). This fitness evaluation is done twice a year for record and all soldiers compete against a scale. The test is two minutes of pushups, 15 minutes break, two minutes of sit-ups, 15 minute break, followed by a 2-mile run. There are minimum numbers and times required to just pass and there are maximum numbers and times for 100% scores. 300 is a perfect score. For my 45-year-old age group 66 pushups (you can't pause and rest on the ground), 72 sit-ups (same thing) and 14:06 run are the maximum scores. I came in at 65, 70 and 14:48 for 291 points out of 300. Pretty good but still room for improvement. It was very pleasant not running in the heat of the day.

Jim McHenry, Topeka super-star library fund-raiser, asks: "I'd be curious as to whether or not public libraries are able to function in Iraq. Are they weathering the storms or have they become institutional casualties of the domestic unrest? I'm hoping some of them escaped the looting and are finding ways to keep their doors open and to continue providing services."

Informally only, from just asking around at meetings, the news is mostly good. There are about 10 lending libraries in Baghdad and many others in other cities. There were more before the war but they were heavily looted and all closed for some time. This is a big improvement over the past two years. Libraries are high on the list of things to do at the Ministry of Culture and the

Ministry of Youth and Sports, and with the help of American and coalition forces additional new ones are popping up in smaller towns and cities that have never had them before. In some cases local citizens are taking it upon themselves to create reading opportunities for kids. That's a great sign. The more the Iraqis figure out they can help themselves in many ways rather than waiting on someone else to do it, the better for us all. Additionally, the overall state of research, university, teaching and medical libraries is reported to be good. A few were looted or burned but most survived the war intact and were less targeted by looters.

Cards and letters from Pop x 3, dear Dorothy Hamler, Jean Crouse in Nebraska,

American by birth. Soldier by choice. Volunteer by God!

Roger T. Aeschliman
Major, Armor
Deputy Commander, First Kansas Volunteers

Eric Hyler 14 May 2006
2213 Riviera Dr
Lawrence, KS 66047-1990

Dear Eric,

Just a quick note from Baghdad to say congratulations and thanks for a wonderful teaching career. I don't know if you had Rick at Perry Middle School, but I know you had all the rest of the Eldon and Mary Jo Aeschliman litter. And I know we all came out of your classes both more knowledgeable and better people. Hard to ask more from a teacher than that.

I hope as you look back that these years were rewarding and fulfilling for you. There is no higher calling than a life spent in helping others become better people. Teaching is the epitome of this service. The effects of your life in teaching will ripple on for generations. My retirement wish for you is that you truly understand and believe this and feel great joy in your lifetime of achievement.

With your agreement I look forward to a visit upon my redeployment and the beer or coffee (or whatever) is on me.

With greatest affection and respect,

MAJ Roger T. Aeschliman
Deputy Commander, 2-137 Infantry
Kansas Army National Guard

From: raeschliman
Date: Sunday, May 14, 2006 5:55 am
Subject: job thoughts

Hey Darling,

Regan says to not take the job and Ryan says to take it. Go figure. I've been agonizing over this off and on all day. Even called Amy and talked with her for about an hour and a half. Not just me; her stuff too. After listening to me she said not to take it but that she understands my indecision. Ugh. I don't like that God threw this in my path. I was ok with not getting the other job and had sort of mapped out next year in my mind with completing some old projects, beefing up my subbing, and continuing with volunteer activities. This is really throwing me for a loop. I really like this opportunity but am not sure I really want to go back full time permanently. But I don't know that I can say no to this. My indecision is partly selfish in that I miss not having my own time to work on projects, run errands during the day, and have lunch with friends. It also really killed me when I had to call Lezlee to pick up Regan yesterday at school and bring her home. Just a mom thing. I wish I could figure out what would make me happy. I think that might be subbing for now since it gives me some flexibility and brings in some money but I hate turning down this job and not using the degree I've been working on. I'm going to sleep on it and see how I feel tomorrow.

I love you and thanks for letting me continue to vent with you. I'm sure I'm driving you crazy. One last thing, what is your gut feeling.....want me home with kids or picking up my career? Really, I know you want me to do what would make me happy but what would make you happy? Not a trick question, it's the same one I asked Ryan and Regan, and it does play a part in my indecision since I want to do what is right not only for me but our family.

Robyn
XXXOOO
**

My gorgeous wife,

I think for the sake of my motorcycle you should take the job. For every other reason I think you should graciously pass and be happy being a mom until the time and job of your choosing.

Love you regardless and support you regardless. rog

GEN (R) Barry McCaffrey 16 MAY 2006
2900 S. Quincy St. Suite 300 A
Arlington VA 22206

Dear General McCaffrey (and Christi!)

Thank you so very much for the huge box of goodies! It was a great day brightener and the men greatly appreciate it. There really is something in there for every taste and the pile is rapidly disappearing. Your kindness will be remembered.

Forgive me if I mentioned this earlier (just don't remember…hell getting old), but the troops here have read your report and think you got it exactly right. Every day the Iraqi Army and Police stand up a little bit more and recently have slugged it out toe to toe and gotten the best of the AIF. This is a great shift in standards from their "cut and run and hide" reaction only four or five months ago.

Please just keep telling the truth about what you've seen over here. You are once again making a difference in the lives of American soldiers and the affairs of this great nation.

Thanks for your service and, again, for the wonderful gift box.

American by Birth; Soldier by Choice; Volunteer By God!

MAJ Roger T. Aeschliman
Deputy Commander, 2-137 INF (First Kansas Volunteers)
Kansas Army National Guard

To: Roger Aeschliman
From: raeschliman
Date: Tuesday, May 16, 2006 1:57 am
Subject: more job....

Hey Babe,

Called Warren Watson this morning and declined the position and he immediately turned around and said, "what about part-time -you can choose which days you want the program to run." So....I told him I'd get back to him in a few days. Your thoughts?

Robyn
**

To: "raeschliman"
Sent: Tuesday, May 16, 2006 12:55 AM
Subject: Re: more job....

My dearest,

Part-time sounds much better. Great opportunity to get into the system and position yourself for the future. May learn you love high school (or not). Doesn't eat up your whole life right away.

Down-sides: You will have to schedule "working days" this summer in order to be ready. Not all summer, but enough to run with the ball in August, so you won't have all summer to be lazy, catch up with home maintenance, etc. Second, part-time still won't enable you to always "take Regan home" or whatever else happens. Sometimes you just won't be able to leave.

It sounds like you are desperately wanted and needed. I think you should do it and I'll settle for a very old, used motorcycle that we can pay for in a year or so.

Love you!!!!!!!!!!!!!! rog

P.S. Call Bob and Jeff to come and replace the Garage door opener. The two of them and Billy and Ryan could bang it out pretty quickly. All you do is pay for it and provide a couple of beers for Bob and soda for Jeff. What do you think?
**

To: Roger Aeschliman
From: raeschliman
Date: Tuesday, May 16, 2006 1:57 am
Subject: I sure do love you! :) XXXOOO

May 18, 2007

Hello Gentlemen! Please share this with your soldiers as you see fit.

Happy Birthday to the 137th Infantry Regiment! May is a special month. It marks another birthday of the 137th Infantry Regiment. I hope you have a moment to celebrate that birthday and reflect on the honorable and distinguished history of our Regiment.

Since 1861, Kansas Guardsmen have proudly and honorably served in our Regiment. In every major conflict their presence has been felt by the enemy and appreciated by our citizenry.

In 150 years, the 137th and predecessor Infantry units in our lineage have accomplished every mission assigned. From defending the Kansas Territory, to protecting lives and property of Kansas Citizens during natural disasters, to defending freedom and the ideals of the United States, the Regiment has remained constant --- Trained, Ready, Available and Capable.

You continue that heritage today. As you execute the difficult missions assigned to you in Iraq, remember the sacrifices of the brave citizen-soldiers who went before you. They too suffered intolerable heat in the Phillippine Jungles. They engaged in horrible close combat in the trenches during WWI. They fought terrifying battles in the hedgerows of France in WWII. Through their honor and character, they overcame the obstacles to complete their missions and wrote new chapters in the Regimental History.

You are writing the next chapter. Your chapter continues the tradition of mission accomplishment through the character of your soldiers, the dedication of your NCO Corps and the professionalism of your Officers. I am certain that when this mission in Iraq is completed, you will have reminded America that the FIRST KANSAS VOLUNTEERS are a capable and professional force dedicated to mission accomplishment and taking care of its soldiers. I am extremely proud of you!

Patty and I pray for your safe return and thank you for your service to our State and Nation.
God Bless the 137th Infantry Regiment.

FIRST KANSAS
Lyn Smith
**

COL Smith,

Thank you for these meaningful remarks. I will read them to the JVB team at our battle update briefing today. I want you to know how much I and everyone here appreciate your continued support and affection for the unit and men.

Things are going well country-wide, despite the IED and murder sprees. The SWEAT-M analysis continues to improve every day, the government is standing up and especially noteworthy from my perspective is that everywhere there is a fight the Iraqi Army and Iraqi Police are standing to fight and are winning. This is a big change from the running and hiding of six months ago.

Our soldiers are on their toes, both JVB and battalion-wide, and the combat patrol-missions are keeping everyone edgy. We own some hot property that is heavily targeted for IED drops and our men are finding most pre-det. Our biggest concern at the JVB is the surge of surface to air fire on helicopters of the past two months, and the ongoing threat of a rogue Iraqi security agent deciding to emerge while one of our dignitaries is meeting with their Iraqi VIP. We take a lot of crap from people about wearing our IBA all day on missions but if a sleeper decides it's time he won't give us the opportunity to suit up.

Well, again, thank you for remembering us. Looking forward to seeing you all upon return in five months, one week and two days (but who's counting?) (just kidding...we don't know...) rog

MAJ Roger T. Aeschliman

Greetings All,

"You'll notice in the photos this week that everyone's hair is appears to be gone. I'm assuming Roger's is shaved off at this point too. With the temp as high as it is there it is one thing you can do to try and cool down your body. We haven't been able to webcam with Roger for a few weeks so haven't seen him lately and didn't think to ask today when I talked to him if he had finally decided to shave it all off. I'll let you know if he has and as him to be sure to include a photo of himself in a future update.

"Robyn"
**

Howdy everyone, 21 May 2006

The tremendous news from Iraq is the new government is approved and seated! Despite all the yelling and screaming from the media back home, they have put it together in their own manner. While not an Arab/Iraqi expert I have learned a few things since November. The people in this region come to agreement through talking to exhaustion while maintaining "honor." They also solve problems through bluster and loudness including gunfire. For example:

If there is an argument over something, they yell at each other and bluster. Then they go get allies and all the allies yell at each other and posture. Then they all get guns and wave them at each other and yell. Then they all back off 300 yards, hide behind walls and shoot (mostly into the air) without aiming. Then, having proven they are not afraid and can't be intimidated, they all declare "victory" and go home. This cycle continues until one side figures out that if it really comes down to true violence they will be the losers. Then they talk some more, reach an agreement and all love each other again. It kind of depends on the realization setting in that there is more to be gained through agreement than through disagreement. There is a parallel in the wild kingdom with hyenas and lions. Hyenas will run from lions generally as lions are bigger and stronger. But if the mass of the hyena pack outweighs the mass of the lions then the hyenas will attack and fight, and have been caught on film killing lions by nipping them into stupor then overwhelming them.

So, back into Iraqi terms, the Sunnis (and others) will continue to yell and posture (and build IEDs and murder people) over every perceived loss of honor and power, but every time they are forced back into the discussion because the critical mass of progress is against them and they are wise enough to see that open and total civil war would mean their extermination. So they fight kicking and screaming for every scrap they can get but they keep moving ahead and keep coming back to the table. It just happens in an Arab way and their sense of timeline and urgency is different than in the USA.

I think it is very significant that the appointment of the ministers was ahead of the constitutional deadline. The new Prime Minister Maliki (sounds like Maleekee) is a hard charger and is going to make things happen.

There was concern the appointments would be met with massive attacks by the Anti-Iraqi Forces (AIF) but it really did not develop. Friday-Sunday saw pretty normal levels of booms, bullets and bad guy killing bad guy.

We had a short mission Friday and Saturday with Senator Orrin Hatch (Utah) and Senator Gordon Smith (Oregon). They arrived late to learn flights and air space were heavily restricted due to the seating of the government. The mission was chopped in half and the two Senators wound up meeting with US Ambassador Kalizad and Iraqi President Talabani and then flying right back out. Turns out our helicopters were the only things flying over Baghdad Saturday morning (exactly when the ministers were being named). That's a pretty obvious target and I was pretty keyed up but it turned out uneventful. Hatch and Smith were both very pleasant, perceptive and bright. I suppose we should expect that from our Senators and Congressmen but I've met enough of these folks to know they didn't all emerge from the deep end of the gene pool…

Temperatures this week: 103, 105, 111, 109, and a very mild day in the high 90s. At twilight the temperature drops 20 degrees and I swear the mid-80s feels cool. If it's 85 with a breeze some people put on sweaters or jackets. As dusk deepens the bats come out. It's a joy to watch them dance. For a few minutes they and the swallows are in competition then the swallows go home to roost and the bats have air superiority. During the day the diverse and abundant dragonflies rule the lakes in shimmering yellows, greens and blues. All together the bats, dragonflies and swallows help control the mosquito population which would otherwise physically carry us away to their secret lairs and suck us dry.

Last Sunday I spoke with Robyn and Mom on Mother's Day and thanks to the Internet was able to send roses for home delivery. How cool is that?

We have many partners and collaborators in our daily work. Two primary ones are the Air Force protocol staff at the Baghdad Airport (who receive all the incoming VIPs) and the people at the Visitor Operations Bureau (VOB) – the people who plan the VIP trips that we in turn execute at the Joint Visitors Bureau. May brought the nearly complete turnover of personnel at the airport and at the VOB. All new faces. The outgoing crew helped train us when we arrived and now we are the senior people helping train all these newbie's. The Circle of Life . . .

General McCaffrey as a thank you sent two giant gift boxes full of treats, books, magazines. Hundreds of dollars of goodies. What a very nice gentleman. I've said before most of our visitors will *say* thank you as they leave but only a few have bothered to write a note and none has before sent anything like this. McCaffrey issued his report and you can find it on the Internet by typing "General McCaffrey Iraq April 2006" into a search engine. It is a powerful report, clear, concise and well-written. I'd recommend everyone read it to hear what this smart straight-shooter thinks about our progress.

Cards and letters from Pop x 3, Mom's thank you note for Mother's Day flowers, Rose Blair and the Adriel Class at TBC, Aunt Janie Evans, pal Susan Anderson, goodie box from Mom that arrived on Mother's Day, great goodie box from Commerce co-worker Carol Jacobs, and the two huge boxes of treats from Gen (R) McCaffrey.

American by birth. Soldier by choice. Volunteer by God!

Roger T. Aeschliman
Major, Armor
Deputy Commander, First Kansas Volunteers

Dear Ed, 23 MAY 2007

Thanks for the box of goldfish! Can you write them off on taxes?

They are hugely popular so thanks for the resupply.

You've probably heard through Beck that Robyn is going to work half-time next fall as the gifted coordinator at the Senior High School. She is excited and angst-ridden at the same time. 14 years is a long time to be mostly out of the workforce and she knows she will miss the time with the kids and the chance to do the volunteer work and to read smutty romance novels. I feel very fortunate she has chosen to be at home all these years and know we have better children and a better lifestyle than so many others who don't have a two parent family or have chosen to have two incomes/two careers. (I have one friend who decided to downsize their home and move to a lesser but still safe neighborhood, in order for the wife to stay home and raise the kids. I think that substance over style selection is one more people should make but don't)...

Tell the Cat that I'm proud of her athletic accomplishments and that she has learned so early that mental and physical fitness go together.

You know you are getting old when you hurt yourself getting out of the golf cart! I'm running nine miles a day now, sprinting all over airport runways, crawling into and leaping out of helicopters just fine, and yet, sometimes I twist something just getting out of the bunk in the morning. I've said this before: there aren't many 45-year-old that could do this mission day after day. There's probably a lot of X-Box playing slackers in college that couldn't do this stuff...

Please don't let my kids see the big TV. We simply have no room for one and (frighteningly) we're going to need the money to buy a vehicle for Ryan! soon. Or more likely something new for Robyn or my work and the kids will use the Toyota Tacoma for school.

Your new house sketch looks good. A style I would love to have. Will it overlook a pond with bass? Can I kill a deer and turkey from the porch?

Love and thanks, rog

From: Jim McHenry
To: Roger Aeschliman
Sent: Tuesday, May 23, 2006 11:06 AM
Subject: Thanks for the library update

Rog, thanks for your very interesting reply to my inquiry. It is gratifying to know that libraries are seen as priorities in Iraq, particularly in such difficult times.

Congrats, too, on your APFT test score. I'm trying to gear up to swim in the Sunflower Games this summer, so I've begun training with Linda, our family's three-time national champion. She really whips me into shape. Right now, I'm still at the stage of hanging in the gutters and gasping for breath as we swim through consecutive 100 yd. repeats. Like you, however, I can see definite progress, which is encouraging.

Here's a wish for you straight from the roll call of Hill Street Blues: "Let's be careful out there!!!"

James McHenry, Ph.D., CFRE
Director of Development, Topeka and Shawnee County Public Library
**

Dear Jim,

I liked the original Hill Street Blues line: Do it to them before they do it to us. In much of the country Americans and Iraqis are aggressively out there doing it to them pretty successfully with little media attention. In my specific work we have little chance of deliberate military actions so no chance of doing to them first, but we exercise the "be careful out there" part intensively!

Keep up the exercise and enjoy the pool time. I will plan on reviewing your gold medals later this year. I, sadly, do not float. I sink, so pools (other than watching Robyn tan in her bikini) hold little interest for me.

Thanks, and looking forward to renewing my library card when I return.
Rog
**

From: Jim McHenry
To: raeschliman
Sent: Sunday, May 28, 2006 8:46 PM

Subject: RE:An offer you can't refuse

Roger, I acknowledge that some people float better than others, but most people can become good swimmers with just a little of the right coaching. At a future date, we'll arrange to meet at a Topeka pool for me to eyeball your strokes. Chances are very good I can change your aquatic self image in less time than you imagine. Most people make a few fundamental mistakes, and they exhaust themselves very quickly as a result. Not much fun to be had in that scenario.

It goes without saying that even on my best day of coaching I will not remotely compete with the allure of Robyn tanning in her bikini; however, we swimmers have a saying: "Sooner of later, we will get them all." The meaning here is that runners, tennis players, B-ball players, all manner of track and field participants as well as baseball players will, sooner or later, end up in the water for PT. Why not move ahead of the crowd and learn to really enjoy and benefit from fitness swimming?

Keep my offer in mind while you are "being careful out there."

Jim
American Swim Coaches Association (ASCA), Past certification--Masters Level 2

From: Pat VanHooser
Date: Monday, May 22, 2006 7:06 pm
Subject: voting

Hello Roger,

How are you enjoying your last summer in the furnace?? It's supposed to be 90 today in Kansas. Bet that sounds like a cold front.

Here is the current question I'm pondering now. I'd be interested in what you think. My Senator, Lindsay Graham, is a pu… ah, coward. He becomes more liberal by the day. Rush Limbaugh made a point on Friday to say that if you want conservative votes you must vote conservative. Of course, the problem is there is no conservative running against Graham. If we vote for him there is the reward factor that says you can do most anything you want and the people will return you to your seat.

Is it better to vote for the really bad guy in order to send the message that we won't stand for this? I just don't know. Florida was great. It was fun to sit in the ocean and read in the sun.

Wednesday night Pat, Mike and my boss Jeff are going to the Fair Tax rally in Atlanta with Neal Boortz, Sean Hannity and John Linder. Should be fun and informative. If anything really cool happens I'll let you know. Think over my question and send me a smart answer if you can.

God bless you and thanks,
Pat
**

Howdy Pat,

114 degrees yesterday on a mission in the desert, then the wind kicked up a dust storm. Really truly miserable...

I met Graham over here. Bright, pleasant, and rumored to be presidentially inclined. Strictly according to the PR value of his "package" he is unelectable. Too short, too bland looking, too guarded and measured in his opinions. Reagan, Clinton and Bush all prove you must at least make the public believe you believe in the same things they believe in in order to be elected. Their opponents all lost because they either believed in nothing and that came across, or they did believe in something and the majorities didn't want it...

There is a "law" that says all organizations that are not explicitly chartered as right wing will eventually become left wing over time. I believe the same is true of elected officials. Once in they become so enamored with "running the trains" or "reaching consensus" they almost always fall into trap of the slogan that says "Politics is the art of the possible," - the old half a loaf theory. Well, all of that is crap. Politics is 51 votes in the Senate and people with enough guts to vote the way they believe and not what they think the NY Times wants to hear or what sells best at home.

So, to the point, once elected a Senator the money machine is almost indestructible. Unless they have sex with goats and post the video to their homepages, a seated Senator does not lose. End of story. Your potential "against" vote will be a token effort and serve no purpose UNLESS you tell him you are voting no, tell him why, tell him you are going to tell a thousand friends to vote against him and then do it all in a highly visible, public manner. And all that just gets you painted as a crank. If you are successful then you wind up electing a left-wing dofus for six years. Pretty harsh results.

You may want to consider buying some influence. $1,000 at the right time can make you a visible partner with a chance of becoming an advisor over time. Advisors can change the behavior of elected officials when almost nothing else can.

Voting for the really bad guy is a wasted effort. You can't win either way.

Try to get in on the inside over a year or so. Senators are usually a lot more approachable than they seem from the public persona.

Related subject: I think we are closing in on another round of populism. The Gingerich era almost reflected this but not quite. With the fundamental issues of too big of government, too intrusive of government, an out-of-control judiciary, immigration problems, and a generally un-solid foreign policy Joe MiddleClass just won't take it much longer. It will be a strange sort of populism (middle class instead of the traditional farmer/lower classes) but it will reflect a strong swing toward the right/center and a big government lash back. God please let it happen soon.

Best to you and the GA gang. rog

To: Pam Crane
Sent: Monday, May 22, 2006 9:39 AM
Subject: flat matt is on the way home

Hi Pam,

Matt is in the mail with the camera and the journal. I hope it meets your expectations. It turned out to be both quite a chore and fun at the same time. Attached is a photo taken today of Matt at the Victory Base Post Office with Lt. Osborne, Lawrence. rog

"Hey All,

"Happy Memorial Day Weekend to everyone. The kids and I have been busy with yard work and opening the pool. Quite a job without Roger. I didn't realize how much I relied on him for some of the heavier jobs. Ryan and Regan were troupers though and have been a huge help. They will probably spend most of the weekend in the pool now that it is finally clean. Enjoy the weekend and remember to pay tribute to those who have gone on to a better place.

"Robyn"
**

Howdy everyone, 28 May 2006

I could say that the best thing about this week was a great mission with the Governors of Montana, Missouri and Massachusetts. Or I could say it was the Danish Prime Minister's mission that went without a hitch despite the Danes being despised by much of the Muslim world.

But really, the best thing about this week was whipping up a batch of no-bake cookies for all the guests and soldiers here at the Joint Visitors Bureau. Commerce Bank & Trust co-worker Joyce Merryman sent most of the ingredients in the mail. I added milk and butter, boiled and stirred and wound up with great-tasting blobs of goo that just didn't quite set up in this heat. They still disappeared quickly. Will try a little less milk and butter on the next batch...

The Governors' mission was a good one. Two days and no glitches that they saw - just the normal dozens of glitches all day that we fixed while they had meetings. It was 114 degrees while I watched the Governor of Montana pass out awards to Montana National Guard Airmen up in Balad and that was just plain old hot. We got back to Baghdad and all three Governors were given a firepower and training demonstration by the Iraqi police (ok with me in a very controlled environment) and then the governors were given the chance to shoot a variety of weapons (not ok with me at all but the train was rolling and I could not stop it as the governors had loaded automatic weapons and I did not).

The Governor of Montana (masters' degrees, agricultural engineer and irrigation/aquifer specialist, old hunting buddy) was as comfortable as a hog in a puddle and filled the targets with lead. The Missouri Governor (Navy Reservist) looked fine but is not very big and kind of got bounced around by the recoil. The Governor of Massachusetts looked very comfortable and pleased with himself as he put lots of bullets on the targets. I suspect the blue-state population of Massachusetts would not be pleased to see photos of him hammering away with a Soviet AK-47 on full auto.

Well, Governors with guns. Turned out fine.

We were hit with a dust storm just then and the Danish airplane coming to take the Prime Minister away could not make it into Baghdad. So, because a coalition partner head of state out ranks the governors the Danes took my airplane away. After a lot of teeth gnashing and hair pulling we came to an agreement to share the airplane. Then it was just a matter of convincing the Governors to get on board the hot C-130 before the Danes arrived. Protocol says they needed to be on board and ready to go when the Danish PM arrived and I kept them off and in the air conditioning as long as possible but then just had to tell them to go. They were a good three governors. Smart and nice.

One little side tour took us onto the roof of the Water Palace main command post. The view is spectacular but the pleasure wore off quickly as the heat there was magnified by the concrete and black roofing and we were dripping in a minute.

As we flew around Iraq this week it is amazingly green considering the heat. I guess if you water things enough they will grow. There was a peculiar smell coming off the date palm orchards - fruiting now. It is intense and queer – sort of musky. One of those smells you will never forget, but the trees are just pouring it out.

The noise over here is ubiquitous. Generators of all sizes. Helicopters flying all day and night (and tragically in a pattern right over my hooch). Airplanes taking off at all hours (and roaring right over my hooch if they turn east). Vehicular traffic. Small arms fire continually. IEDs and controlled detonations. The ambient noise is like the heat – always there. I mentioned this to Robyn when I was home in March. Kansas was so quiet and peaceful.

We wear earplugs in the armored Humvees we use and especially in the Blackhawk helicopters. You would suffer hearing damage in short order without them.

In the morning and evening twilight, there is about one hour when it is too dim for the helicopter pilots to fly without night vision devices, but too bright outside to use them. So the helicopters just set idle for an hour twice a day (unless there is an emergency). This is the most peaceful time of the day and you can sit outside in the gathering dusk, watch the bats eat bugs, and think about being someplace else. It is a rare, nice, quiet time.

My sister Ronna in Costa Rica asks: "I'm just really curious, seems like almost everyday I read, see, hear of explosions in Baghdad by suicide bombers. Some roadside bombs that destroy vehicles, others on persons entering public places. Do you HEAR these explosions? Are they something that they just get USED to? When you hear one, can you tell how far away it is, what part of the city, what TYPE of bomb, how big, etc?"

Yes, we hear them. Baghdad is geographically just not impressive, certainly smaller than metro Kansas City. One artillery shell (what they commonly use for Improvised Explosive Devices) is really, really loud, and if they use two or three it booms for a long, long way. This is the root of the old military saying "When in doubt move to the sound of the guns." A really big one two or three miles away will shake the walls of the hooch and rattle the windows of the command post. Because I am a lousy sleeper from way back a bad night of IEDs means I don't sleep much. A good night means I only wake up a couple times. Most IEDs go off during the day because that's when the bad guys can see a target to shoot at. There is also a controlled detonation site less than a mile from where I live. There are numerous detonations every day as the coalition blows up all the caches the good guys find. We are just so used to booms that no one even flinches any more. It really is hard to identify what they are because a grenade at 500 meters just outside the wall sounds a lot like a truck full of explosives at five miles. We learn what and where things were typically the next day at our daily briefing.

Cards and letters from Pop, Topeka newsletter reader Linda Dale, thank you note from Kim Hinkly (Leadership Topeka 2006 Class Member) (I'd forgotten I'd sent them all congratulatory notes... and now the program must be over already), Grantville Matriarch and friend Juanita Kendall, and goodie boxes from teacher Nancy Lonergan and cards from all her kids, box full of Taco John's kids meal Graham Crackers from Taco king Ed Linquist, and the box of ingredients for No-Bake Cookies from Commerce Bank and Trust buddy Joyce Merryman (just add milk and butter!).

American by birth. Soldier by choice. Volunteer by God!

Roger T. Aeschliman
Major, Armor
Deputy Commander, First Kansas Volunteers

From: KSCranes
Sent: Saturday, June 03, 2006 5:55 AM
To: Aeschliman Roger T MAJ MNF-I JVB Deputy Commander
Subject: Re: [U] flat matt is on the way home

Good Morning Major Aeschliman. Wanted to let you know that "Matt" has made it home safe and sound. I took the camera over and had the pictures developed. There were four that didn't develop. 1 of Matt and Secretary of State Condoleezza Rice; 1 of Matt and Washington State Congresswoman McMorris; 1 of Matt with General Casey and 1 with you, Flat Matt and General Abizaid's combat photographer with her flat Stan....you wouldn't have, by chance, taken any with your digital? Matt's trip was so awesome and he can't stop talking about his experiences and the wonderful people that he spent time with, especially his guardian and his family. There are not words that describe the gratitude that I hold for ALL of you that were so quick to make Matt's journey a success. Be safe and keep the weekly reports coming.... Lyn makes sure that I get them each week. And again, THANK YOU :O)

Pam Crane
Marine Mom

Howdy everyone, 04 June 2006

I don't think you can imagine how hot it is and it scares me to know it will still get worse. I'm writing from the air conditioned comfort of the US Embassy, in the heart of Baghdad, on the banks of the Tigris at 2000 hrs (8 p.m.) Saturday night. I'm escorting a group of Congressmen who are in a three hour meeting with a group of US Embassy staffers discussing how things are going with trash, sewers, water, education, electricity, highways, oil, and the development of the national government. This follows a full day of meetings with the US Army and the Iraqi Army leaders talking about how the military is doing and how the Iraqis are performing. All in all it's another typical mission.

Except I did mention that it's hot?

Today was between 115 and 118 at our various locations. On the runways, asphalt, and sidewalks it radiates upwards of 130. In Kansas we know the day is going to be hot if it is 80 degrees by 8 a.m. Here we expect it to be hot if it is 90 degrees by 0600. And that happens almost every day now.

The heat is palpable; tactile. It is a living presence. There are signs up every where that say "drink water – heat kills." So we drink water and sweat. I have already confessed that I am a sweaty guy. Over here I step out of any building and I start to drip. I began exercising the day I arrived here and have continued to run during the heat of the day just for the purpose of being able to work non-stop for 90 minutes in the heat. That's proven to be wise as even though I did all that there are days I am barely making it. Sweat, sweat, sweat, drink, drink, drink AND eat, eat, eat. The caloric requirement to survive in the heat while working is enormous.

Helicopter rides are nearly unbearable. At 160 miles per hour, with the windows off the helicopter, the air rush and the rotor wash is a blast furnace. If you can remember sticking your head out the window of the family station wagon as a kid, and if you have ever sat in a really hot sauna, and can put both of those experiences together and double the miles per hour, that might be what it feels like to ride in a Blackhawk over the desert – or the city for that matter. The two furthest outside front-facing seats are appropriately nicknamed the "hurricane seats" as the rotor wash is exceptionally vicious. If you open your mouth it sucks your spittle out and splatters your neighbor. It will tear the glasses off your face. It makes my terribly broken nose dance around my face. None of that is exaggeration. Just the facts Ma'am.

Since last report I have had five missions and am on one now. I'm amidst a 15 traveling/mission days out of 17 day window. During this time a good night has been four hours sleep. The Congressmen have just been flooding into the country. Since the Governors left I worked on Elizabeth Dole, Speaker of the House Hastert, three US Senators and another 20 US Representatives. There are four here today that I can't name until 24-hours after mission completion when their agenda becomes public. Of all the aforementioned the most notable were Dole, Hastert and Senator Warner of Virginia, frequently cited as a Presidential candidate. His is tall and attractive but we did not interact any significant way so I have no opinions for you. All of these missions had one thing in common: very smart people who are elected to Congress don't always take advice. On every one of these missions one or more of these elected leaders chose to sit in the hurricane seats (because it is the best view when the windows are in) despite being told not to. Every one of them said I was right afterwards. Usually I take one of the hurricane seats and I wear my flame retardant gloves and my tight fitting goggles and I cover my entire face with my hands for the entire flight. It looks like I'm praying. And I am: for the flight to be over!

But you have to take the windows out or it would be over 150 degrees inside the birds.

Did I mention I sweat a lot on the helicopters too?

Elizabeth Dole is now 70-year-old and looking just as pretty as she did when I met her at a Republican to-do. Bob Dole brought her to Kansas for the first time and introduced her as his fiancé. Elizabeth was very nice and pretended she remembered me. She said she would say hello to Bob, Sam Brownback and Pat Roberts for me. On her trip she met with the three Iraqi women just appointed to ministerial positions in the new cabinet. This was at the notorious Al Rasheed Hotel from whence so much of the two Iraq wars were filmed and videoed by the media. It is a decent looking hotel and in business today. There is a smallish sort of Crown Center there with little shops of expensive things.

With one congressional group we went on a tour of the Tomb of the Unknown Soldier (which the Iraqis kind of like and think is an appropriate memorial to all the soldiers who died in the Iran war), and the Swords of Qadisia (which most Iraqis think is a monument to Saddam and should be torn down). The crossed swords are cast from thousands of captured Iranian weapons and thousands of Iranian helmets are set into the concrete so that to walk or drive under the arches you must step on the helmets. Feet on a head are very offensive so this is a great insult to Iran. The swords were intended to be a taller arch that the Arc De Triumphe in Paris but there were mistakes made in measurement and construction and it wound up shorter. The architects and engineers were killed (at least that's what the official tour guide said).

We went north to Irbil for a day – the first time ever to the Kurdish Capitol City. The Kurds have their own regional government with their own parliament and prime minister. Things are booming and prospering. There were not armed guards on every corner and there was not a single loud noise the entire time I was there. The surrounding countryside looked much like Kansas around Salina and the wheat was in harvest by COMBINES! I was at that moment as homesick as I have ever been. (It was still hot up there too...)

Mel Blunt, the Congressmen from Missouri was in and we visited a little bit about his son, the Governor of Missouri, who was here last week.

Well, I need to run as the meeting will break up soon and we need to fly back to the JVB hotel for the night. I finish up with these guys elsewhere in Iraq tomorrow, get home late Sunday night and then have no missions planned for 48 hours.

Cards and letters from Pop x 4, Mom, aunt Nancy (Tennessee) and a magazine, goodie box of coffee and candy from Topeka friends and State Farm retirees Judy and Jim Wood, goodie box from Mom and Pop.

American by birth. Soldier by choice. Volunteer by God!

Roger T. Aeschliman
Major, Armor
Deputy Commander, First Kansas Volunteers

Pop, at the end of May: 11,475 miles in the air and 535 on the run.

A group of Congressmen and United States Senators at the great parade field and Crossed Swords of Qadisia. This was one of the most common stops for any group of dignitaries, both for the history lesson and the photo opportunity.

From: Lyn_Smith@cargill.com
Date: Tuesday, June 6, 2006 7:38 pm
Subject: GEN Flatt Matt

Rog --

Thanks for taking on the Flatt Matt mission. I just saw the journal and pics. It's great. Pam is excited and very happy with the results. I'm guessing it was sometimes a real pain in the ass to do, but ... as always ... you accomplished the mission with an ACOM level of performance.

Thanks very much for doing it. It really means a lot to Pam and I'm sure the results will be widely communicated within the Marine Moms organization. How are you doing since the Iraqi summer has ramped up? Hopefully all your soldiers are doing well. God Bless and take care!

Smith

ps: When you get back, we'll have to arrange a get together with you and Pam. I'll buy!!
**

Dear COL Smith,

Don't tell Pam, but Matt was a real pain in the ass and in fact got me into trouble one time. When Congressman Tiahrt was here, he came out of a meeting with the ambassador and I perhaps unwisely asked Todd if I could get a picture of him with Matt at that point (as it was convenient for me then and perhaps not later). Todd said sure, then the other congressmen came out and the Ambassador followed and suddenly they were all in the photo. It was a nice picture and I forgot about it. Two days later I was getting yelled at by O-6s and told never to talk to Congressmen again because (as perceived by the department of state agents) had very nearly "assaulted" the Congressmen and Ambassador. I tell you Lyn, the sensitivity levels over here run into the absurd from time to time. I was taking a picture of Todd, the Ambassador ASKED ME if I wanted him in the photo and then I get skewered. Geez.

Well, glad Matt's gone.

We are doing well and morale is high in the JVB. The morale is a little lower, but I believe still good, in Slayer. In Slayer there is a little bit of the "they attack us but we can't ever get back at them" going on due to IEDs and lack of positive ID to shoot back, but generally still good. The force protection stuff works! There have been several IEDs detonate prematurely due to the right equipment and several detonate after convoys because of jamming. This stuff saves lives but the close calls keep the men edgy. Lot's of CIBs and CABs for the troops though. (not many purple hearts and that's a good thing).

It is hot. Our new scale according to Trafton is anything 100-115 is hot. 115-119 damn hot. 120 Fucking hot. And 121 and up is damn fucking hot! We remain damn hot right now around Baghdad but last week I was damn fucking hot in Tikrit!

Hydration is essential and the soldier care by the NCOs is very good. When we travel as an escort team I take care of the guys and they take care of me so we all stay in the game. It really is hard work to stand up all day on guard in the full battle rattle when it is damn hot. We are so joyously happy when the DVs fly away so we can drop all the gear and just sit for a few minutes.Wishing you a great summer! rog

Dear Regan, 09 JUNE 2006

Just wanted to send you a note telling you how proud I am of you for your hard work and achievements this school year. I know it must have been difficult for you to get along with only one parent and that you probably missed some fun events because there just wasn't any way for Mom to get you there. I'm sure there were times you would have liked to have visited with me about homework or boys or something, face-to-face. Sorry I wasn't able to be there.

But despite the barriers I know you did a great job in 6th Grade and are now a graduate of Elementary School! And with very high grades the entire time! Congrats.

You also excelled on the William Allen White reading program. I think that shows your drive and commitment to be a high achiever and proves you have the ability to do anything you want in this world. It's only a matter of figuring out what that is. Don't worry . . . you have plenty of time. Most people are in college before they really think they know what they want to do and most of them are wrong at that time. I think most people are out of college and are already working before they really get a grip on what they want their lives to be like and what kind of person they want to be.

I think you already know what KIND of person you want to become: smart, kind, willing to solve problems and get things done. I have no doubt you will move right into middle school and do very well there too. Your ability to make friends among all types of people is a good one and will serve you well next school year.

So, again, congratulations on a tremendous school year. I am both proud of you and also grateful that you were such a great help to mother all year.

You are a very impressive young woman and I love you very much.

Have a great summer and I look forward to being home before the first semester of middle school is over.

Love,

DAD!

My very dearest wife, Robyn, 09 JUNE 2006

I don't think you can imagine how incredibly proud I am of you. You are the most remarkable person I know. I not only love you deeply and completely, I respect you more than anyone else in the entire world.

Specifically I am amazed at how quickly you achieved your master's degree and the determination you showed in slogging away at it with multiple classes per semester. It seems like you began just yesterday and here you are completed with perfect grades. I further know that you worked very hard at it. You cut no corners and earned every grade. You are amazing.

I am amazed at how you integrated the program into the rest of your life. Our children did not suffer any loss of attention or pain of any kind from your school work. Our household was maintained. Our lifestyle did not suffer in any way. Thank you for being able to do so much so well over such a long time.

And you worked so many days and weeks on top of everything else. Remarkable.

I know you miss me. I know you are fearful from time to time. Yet I never hear it in your voice and I know from the mannerisms and communication with the kids that they don't hear or see it from you either. It must be terribly hard to hold that in when we are talking and in not letting the kids see it. That is incredibly strong of you and harkens back to a stronger generation. I cannot begin to thank you enough for NOT being a crying, whining wife on the phone demanding that I solve problems from overseas, complaining that I'm not home and stirring the fears of the children up. You may not be able to understand how important and meaningful this really is. But it happens all the time. I hear the telephone arguments and learn from counseling soldiers of spouses spending into bankruptcy, having affairs, filing for divorce and moving to other states, or intentionally turning the children against the soldier. I love you all the more for your steadfastness and grit and ability to do everything at home (whether you think you can or not, and whether you want to or not).

I can list dozens of reasons why I love you. I'll save some for another day. For now, please know I am more proud of you than I can say and honored that you chose me for your husband. Thank you for everything.

I Love You!

rog

Dear Son Ryan, 09 JUNE 2006

Just a note to make sure you know how proud I am of you!

First, completing middle school . . . with perfect grades! Very few people have the intellect or the willpower and drive to sit down and do the hard work day after day in order to achieve at this level. Lot's of people have the brains, but are too lazy. Others are willing to work hard but don't have the determination to keep working hard long enough to get the job done. Others just don't have the raw brainpower to comprehend complicated things or to process disparate bits of data into useful information. You intellect is keen and powerful (thank genetics for that ☺) It will serve you well as long as you remember that a high IQ is a gift from God and not something to remind other people about.

Second, your extra-curricular activities this year were quite impressive. The lead in the musical, the honors band, first chair, pep band, playing two instruments, scouting, church, track. Well, quite a list. I am pleased you were willing to try so many things and showed the guts to stick them out. When faced with choices of conflicting events, it appears you chose the ones that helped others and got things done rather than the ones you might have preferred. That is a great sign of maturity.

Third, your emotional growth is also good. You may not remember being a high strung kid who burst into tears easily and was frustrated pretty often. But you were. Even as recently as 7th grade you struggled emotionally with the homework load and had a few crying fits. Your growth here is a good sign; things will be hard and may be painful from time to time but just dealing with it and getting it done are much better approaches than letting it get you down and wasting time worrying and crying about it.

You had a great year and I'm sure you will have a rewarding and enjoyable summer as well. Best of luck with all your activities and have a good time with your friends and the swimming pool. Looking forward to seeing you before Thanksgiving, maybe sooner.

Love,

Dad

"Hey All,

"This week's update has lots of news in it. I think Roger was standing on a soapbox for the first part.

"Robyn"
**

Howdy everyone, 11 June 2006

I try to avoid superlatives so when I say this was a *monumental* week in Iraq please know I mean it:

1 – The killing of the butcher Zarqawi.

2 – The uncontested appointments of the final three ministers (defense, interior, and security agency).

3 – The announced release of 3,000 Iraqi detainees by the Iraqi government.

4 – The successful handover of the Habbinyah area to the Iraqi Army (in Al Anbar!).

Any one of these was big news. All together they are incredible good news for the government and people of Iraq. Zarqawi was a pimple on the ass of humanity, now popped. Good riddance. You may not have read about nearly 100 raids and attacks by coalition and Iraqi forces since then, with many bad guys killed and many more captured. Killing this guy is historically on par with the shooting down of Yamamoto during WWII. And this will lead to many, many more raids and killing many more nasty, foul creatures. With a bit of luck it will also lead to these creatures turning on each other in a struggle for power. Wouldn't that be just too bad?

Two weeks ago the US national media was screaming that the failure to appoint the three ministers was a disaster, the death blow of the new government. Now, they are appointed and seated and working (we just met with them all today) without dissent in the parliament and what is the US media saying? NOTHING! Lost in the Zarqawi news maybe, but probably just too embarrassed to admit they were wrong again. I said a few weeks ago that Iraqis get things done on a different sense of time and urgency than we westerners. They talked, they yelled, they haggled and they got it done their way.

Releasing 3,000 people back into society. This is restoring honor to many families and is making allies for the new government. More will follow. These are not the bombers and killers, but they were involved in the wrong side at some point. Now, they have an honor debt to the government for restoring theirs. A huge coup for the prime minister.

And you never heard of the Iraqis taking over Habbinyah. This was a terrible town on the edge of a major US base. Iraqis have it now and are doing fine, thank you very much. So, even the worst part of Iraq (Al Anbar province) is making progress.

Despite all this good news I don't believe it is THE turning point. THE turning point was reached 18 months ago with the destruction of the widespread defense and culminated with the elections in December. Iraqis want one Iraq. It is only these fetid, power-seeking terrorists who want to control the entire Arab world (by their own admission!) and they are using the tools of terror to try and inflict their will on an unwilling Iraq and the world. Well…they lost this week!

The only thing I had to do with Zarqawi was to prevent one senior dignitary from actually going to the site of his killing today. We had a pop-up mission (very short notice – I learned about it at 10 p.m., was on a helicopter at 2 a.m. and escorting in the morning sun) for a pair of Senators who were already in the region and decided to come into Iraq upon the announcement of Zarqawi's death. Good guys, good mission, but bad, bad, bad idea to go deep into hajjiland where many bombs are going off daily and helicopters get shot at. I finally spoke with one senior department of defense official on the trip and said it this way: "Sir, you need to tell them that we will take 20 young soldiers with wives, girlfriends and children (including me but no girlfriend) on roads that are blowing up every day, for no reason other than a trophy photo. If the Senator dies or is wounded the whole Zarqawi victory instantly turns into a PR disaster that the US can't even protect a US Senator. It's morally and strategically wrong." He got it. He passed it on and we didn't go.

The Joint Visitors' Bureau – winning the war by preventing one stupid thing at a time.

Did I say Flat Matt has gone home to Kansas?

Check out www.mnci.centcom.mil to read all about what's really going on in Iraq.

I interviewed over the phone for command of this incredible battalion: 2-137 Infantry. The finest men in the Army. Wish me luck!

The Army now has a gee whiz, hand-held Arabic translation device straight from a sci-fi novel. GI's talk into it in English and it speaks Arabic right back out to the Iraqis. Wow...

I was so tired I forgot to mention last week that one of our helicopters was taking off, blew some sort of hydraulics and landed hard from several feet high, wheels collapsed, belly-flopped. No injuries. The JVB soldiers performed brilliantly. Securing the DVs, moving them into a safe area, lining up additional birds and getting back into the air and on schedule. Could have been bad. Turned out only to be something the dignitaries get to brag about at home (how I survived a crash in Iraq).

I had fun on a C-130 last week too. On descent we went down so steeply that we nearly exceeded the speed of falling. I floated my 10 pound Kevlar helmet up into the air a few times and it ever so gently drifted down. It really did just hang there in mid-air. It was cool. People would pay a lot of money to get that at an amusement park.

Cards and letters from Pop x 4, my Perry Middle School teacher Eric Hyler, dearest grandma Dorothy Hamler, Wilbert and Jean Crouse, hand-made card from Peggy Bukovatz, goodie box from friends Lezlee and Jeff (who just fell down and cracked his skull so say a prayer please but he is doing good) Heryford, goodie box from Mom and Pop, and three goodie boxes from First Baptist Church buddy Greg Mclaren and his six amigos at the FHL Bank in Topeka!

American by birth. Soldier by choice. Volunteer by God!

Roger T. Aeschliman
Major, Armor
Deputy Commander, First Kansas Volunteers

PS – Uncle Harold and Aunt El want to know what the "Volunteer by God" means. In the Army you have a slogan greeting and counter-slogan response. In our Battalion the official greeting is "FIRST KANSAS!" in honor of our Civil War heritage as the First Kansas Volunteer Regiment. The response is: "VOLUNTEERS, BY GOD," a double meaning one, we are all volunteers and dang proud of it; and two, we are in this great historical "Volunteer" unit by the grace of God. The whole "American by birth. Soldier by choice. Volunteer by God!" is my own personal spin.

Howdy gang,

Per A.J.'s question: I have zero experience with Iraqi food. All military here are subject to GENERAL ORDER NO. 1 which bans alcohol, porn, sex, pets, buying most Iraqi stuff and also consuming local food or beverages. In part this is intended to keep us all healthy as previous wars show massive infections from bad food, water, sexual relations and animal borne illnesses. Historically illnesses put more soldiers out of action than wounds...

Here it is also intended to keep us segregated as much as possible from the Iraqi people so we don't inflame their tender passions in some unintended way. We are here, we do the job, we eventually leave and they carry on in their own way without us destroying their way of life by USA contamination.

I do know from asking around that the Iraqi diet is heavily fruit, vegetable and nut based. Chicken is the most common meat with lamb and goat also eaten. Beef is more exceptional but there are lots of cattle around. Even in the mess hall there is no Iraqi style food. We can get soul food, Cajun food, Mediterranean food, Italian, Chinese, Bosnian, Greek, and sad to say not very good Mexican food. But no Iraqi food.

RE. politics, All I can say is that the least interesting political thing over here is more interesting than even the Presidential posturing going on. This is really circa USA 1880s with people killing each other for power. I have been able to watch the birth of a brand new democracy from election day to seated government making decisions about their country. It has been fabulous. What we take for granted in the USA is incredible . . . Still I hope we get to see a good Presidential showdown between candidates with different philosophies, not just twins in drag.

I still believe that House of Representatives races are about individuals, not political parties so am interested in seeing November roll around to validate or invalidate that. If Iraq is really what it is all about and the president is some kind of anchor dragging people down then both the house and senate are lost. If the race is about individual candidates with thoughtful positions then it should still be Republican time.

Your thoughts at a convenient time? love rog

"Happy Father's Day to all the dads out there. No photos this week – just the weekly update. Enjoy!

"Robyn"
**

Howdy everyone, 18 June 2006

I know it was a super secret surprise in the United States but in Iraq we knew Bush was coming. And, no, sorry, neither I nor the Joint Visitors' Bureau had any role to play. Some of our junior soldiers were kind of insulted that the JVB was not asked to support the mission in some way – they felt we had earned it.

Matters not. Bush came, he saw, he conquered. The boost to the Iraqi government was huge and we were all inspired by his presence and words.

At the JVB we had a warning order a week before he arrived to be prepared to support a "close-hold" dignitary. We understand this to mean a cabinet secretary or higher and the rumor mill said the President was coming. Thus prepared, no mission ever came. Throughout our area of operations we saw many portents and it was clear to all that it had to be him coming in. At the airport there were 40 gun trucks lined up with hundreds of soldiers on the ground. We could not get our normal dog sweeps for our work. Roads were closed. Flights were canceled. At the Embassy all of the local national workers and third country workers were escorted away and many of the normal functions (the coffee shop and snack bar e.g.) closed. Two major meeting areas were closed and gutted. Every contractor security officer in the International Zone was brought in and placed on hallway guard duty.

During this time I was again escorting General Abizaid, theater Commanding General. We had a full two-day agenda and when he touched down his most senior aide shouted over the jet engine noise: "We need to cut six hours off!" That clinched it for me. The only reason to shorten his visit was in order to take off BEFORE the president arrived and all the airspace over Iraq was frozen. And it worked out that way but it was incredibly difficult to work new appointments on short, short notice. At one point I had the modern version of the walkie-talkie, a cell phone and a secret land-line all in my ears at once, with the senior aide giving me instructions.

General Abizaid, General Casey and the ambassador all spent about seven hours on secret two-way video conferences with the president, vice president, Rumsfeld, Rice and other cabinet members from Camp David. This continued until midnight our time. I was obviously not in any of these briefing and preparatory events but as they took breaks, entering and exiting the briefing room I was able to see glimpses of the president and others on the screens. Kind of cool to see history happening.

The only interesting thing at all from this mission was when we lost General Abizaid and Casey. We landed in Blackhawk's around midnight at the pad near Casey's residence, motorcade ready to go, guards standing by. Without telling anyone, Casey and Abizaid decided to have a late night visit at Casey's residence and just walked away from the guards, the motorcade and me. You just can't let Generals hang out together as stupid stuff always follows.

Final result, in bed by 0200, up at 0500, Abizaid successfully in the air and away before the airspace froze, we saw Air Force One land from our command post, Bush came and went.

I want to thank everyone for your wonderful gift boxes of coffee and Gatorade. I believe I have written thank you notes to everyone sending anything. If I have missed you please forgive me. At this point I would like to request no additional gift boxes of any kind. My personal supply of Gatorade looks good enough to last the rest of our time here, and the coffee pile appears big enough to hold up in the command post as the new night shift are not coffee drinkers and it's just too dang hot for most people (except me) to drink coffee other than one cup in the morning.

If you really feel you must send something, I would really just like a nice letter telling me about your NORMAL life on a NORMAL day. What did you eat? Who did you visit with? Aunt Edna's gallstones acting up again? Did your kid's T-ball game not get blown up by terrorists again? Normal lives in the USA equals meaning in our lives over here...

I am still trying to run every day I am not out on an active mission. It is hard to work in the heat. I typically drink a liter of water before starting, run about five miles, drink another liter and walk ¼ mile, then run the final 4-5 miles, shower and drink another liter. Not many people running mid-day now. But I'm not running for miles or time, I'm running to be capable of working for an hour in 115 degree weather wearing 60 pounds of gear. You have got to train what you do.

I've forgotten who asked this but the question is: "You've mentioned Poland, the Ukraine and Australia but what are the other coalition nations and where they are serving?"

In some ways the answer is classified, but open Internet sources show Korea, Italy, Romania, Georgia, Japan, Denmark, El Salvador, Bulgaria, Mongolia, Albania, Latvia, Azerbaijan, Slovakia, the Czech Republic, Lithuania, Armenia, Macedonia, Bosnia-Herzegovina, Estonia, Kazakhstan, Moldova, the Netherlands, and Portugal in addition to the US, Great Britain, Poland, Ukraine and Australia - 28 total right now, and Tonga is coming in. Some of them are only a platoon of 30 or 40, others run into the thousands. While some are part of the multi-national division run by the Poles in the south, most are scattered all over Iraq, assigned as subordinate units to the American Division commanders. All nations are represented right around here in the HQ area so I have run into and visited with soldiers from all of these except Armenia, Albania and Azerbaijan.

Finally, last night I went to a USO show of three comedians. Very funny, mostly sex humor. A team of my guys were the escorts and security for them and made sure the comedians knew who I was and where I was seated so I was the target of many slings and arrows…well, he who laughs last … etc.

Cards and letters from Pop, goodie box full of Gatorade from boss Kirk Johnson, magazines, treats and Fathers' Day present from Robyn, Ryan and Regan, box of goodies from Topeka buddy Jeff Wagaman!

American by birth. Soldier by choice. Volunteer by God!

Roger T. Aeschliman
Major, Armor
Deputy Commander, First Kansas Volunteers

"Hey all,

"I've heard from several of you in regard to Roger asking that all goodie boxes be stopped at this point. I asked him about it on Sunday and he indicated that they have plenty of junk food, Gatorade, and coffee to last for quite some time to come. Most of you have told me you *still want* to send packages. If you feel the need to send items anyway, please feel free to do so. What Roger and his guy's don't use they can leave for their replacements. On his behalf, I have to say a huge thank you to everyone who has sent packages, letters and cards. It has certainly helped me – I have concentrated on his magazine subscriptions, school items from the kids and personal items. Because of your support I haven't felt guilt for not sending homemade goodies!

"As an aside, I sent him a package of malt balls last month and asked if they made it or not. I was curious because of the heat and how the chocolate would travel. Roger said the chocolate part was fine, but…the wax cardboard container melted and fell apart and the malt inside the balls evaporated. He had to clean oozy wax stuff off of the rest of the items in the box. Too weird. Makes you wonder what's in the chocolate that it didn't melt but everything else did.

"Feel free to drop Roger a note or a card. Send a photo and he'll put it on his big "homesick" board. If you look at some of his past photos you can see the board in the background. Ryan and Regan have had fun pointing out different people they know in the photos.

"We still have several more months of this deployment but we are starting to see the end of the tunnel. Thanks for all your prayers and support.

"Robyn"

Dear Karen, 22 JUNE 2006

Thank you for your so kind and caring letter. It is thoughtful, lucid and passionate, - just like you. I have pondered a bit before responding so as not to give you some sort of flip, softball answer. I will try to tell the truth as I see at happening and as I feel (and the feel part will be a bit hard as at my deepest personality and being I am truly introverted and I don't like to talk about my feelings and I generally don't want people to know much about me).

I'll start by telling you who I think I am. First, I was a typically terrible kid. I was a slave to my hormones and chemical imbalances as a teen and then a party animal through college and for a couple years afterwards. In retrospect I was a piece of shit. I'm lucky to be alive and can recite a dozen times when I could have died ½ second either way. At the same time I see I was a high achiever compared to most and I still struggle with this dichotomy. How could I have been so rotten and so successful at the same time? Talent? Education? Genius? Luck? Persistence?

Well, whatever, I grew out of it and became a man. I am an unmitigated man, unrepentant male, and typical guy. I believe in fair play, honesty, integrity, human kindness, and pulling yourself up by your own bootstraps. I believe the world would be lots better if people stopped whining and just got on with it. If people just accepted where they were and started moving ahead from there. If people took more self-responsibility for their own actions and the results of those actions and stopped blaming others. Instead too many people blame others for their current condition and can't seem to leave that behind. Thus they never move ahead. It doesn't matter where you go, there you are. That's where you have to start from. I believe in putting one foot in front of the other, gritting your teeth and taking the pain, and especially, especially just doing it.

So, all of that helps me over here I suppose. I don't fear death. I am comfortable with my understanding of life and death and while dying don't sound like all that much fun, being dead doesn't bother me. Lots of life insurance; the kids and Robyn cry; life goes on, perhaps a bit duller than having me around but 100 years from now every one of us and everyone we know will be dead too, names on tombstones no one goes to see.

I fear pain a little bit and I fear causing people I love pain a lot. I don't think I could ever be captured over here. The evidence of what these criminal assholes do to prisoners is simply too terrible to inflict upon my family. I hope I would have the courage to fight to the death rather than surrender.

Doesn't matter though, having worked you into a dither now, let me calm you down by telling you I am in so little danger and face so little risk it is hardly like a war at all. I try to say that in my letters and to Robyn and the kids. And yes, I softball it a little bit for Robyn and Mom and Pop, but the truth is that no one has ever specifically shot at me over here, no one has aimed at me, I am not a specific target for anyone.

So far we have had the bullets fall out of the sky three times from celebratory gunfire (and that could kill you I suppose if you were very unlucky); I have seen bullets fall into the lake or skipped off the roads in front of me or behind me while jogging from more random gunfire (none closer than 25 meters or so), have had half a dozen rockets or mortars explode from 100 meters to 300 meters away (you don't even duck at those); and have twice seen bullets tracers fired blindly in the night in hopes of hitting my nearly invisible helicopter (both in December). A couple of IEDs have blown up near Camp Victory (1/2 mile or so), loud but no risk to me.

So, the biggest risk I face is a car crash or a helicopter malfunction. And that's pretty much like being home. You just don't get into the car or public transportation and instantly worry about a crash. You just get in and go.

Sometimes, when I am very, very tired after 2-3-4 full days of hot, hot missions my emotions run a little closer to the surface (normal human thing) and my psyche intrudes into my normal brainwork. At that point you have to know enough human psychology to understand you are not a loser, you are not a moron, the world is not out to get you, that it's really just time to go to bed and get some sleep so your brain can sort it all back out and you can wake up ready for another day.

I have had days over here where I was so tired that all the nagging concerns pushed into the forefront and I was sure I was a dirt bag, wondered why I was here and needed to go home right then. I am very close to that right now so perhaps there is a risk in writing today…I was again recently yelled at by a senior official in the theater for doing my job (and he doesn't understand what my job is), I learned only minutes ago that I was not selected for the command position, and that my promotion to Lt. Col. will not happen until some time after I return home (two full years after being selected). I know I deserve to be a Lt. Col. and that it will happen some damn day when someone cares enough to make it happen. I know that I was the best choice for commander but that telephone interviews don't allow the interviewer to see the whole man and understand all that man brings to the table. I know all that, but when you are exhausted all that spells out: The world thinks you suck! You are nothing! Last night I was sure I was the most worthless human on the face of the earth and both my chin and my ass were dragging on the ground. This morning after a decent night's sleep I'm much better and tomorrow I'll be fine. 95 % of the time I am better than fine and spend a lot of time helping other people feel fine too.

I guess I really do believe in this old saying: When I was 18 I worried what everyone thought of me. When I was 30 I decided I didn't care what anyone thought about me. By the time I was 40 I understood that no one was ever thinking about me in the first place.
I know the world is not out to get me. There are nearly 6 billion people on this earth and some 5 billion, 999 million, 950 thousand have never heard of me. Of that remaining 50 thousand who may have bumped into me at some point or other in my life, 49 thousand never think about me unless our paths cross, and of that final 1,000 there are fewer than 100 that think about me daily, if that. The world does not care about me, or you, or our kids. I understand that life is not about me: It is about what I can do for others. I don't know when I made that turn from child to adult but I truly believe it and try to live it.

So, grit our teeth and take the pain of life, search for all the enjoyment it offers through friendships and love and just keep going.

I'm sure all the preceding sounds so negative and down that I can't leave it there. I am generally happy and I love life. It is important that I be here because I truly believe that if we were not here, they would be over there blowing up the Simons and Ronnas and Palins of the world, just like they are doing over here. This is where the battle is and I am honored to be here on behalf of your kids and mine.

I think a lot of your fears are based on several common misconceptions about the Vietnam War and the brave heroes who were there. Most of them are not messed up. Most of them are so normal they are just woven into the fabric of our society. Most of them are civic leaders and businessmen and women and the people who sit in the front row at church and the people who we brush shoulders with in the grocery store. They are just normal.

And like normal people they have a huge range of feelings about their involvement in the war. Most are proud and honored to have done their duty. Like me. Others are suffering from a variety of physical and emotional wounds. Those few are the ones that get all the media attention. The media sucks. In the big picture the Vietnam Vets are doing just fine and they are pretty much running this country and making the world go around right now. There are many studies available and they all say the same thing: Since the Civil War the percentage of people who suffered emotional harm from the conflict has been the same whether it was called malaise, shell shock, battle fatigue, or today's post-traumatic stress syndrome. It's all the same thing. Some psyches don't take war very well and are wounded just as surely as by a bullet. The most messed up person I ever met was a WWII veteran who spent his entire tour as a typist in England. Never saw a bullet or a bomb. But he was wounded.

Yes, I will be different when I get back. I will be a year older. I can't say if I will be different in any other way. I'd really like that motorcycle but I've wanted that ever since I sold the old one in 1990.

I suspect most of the vets from this war will return home, be normal and be happy, and many of them will seek to find the same sense of purpose that previous generations of warriors have done. They will seek leadership roles in business and industry, in church, in civic organizations and in elected office. Just like previous generations have done. I hope I still have something significant to offer my community, state and nation. Right now I remain focused on being the best husband to the most perfect woman in the world and the best father I can to two wonderful children.

I am an unlikely candidate for suicide. Please let me know if you see warning signs.

I believe Robyn and I have a strong and robust love and relationship. We talk a lot about the big things and I let her have her way almost all the time on the small things. She is an incredible and powerful person. I think I will fit back in to home easily. The biggest challenge will be having missed a year of common experiences with the children. They have both had such explosions of growth and maturity in my absence it scares me. If this had been a different kind of war with no telephones, no webcams, I would not know them when I get back. As is I get to see them growing.

Hard to imagine the vets of WWII especially. Many left home in the National Guard mobilization of 1939 and did not return until 1946. Left childless and returned home to a six year old. Hard.

So, feel free to ask me how I and my family are doing at any time, but do it this way: Hey, Rog, let's take a walk, just you and me.

Either that or a pitcher and a game of pool. That opens up lots of time for talking while pretending to do something else.

Thanks also for your nice NORMAL update. I so miss the little children. We are not allowed any real contact with kids and it is not available even if we were. Pets too for that matter.

Please give my love to all your family. They sound like they're doing great.

You asked so many questions and had so many concerns I probably didn't answer them all so let me know and I can try to elaborate. Unless something dramatically changes I will not be shot at or shoot at anyone and my stories about this war will be amusing little tales about overblown VIPs who don't understand how insignificant they are in the big picture of life.

With much love, your adoring brother,
rog

Dear Lea, 22 JUNE 2006

Thank you for your very nice letter of June 9 and the prayer card. I have added it to my wall where I and everyone else can see it every day.

Hope your dad is doing well now. From talking with Robyn and Regan it sounds like he is doing fine. I'm very glad. Hospitals are so scary when someone you love is there.

Sorry to hear about your aunt and uncle. Jeepers Creepers! Sometimes it seems like bad things all happen at once. That's not true of course but it seems like it some times. Usually life is a mix of good things and bad things and it's strange, but we forget the good things and remember the bad things. That's why it is a good idea to keep a diary or journal, just to write down the good things. Then when you have one of these times when all the bad things seem to be happening you can look back at your notes to remind yourself of how the good things and good times are more frequent and most common.

Solomon wanted to know the best advice in the world and his wise men told him to always remember that "This too shall pass." That's pretty good advice. It reminds us that whatever is bothering us now will one day be gone and things will be good again. It also reminds us that when things are really going great to not get too proud or cocky because things will get bad again and we need to be prepared to deal with that.

I sure miss you and your wonderful family, like I miss my own. But I know that this too shall pass and I'll be home again to splash in the pool and watch you and Regan grow up.

The summer is already about half over. How fast has that gone? Are you getting excited about moving into Middle School? It will be very exciting and you will have many new opportunities for sports, music, drama, friendships and education. It will be lots of fun.

I look forward to getting home and seeing you and everyone again. Hope you have a great summer and spend a lot of time at the pool with Regan.

Your friend,
rog

Hello Amiga Pat, 23 June 2006

We have a new measuring standard for the heat over here. It is not even officially hot until 110. 110 to 115 is hot. 115 to 120 is Damn Hot. 120-125 Fucking hot and over 125 is Damn Fucking Hot! Pretty simple really and it does away with the confusion over centigrade and Fahrenheit. Even the most doltish lout among us can understand that Damn Fucking Hot will kill you if you don't take care.

Please do tell me about the Tennessee cave country. I'd love to hear about GREEN and COOL.

I too hope that the accused Americans are proven innocent of these charges. If they actually did it, with no mitigating circumstances whatsoever, then I'd be first to call for their hanging. This war is a hard one and different (just like they all are hard and different) and if these men killed innocent women and children execution style then they will have to pay the price for STRATEGICALLY hurting the war effort. If it turns out that there were shots being fired at them from these houses and they raided them in the dark, and that innocent people were shot while they were clearing room by room in the dark, well, that is totally different and falls under the war is hell category. I hope that turns out to be the case. Somehow we in the USA continue to be held to a higher standard than the rest of the world. If Saddam erases a village from the map, that's just what an executive has to do sometimes. If the Tutsi and the Hutu chop each other's women and children to bits with axes, that's just ethnic strife. If Palestinians blow up innocent women and children in Israel then that's just a natural release of rage from 3,000 years of repression (mostly by other Arabs). But GIs can't make a mistake of any kind...

So, hope they didn't do it; if they did I hope it's not like it looks and that there were factors that make a difference; and if they just flat out did it I hope we hang them.

We in the USA also are so inured against death of any kind now, military or civilian. Would our country have the guts and willpower to fight World War II again today? In the face of 10 million dead Russian civilians, 30 million dead Chinese civilians, 250,000 US soldiers killed, more on D-Day alone than have died over here in 4 years? I question our national will and common sense. We are now in World War III and there is no room for equivocation. You are with us against the non-state players who wish to enforce their will over the whole world, or you are against us and are willing to let them have their way. There is no middle way. Bush gets it but he articulates it so poorly and the US national media doesn't get it. Help...

Well, other than being temporarily depressed over lack of promotion, non-selected for command and yelled at by people who should know better I'm really fine.

All the best to you back in the greatest nation on earth (Mr. Franklin, what have you given us? "A Republic, if you can keep it!") Your friend, rog

Howdy everyone, 25 June 2006

This week we're going to talk about a great speech, a bad congressional delegation, wallowing in self-pity (only a short while), and some odds and ends.

Prime Minister Maliki made a nationally televised speech today about reconciliation. It was very well received around the region and offers amnesty for nearly everyone not guilty of killing someone, but a fist to those who continue terrorism here. Very bold. Some here are saying it is an Arab version of Roosevelt's "nothing to fear but fear itself" and Churchill's "we shall fight them on the beaches, etc..."

I was downstairs in the great conference center that serves as the parliament building while Maliki spoke upstairs. The medic and I were escorting four US congresswomen as they met with a group of Iraqi parliamentarians and cabinet ministers. The Doc and I were the only US uniformed personnel in the building as Iraqis have their own security there in hand. Doc said on his 2004 tour anytime they were in the same building it took a full company of soldiers to guard all the doors, rooms and motorcade. 100 then, 2 now...

Anyway, the Congressional delegation was not a good one. Three of the four were not physically fit to be in the heat and on helicopters. They whined all the time. It was hot, the toilets are foul (I told YOU that nine months ago!), it's hot, the Iraqis are late, it's hot, the beds are uncomfortable, it's hot, who's going to carry my bags? ...

They came specifically to do a women's program and to train the Iraqi women how to be good parliamentarians and to be women's rights leaders. Guess what? The Iraqi women didn't want to be trained. Shortly after the Congresswomen began speaking the Iraqi women sort of shouted them down and told them to pretty much just listen. Downhill from there. Four hours later the Americans were shell shocked and pleased to get back on the C-130 to Kuwait and air conditioning. This was a rare case of the staff members being great and the actual Congress members being less than great. It clearly points out the danger of not knowing your audience and of having too many preconceived notions.

That Codel (congressional delegation mission) followed a Govdel (Governor's delegation) earlier in the week. Had governors from North Dakota (very bright and informed but knew he was), Alaska (formerly US Senator, a little too old and too heavy for comfort in Iraq heat but he hung tough), and South

Carolina's Mark Sanford. I was fortunate to spend a lot of time with Sanford and we talked about our mutual friend, former Topekan Mike Ryan, Augusta Ga. Chronicle Editorial Page Editor (lots of Augusta readers in Southwest South Carolina). Sanford is very bright and a nice guy. That's pretty much like an A+ from us over here. If you can be smart and pleasant we like working for you. Anyway, Sanford praised our guys tremendously and I was pleased to take a photo with him. See attached shot from inside the outbound C-130. Sometimes it is hard to get off the airplane before it leaves for the USA.

After that great Govdel I arrived back at the office around midnight and logged into the computer system. I should have just gone to bed as bad news piled on top of bone-weary tired is bad juju but I read my email: One) I was once again stupid and a mission was messed up as we made (self) important people wait; Two) the action step I need to be promoted to Lt. Colonel will not happen until mid-September meaning we will be long home in Kansas before I see a Silver Oak Leaf; and Three) the battalion command went to a fine officer who is not me.

Now I am generally a pretty sturdy fellow and don't wear my emotions very far away from my skin but this combination of disappointments on top of end-of-mission exhaustion was just too much. I kind of tossed and turned the rest of the night with too many thoughts rushing around, and spent the next day feeling worthless. Then I spoke with Robyn and Regan, got a couple of very nice letters from people who love me, got a good night's sleep and got back to work.

I'm fine again. I don't wallow too well.

The dining facility has an advisory council. The council's last report included the following complaints: 1 – How come we only have five flavors of ice cream? 2 – How come we can't have our lobster tails cut in half? 3 – How come we can't have flan (Mexican custard)? Answer: we DO have flan three nights a week. Follow-up question: I mean how come we can't have flan every night? 4 – It's so noisy I can't hear the big-screen TVs; and that followed by: The TVs are too loud, we can't hear our conversations.

I'm not kidding.

I've told you what a Fobbit is haven't I? A military person who never leaves the Forward Operating Base (FOB) but thinks they can dictate to those who do.

Got to see my father (mother, brother, wife and kids) by webcam on father's day!

A special hello today to Dave Phillippi, my dad's college buddy and best man. Dave is fighting lung cancer and I know is facing it with true grit. Prayers from Iraq Dave!

I voted by mail today in the August primaries. Pretty easy process and great help from buddy Libby Ensley and her team at the Shawnee County elections commission.

Cards and letters from Pop x 3, sister Karen, friends Lea Heryford and Susan Anderson, goodie box from Fiji brother Jeff Wilson, box of yummies from the Linquist clan including those graham Goldfish that the boss loves so much, and a goodie bag courtesy of Fletcher, a Cub Scout with Pack 3118 in Ottawa! If any reader out there can get me the address of Fletcher or the Pack, I will send a thank you note.

American by birth. Soldier by choice. Volunteer by God!

Roger T. Aeschliman
Major, Armor
Deputy Commander, First Kansas Volunteers

June 22, 2006

MAJ Aeschliman,

MAJ Anthony Mohatt has been selected as the next 2-137th Commander.

You did an excellent job on your interview. I told BG Small that I felt you would best be suited for the upcoming MTF Command. The details of the selection for this command are not solidified yet.

Recommend that you seek a position with TCTF or JFHQKS that keeps you close to the MTF planning process. I would be glad to sit down and discuss your future career plans anytime.

COL Braden
**

COL Braden,

Thank you for your consideration and your kind words. You have made an exceptional choice in MAJ Mohatt. Tony is a fine officer and will do a great job for you and this tremendous battalion.

I welcome your counsel on my 2007 assignment. I would prefer doing something useful at the BDE under your guidance over STARC or 35th DIV HQ and look forward to exploring the options.

Please let me know if I may assist you and the Trafton/Mohatt transition in any way and I look forward to seeing you at our return home ceremony!

Most sincerely,

MAJ Roger T. Aeschliman
**

Dear Tony,

Congratulations on your selection for Battalion Command! You are a highly gifted officer and it pleases me greatly to know you will lead the 2-137 Infantry on to even better things in the future.

Please let me know how I may best assist you and Trafton in the transition be it publicly and visibly, behind the scenes, or out of the way and silent. I'll be pleased to help in any way.

I look forward to congratulating you personally. Your friend, rog

June 27, 2006

Roger,

We love your reports. They should appear in a newspaper to give a view from the ground in Iraq. We saw your mother in church today. What a lovely lady! I told her that I talked with Jim Inhofe from Oklahoma who I believe you recently hosted. He appreciated your good work!

As I hope you saw, we debated the war in Congress the last two weeks and had strong vote totals in favor of seeing this thru. This is a very important mission in the war on terrorism and must be concluded on our terms. Proud of your work! We will pray for you!

Mary and Sam Brownback
**

Dear Sam and Mary,

Thanks for your nice note. I did see the good news on the war vote and I often think of you fighting the war for us in Congress. Thanks as I believe the home front is the key theater and the big national media is now the critical overall enemy.

I know that sounds Limbaughish but we believe it over here.

Thanks and looking forward to seeing you over here one of these days (before November or it will be some group of Kentucky guardsmen instead of me greeting you at the Baghdad Airport).

rog

Dear Terry, 28 June 2006

Thanks for your wonderful letter of 20 June. It is a joy to read about how your friends are doing back at home, all the good and the bad.

I think I am ready to retire right now but I haven't yet worked out the funding mechanism. If I had an agent and a publisher I think my final career field would be writing children's books and doing school tours reading my fun little bits of poetry to grade-schoolers. Well, you will know when the combination of financial math and "it's just not much fun anymore" equals the right time. If you are like my father I suspect you will find yourself never doubting it was the right time to retire, but also wondering how you every had time to work in the first place as you will be so busy around town doing all the things you want to do rather than the things you must.

As a trust officer at the finest bank in Kansas I would suggest to you that you go visit with Kirk Johnson at Commerce Bank & Trust. Do you already know him from community involvement? Kirk is my boss and I think he could give you some clear thoughts about both of the aging parents and your daughter. I'm sure you have some familiarity with Trusts from all this time in the accounting world. They are powerful tools...Not meaning to intrude into your personal space but I do believe in what I do and have seen the difference in quality of life between those who planned and those who didn't.

Preacher Jim C. and I go way back to basketball at the Y and he had a great jump shot. He also had a bit of argumentative streak. I don't know if that's a surprise. He was NOT very forgiving on the basketball court.

Like you I have married beyond my station and am so grateful. Robyn is so very, very good and talented that I worry about nothing over here, except about here. So many soldiers I counsel and mentor are not in the same position. They are in constant telephone arguments over money and children and household affairs. Very sad.

Glad you are on top of the fitness game now. I continue to surprise myself with my exercise. I really don't like to run and if you had told me at Fort Sill in September that I would be running nine miles a day in 110 degrees I would have laughed at the notion. I didn't set out to do that; the distance just kept adding on in about the same time frame.

Please tell Keith hello for me and I look forward to jogging with you both!

rog

5.11
4300 Spyres Way
Modesto CA 95355

Dear Gentlemen and Ladies, 01 JULY 2006

I'm writing to express my concern about the quality of the 5.11 tactical desert boot I recently purchased through the PX in Iraq. The leather upper heel of the left boot split after about ten days of wear on fairly routine missions in Iraq.

The PX will not refund or replace without the receipt and would also charge me for two months of wear on the boot. (I sent you the receipt to get the free pair of socks☺)

Your web site indicates boots purchased through third parties will not reimburse postage and frankly from the narrative on the web site I'm unsure whether the boot would be repaired or replaced at all.

I do like the boots tremendously; they are comfortable and take a burden off of my old man knees and hips. They are my favorite boots now and I wear them exclusively on the hardest, longest field missions that require me stand around for long periods several days in a row.

My bottom-line is that I cannot afford to put them in the mail to you with the hope that they would be replaced or repaired and returned to me before we redeploy to the USA. Further, I do like them very much and would rather wear them defective as they are than the more unforgiving issue boots. I don't want to be without them for two or more months. So I've superglued the ragged edges together and will try to stay out of puddles (pretty likely through October here now).

So, please consider this a friendly piece of advice. Check the quality control of the leather on the heels. Otherwise you have a good product and a number of my soldiers use these and other 5.11 products.

Thanks,

MAJ Roger T. Aeschliman
B Co 2-137 INF
APO AE 0934201400

From: Mark Sanford
Date: Saturday, July 1, 2006 0:35 a.m.
Subject: Thanks

Roger,
Just wanted to write a quick note to say thanks so much for all the help. Take care. Sincerely,
Mark
**

Dear Governor Sanford:

You are so very, very welcome. Please say hello to Mike Ryan for me and may the grass always be greener on your South Carolina side of the fence. rog

"Happy Fourth of July weekend to everyone!

"I spoke with Roger earlier and asked if he will have any sort of celebration there. He was unaware of any planned activities but assumes the food will reflect the holiday – hot dogs, hamburgers, apple pie, etc...I wish all of you a happy holiday and safe firing and viewing of fireworks.

"Robyn"
**

Howdy everyone, 02 July 2006

In the calm before the storm I had an uneventful week with no missions. I ran, slept, did laundry. I'm writing on Saturday with missions planned for tomorrow and then 18 of the next 27 days (and more yet to come). The JVB as a whole is maxed out through the first two weeks of July meaning we simply cannot transport, guard or house one more person than currently templated. It's going to be hot in July.

We see on the news here that some politicos continue to cry for a partition of Iraq into three separate nations (Sunni, Shia, and Kurdish). In March, on leave I discussed this with several people. This week here are some thoughts as I understand the situation in Iraq from observation, meetings, briefings, and from historical readings.

Most importantly there is no homogeneous insurgency out there. Many divisions fracture the country. Some are:

1 – Baathists. The Baath movement wants a unified *Arabic* state in the Middle East. It would stretch from the Atlantic to at least Iran and maybe to Pakistan. There was an effort toward this end in the 1970s when Egypt and Syria accepted overtures from Saddam but Jordan refused to play. This helps explain Saddam's attacks on Iran and Kuwait.

2 – Wahhabists (including Al Qaeda). The most fundamentalist, least tolerant version of Islam. Founded and financially perpetuated in Saudi Arabia it says the world must be one caliphate under Islam, *their* type of especially repressive Islam under Sharia law. And there are at least three major splits in Al Qaeda: Bin Laden, Zarqawi (now dead☺), and Zawahri who don't follow one another any more.

3 – Saddamists who had a good thing under Saddam and would like to have him back or at least their sweet lives of dominance and control.

4 – Agginers. Western Iraqis and scattered others who just want to be left alone to live their own way. They were a problem for Saddam and will oppose anyone who tries to impose a non-local, non-tribal system on them. They don't hate us or the forming government, they just want us gone.

5 – Kurds. 30 million strong scattered in Jordan, Syria, Lebanon, Turkey, Turkmenistan, Iran and Iraq, with 4-6 million in Iraq. A minority is willing to risk wide-spread war in order to consolidate a greater Kurdistan. A second larger group following Talabani sees hope in one Iraq with significant local control, and a third equally large group follows their own regional Prime Minister Barzani. They thought they were promised and did not get a country of their own after both world wars. They have half of Iraq's oil.

6 – Southern Shia. The Southeastern group is Persian, pro-Iran, Farsi speaking. Historical ties were cut by the artificial borders drawn post WWI and WWII. Oil, industry, port, and navigable rivers centering on Basra, the second city of Iraq. Southwestern Shia are less interested in Iran and have oil, but nothing else. They live in the desert - the real desert.

7 – 40-50 tribal divisions. Sheiks (SHAKES) still rule informally and still control much wealth in many cases. Most still have their own tribal militias. In the absence of higher control the country will fracture this way. In desperation clans will protect their own turf and fight over the boundaries just like they have for 10,000 years.

8 – Mafia or the equivalent. Who knows how big, where and what? But they are real.

9 – Street gangs or the equivalent. Younger than the mafia, perhaps working for them, perhaps the sheiks, perhaps the clerics. Control life on the streets in some limited areas. Non-existent in others.

10 – Clerics and their militias. Most notably Sadr in his slum. A few of the big ones can call up forces. If the local sheiks are weak the clerics can be more powerful.

So, a three-way split is problematic. None of the three could be self-sustaining in terms of economy and self-defense against Iran and Syria. Baghdad is especially problematic. How do you partition a vastly integrated city of 10 million? Walls? The Tigris? Who gets to use the airport? On alternating days? The entire middle area is a tossed salad of groups. Creating the middle country in Iraq immediately craters into sub-units. North and south follow. You wind up with 40 turfs of tiny nations that squabble with each other, fight over resources and probably the oil stops flowing.

The only successful partition in history was India. Considered a *friendly* partition, still one million people were slaughtered in the process. Sixty years later India and Pakistan remain on edge and Bangladesh is an endless bog of poverty. The partition of Iraq would not be a *friendly* one.

If you start to partition Iraq it quickly degenerates into 30-60 small kingdoms with ongoing border strife. Iran and Syria step in to gobble up oil wealth, the Kurds are forced into their own nation and Iran, Syria and Turkey attack to destroy the Kurds. I think partition is THE GUARANTEED recipe for civil war and regional disaster rather than the prevention.

I've spoken with many Iraqis from all over the country and they all want a single, unified Iraq. Period.

Jeff Moe, executive director of the Jayhawk Area Council Boy Scouts of America found me an address for Cub Scout Fletcher of Ottawa. Thanks Jeff.

Miracle of miracles! TWO notes from VIPs this week, a nice card from Congressman Frelinghuysen (NJ-who was one of the nicest people ever here) and Gov. Sanford (SC – also very nice so perhaps nice shows in common courtesy as well); cards and letters from Pop x 3, Adriel class at TBC, info packet from proud papa Jim McHenry regarding his son's publication and poetry reading at the fabulous Topeka and Shawnee County Public Library, longtime pal Terry Kimes telling all about his normal day, card from sweetie Robyn, letter and goodie box from Linda Crandall, and goodie box from Mom and Pop.

American by birth. Soldier by choice. Volunteer by God!

Roger T. Aeschliman
Major, Armor
Deputy Commander, First Kansas Volunteers

POP – end of June: 693 miles on the ground and 12,840 in the air.

Dear Fletcher and all your fellow Cub Scouts in Ottawa, 03 July 2006

My name is Major Roger Aeschliman (Ash – L – man). I am the Deputy Commander of the 2nd Battalion of the 137th Infantry Regiment of the Kansas Army National Guard. That means I am the number two person in charge of about 500 soldiers.

I am so very pleased to receive your very nice goodie bag full of treats. I have taped your nice card to the wall over my desk in Baghdad as a reminder of how important our work is here. There are about 120,000 American soldiers over here, doing everything they can to help make Iraq safe and free. If Iraq is safe and free, then chances get better that you and all your friends, and my children in Topeka and all their friends, and lots of other children all over the world will grow up free in a more peaceful world.

I know it doesn't seem to make sense that people should have to fight so there will eventually be peace, but the history of the world shows this is true. I thank you so very much for thinking about me and all of us over here.

My children in Topeka are a 12-year-old Girl Scout and a 14-year-old Boy Scout.

Please read everyday. Reading is really the secret to a great life (reading and eating Oreos). My best wishes to you and everyone in Cub Scout Pack 3118 in Ottawa.

Major Roger T. Aeschliman
B Co 2-137 Infantry
APO AE 09342-1400

From: Joyce A Merryman
Date: Tuesday, July 4, 2006 1:19 am
Subject: Thanks

Tomorrow as we celebrate our country's birthday, I'll be thinking of you and the other soldiers who are still working to allow people to have their freedoms.

Thanks you to all of you. God Bless and stay safe.

Joyce
**

Dear Joyce,

You are so very, very welcome. I truly appreciate your kind words as this is my most melancholy day of the year. Even worse than Christmas.

I am so unabashedly patriotic and admittedly jingoistic (and I don't think it's a bad word like the Hollywood goofballs do) that the meaning of this day looms large in my mind. While it is a totally American holiday it should be celebrated world-wide by all those who enjoy individual liberty and freedom. It is on this day that men for the first time drew a line in the sand and said we shall not be ruled. How remarkable! Freedom followed country by country and its march continues today.

So, today as I miss the big family pool party and hot dog feed at home, then the children shooting off fireworks in the dark, and even my mutters and cursing as the noise continues long after all sane people would shut it down, I will think of you and everyone else enjoying the freedom to associate, celebrate and relax, safe and sound in a great land of plenty and feel good about my choice to come here.

Looking forward to seeing you and getting back to work! Your friend, rog

Dear Mike, 04 July 2007

A very happy Independence Day to you! Kiss the wife, hug the kids, pet the dog, drink a beer, nap on the porch, shoot some fireworks, and dance in the moonlight. Freedom is a remarkable thing. Enjoy it for me please!

I believe most Americans are not tuned into the key issue: that we are in a long war, hot and cold, here and all over the world for 40 years. Two generations of kids in these places have to grow up in a freedom-evolving-into region where they see the good of liberty and freedom and want it and will take it forcibly from those mullahs who deny them. They must move from sheiks, mullahs and the rule of one strong man (and the horror of honor society and vendetta) to individual freedom and property rights. And it's going to take a while.

The nationally prominent Democrats don't get it.

Thanks for the ongoing contact and thanks for fighting the good fight on the home front!

rog

Dear Robyn, Ryan and Regan,

Happy Independence Day!

I love you all so very much and truly wish I were home with you today to enjoy all the family, friends, food, fellowship and ice cold beer and pop! While there have been many special days gone by this past ten months and so many family moments missed I have to tell you that missing this 4th of July celebration really hurts me the most of all. I have been moping around all day and wishing, wishing, wishing I were home for good.

I think it's the fact that this holiday is special to me in so many ways. First, it brings back so many pleasant memories of childhood. Blowing up little green soldiers and little lumpy toads with firecrackers, bottle rocket fights with Uncle Rick and neighbor kids, kicking rocks down the dusty road waiting eagerly for the sun to go down and the Rees's to come over to shoot off fireworks. I even have a memory of my little 4-year-old self waving a sparkler around in Superior Nebraska. I have another memory of being a young teen I think, in Colorado watching the only major fireworks display I have ever seen at Greeley while visiting grandma's parents. That's pretty sad isn't it, to have only seen one big show in 45 years...maybe the two giant celebratory gunfire nights we have seen over here count too ☺

Second, this celebration we do at out house is so special as it was something that Robyn and I did together, as a new family, and in my mind it is a thing that has brought us closer together, our own family tradition. To miss it digs deeply into my soul and I envy you all the fun, laughter and smiles.

Third, I hate to miss seeing you two children shooting the fireworks tonight. It has been a benchmark event each year to give you more and more responsibility and freedom with these dangerous devices. You have matured and acted responsibly, taken instructions and listened and learned. I am proud of you both. It is a little like Halloween, Scouting and hunting. Each year you have grown, taken more responsibility and acted more grown-up. Missing you this night just especially seems like a giant nail in the coffin of this missing year of my life. By next year you may be too grown up for sparklers and smoke balls and tank races and that will break my heart.

Fourth, this is a uniquely American holiday created for the purpose of recognizing the birth of our great nation. Although it is an American holiday it should expand around the world and be celebrated by all free peoples as the moment in history when a small group of people stood up in the face of a dictator and the rule of absolute power to say "NO MORE." People by natural law have the right to be free. All over the world since then, people after people have shrugged off the yoke of kings, czars, mullahs, and emperors to become free with all the rights, duties and responsibilities that come with liberty. That is so worth celebrating that one day a year is ever too little recognition.

Even though I am over here I celebrate with you in spirit and emotion. I will be thinking of you throughout your day and remembering years past as we scrambled around to make the ice cream, clean everything a final time, set up all the drinks and food, fish all the leaves and seeds out of the pool, and finally, let you kids into the pool to enjoy the fabulous day. If you will just pause at some point to think of me then at least for a while I'll be there with you, smiling, having a piece of gooseberry pie, going to get the chicken, and eating the last of the ice cream late at night, after the fireworks, with you kids finally in bed, looking at Robyn and wondering how someone like me could be so blessed to have such an incredible woman and two such awesome children.

With all my heart I love you and miss you so. Have a glorious and fabulous fun day, tell everyone hello and hug them for me.

Your adoring husband and father, rog/dad

From: Bloomquist, Robert COL
Date: Wednesday, July 5, 2006 11:28 pm
Subject: 4th of July

Roger,

What a nice party Robyn organized. It was great to see some super people. Tons of questions from numerous folks about mobilizations, coming home etc. Of course John could talk the conditions in Iraq and I could relate to how important your job is and how many folks travel to places to see for themselves what is really happening. Your Dad asked many questions about your promotion. I did tell him I had great respect for COL Braden and thought you were the Ace in the hole to get this new organization off the ground. I clearly think you are the best candidate for command and therefore, would wait to put you in at the most critical time.

As you know, Robyn is as beautiful as always and Ryan and Regan are growing up quick. I do still have an inch or two on Ryan but not much. Anyway, Robyn put in an order for firewood later this fall, so Billy and Ryan have some work to do. It was great going, but sure was different w/o you. Everyone made Betty feel so special and remembered she was there alone last year. You are blessed my friend, now keep your focus and get through this summer heat and desperate efforts of the terrorists.
**

Dear Bob,

Thank you for this great note. I had been planning on a miserable, lonely 4th of July, wallowing in misery and instead got a frago move out in order to be elsewhere ASAP. Wound up in Balad overnight in order to meet up with Congressmen early the next day, with no time to be miserable.

I enjoyed visiting with you and Betty on the phone. I hope you had some great pool time with the tadpoles. They are all growing so much, so fast.

I will miss the firewood labor. It is a tremendously satisfying feeling working with firewood, honest and clean work. Please don't let Ryan saw his arm off.

Wishing you a brilliant Kansas summer! rog

Dearest Robyn, 06 July 2006

Happy Anniversary my darling! These 18 years have been so wonderful for me and have passed so very quickly. I have to wonder if perhaps the price of joy and happiness is that it goes by so fast. I look back on these years together and I can only kick myself and know I was so stupid not to have pursued you sooner and more vigorously – we could have had an additional two years together by this time…

Most likely though the timing was perfect. I needed time to grow up and basic training in a way did its part. Had we dated much earlier I doubt my maturity level would have supported a relationship. I was too self-absorbed and interested in just having fun.

When we finally began dating I realized with you I could have fun and enjoy the company of a fine and intelligent woman at the same time. I knew from the first date that you were the one for forever. There was never a moment's hesitation for me after that and other than the unbidden, common, primal sexual thoughts that all men suffer that we have talked about, I have never even looked at a woman with thoughts or intentions of action since our first date. You have been the one and only woman in my life and you always will be.

I have never in these 18 years had one single doubt or even one moment of wondering whether our marriage was the right thing. I'm sure you did, especially in those earliest times when I was such an arrogant twit. I apologize and wish I had been both kinder and more considerate of you and your feelings. I hope I have made up as the years have passed and that you don't feel robbed of time.

For some years I have tried to tell you that you are the most remarkable woman that I know. I have told many friends of ours the same thing and they agree. I no longer can say that about you as it understates who you are. You are the single most remarkable PERSON I know. It is not being female that makes you special; it is the totality of who you are. You are strong, courageous, adventurous, wise, intellectual, charming, kind and considerate. And that is on top of shockingly beautiful, curvaceous, and so terribly innocently sensual. It amuses me that after all these years of me telling you, you still don't understand that you are a man magnet: lovely, intelligent, and sexy. I don't know why you picked me but I am so eternally grateful you did.

I cannot say enough times how much I appreciate your strength, resilience, toughness, and ability to tackle anything at any time. The number of men over here who are struggling at home with wives they controlled and dominated, or never encouraged to grow is sad. The men did it all and now can't understand why things are not going well at home. Somehow they thought they could run their families from Iraq…sad. There is much open yelling and screaming over the public phones as their anguished passions make them forget the public setting. I am so lucky you are there, taking care of it all. I knew you could and have never worried about it this entire time. I am glad you include me in some of the decision-making but I know my input is not truly needed. You have made this separation endurable and have lessened my worries to nearly nothing.

I think about you often during the day and wonder what you are doing then, what typical activities have you engaged? Just idle daydreaming remembering you and my wonderful life there.

There are of course women over here and many a young folk are foolishly engaged in sexual antics. It is unwise for anyone to do so for so many reasons but it does occur. Please know and trust that I am true to you and faithful to our vows just as I so deeply trust you.

We must have been separated on our anniversary at some time or other over the years but I can't remember when. I'll remember missing this one and we'll add it to the list of sacrifices we have together made for freedom and the future of our children and grandchildren. Birthdays, weddings, funerals, parties, holidays, receptions, events, children's activities of all kinds, family trips, all missed due to all these years of Army commitments. This deployment alone the list includes the first day of school, Ryan's musical, Regan's programs, musical performances, three graduations, Halloween, Thanksgiving, Christmas, New Years, the Superbowl, Scouting advancements and events, skiing on snow and water, church programs, Regan's William Allen White achievement, two birthdays, all the babies and children in our lives. Few people outside of the Army could understand how all these add up to irreplaceable lost time. It is not just the soldier missing things; you miss them too and I thank you for your tolerance and your sacrifice.

I wish I could promise you now that I'll soon be home and never gone again. The odds are extremely good that I'll be home in November, safe and sound. The odds are pretty bad that sometime yet in my National Guard career I'll be off again somewhere. I hope not but likely so. We'll have to discuss the whole thing in small detail when I'm back. All the hard costs and sacrifices compared against all the benefits and the need for good people to stay in and do the hard jobs. It would be so very easy to just hang it all up in December, our 20th year at this work, and go find a part-time job at Wal-Mart or a bookstore to make up the income. The lack of appreciation or even coaching these last four years has been nearly debilitating and now these twins of non-promotion and the non-selection for command really sting. Only you and Bob have kept me going. We'll really have to talk about it ...

To not end poorly, please know that I was a worthless and unworthy self-centered twerp (and that's a kind word) before you chose to love me. It is you and you alone who have turned me into whatever kind of man I am today. Without you and your love and your patience and guidance I know my life would have been totally different – wasted and fraudulent. Thank you for saving me and turning me into a good person.

On our anniversary I will invariably be out on some sort of mission or other and it will be a most dangerous day as I will be horribly distracted with my thoughts ever turned toward you.

I love you, respect you and miss you beyond your ability to understand how much. Happy Anniversary my lover, my friend, my wife!

rog

Howdy everyone, 09 July 2006

After last week's sermon here is a hodge-podge.

My own Topeka Congressman and famed miler Jim Ryun was here for two days. He is a true gentleman, kind, devout and sincere. Love him. He came with House Majority Leader John Boehner (no, it's not "boner," it's "bayner"). Uneventful except that Boehner and one of the other six Congressman smoked like fiends, adding five minutes to every meeting and every stop. Our planning from now on includes asking about smoke breaks so we can properly plan times.

Augusta Georgia Congressman Charlie Norwood was here, notable for his missing lung and our first time ever requirement to haul a wheelchair around. I carried a defibrillator around for two days (another ten pounds!). We were so over hyped about him that it was a great relief to actually meet him as he turned out to be no problem at all (except humping the wheelchair into and out of vans and buses). He was a trooper and carried his own weight except one trip up a circular palace staircase where we carried him up.

Norwood's group were all health committee members and did a medical services tour. I saw for the first time places that produce military eyewear and the central medical supply facility. And it was here we found the first working drinking fountain I've seen in Iraq. I took a deep drink. The water was hot…

I expected to be miserable and homesick on the 4th of July, my favorite holiday. Instead I was ordered out on a mission early and traveled most of the day to stage for the July 5th workday. Too busy to be homesick. I did stay up late and called home to visit with family and friends at the annual hotdog, fried chicken and homemade ice cream feast. Still a little homesick and feel worst that I missed Marilyn Rees's gooseberry pie, especially that last piece reheated in the microwave, topped with the rich vanilla ice cream, late at night after the kids have finished fireworks.

I vow to never again complain about the morons who shoot off fireworks after 10 p.m. the week before and after the 4th. That is truly the sound of freedom.

Neil Gibson, a Vietnam-era veteran, and my college fraternity brother Joe Graber, sent five boxes of soldier-requested things. Thanks to both, and to Ranger Neil, especially, for your service to this great country.

The soccer world cup is nearly over. Ho-Hum...

Took US Senators Biden and Reed all over the country but most fun for me was a concert by the United Kingdom's Royal Marine Band. Classical, marches, big band, naval and a smudge of straight ahead jazz tunes. Drum and bugle team was a hoot with very dramatic arm movements raising the drumsticks to upper-lip level looking for all the world like walrus mustaches.

Went to the British mission in the International Zone for a social hour after the concert. There guests enjoyed Guinness, Fosters, Carlsberg and other tall, cold beers. I stood helplessly by, nose pressed against the window glass, drooling.

Biden is interesting. Tall, trim, tanned and very, very good one on one, making you feel loved and appreciated. Especially good with women, but gets too close into your personal space for most men. Kind of Clintonesque in appeal but one would hope not so revolting inside.

Final Biden mission thought: when the Senators flew away, we were stuck at the giant Marine airbase of Al Asad in the western desert. Sat around for four hours then caught a late Chinook helicopter home as it routed all over western Iraq for FOUR more hours! Our butts were sore and bladders full. The landing pad here at Camp Victory looked wonderful at 0230 hours. (I forgot to turn OFF my travel alarm clock so awoke angrily at 0530).

There is a young soldier checking IDs at a dining facility here. His running patter: "Thank you. YOU have a great day, and YOU have a great day! Thank you, and you and you and you and YOU too, have a great day." It so silly but it makes you smile and his time passes more quickly.

The official word on the insurgency now is that it has morphed into a criminal/mafia like operation, with hijackings, smuggling, black market sales, fuel theft and sales, contract fraud, extortion, kidnapping and protection rackets as the primary focus of their efforts. That's because their exterior funding has been pounded so badly by the financial investigations and efforts back home. That's why the New York Times is so terribly, horribly on the wrong side of the war. To give away key wartime secret strategies is treason. It just proves the national media doesn't understand the nature of this 40-year world war and that the financial theater of this war is just as important as our combat theater.

The national media probably hasn't told you the "suicide" drivers are now being kidnapped, drugged, then tied, chained or super glued into the vehicles with orders to go kill themselves. If they don't then their families get butchered. The enemy is evil.

Just got the first draft planning documents for our return to the USA, with target dates and instructions for packing shipping containers. YAHOO!

I ran into General Caldwell, the handsome fellow you saw on TV announcing Zarqawi's death. He had an enormous cold sore and was perplexed as he'd never had them before. As a life-long sufferer I gave him some of my own stash of the stuff that works. I pondered and was pleased to realize I'd not had a cold sore for a year! Thus I immediately developed a sympathy sore…I'm ready for the miracle cure if anyone out there is working on it.

Cards and letters from Pop x 2, Mom, Topeka attorney and work associate Craig McKinney, co-worker Joyce Merryman, California dad Roger Reimer, Topeka buddy Margaret Telthorst, co-worker Peggy Bukovatz, Ed Linquist (you can feel free to go ahead and keep sending the giant goldfish grahams…) and the boxes from Neil and Joe!

American by birth. Soldier by choice. Volunteer by God!

Roger T. Aeschliman
Major, Armor
Deputy Commander, First Kansas Volunteers

Hello my friends, 09 July 2006

I hope you are not all worked up about the most recent North Korean pronouncement to launch a war because they feel "threatened." I assure you I will personally go there and cut the nuts off that Don King wanna-be if he keeps flapping his gums.

I have already told my children that any nation with the word People's, Democratic, Republic, or Workers in its name is guaranteed to not support or defend any of the four...

Also, any land with public displays of the living leader is assured of rebellion and fire. It's just a matter of time.

Had a mission with Congressman Norwood who indicated he knows you both. He struggled a bit with the heat and long movements (first time we ever used a wheelchair on the mission-actually moved it around on helios and carried him in it up a circular stair in the palace) but was a trooper and not really a burden. He said he so was so grateful that Mike had arrived in Augusta and turned the paper around compared to previous editorial positions. Honest and truly... I did not pass on any embarrassing stories but did make him promise to say hello. Also had Deal on the same mission and couple from Texas.

No, of course there were no protests against Hajji and his pals for the slaughter of the three troops. Don't know what America heard but they were eviscerated, castrated, partially beheaded and burned still alive at least technically. The enemy is evil. Period. We've had discussions about capture among a few of us and there is no agreement. Fight to the last bullet and then keep fighting hand to hand with the hope of hurting as many of them as possible to the end, risking capture, pain and the media feast, or eat the last bullet and spare yourself the pain and the US the torment of knowing you suffered? For us it is so hypothetical it's too easy to say what you would do. History shows everyone reacts differently; some fight insanely tooth and claw and others freeze up even with weapons and ammo watching the enemy walk right up to shoot them in the face.

So, again, no protest in our favor over this, but there was a goodly amount of intel and support from locals to resolve the case. Lots of bad guys got outed down there and lots were killed. This week the Iraqi Army went right into Sadr City and kicked butt. That didn't get much news either.

I met a 23-year-old Major in the Iraq Army that now works directly for the new minister of defense. He speaks great English with a Mexican accent as he learned through total emersion with the Marines out west. Very smart. He said so many of the youth of Iraq are so pissed about things right now that they are turning their backs on tribe, clan and honor and want to westernize rapidly. He said he would eagerly go to his home area and fight against his own tribe if he could as they are a nasty bunch killing other Iraqis and holding the country back. He has no use for secular conflict and says the Army is fusing into the same mindset; Army and brother in arms first against all the bad guys regardless of stripe. A hard long, slog he said but it will work. He also said in another year or so the Army will have to go do ruthless terrible things and the libs will scream and gnash teeth but after about a week it will all be over with the government in control. Interesting conversation.

I don't have access to top secret stuff but I continue to chat with the top spooks who are hunting and killing the bad guys. There is great success exploiting Zarqawi's cell phone, computer, etc. And each success leads to more computers, cell phones. Going good. Flattening whole towns sounds like a nice idea but eventually you wind up swallowing poison and a bullet in your head (Hitler) or on trial and in route to a good hanging (Saddam). You would have to eliminate an entire tribe because if you leave any alive they will have to come get you for blood debt/feud/honor. The court of international opinion (which I as president would totally ignore and tell to kiss my ass) would convict us and our own national media piles on. No win approach in the long haul.

And for no reason other than I just like saying it: The UN sucks and we should close it down and start all over.

I love you guys and appreciate your support. Happy summer to you.

WHY SOCCER IS COMMIE (and other reasons why it is the worst game)

Roger T. Aeschliman
11 July 2006

Let's be perfectly clear right up front. Soccer sucks! It is the worst game in the world and the fact that the United States remains out of step with most other nations on this is to our credit, not our shame.

The athletes we send onto the global soccer field are truly the seventh or eighth string of American talent, lagging somewhere behind professional lacrosse and those US expats in the Italian or Spanish Basketball Leagues. Our children still grow up saying "I want to be Barry Bonds" (except for the steroids) or "I want to be Priest Holmes" (except for the injuries). No one says "I want to be Ronaldo," or "I want to be Beckham" (although the latter does come with the arm candy former Spice Girl).

No, in the USA it's still the football captain who gets the girls, the baseball pitcher who never strikes out and the basketball forward who scores most often. But I already digress.

Soccer is first and foremost the ultimate communist sport. It is a very small game played on a very large field cluttered with self-important nabobs trying desperately to fill all the gaps with the semblance of progress. It is all appearance and style with no real action and very few results. Communist. In the highest level of soccer the scores are most commonly 0-0, 1-0, 1-1, and the occasional 2-0 rout. All sound and fury signifying nothing.

Soccer is in theory a team sport where success depends completely on everyone offering their best effort all the time, sacrificing their own achievement for the greater good of the team. Sound familiar? Nee: From each according to their abilities, to each according to their needs. And, like communism, it sounds so nice but the reality is always, always skewed toward the cult of personality, the so called striker who scores the goals. When the game is over it matters not who made the pass, who set up the ball, who blocked the shots. All that matters is that one superstar scored the one point of the whole, terribly long and dreadfully slow-moving 90 minutes or more.

To see the frantic and desperate celebratory search for attention after a goal is scored is to watch the search for individuality and recognition that lurks unfulfilled under communism. Some one scores, they run around with bursts of energy they seem unable to muster during the actual play, they prance and mince in order to draw the attention of the crowd, they psychically scream "for God's sake, someone look at me please!" All of the lesser beings who contributed to the score are abandoned, and if they seek to join in the celebration the one who kicked the ball into the net physically runs by or *through* them, sometimes even violently pushing them out of the way in order to keep the limelight solely focused on himself. The team becomes very unimportant at the moment of glory. Only the figurehead is allowed to have the public's adoration. He has *earned* it; it is a *right*. And he jealously keeps it from all the others. Commie, commie, commie.

Soccer is a game that promotes whining, lying, and blame-placing, three of the less attractive traits of mankind, all featured in communism. Unlike football, baseball, hockey boxing and other truly physical tests, no one is ever really injured in soccer (a reason why so many misguided American moms encourage their children toward this sissy sport these days). In our American professional sports the danger is very real. People are seriously and often permanently incapacitated (there are even occasional deaths from contact and blows). Real men and women take the pain, get hauled off the field and get treatment, hopefully to recover in six months or for next season.

Not soccer. In this silly sport a large part of the game is whining about every minor bodily contact, followed by feigning injury in order to gain field position or, even better, one of those penalty kicks that so often decide the otherwise uneventful game. To see the replay of the accidental grazing of a foot that may or may not have actually *touched* the opponent, followed by he so "fouled" rolling on the ground in agony is to see into the heart of communism. To whit: "I failed because someone else made me fail." Under communism and soccer no one ever messes up and no one ever takes the blame. It is always, always, always someone else's fault and someone else who conspired to destroy you. One of the most endearing things about historically great American athletes has been their willingness to accept the blame. Not in soccer. It is always "I was fouled," or "the referees were blind." In soccer, no one ever says "the better team won," because it is not honestly about the team, it is all about the cult of personality and avoiding the blame and the subsequent execution or exile to Siberia.

So, they roll on the ground in terrible pain, unbearable pain; surely they've a broken femur or a ruptured spleen. But then, one of two things happens. First, the referee ignores the display, content to let the play continue. In that case, some teammate hollers over: "Get up man! It's not working. Get back in the game." The victim recovers his feet, limps around for five seconds to maintain the pretense of dignity and then is miraculously cured and going full-speed again. Or second, the referee does see the "foul" and subsequent acting and is so moved by the performance that a penalty is awarded at which time the poor abused victim totters to his feet, staggers about a bit, has a drink of water, pulls up his socks, kicks the winning goal, then runs about at lightning speed, basking in fan adoration, pushing teammates aside to avoid sharing any credit. Amazing recuperative powers these soccer wimps, from cripple to 100-yard dash man in six seconds.

The fraudulence of the drama is horrific in that someone who didn't do anything wrong is accused, condemned and executed in the court of public opinion. This is so historically accurate for communism and other forms of socialist dictatorships where the actual guilty person refuses the blame and successfully throws it at another. Innocence is irrelevant. Facts are useless. Blame is important. Survival is all.

Soccer is also a game created by the low IQ for the low IQ. We may confess to moments of graceful skill and athletic talent, but they are overshadowed by the mind-numbing banality of the game. Soccer is the sports equivalent of tic-tac-toe. There is nothing intellectual there. The rules are simple, the tactics are simple, the strategy is non-existent.

Well, that may not be totally true. There appear to be two piddling strategies in soccer. First, the offensive strategy in which in the cult of personality figurehead (supported by the unappreciated and unrewarded team) attacks repeatedly at the point of weakness – the least talented defender, a basic strategy that is only the first step in a game plan for all real sports. Second, the defensive strategy which recognizes the inability to attack successfully due to a lack of talent and just hopes to keep the enemy out of the goal. If defense is successful long enough, it gives the actors and drama majors a chance to whine and act their way into a penalty kick and potential 1-0 victory over the better team.

There is nothing else there. Stop looking.

Compare this to the NFL. It is an extraordinarily complicated game with plans, sequels and branches, multiple strategies, and an endless inventory of weapons, tools and personnel to enact the multitude of strategies throughout the dynamic and ever-changing conflict. Players with different skills rotate in to confuse and imbalance the foe. There are numerous points of weakness to exploit and numerous ways to do so, but always in the face of the opposition who seeks to exploit the weaknesses they sense.

Any person exposed to soccer can understand the basic game in 10 seconds and master the nuances (mostly involving lying, whining and blame-placing) in 10 minutes. NFL football requires a lifetime of observation, continued education regarding players and talents, and a practical knowledge of physics, meteorology, and the laws of thermo-dynamics. Anyone unexposed to the NFL could watch it for a full season and not yet grasp the basics. The strategies of team versus team are learned and relearned but never mastered.

Soccer is so loved world-wide specifically *because* it is so easy to understand. It does not discriminate against anyone. Everyone is a master of the game. Everyone is a critic.

Hence the befuddling antics of the uniquely American "Soccer Mom."

And it *is* befuddling. A parent who would never dream of walking onto the basketball court yelling "pass the ball to Tiffany you moron!" will run tirelessly up and down the soccer sideline screaming at Billy, Jessica and Nicole to head the ball in from the mid-line, or to center the ball from the corner to their son Ja'wan who will surely fire it into the net if the lesser talented kids would just get him the ball. A football parent who understands deep inside that their son is a third string offensive tackle at best, and accepts the coach's decision as fundamentally wise turns into the ultimate, evil stage mom, demanding their end-of-the bench, overweight, untalented brat start the soccer game and be given the ball at every opportunity.

Assaults upon coaches and umpires from football, basketball and baseball are rare. They are modus operandi in the youth soccer world. The game is so simple, the communist feel so close to the surface, that THEIR child cannot possibly be wrong so the coach or umpire must be intentionally harming the kid and THAT draws out the instinct to defend the offspring. It is primal stuff and dangerous.

And it's not just parents. Soccer brings out the worst in everyone. The game is so mind-numbingly dull that one simply must drink to excess to get through it. Too much booze, too little action, all those inflamed nationalist passions (with no national achievement to justify it) all add up to soccer hooliganism. When your country has absolutely nothing of which to be proud, you can hang a lot of hat on a few soccer wins over Mali, Panama, or Estonia. And victory on the field drunkenly entitles you to victory in the stands and brawling in the bars.

If the game were more complex it is possible the thugs would tip back another pint, pause to analyze the results and vent like this: "If only Zembosa had performed the Titian Maneuver at the schwerpunkt," or "their entire strategy was wrong; it called for the double envelopment using the traditional impi formations of the Zulus." People who think like this don't smash windows and knife each other in the in the streets.

The only USA parallel to soccer's post-match violence is the inner-city rioting that occasionally follows the NCAA basketball championship. And those happen exclusively in pathological urban communities or randomly amongst the drunken college preps who stayed up two beers too late.

Finally, even the World Cup trophy is a sissy communist icon and a lie: two strikers, both celebrating (which assuredly never happens), prancing in different directions, with the whole world on their backs. In only a moment they will spring apart and the world will fall. And it's not even a cup. The metaphor is complete.

Howdy everyone, 16 July 2006

Happy 18th Anniversary today to Mrs. Robyn Aeschliman, the most remarkable person on the face of the earth! She deserves so much better than me and I am eternally grateful to have her (and our two adolescents – whom I will embarrass by saying we called them Doodles and Pooky when they were little) as the focal point of my life. Despite the National Guard work we have spent nearly if not all of our Anniversaries together. Even the first one, when I was attending a four month military school at Fort Knox, Robyn flew out to Louisville and we spent a week together, the lowlight of which was me splattering prime rib au jus all over the wall of a pretty swanky downtown steak joint. Even the normal drill weekends and annual trainings have required so many sacrifices from Robyn, Ryan and Regan: missed birthdays, school events and programs, church activities, family get togethers, sporting activities, civic/social nights, outings with friends and neighbors, reunions of all types. Now this whole lost year ... Love you guys!

My specific work here has evolved into a sort of mad week or ten days followed by a slow week or so. We seem to have this flood of Congressmen, Governors, and foreign dignitaries (all my responsibility) during which I am just insanely busy and away from the base, followed then by nothing.

The work has gotten harder and harder as the weather worsens. After soaring into the 120s in June, we had a long week of 110s in July. It felt positively balmy. Now the temps are creeping up again and the 118s and 119s are searing. We've had teams in places where the desert temperatures were in the high 130s. It's impossible to function in that heat. You just can't move. The work involves sitting very still while traveling, slowly walking into an air conditioned building or tent for a meeting and then sitting still, drinking a liter of water per hour. Even standing still in the shade on guard is onerous under the weight of armor and gear.

After two, three or six days of 120-degree missions, three, four or five days without a flying mission are just great. The first two or three days are just sleeping, eating and recovering strength. I feel for the young troops who are out patrolling the streets and farms, especially the gunners riding out the top of the armored Humvees, with all their gear on and 120-degree wind blowing in their faces. Those soldiers are real warriors.

People don't walk briskly around here. Everyone ambles or saunters. Too sweaty to walk at the normal Army quick time step.

I now secretly wear a sweatband underneath my helmet. So far no one has yelled at me.

It is impossible to take a cool shower. The water storage tanks heat the "cold" water to a nearly intolerable temperature. By mid afternoon and into the early evening it is dangerous to take a shower at all because the water is too hot.

The wind blows steadily now out of the northwest at 10-20 MPH and gusts higher. Eases off in the evening and kicks up mid-morning. Dust and sand storms are common and cause regular delays in our missions due to grounded helicopter flights.

I've heard from several people who questioned my sanity in regards to my "positive" impressions of Senator Biden. I re-read what I wrote last week and perhaps I was too subtle. Please forgive me. I thought the "Clintonesque" statement was damning in that I personally believe the ex-president is the lowest form of life on the planet, a despicable, evil man who sacrificed our national security in favor of an ill-conceived effort to expand the nanny state and to sate his own juvenile, carnal instincts.

Here's what I wrote to a friend:

"I watched Biden work closely this time and he has a lot of Clintonesque qualities. He is GREAT with women. Stands close, holds one hand, grips an elbow or upper arm with the other, looks deeply into eyes, smiles, really gives all his attention. They swoon. He is tallish too, 6 1, 6 2 or so. Tanned and trim. He misses with men because he does much the same thing and it comes off really gay. Way too close into male personal space. Also, he talks about himself almost entirely. I saw this, I did that, what you just said reminds me of what I once said and let me tell you. In all the meetings and events he dominated the discussion and listened much less to what was said than for the opportunity to respond. Still, he has a lot of style and charm and could do well if he could break the code on talking to groups. One on one he can tailor his message and sell it. In a group he has to sell them all at once. Harder for his intimate style. Interesting. He is terribly bright and reasonably pleasant to be around. Said thanks etc. He grudgingly said a lot of nice things about how well things are going since his December trip. He never said he was wrong earlier, but that things were better now. Also, to a group of Marines he said there was "no one seriously talking about cutting and running. We all know we have to finish this thing." No media around to record that..."

Does that add clarity?

Last Sunday, crossing a big swath of desert we flew over what I took to be an ancient cemetery in the middle of nowhere. Pure desert with no signs of life. There were many large rock stelae rising from the sand, roughly in arced rows. There were not even signs of abandoned canals or irrigation ditches. It was at least 50 miles from anywhere. What, how and why there?

Cards and letters from Pop x 2 , Mom, talented big brother Rick who is now in business for himself in the Topeka area doing ANYTHING in the home-building and carpentry arena, running pal Terry Kimes, college fraternity International Executive Director Bill Martin (that's pretty cool . . .), Aunt Nancy (Tennessee), and a post card from Melba Waggoner.

American by birth. Soldier by choice. Volunteer by God!

Roger T. Aeschliman
Major, Armor
Deputy Commander, First Kansas Volunteers

From: Joe Kutter
To: Roger Aeschliman
Sent: Monday, July 17, 2006 10:03 PM
Subject: Re: weekly report

Roger,

I have read your epistles with great interest and look forward to a time when we can sit face to face for conversation. You are a terrific writer and your descriptions of people, the places and events have been wonderfully helpful. Your observations about Senator Biden are a case in point.

All I want to say is that never a week goes by that you are not mentioned in our prayers and you occupy our thoughts more frequently than that. Without fear of contradiction, I can say that FBC/T is proud to count you as one of our family.

God take care of you and your family. Happy anniversary-- belated.

Joe Kutter
**

Dear Joe,

Thanks for your complimentary and encouraging note. Writing was my first career and I still enjoy telling a story orally and on paper. I have over the past three months written a novel for Regan about a little island boy who survives the great tsunami and has many adventures returning home. Regan is my collaborator and we are at loggerheads now whether the boy's mother survived the disaster. I think not. Regan thinks it would be a good twist to have her live as the reader expects her to be dead. Decisions, decisions.

Either way it is a story of grit, determination, pulling yourself up and just getting on with it. Fun to write and pass a few hours...

I appreciate the prayers and recognize I am wrapped in a blanket of protection from the hundreds of people (maybe thousands) who are interceding with God on my behalf. I don't deserve such attention but I am grateful for it.

Likewise I am appreciative of the kindness everyone has shown to Robyn and the kids in my absence. As much as I wish it were "if you love me then love my family," as contrary and remote as I am I know the truth is "love Robyn and the kids so help them despite Roger." And that's ok.

Always enjoy visiting with you Joe, limited as it is. Thanks for writing and thinking about me at all.

Most truly yours, rog

Howdy everyone, 23 July 2006

This week I completed four missions and the entire Joint Visitors' Bureau handled twenty more. We housed over 700 hotel guests and fed over 1,000 meals in the hotel mess hall. Had another 20-30 brief driving missions taking some general, ambassador, high mucky-muck or other to the airport or helipad. The rest of the 2-137th Infantry Battalion guarded twenty miles of walls, six gates and entry control points, supervised 200 Ugandan contractor guards, ran a dozen combat patrols around Baghdad and put several dozen hours into the infrastructure development of a nearby village called Makasib.

I think our plate is full.

Congressman Hoekstra, Michigan, chairman of the House Intelligence Committee was here with four others. They were generally fine but one aide was the biggest jerk I have seen over here. It's always the aides...With this group we wound up in Irbil, Kurdistan. I celebrated my anniversary eating an incredible meal at the security guards' "kiddie" table while Hoekstra and others had lunch with the Kurdish Prime Minister. Real Kurdish/Iraqi food for the first time here and it was delectable. Our package flew away from Irbil and we were left to find our own way 300 miles home. This is hard in Irbil as the region is so peaceful that there is almost no US military presence. The airport is run by Kurds, the security is Kurdish and the communication system is Kurdish. Our planned plane never arrived but we rerouted a C-130 at 2 a.m. for a 3:30 landing at Baghdad. This region and the Kurds are a great example of what this country can become with freedom, self-responsibility and security. There is a tremendous housing and commercial building boom and the city looks more European than Middle Eastern. The Citadel of Irbil is reported to be the oldest, continuously inhabited place in the world dating at least to 2,300 BC and maybe 6,000 BC. The middle of the city is an enormous mound (mostly likely ruins and garbage from 4,000 years as the rest of the region is flat) with a fortress on top. Irbil spreads out in concentric circles from this tell. Alexander the Great is reputed to have set a large stone in place atop the hill upon the final defeat of Darius in 331 BC and the fortress, stone and the Kurdish Museum of Carpets compete for tourist honors. We saw the fortress and stone in passing but not the carpets.

I saw a young soldier awarded a Purple Heart at the Balad Hospital. He was surrounded by Congressmen and a pile of Generals and Colonels. His wounds were real but relatively minor and he was drugged up and marginally coherent. From the look on his face I know he really just wanted to be left alone for a nap.

Still, the ceremony at bedside was moving and it really made me appreciate how easy I have it.

Well, I never went to bed at all Sunday night and greeted US Secretary of Commerce Gutierrez at the Baghdad airport at 0800 Monday. Very busy one-day schedule including a business showcase and sort of Iraqi Chamber of Commerce luncheon. The Iraqi economy has grown about 30% since I've been here. Another one of those unreported successes. Secretary Gutierrez was followed Tuesday (I got a little sleep Monday night) by Energy Secretary Bodman who met regarding oil, gas, electricity, etc.

Having other cabinet agencies coming is brand new and I suspect in direct response to General McCaffrey's April report criticizing the lack of such support and involvement. Expect to see more. There was lots of good media in the Arab world over these visits. The US reporting I read on the Internet mentioned the trips but only second or third after minor bombings.

Secretary Gutierrez was talking before TV cameras when a rocket launched from across the Tigris, went overhead and exploded a goodly distance away. One hyper security guard shouted warnings and the Secretary was embarrassed on camera by running back into a nearby building as his suited aides hit the ground. I knew better as the rocket was softly going by "shoo-shoo-shoo" and could tell it wasn't close. The close ones go "SHWOOOOSSSSH" before they go BLAM!

Another positive is all these Iraqi officials are taking charge of their own agenda now. We've seen meetings start late, end early and canceled on short notice. They still want to meet with Congressmen and others but they do have a country to run. This has irritated some of our visitors but I look at it this way: If an Iraqi congressman came to the USA would President Bush or any of our cabinet secretaries even think about meeting them? No way! It's pretty presumptuous for a back-bencher junior congressman to demand time with the head of a nation.

General Abizaid came to town again. Typical mission for him: land, change everything right away then change it five more times over the next two days. The day goes really fast when he's in town. Flew back from Balad in a sporty C-12 and once again had a nearly stomach emptying thrill ride dropping 5,000 feet in two or three minutes to land at Baghdad.

I was awarded the Army Physical Fitness Badge this week.

A team of our replacements came and went this week to review the mission and look around. Not counting chickens but sure a smile-bringer to see them.

Here is a "what can I do" possibility for anyone who wants to send me something. The little town of Makasib is very poor with limited infrastructure. Our Kansas guys are working on electricity, sewage, and water and making progress. But the people can really use some help in small ways too. If you would be willing to fill one of those $8.10 postage boxes with hygiene, first aid, health, or toys/games and mail it over our Kansas soldiers could distribute them to great lifestyle improvement for the Iraqis and great PR for the USA. (See below if interested).

Cards and letters from my very own Congressman Jim Ryun with an autographed photo of the two of us (he left me an inscribed Bible when he was here!), Pop x 4, Mom x 2 (including anniversary greetings), grandmother Dorothy Hamler, the Crouse's (Nebraska), Aunt Nancy (Topeka), nifty little hand-made mementoes/photo book of the 4th of July from the Telthorst's, box and photos from Robyn.

American by birth. Soldier by choice. Volunteer by God!

Roger T. Aeschliman
Major, Armor
Deputy Commander, First Kansas Volunteers

MAKASIB BOXES

Fill one $8.10 flat-rate USPS box with any of the following:

Hygiene products: toothbrushes, toothpaste, soap, shampoo, hand sanitizer, cotton swabs.

Health products: multi-vitamins, aspirin and other pain/fever reducers, cough syrup or cough drops, cold medicine,

First Aid products: Band-aids, hydrocortisone cream, bacitractin ointment, medical tape.

Toys etc: Any little things you might get at Walgreens or a grocery store, and, if willing, an inexpensive, deflated soccer ball. Soccer balls are GOLD over here (even though it is the worst sport in the history of mankind)!

On the exterior customs statement please detail the contents so we can figure out what best to give whom and somewhere on the bottom of the box in big print write "MAKASIB."

Mail to me at:

MAJ Roger T. Aeschliman
B Co 2-137 INF
APO AE 09342-1400

DATE: July 24, 2006

"I have received your article, "Victory Over America." The article has been reviewed and accepted for publication contingent on an operations security review certification. The enclosed form, "OPSEC Review Certification" should be completed by your G2/S2 and public affairs officer. The attached instruction sheet provides a step-by-step process to help complete the security review. Once the article is cleared for publication by the G2/S2 and PAO, it will be published; however, I cannot give you a definite date of publication. If this is acceptable, please complete and return the enclosed permission to publish form and biographical worksheet.

If you should move or change jobs before your article is published, please let us know so we can update your bio. You can email the information to us at armormagazine@knox.army.mil or phone DSN 464-2610/2249 or commercial (502) 624-2610/2249.

Thank you for your interest in ARMOR.

Sincerely,

Kathy Johnson
Armor Magazine
**

Dear Kathy,

I'm sorry to report that my previously submitted article "Victory Over America" WAS NOT approved for publication. Thanks for your consideration and I would appreciate it if you would delete the original submission and send me an email note to that effect so I can prove my compliance with the rejection.

Thanks again and regrets,

MAJ Roger T. Aeschliman

FROM:Anti-Iraqi Forces Headquarters
DISTRIBUTION TO: List Zulu (not lower than selected cell leaders only)
OPLAN 0601
CODE NAME:VICTORY OVER AMERICA
DATE:01 AUGUST 06

SITUATION:Militarily and in terms of the civil environment we have lost the war. There is no hope for a military victory over America and no hope of winning the hearts and minds of the Iraqi people. We must accept these facts in order to fully prosecute the plan that follows. The only hope for our victory and the spread of our true Islamist/Baathist agenda is to defeat the United States *will* through their own media as occurred in the Vietnam War. Fortunately the Americans do not know their own history and are thus totally unprepared for our plan.

To review the historical parallel, the United States had won significant tactical and operational victories in Vietnam. The Information Operations campaign of the Americans was successful in the villages and provinces. The North Vietnamese and Viet Cong through their unending murder, torture and terrorism had lost the hearts and minds campaign. The war was nearing an end militarily. If not for the incessant carping of the United States media feeding the "peace-at-all-costs" movement in America the war would have been formally lost by the Communists in late 1968. But that media carping created the single point of STRATEGIC weakness necessary to turn defeat into victory. The Tet suicidal communist attack on multiple fronts had minor and temporary tactical successes, but over two weeks turned into a tactical, operational and strategic disaster for the northern forces. The Viet Cong were destroyed in the south and the North Vietnamese regulars were decimated on the border. At that point aggressive American action would have overrun the north and concluded the war in short order. Instead the US media turned the failed Tet offensive into a strategic victory for the north. By attacking the US government polices and elected leaders for failing to protect US troops and the civilian population (even in their most secure areas: Saigon, Hue, Khe San), the media outcry led to a cessation of US aggression and renewed promises to bring the troops home. In the minds of the US citizen, the war was lost, despite the tactical and operational failure of the communists' Tet offensive.

Thus, the parallels between then and now are remarkable. We too have lost the military war and hearts and minds efforts. We too are fragmented and on the verge of disaster. We too have less than one year of organizational coherence and ability to strike with any coordination and to any effect. What we do have is good intelligence from the hundreds of spies we have working on American camps, and a cadre of willing fighters eager to sacrifice themselves for heaven. And we especially have the US media and a Congressional element on our side eager to prove the failure of the President's war and to feed the "peace-at-any-cost" movement. We can win the war strategically with one blow now. It is all or nothing.

MISSION:On D-Day, H-Hour all cells attack forward operating bases, the International Zone, and the strategic hub of the Baghdad Airport/Victory Base Complex to penetrate the defenses, disperse among the housing, killing or wounding as many Americans as possible in order to turn the US media finally and totally against the war and raise public outcry to force the withdrawal of US troops from Iraq.

EXECUTION:Upon notice cell leaders will gather all assigned fighters for hasty purification rites and prayer. Leaders issue American uniforms in either DCU or ACU style, 200 rounds of ammunition and all manpackable explosive devices (grenades, satchel charges, improvised devices), then move to their lines of departure. Leaders will assign martyr truck bomber drivers, snipers and rocket-propelled grenadiers and issue that appropriate pre-positioned equipment.

H-Hour is dependent on the nation-wide celebratory gunfire expected at the conclusion of the Iraq National Team soccer victory over Iran, or upon the verdict/sentencing of Saddam. This firepower display will provide significant cover and confusion as Americans will be notified in advance that massive celebratory gunfire and even some explosions are to be expected from the "non-hostile" civilian population. At H-Hour all cells attack their assigned towers with sniper teams. RPG teams attack the same towers under the cover of sniper fire. The massing of RPG fire only on the targeted towers will destroy the enemies' ability to immediately respond and remove the eyes and ears from the targeted section of wall. Martyr vehicle bombs will move aggressively upon the launch of the RPG attack. The critical wall sections are identified. In each case we have templated the least observed and most secluded portion of the defensive walls. Once the guard towers covering these sections are destroyed our large martyr vehicle bombs will rubble the walls. Then assault elements attack on foot through the wall and into the living areas of the Americans.

Haste, shock and violence of action will win the day. Our soldiers will attack with great speed toward their assigned targets, shooting everything that moves. The speed of the attack will have our fighters among the housing before most of the lazy Americans are even out of bed. In the event of challenge our soldiers must use their training to respond in American accented English "This is Bullshit man!" or "What the hell is going on?" or "Jesus, they're right behind me!" These slang terms will provide a few moments of confusion as will the American uniform. Remember that there are no innocents in these areas. All are the enemy of Wahhabist Islam and must be destroyed. Shoot to kill or wound as many as possible. Remember the total number of casualties is more important than the number killed. Horrific wounds and inhumane treatment are also effective for the success of the plan as the US media will call us insane and ruthless and thus undefeatable.

The special operations teams will move with extra speed to the homes of the Generals and the headquarters of all brigades and higher. With the same shock, speed and elements of confusion they should penetrate into the command operations centers and detonate their explosive devices. This will further disrupt communications and command.

With an estimated 1,500 fighters and 20 vehicle bombs we can attack 10 locations. With 200 rounds and explosives, and judicious rate of aimed fire we estimate an average of 10 casualties inflicted per fighter prior to death. Additionally the surge of Surface to Air missiles now received will allow us to defend ourselves during this attack and destroy an estimated 25 helicopters.

As all this occurs in the middle of the night it will be at least 1000 hours the next day before the Americans can organize an effective defense or counter attack. Elements of the attack may still be operational into the next night and should use the cover of darkness to renew the assault. The longer the attack continues, the better, but again, the primary objective is mass casualties across Iraq. Do not sacrifice yourself too cheaply but do not hesitate to martyr yourself with explosives when a mass target presents itself.

CONCLUSION:We recognize that all our warriors will perish for the glory of Allah. The purpose is not to seize or retain terrain, the purpose is to kill and wound as many as possible in as horrific manner as possible. The result will be all or none, just like Tet, a minor and short-lived tactical success, total operational failure and the devastation of our fighting forces and organization weighed against the anticipated strategic victory of the Information Operations campaign. As the US *will* crumbles we expect to see a resurgence of recruiting among foreign fighters as they see the vulnerability of the Americans and see the then proven opportunity to strike and die for Allah. Thus as the Americans leave, our ranks will grow just in time to resume a national offensive over the non-cooperative Sunni, the Shia and Kurds. The sacrifices of our heroic fighters on D-Day will lead to the renewal of our Wahhabist/Pan-Arabic plans to spread the rule of Sharia law across the entire world. Inshallah!

——————

The preceding plan is based on facts.

- There are areas of weakness on the perimeters of many FOBs
- Many FOB soldiers are so used to explosions and gunfire that reaction times to such an attack will be slow
- Challenges and passwords are not used *once inside* FOBs
- Tower guards are used to being approached by civilians of all types and appearances and do not have standoff range
- Escalation of Force restrictions are so ingrained in tower personnel there is a great risk they can be put out of action by snipers and RPG teams without defending themselves.
- Plans for defense *within* a FOB are fragmentary
- The enemy is dedicated to his cause and has access to weapons, ammo, explosives, missiles and manpower
- The enemy is organized

Most soldiers today have never heard to Tet and if they have they believe it was a military loss for the United States. They are sadly unaware that Tet emasculated the Viet Cong and the forces at the border. They are ignorant that an aggressive post-Tet counterattack would have taken Hanoi.

But our enemy knows this history and the enemy have reached a conclusion. The enemy believes an attack will break the will of the United States.

I am concerned about the United States public positioning regarding the potential attack on the Victory Base Complex, other FOBs and other high profile "secure" areas (the International Zone and several prisons come to mind). I am not concerned about the success of these potential attacks. They will fail, the enemy killed and routed. I am very concerned about the historical precedent for theses types of highly visible attacks and how they play out in the US media.

During WWII there was clear intelligence of the pending Nazi attack into the Ardennes. It was not a surprise when the attack occurred. Even Eisenhower commented in the early stages of the battle that the attack presented a great opportunity for the allied forces. Yet because of the lack of a public IO campaign that attack was seen as a surprise and a great initial victory for the Nazis and fear that the war was now lost.

During the Korean War as the United Nations (overwhelmingly US) forces closed on the Yalu River there was significant intelligence that the Chinese were prepared and massed to join the war. Yet due to the lack of an IO campaign (and some terrible generalship or mental illness on the part of Macarthur) the attack was perceived as unexpected by the American public and that the war was now lost.

During Vietnam there was significant and credible intelligence about the massive Tet offensive. This was apparently ignored by higher headquarters as improbable and there was no public IO campaign. Thus the Tet offensive was seen publicly in the USA as a tremendous surprise and a great victory for the North when the truth is that it concluded as a tactical and operational disaster for the Communists. This is clear: in the case of Tet a great military victory (of which the USA had advance knowledge) was turned into a strategic/public relations defeat and led directly to the abandonment of the SE Asian Theater. America did not lose in Vietnam. Our nation walked away after this terrible public relations loss.

I believe the potential for a public relations disaster due to an attack at the airport, the Victory Base Complex, the International Zone and other "secure" zones is tremendous even though the military result will be a failure for the Anti-Iraq Forces (AIF). The Tet parallel is nearly perfect.

From previous career work and experience I believe in the strategy of "Hanging a lantern on your problem." Share it, make others aware of it and explain the result of it BEFORE the bad thing happens. The contrary position which seems more common in the military is "Never show your ass." I believe an Information Operations/Public Relations effort to explain the intelligence and our preparations for it, then explain the result and how it is strategically and operationally insignificant IN ADVANCE of any attack is the right course of action. If this is not done and the attack occurs the US media will paint it as a great surge of the AIF and show how it proves the war cannot be won. The enemy will prove it can strike even the most secure areas of the coalition and that they can mount organized offensives.

The lessons of history are clear. Must we be doomed to repeat mistakes?

From: Mary Jo Aeschliman
Date: Wednesday, July 26, 2006 5:24 pm
Subject: dictionary

Hi Roger. You send me to the dictionary often. This time is was for leviathan. I didn't know that it meant "any huge thing". I LOVE THAT YOU HAVE SUCH A GOOD VOCABULARY. I remember teaching lists of vocabulary words to 4th graders, taken from their reading book.

Caroline Bigham sent a nice note to Ash in thanks for all the garden goodies. She used the work "largess", so off to the dictionary I went - and the word sure "fit". I'm sure you know that it means a gift generously given.

I hope you are sleeping WELL at this very moment. Love you lots, MOM
**

Dear Mom,

I hope the dictionary thing is ok and not off-putting. I just try to use the right word for the right moment. English is such a great language because we have stolen so ruthlessly from all other languages and have so many words that mean NEARLY the same thing but not EXACTLY the same thing. We can nuance with a specific word far beyond what other cultures can do. They must depend on context, body language, accent, emphasis and inflection in order to determine the meaning of a specific word. English, if you read and ponder, lets you be accurate and precise with the specific meaning of the spoken word. That's why the international diplomatic community hates the English language; it takes away their wiggle room. (That's why they hate Bush and hated Reagan too, because they both say/said what they mean not vague diplo-speak).

Anyway, leviathan is biblical, a reference to a great sea beast that is evil and can't be resisted or defeated, similar to the behemoth. It is also a metaphor for Satan, or the Ocean as a whole. It goes back to the beginning of written history and is found in many cultures, eventually winding up in the Bible.

So, stop using big words or are do you think people are ok/entertained/challenged to see them?

Largess is a great word too. Seldomly used anymore except by us Trust Officers who get to say nice things about the deceased who benefited others through their largess. In English we can say "liberal" "generous" "giving" "benefactor" and "sharing" as well as "largess" to dance all around the idea of giving something to others and they all mean slightly different things. Cool huh?

I am at this moment exhausted again. Had four days of flying missions out of the last five. Got back in early this Thursday morning at 0300 after flying all over the country yet again. Tired as I was I still tossed and turned from 3-9 a.m. then forced myself up to face the day. I'm sure to sleep soundly tonight. Over the past two weeks the acoustics of the war have changed and we are hearing the many explosions more clearly. There hasn't really been an increase and they aren't really any closer we are just hearing them more and feeling them in walls. I don't know if it is a result in a shift in the prevailing winds or a heat effect in some way, but the bottom-line here is we can both hear and feel the booms more than before so my sleep is even more interrupted. I have reached the point of just being tired all the time. I need more time to recover from each mission and really don't mind having several days without missions in order to just idle about and physically rest.

Despite how that may sound my spirits are good and I feel healthy and robust. Just tired. Kind of like basic training.

August now looks to be very busy for me especially and the entire operation overall. Another month will go fast.
Love you guys and looking forward to heading home. rog

Dear Pat, 27 July 2006

Thanks for the great joke! I've shared it at our battle briefing and I intend to send it out in a newsletter home too. Really funny.

Re. Israel and the Arabs. I have for nearly my entire adult life said it is time to get it on over there. Kind of like the original Star Trek episode where two cultures are fighting a virtual war but have real casualties report to be evaporated and CPT Kirk destroys their virtual war machine and makes them put up or shut up. The Arab/Islamo-nazis insist that Israel is a lackey under the control of the USA. I believe we have a tiny bit of RESTRAINING control over Israel but ZERO enabling control and the Arabs ought to be singing our praises for restraining that nation over the last 50 years. Otherwise they would all be living in the free and democratic magnificent nation of Greater Israel stretching from the Sinai to Iran and maybe Afghanistan. How awful that would be! 300 million people living in freedom for the first time in 10,000 years. Maybe that is exactly what they are afraid of...

Anyway, Israel could roll through Syria, Lebanon and all of Gaza in about two weeks.

There has never been a nation of Palestine. Clearly after the last 50 years there is a real and legit nation of Israel. rog

"Greetings All,

"I have a request for each of you this week ....Please find a moment to drop a note in the mail to Roger. It can be a funny Hallmark Card, scenic postcard, personal note, etc...Just put something in the mail to him showing your support. I can hear how tired he is in his voice when I speak with him and he is sooo ready to come home. I think the job is extra hard right now due to the heat (upper 120s) and the novelty of escorting VIPs no longer holds the same appeal it did six months ago. Roger really needs a shot in the arm to help get him through the next several months.

"Thanks!!! Robyn"
**

Howdy everyone, 30 July 2006

A year ago (August 1) I said goodbye to co-workers, family and friends, heading out onto active duty. . .

I had ten missions this month. Most were two days. That's running hard. (August already looks worse!) And it is now 125-plus at some of our most frequent stops.

After all this time there are still "firsts" to see and do. I escorted a couple of Senate Appropriations Committee staff members to the construction site of the new US Embassy on the banks of the Tigris River (see attached photo of the forest of cranes). There are a dozen or so buildings going up simultaneously on a large campus right across the street from the Iraqi Judicial Center where the Saddam trial is nearing completion. Round the clock shifts by mostly Indian contractors, doing what appears to be quality work based on the volume and weaving of rebar going in. I was told recently that doing good concrete work in Iraq requires extra diligence as the readily accessible sand is so smooth after thousands of wind-blown years that it has no edges to which cement can bind. After only a few years concrete made of this typical sand will simply crumble. I have seen this happening in many buildings all over Iraq (including my hotel).

With the same delegation we caught a flight to Al Asad, the giant Marine Air Base in western Iraq. We rode in solemn honor with the flag-draped casket of an American soldier slowly making his way home.

At Al Asad we took a short flight to a tiny camp, about the size of my folk's 1 acre Grantville homestead. Camp Lueken is a primitive place where a small group of Americans live, train and work with the Iraqi Army and police to improve things along the Euphrates River between Ramadi and Haditha – two hot spots. They have limited air conditioning, and a three-holer outhouse latrine with a sign that says "NO SMOKING OR YOU WILL DIE" as the collection drums are partially filled with gasoline. I met some young Marine tankers there and they let me pet their M1-A1 Abrams tanks. These are remarkable young men doing remarkable work and we must be proud of them.

Their commander, Lieutenant Colonel Cooling, described the work out there as "whack a mole." The western region is so vast that there is always someplace where the bad guys can flee to without Americans around. So they whack them here only to see them pop up again over there. This is improving as this incredible LTC and his young Captains and Lieutenants continue to recruit and train police chiefs and policemen and to actually build police stations themselves. This is another area where the "insurgency" is really about criminal enterprises rather than politics or governance. A few thousand jobs would go a long way to fixing the whole region.

The Euphrates (see photo) is a smallish river at this point in the country and you can see the irrigated "green zone" only extends a few hundred yards from the banks. Renewed development of the ancient canals and aqueducts could spread this to tens of miles and restore this once abundant farming area.

Much of the violence in Baghdad today is based on vengeance and honor killings rather than politics and governance. In meetings with several commanders our dignitaries heard that the code of honor requires a significant payment for the death of a family member. If the financial payment is satisfactory then the death is waived off. If the price is not right or none at all then vengeance is required or the whole family and tribe is shamed. We have nothing like this in our culture. Introducing the rule of law remains a hurdle. That is why the adjudication of Saddam remains so critically important to the national psyche. If the courts can take care of him then people may be able to see the law can take care of them too. Right now people are killing out of vengeance more than sectarian hatred.

I finished writing a book for my daughter Regan, a voracious reader. It is about a sea gypsy child who survives the 2004 tsunami and many follow-on adventures. It was great stress-relief and Regan motivated me by begging for each chapter. In my remaining time here I think I'll focus downtime on reading which I dearly miss.

Sharp-eyed horticulturalist friend Randy Crandall pointed out the pretty pink blossoms from last week were: "Bougainvillea. We have them in KS but they are not hardy to be able to survive our winters." Thanks!

Here's a wonderful joke sent to me by Georgia friend Pat VanHooser:

When terrorist Abu Musab al-Zarqawi died, George Washington met him at the Pearly Gates. Washington slapped him across the face and yelled, "How dare you try to destroy the nation I helped conceive!"

Patrick Henry approached, punched Zarqawi in the nose and shouted, "You wanted to end our liberties, but you failed!"

James Madison followed, kicked him in the groin and said, "You are why I allowed our government to provide for the common defense!"

Thomas Jefferson was next, beat Osama with a cane and snarled, "It was evil men like you who inspired me to write the Declaration of Independence."

The beatings and thrashings continued as George Mason, James Monroe and 66 other early American leaders unleashed their anger on the terrorist.

Zarqawi lay bleeding, wept and said, "Allah this is not what you promised me."

God replied, "I told you there would be 72 Virginians waiting for you in Heaven. What did you think I said?"

Cards and letters from Pop, a full week (!) of 7 (including photo of a lovely 8.5 pound channel catfish and news that the cattle did not die in the 105 Kansas heat), Mom, little sister Karen, Adriel Class at TBC, new correspondent Evelyn Damron, Kansas Congressman Dennis Moore (who hasn't even been here but returned a "howdy" I sent through another Congressman), and Commerce Bank & Trust co-worker Carol Jacobs.

American by birth. Soldier by choice. Volunteer by God!

Roger T. Aeschliman
Major, Armor
Deputy Commander, First Kansas Volunteers

PS – At the end of July 16,225 miles in the air and 791 on the ground.

Dear Cathy, 30 JULY 2007

Thank you for your very prompt response regarding my boots. Based on my experience at the PX I wrongly assumed I was screwed and would hear nothing. I am very pleased that 5.11 will take care of this. Wow!

The boots are the HRT Boot, 310 Desert Sand, size 10.

My address is:

MAJ Roger T. Aeschliman
B Co 2-137 INF
APO AE 09342-1400

I will be here another three months or so.

Please pass on my praise to the entire organization. This is remarkable customer service.

Also, at a personal level please accept my deepest regret and condolences for the loss of your loved one. So many people are so far removed from this war that they don't understand how important this is. I pray that God will give you peace and comfort and fill your heart with joyous memories.

Most Sincerely your Friend,

rog

(Advertisement posted in National Review – hoping to find a publisher for this book and other creative endeavors. 01 July 2006)
**

Creative conservative deployed Baghdad seeks entrepreneur/angel to publish, manufacture projects upon return USA.

From: Lyn Smith
Date: Monday, July 31, 2006 8:13 pm
Subject: Tour of Duty

Guys - I just wanted to touch base and make sure "my guys" are doing ok and to philosophize for a minute.

Roger, I really appreciate your weekly updates. Robyn forwards them faithfully. I look forward each week to learning what's happening in the JVB and how your team is getting along. These notes are invaluable and I share them with others in my office who have loved ones deployed. The feedback is that your notes help keep them level-set and also help them ignore the negative news reports. Your efforts have a much wider impact than I think you know. Keep it up.

You guys are nearing the homestretch of your tour. You should be proud of your accomplishments to this point.

Having said that, I feel compelled to make a couple of comments and offer some unsolicited advice. Jim I know you are on top of this, but I'm gonna remind you anyway.

You are entering what is possibly the most dangerous part of your deployment. Many of your soldiers feel like combat veterans and will act like they know everything --- they don't. This will be especially true when you begin the transition process with your replacements. You know it is dangerous for your snuffys to have that mindset. It is more dangerous for your leadership to develop that mindset. Be certain your Company grade officers and Sr NCO's keep their focus. These last few months are going to be much like the last two or three days of AT. It will be easy for them to begin to let their minds wander to life after Iraq. Don't let them do that until they get off the plane at home.

It is also easy for you to become overwhelmed by everything on your plate. You gotta keep doing your regular missions while picking up the missions of other units that rotate with no replacements. You gotta plan transition activities for your replacements while preparing to redeploy. Not to mention the added tasks of trying to keep Kansas Leadership (and Staff) happy with all their requests plus the information needs of the various FSG's. Please remember that every soldier in the unit is counting on you to provide the leadership and well developed plans. To do that, you've got to take care of yourselves (eat, sleep) and ensure that your subordinate leaders are doing the same.

I fully understand how the mission-load and task list can overwhelm you. Just hang in there and do the things you know how to do with the same intensity as when you started. The priorities have not changed --- it's still mission accomplishment followed closely by soldier care and then everything else. Bring 'em home safe. Thanks for your patience and for allowing a crusty old Infantryman to philosophize. More importantly, thanks for your incredible service and sacrifice to our great Nation!!!

FIRST KANSAS
Smith
**

Dear Col Smith,

Thanks so much for your faithful and refreshing notes. It is nice to get a long-distance pat on the head and your thoughts are always timely and cogent. LTC Trafton read your remarks to the command and staff team yesterday and it helps for the younger leaders to hear another version of the same sermon then they know it's not just Jim and Roger yammering once again, but real and important.

I think the overall morale is good now that the Slayer team has got off of 12 hours shifts and is getting a little down time. JVB morale is high.

I am personally grinding down. It has gotten so hot that the six or seven days in a row I could do in Feb and March has dwindled to three or four MAX! And then I need two or three days off to just sleep and eat. It's hell getting old! CPT Denney and a LT will be on leave during August so I'll just suck it up and get it done under the August mission surge but I will be pretty beat up by the end of the month.

Nevertheless, good spirits here and looking forward to a beer with you.

Any thoughts for me about possible LTC assignments after we demob? Right now I appear homeless and starting to ask for advice from key folks like you.

Best wishes. rog

From: Neil Gibson
To: raeschliman
Sent: Tuesday, August 01, 2006 2:58 PM
Subject: Topeka in August

Roger.

Thanks for the nice letter. I am surprised that you had time to dash off a note with the agenda that I read about in your last email.

The heat sounds brutal over there. In 1998 I spent 7 weeks in Africa with heat from 110 to 120 each day. We hunted everyday except for three travel days so I have an idea of what you are going through now. We were constantly on the watch for armed poachers so, in a smaller way, we had some of the side amenities that you guys have over there.

The media here is making it sound like there is no bright spot in the whole Iraqi stage but we all know that isn't right. It will take some real action in Iran to stop the Shia death squads sponsored by Iran and some action by snipers to stop the Sunni death squads. Would like your candid view of what the odds are that the Iraqi Congress can survive. If it does not I fear for conservative elected officials over here in 2008. Am sure that the Sunnis and Shea know that and are pushing hard to dissolve the Congress. There is the Vietnam example of this nation's long term resolve in the face of conflict that is not a direct threat to us. Our national attention span is about that of a gnat. Our overweight and spoiled kids have their Ipods, cell phones, text messaging etc. and have no idea of how fragile our democracy is if one generation flakes out on us. And that looks as if it is going to happen. Can only hope that the next generation will knee jerk the other way. I am anxious to see what these kids do when the Boomer parents die off and they have to provide for themselves. Gentile poverty might be the outlook for most of an entire generation.

I have another box coming that will speak to some of the issues you mention in your email.

Thanks for taking the time to write. The pictures are excellent and enjoyed by a large group that you don't even know about. You write well and may others enjoy your views and experiences.

Hang in Major!

Neil Gibson
**

Hi Neil,

Thanks for your note too. For me writing is fun and therapeutic, so not very hard to do. We surged again since we've corresponded then faded yet again. The tempo is odd but we're getting used to it and take the reduced pace eagerly now. You know a little boredom is a good thing.

My dad sends me copies of American Hunter and Kansas Wildlife and Parks so I get to keep up to date on the hunting scene. I envy you your trip to Africa for whatever game you hunted. I devour the African big game articles and look forward to that opportunity one day. I do go crazy when I read about the No-hunting policies in some of our national parks, then read about the government issuing million dollar contracts to thin the overpopulated herds of elk. Just open it up to hunters and MAKE MONEY for taxpayers instead of spending it. Are our priorities screwed up or what?

I want you to feel good about the young'uns out there. The fine young men I work with are top notch, good thinkers and they get it. I think they clearly represent the typical American youth, even if they are not flocking into the military. IF they were told by our president that military service now is important and if he told them why I think you would see them pour into the service in numbers like WWII enlistments. I think most of them are nearly totally restrained by their parents who are failing them by coddling them so and are reflecting their flawed memories of growing up during the Vietnam era. They know nothing of that war and have taken the wrong lessons from the 60s all together. Sorry to rant...

Universal service could be the answer. That way, no matter what else happens the rest of their lives they would know that they CAN be in shape, they CAN control themselves and their impulses, they CAN follow directions and orders, and CAN perform beyond their pre-established limits. Eight weeks of basic and skills training followed by two years of hard work can set a lot right and would certainly produce a better crop of college freshmen.

Sorry, ranting again.

Over here is both terrible and great at the same time. On the large scale there is continuous and dramatic improvement in the ability of the Iraq Army and

Police, the national government, the economy, the education system, the water, sewer, trash, power, oil infrastructure, on and on. It is in the security arena where it ebbs and flows and that is of course the only arena the media cares about. Regarding the national parliament, these folks are taking their work pretty seriously and their security very seriously. They are murder and kidnap targets but there have been few incidents. They do posture and bicker but that is normal for any government. They have lots of work to do as there really is NO body of law in existence over here or in any Arabic country. They will have to establish laws and justice themselves. Hanging Saddam will help a lot I believe. Hope they get around to it soon but I've heard they are adjourned until October now to consider the case.

You probably saw the news last few days of Abizaid saying civil war could break out IF security doesn't improve. I'm sure he is right as he is a true expert in this region and fluent in the language but he also knows and said it shouldn't happen as Iraqi and American forces are surging into Baghdad now to quell the cycle of kill, revenge kill, revenge kill, etc. We'll see how it all looks in early October. The mess in Lebanon is worrisome around here as the hatred of Israel is irrational, deep and lasting. There is no argument or discussion about it. They just blame all their problems on the Jews and that's that. Maybe we should just encourage Israel to go ahead and wipe out a few million Arabs and triple the size of their country. It couldn't get worse there than it is now.

Well friend, thanks for the note. rog

From: Bob Caplinger
To: raeschliman
Sent: Thursday, August 03, 2006 9:34 PM
Subject: Boxes

Hi Roger,

I attended Rotary today. Al read your most recent message and it was well received; they all are.

I wish I could adequately express our appreciation for your weekly messages. Our Jesse is not given to expressing his activities or what happens around him (maybe that's per instructions; if so, he's really doing a good job of following orders.)

Helen and I have finally gotten around to getting the PO Boxes and the stuff to go in them. We will take them to the Post Office tomorrow. It sounds like a great idea.

Take care of yourself.

Bob & Helen Caplinger
**

Dear Bob and Helen.

Thanks so much for your nice note. I will thump Jesse on the noggin and tell him to write or call more often.

I enjoy writing the weekly update as a chance to exercise the old newspaper skills from way back so it's not a strain. In many ways it's therapeutic.

Thanks in advance for the box. I can hardly explain how much it will be appreciated but I'll try once we start deliveries.

With much affection, your friend, rog

"Greetings All,

"Thanks to all of you who put a note in the mail to Roger this week. We just got off the webcam with him and he is in the good spirits – just complaining about the heat but then I'm doing the same. ☺

"Robyn"
**

Howdy everyone, 06 August 2006

The birds here all mope around, tails dragging, beaks gaping, tongues hanging to cool themselves. We have not seen south of 90 degrees (even at night) for a month. I can no longer exercise noonish as the temperature (AND surprising occasional high humidity plume from God knows where) is prohibitive. It is better at 0700 or 0800 as it is only 100 or so degrees by then and one can put in a few miles without collapsing.

So, it is hot. All the sources say August is yet hotter. Something to look forward to.

Have you seen the movie "Groundhog Day?" It is a funny and robust film with an architecture to support any metaphorical position you want to hang on it. A cynical and shallow newscaster becomes stuck in time covering Groundhog Day over and over perhaps into infinity. Well, that's what it's like here. The dignitary changes but everything else is exactly the same. The same airplanes drop them off at the same places. The same helicopters take us to the same meetings with the same presenters covering the same topics using the same slides. We visit the same troops at the same mess halls and send them away from the same airport pads to find our own way home late at night. Over and over and over and over and over and over and over and over and over until we are redeemed and allowed to go home to Kansas. Amen.

We hade five Congressmen this week, then the Secretary of Agriculture, Mike Johanns, formerly Governor of Nebraska. Johanns was pleasant and a good mission. I helped by giving camera batteries to a newsman traveling with the group and by providing a roll of heavy tape to a whole gaggle of media to secure their cords and cables at a news conference. It's all magic pulled out of the rucksack that a good escort officer carries. On demand I can produce heavy string, five kinds of batteries, two kinds tape, two sizes of baggies, five kinds of gum, breath mints, superglue, extra earplugs and goggles, flashlights, lighters, pens, pencils, paper, calling cards, calling instructions from any kind of phone to any other kind of phone, bug spray, sunscreen, laser pointer, basic hygiene products, eating utensils, wet wipes, spare gloves, three forms of communications and enough food and water for four people for a day in a crisis. Sometimes I carry a defibrillator as well, for the people who unwisely choose to come.

During the Congressional visit we went to one of the hottest (as in most active) combat zones interestingly named Area of Operations Topeka. Nothing like back at home. After we said goodbye to them (but before our flight back) I got an informal tour of the giant C-5 Galaxy cargo plane. It is up a twelve foot ladder and you step into a hold half as wide and twice as long as a basketball court. And you could shoot a basketball in there too with the high ceiling. It has a separate troop seating for 75, and a spacious cockpit and crew area, where six of the 12 crew can sleep at a time. Huge! To see one take off is to confound the laws of physics. It looks like the Queen Elizabeth II with wings.

The Secretary of Ag said he would say hello to former Kansas Governor Bill Graves for me. He also brought an interesting travel group with him: Mike Martin, President of New Mexico State University, Terry Harris, Vice President of Riceland Foods, Inc., and Ken Root, newsman for WHO radio in Chicago (who put me on the air live to tell all of Chicagoland about the war effort). They were more fun to visit with than the usual gaggle of aides, and more appreciative. It was great to see the private sector here. A couple of days ago I learned the Iraq economy grew 30 percent last year!

The helicopters and airplanes all sport a suite of flares to defend against missiles. The system senses pressure, heat, light and noise and a computer crunches those sensings using algorithms to determine what a missile attack is or is not. At the right combination of sensings it decides an attack is underway and automatically fires flares. It calculates a billion times an hour. If it senses a car backfiring (noise and pressure) and a BBQ flaring up (heat and light) in proximity it could read that as a "missile" and deploy flares. This happens frequently and despite our briefings and explanations the sudden and brilliant flares are anxiety producing for our guests. We've even seen Congressmen issue news releases that they were attacked in Iraq when no such thing happened. I only mention all of this because one night this week our helicopter was coming in for a landing at the Baghdad Airport simultaneously with a C-130 cargo plane. The plane's computer sensed the Blackhawk helicopters as a threat and fired flares. The helicopter pilots wearing night vision goggles were blinded by the flares and the resulting 10 seconds was the most exciting ride I've ever had. I was wearing a crew headset and heard 30 seconds of the most colorful language I've ever heard, and not one word repeated.

Cards and letters from ALL my parents in one day (Mom and Pop, Mom Mary Lou, and Dad Roger and Mom Audrey in California), Pop x 4, Topeka friend Beth Fager, North Dakota Governor John Hoeven, Congressman Adam Putnam, four cards from new friends in Chester, NE, New Jersey beach vacation card from Pat VanHooser, and a delightful little book called "Dear Soldier," letters from children sent by dear friend Maria Wilson (nee Russo).

Makasib boxes from Pat VanHooser, Augusta, Ga. (3), Rotary buddy Eldon Sloan, Ken and Aleda Berry, Topeka (and a box of cookies for me), LTC Dick Spingler (State Farm!), Topeka, Roy and Gerry Browning, (Rotary) Topeka, Judy and Terry Kimes, (running pal) Topeka.

American by birth. Soldier by choice. Volunteer by God!

Roger T. Aeschliman
Major, Armor
Deputy Commander, First Kansas Volunteers

To: Maria Russo-Wilson
Date:July 7, 2006
Subject: Makasib Q&A

1. What is your title, unit, etc. (I have absolutely no military background? please answer this simply yet completely and with clarity.)

Major Roger T. Aeschliman, Deputy Commander, 2-137 Infantry Battalion, Kansas Army National Guard, and Chief, Joint Visitors' Bureau, Multi-National Forces Iraq.

2. Other than Rotary and Leadership Greater Topeka, what are a few of your community activities?

current Board of Directors Jayhawk Area Council Boy Scouts of America; current United Way of Greater Topeka Public Relations Committee; past Board of Directors of the National Guard Association of Kansas; and president of the USD 450 Board of Education. Many others...

3. When did you get to Iraq? When will you leave Iraq?

I was the first person from the battalion to arrive in Iraq, early November 2005. Return is classified but we anticipate being home in Topeka come early winter.

4. How many other Kansans are in your unit? How many Topekans? Can you give me their names (adds to the personal connection)?

The entire 500 plus soldiers are based in Kansas. Most are Kansans. We have units in Kansas City, Lawrence, Wichita. Only a few of us are from Topeka. I can give names with their permission and I'll check around on this.

5. How does sending the boxes help our soldiers?

See the last answer on the following Q&A.

6. Please describe Makasib.

Same. But it is a small town of single family dwellings sitting right outside the walls of the Baghdad International Airport. The mosque minaret and school peak over the wall. There is an empty swimming pool. Two mosques but one is closed. Many animals live right in the town with the people. It is not uncommon to see sheep and goats and cattle being driven through the streets. There are not many satellite dishes on roofs in this town. They are poor.

7. Please describe the work that the unit is doing there.

The military work is to patrol the community frequently to prevent terrorists from moving in and taking over to create a base of operations. This protects our base camps and the airport. The humanitarian mission is to apply US military resources and state department funding to make their lives better in any way possible within the funding limits we are given. So it's kind of one project at a time. Individual health care is so far down the list that it will never be funded by the US government and it's not safe enough for a non-governmental organization/charity to come in a do something. This kind of work is going on all over Iraq, US unit by US unit.

8. Please describe the Royal Palace Complex and the Family Clinic.

The RPC is a series of Saddam palaces built around a Saddam lake resort area outside of the airport. It is a secure US base area and our Kansas troops both guard it and conduct patrols out of it. Their primary job there is to protect the airport and keep the highways clear of IEDS so convoys can bring materials in and out of Iraq. The family clinic there is opened twice a week allowing Iraqi farm families in for medical treatment, giveaways of all types, and to generally keep the pulse of the area. It is about five miles from Makasib on the southwest corner of the airport wall. The service providers are US medics and physicians assistants. It is strictly a humanitarian mission. Otherwise these people have no care of any kind as they live in mud hut farmsteads or tiny hamlets of four or five huts. The products for these clinic rooms would stay in the clinic and the unit that replaces us will have them available to continue this service in the future.

9. Is there a deadline for sending items?

For my unit to distribute and install these things we really need them by mid-October so a shipping deadline of late September. Sooner is better. There is another Kansas unit that recently arrived and we are in touch so we can arrange for continuity regardless but I and the Infantry get the most bang ASAP. In the event things arrive too late a unit from Kentucky will replace us and we can tee them up.

10. Is there an address to use after you personally are gone?

Not yet but if we see that need then yes, I can set you up with one of the Kansas guys that will be here another nine months.

11. Can I give your name/address to the Topeka Capital Journal?

If you think it would help the cause then I think so but Robyn is antsy still about predators who rob the homes of deployed soldiers. Visit with her and then when the time comes we'll grit our teeth and deal with it.

12. I thought in one of your messages you had also mentioned school supplies (or maybe I'm just confused by all the back-to-schools sales right now). If those are also needed, please describe the educational system and how items will be distributed.

The other Kansas unit (out of Kansas City) is working with school groups and a couple of churches on school supplies and clothing so not needed from your end.

13. How will the personal hygiene items and toys be distributed?

These will be given out person by person by our Kansas soldiers on patrol. It will be planned rather than random but you can still expect to see a mob scene that happens whenever anything is offered. They really have nothing. We have nothing like this in the US. If you have nothing in the US any church and any of ten thousand charities will feed, clothe and shelter you. There is no such support system here.

14. Why should people do this? I, personally, am willing because you are the one asking, so it is a personal and credible request. Also, I have seen that kind of poverty in other countries, so there is a humanitarian aspect that I respond to. Those two factors will hit a number of Rotarians. What else? Why should people who don't know you and who believe all of our resources should stay local and who don't support the war, etc, get involved? What are the rest of my selling points?

These are people who are living in their own tiny little society, barely subsistence. They are open to peace and freedom and liberty and democracy and are seeing examples every day from Kansas soldiers who don't want anything from them except smiles. This is a chance to open the world to them that they have never seen in 10,000 years of settlement in this area. Healthy happy children, women not dying in childbirth, 1000 people who think America is a good thing.

15. To what extent do you believe that after you leave, the items will still be distributed/used as you intend?

100% The transition between Kansas and our replacement unit will be seamless.

16. Could you please send a pic of you, one or two of Makasib and its citizens, one of the Makasib clinic, one of the Royal Palace Clinic? I'll blow up the pics to use as part of the plea to the other clubs.

RPC (not the clinic) is attached seen from 300 feet in a Blackhawk. I'll work on this. Give me a week.

17. What other relevant details have you not told me?

Only that you are incredible and Mike is a very lucky guy!

Q&A part 2

1. Obviously, shipping will be a major factor in this project. If we sent you money, do you and yours have the ability/time/place to purchase what you are looking for?

Money is a bad idea for several reasons. First, most of these things would need to be purchased from the US or Europe anyway and then shipped here. Second, sending cash in the mail is dangerous no matter what. And third, as this is not a formal government/Army program the risk of accounting/fraud accusations is tremendous and we should not taint what will be a great help for Iraqi people with any hint of impropriety. Don't send money. Rotary doesn't hear THAT often does it?

2. What do you see as the pros/cons of us sending you money vs. the items you have requested?

See above. If you actually ship the items here there is a clear and precise custody chain and good accountability. They will deliver right to our doorstep and then our soldiers can deliver right to the need.

3. Our help would be but a drop in the bucket of the help that Makasib needs. Why should we do this?

The people of Makasib are welcoming and like Americans. They have suffered minor intrusions from terrorists but they don't like them and don't want them around. They are isolated from the rest of Baghdad by a few miles and are a totally agriculturally based community. Since 2003 they have been off the Iraq power grid, had no governmental services, no education and no medical care. Until the Kansas unit arrived no Americans even went there as it was no risk. Kansas soldiers have been patrolling there now for six months and have "triaged" the overall needs there. First is clean water and it is nearly completed. Restoration of canals and irrigation for crops is approved and nearly done. School repairs, desks, equipment is approved and underway. Getting the town back on the grid is underway. There are no Army or US government plans to do anything in the health care arena. Funding only goes so far... There is a medical clinic with a table and some chairs with a generator for electricity. Baghdad medical providers used to come but quit because they had nothing to work with. The list you received would furnish a clinic to a level that doctors from Baghdad could come out a couple of days a week, fall in on the clinic and help people. This is clearly a help people to help themselves plan. We already have churches and schools sending clothing, shoes, and school supplies for this town. So the big end cost items are covered or will be, the smallest end is covered, and it is this middle size that government won't do and that kids and churches can't do. The value to your Kansas soldiers to be able to deliver a furnished medical clinic is immeasurable. It would show 5,000 ordinary Iraqis (most very young or very old) that Americans care about them, that US soldiers are on the side of goodness, and that there is a future for them and their children.

FROM: MAJ Roger T. Aeschliman, 510-66-0830

SUBJECT:SURFACE TO AIR FIRE INCIDENT 2230 HOURS 08 AUG 06

At approximately 2230 hours 08 AUG 06 helicopter mission 0808B from Balad to Liberty Main received small arms fire from the ground. I and SPC Brian Martin, Combat Medic, were aboard returning from a mission with Congressional Delegates. The mission was delayed about one hour at Balad. I was in the front left seat near the left door gunner and SPC Martin was behind me somewhere. Also on board were two DSS agents who left Iraq for the USA the next day and Paul Janiczek, US Department of State employee. I was looking forward and out of the corner of my eye saw flashing by the left side of the helicopter. I assumed it was the helicopter deploying flares and turned to see. I could clearly tell these were small arms tracers and I saw three or four tracers go by the aircraft at the 7 or 8 o'clock position about 40-50 meters out. I shouted at the gunner to get his attention as he was looking forward. He turned to look at me. At the same time another streak of tracers went up off the front quarter of the helicopter, about the 10 o'clock position, perhaps 50-100 meters out. I shouted and pointed again and this time he looked to the front. At that moment the helicopter begun to turn left, directly into the path of the tracers and I tapped the gunner on the arm and pointed out of the helicopter at the tracers. As he turned again to look where I was pointing a final streak of tracers went up to our seven or eight o'clock position 30-50 meters out. With his goggles on the gunner could not see anything through the narrow field of view. Each time he looked away from where the tracers were. After the third set of tracers someone on the ground opened fire upon the person who was shooting at us and the person that was shooting at us returned fire at the person on the ground. In a moment several other shooters on the ground all engaged each other and we watched this firefight for about a minute before moving out of sight. When we landed at Liberty Main two or three minutes later I shouted at the gunner asking if he saw the tracers in the air. He said he saw the "fireworks" on the ground. I doubt he ever understood what I was trying to say and point at. The pilots and the other gunner would not have seen anything through their field of vision with the goggles and the direction of view. SPC Martin indicated to me that he observed the surface to air fire at our helicopter. Based on the location of the two burning gas flares that are visible at night from the air, and our direction of travel when I oriented to the Camp Victory landmarks, I would place the location of the ground fire in the Kadhamiyah neighborhood, although it was dark and I am unsure of the route.

"Greetings All,

"We webcammed with Roger this morning and he sends the following message to read before reading this week's update: Please don't be alarmed or concerned about this weeks's report. I am fine and feel great. We just live with these things now." So, don't be too concerned. He assured me that this is pretty normal and you get used to it and it never really felt like he was in real danger. I suppose that is a matter of opinion though. (Says his wife). Please keep the prayers going.

This week's photos are of a soldier-signed 500 pound bomb, the ER at Balad hospital, and wall art at Balad that is self-explanatory.

"Enjoy, Robyn"
**

Howdy everyone, 13 August 2006

Officially this week in Baghdad we hit the 118-119 range. But that's the ambient heat, in the shade. The radiant heat, out in the sun, on concrete or white gravel, with the trees, dirt and barrier walls all radiating pushes the index off the charts.

Early one evening at Balad waving goodbye to Congressmen the movement of my hand through the air actually hurt. About 2230 hours, flying over the desert in the dark, the wind and rotor wash pouring in the helicopter, the air flowing under my seat was so hot I had to sit on my gloves for a while as my tush was burning.

Later that same flight as we entered Baghdad our helicopter took small arms fire from the ground. It is kind of pretty to see the tracers racing up, arcing across the sky. Hajji is firing blind, shooting at the sound as the dark green Blackhawk's are invisible at night. After a few moments the fire shifted down and became a ground battle that we watched for a minute or two as tracers zipped over the city below. This is the first time I've been directly targeted. Everything else has been mortars, rockets and IEDs randomly coming or going, none too close. I feel fine. It's all just so much noise these days.

Mom and sister Ronna ask about medical services. Most units, including mine have a medic nearby all the time. We see him informally for minor things. For anything that would take you to the doctor there is a formal sick call clinic about two miles away. Doctors, nurses, and physician's assistants there can prescribe and treat, stitch, patch and cast. If there is anything more significant – wounds or illnesses – the patients are helicoptered directly to one of many surgical hospitals in the country. There is one at the airport mostly for Iraqi prisoners, and the main one downtown in the International Zone. All big bases have good hospitals so a wounded soldier is only 20 or 30 minutes from aggressive treatment. Once stabilized a severely wounded soldier is transported to the theater hospital at Balad (run by the Air Force) for major trauma surgery. If they cannot be returned to duty from there within a few days and just need more recovery they are sent to Qatar for recuperation. If they are still in need of higher level care they are flown to Germany, and if necessary back to the USA. In the most extreme cases a patient would move to say the IZ, then Balad, then either Rhamstein or Washington, all within about 12-15 hours. The overwhelming majority of US patients are treated locally and returned to duty. Finally, if one of our dignitaries were stricken or wounded we always have our own medic for emergency aid, followed by immediate helicopter flight to the closest major hospital.

With the Congressmen this week we were allowed to watch two Iraq soldiers come in by helicopter and receive emergency work. There were amazing pumps that put two bags of blood into the patient in about one minute. They x-rayed on the spot and had them out of shock and stable in about five minutes. These people are good!

We toured the F-16 Strike Eagle airplanes and watched the Congressmen sign their names to 500-pound bombs slung under the wings. Also saw the Predator remote control airplanes (looking like a cross between a kite and the monster from "Alien").

I had the President of Romania for a day. He was tanned and spoke good English. He and the President of Iraq (who looks like the character actor Wilford Brimley) conversed in English rather than through translators. The universal language. Uneventful and pleasant group. When we do it right no one knows. Talked with a Romanian reporter who studied at Missouri and we argued about whether my dear K-State or his rancid Mizzou had the best journalism school.

Also had 4-star Admiral Ulrich, who runs Navy operations in the Europe area and for NATO. That trip was perfect. The Admiral's aide ran everything on time. The flights were perfect, and our JVB drivers were great. We run aggressive motorcades to ensure the protection of the dignitary and that includes driving straight at unyielding traffic. There is probably a big market for Depends among the Iraq civilians driving around the International Zone when we are transporting a package.

This week the Iraqi National Military Command took charge of the 1St Iraqi Army Division. This marks the first time a major Iraq unit is operating outside of American Command. Yet another great step toward Iraq national integrity.

Cards and letters from Pop x 4, sister Ronna x 2, Mom, Robyn, Congressman Thad McCotter, Jeff Wagaman, Amy and Greg McLaren, Chuck and Helen Worthington, Linda Crandall, Judy and Terry Kimes, Joyce and Dave Phillippi, Jean and Wilbert Crouse, Sonna and Don Alexander, and Susan (?) from San Diego. Mark Yardley, Vera Goodman, Judy and Jim Wood, Peggy and Larry Yingling, Jim McHenry. US Senator George Allen, Dorothy Hamler, Linda Gwaltney, Don and Marie Boaz, Mary Alice Avery, Jane Williamson Pauley, Al Williams, Leasa Huffman, Carole Ries, Mary Lou McPhail, Terry Wages x 2, Steve Caplinger, Wayne and Shirley Daniel, Lew and June Golden, Linda Hubbard, US Congress Sergeant at Arms Bill Livingood, Marge Frederick, Les Krull, Harry Briscoe, Brad Malone, US Senator Jack Reed, Glen and Darlene McLaren, and Jacque Brown. Books from college fraternity brother, Troy Mcvicker, and survival rations from Ranger (ret) Neil Gibson with great letter that all the soldiers are enjoying reading.

Robyn confessed she suggested I could use a picker upper. Wow! I can't possibly write everyone back. Though I am unworthy of such attention please know I am very grateful for your expressions of concern and affection. Consider me picked up!

Makasib boxes from Judy and Terry Kimes, Topeka, Mom and Pop x 2, Mark Yardley, Greg McLaren and the gang at the Federal Home Loan Bank x 4, Gary and Diane Aeschliman x 2, Ken and Aleda Berry, Jim and Judy Wood, Bob Caplinger, and through Maria Wilson and the Topeka Rotary Clubs some interesting and exciting discussion about providing medical equipment for the Makasib clinic.

American by birth. Soldier by choice. Volunteer by God!

Roger T. Aeschliman
Major, Armor
Deputy Commander, First Kansas Volunteers

This wall art at LSA Anaconda near the Iraq city of Balad is a powerful and simple statement of soldiers keeping their focus in despite 130 degree heat!

Dear family, 14 AUGUST 2006

By the time you get this you will all have finished the first week of school (and maybe the second if the mail is slow). This new school year is a big event in all our lives. Mom back to work for the first time since 1992...Ryan into High School...Regan into Middle School...and me over here. This is the first time I have ever missed seeing you two kids off to school on the first day of class. That makes me sad but I know that you won't want me and mother hanging around the bus stop any more now that you are all growed up – just like the Rugrats.

I just want you all to know how proud I am of each of you.

Robyn who worked so hard to earn her master's degree in such a short time and with perfect grades and then facing such difficult decisions about whether to return to work before her desired timetable. For keeping our wonderful family on track all these years and for keeping her own independence and sense of self the entire time.

Ryan for working so hard in middle school and making such great progress in scouting and music and all his other interests. I know you will be a great student in high school and explore all the opportunities there.
Regan for doing such a great job throughout grade school and now finally moving on into the big leagues. You will have a grand time there, learn and develop new interests and make a whole pile of new friends to add to your pile of old friends.

I ask you all to please remember to be nice to each other this fall semester. Each of you will be challenged in different ways and will face difficulties. If you fall into the trap of thinking that you are the only one under stress you will not see that each of you needs a pat on the back and a hug. You all can count on each other and can tell each other what is going on. Share your experiences and help each other to get through this dramatic year of total change.

I wish I were there to help you all and support you but we know that's not possible. So please remember as well that you can talk to me on the phone and I may have thoughts or opinions you may find helpful. Also, please remember to be nice to me and take the time to chit chat about your day or week. I really am living a nice normal life through you guys and when you tell me the normal, boring daily stuff it helps keep me sane.

I am ready to come home but they won't let me yet, so we'll just keep on trucking until the day comes that I get back to Kansas to be with you.

Have a great first few weeks of school and a tremendous first semester.

Love you all,

Dad/rog

Dear Neil, 14 AUG 2006

Thanks so very much for the great letter and box of tuna rats. I am now officially set for the rest of the tour. I've got a couple cartons of tuna stashed in the ruck and am nibbling on the rest for mid-day, post PT snacks. You rock!

I've shared your letter broadly and the troops love it. You are a good writer and they love hearing you dog an ole' dumbass tanker Major.

Officially I can't tell you but unofficially we all expect to be home by Thanksgiving. Yum! I should be home for the deer rifle season and have a couple of local farmers that let us thin the does which my father and I do eagerly to fill the freezers. If you would like to come up you would certainly be welcome but where we hunt the land owners do limit us to does and I doubt you would want to spring for a Kansas non-resident tag for a lowly female.

At your convenience tell me all about BC and what you do up there. The predator control sounds like lots of fun and I am among those who laugh at the ninnies who want to save the wolves and cougars. It is a bit cruel but I can't help but smile whenever I read about some hippies getting eaten by cougars or bears. Same with the tree-setters who get stoned and fall out of the trees...

Please forgive me for not mailing you a thank you. With all the cards and letters and Makasib boxes coming in right now, and with our aggressive op tempo I just don't have the time. I know it's rude but hope you will understand.

With great admiration, rog

My dear friend Troy, 14 AUG 2006

I cannot thank you enough for the wonderfully kind card AND books. Your taste in history is certainly similar to mine and I am already devouring the Meriwether Lewis biography. I've heard of both these books but read neither so you hit the nail on the head.

I would send a personal note in the mail but I am swamped with cards, letters and Makasib boxes. Robyn's appeal for a kind word or two has resulted in many dozen letters to which I simply do not have the time to respond due to our incredible optempo right now. So again, thanks and please don't think me a social dolt for failing to send a thank you note in the mail.

Enjoy your great time with your daughter, the beautiful and talented McKenna, and tell her there is a soldier who frequently looks at the photo of her and her father taped to his wall in Iraq and remembers with clarity why he is there.

With love, rog

From: David Dawdy
To: Roger Aeschliman
Sent: Wednesday, August 16, 2006 8:58 AM
Subject: Dawdy in WI

Roger,

Mighty proud to know that one of us is over there keeping the facts straight!

I corresponded with a nurse from Wisconsin for awhile and she gave me some pretty realistic descriptions of what it was like in her camp, plus she said that everything smelled like wet camels - damn. I'll pray for you to stay safe and keep your sanity.

We're behind you 100%, Roger.

Perge, Brother!

David Dawdy
**

Brother Dave,

Thank for the note. I've never smelled a wet camel so I'll have to believe her but I can vouch that the sewage system critically lacks the "system" part. Looking forward to seeing you at some delightful reunion. rog

Email chain 18 Aug 2006
**

Tom,

I think I know Roger! When I was little (7-10) we lived in the little Eastern Kansas town of Grantville where my dad served as pastor at the United Methodist Church there. There was an Aeschliman family who lived there and were members of the church. They had two sons, Rick and Roger along with three daughters, Ronna, Ruthann, and a younger daughter whose name I don't remember (Karen maybe), but who Les was kinda sweet on and was his age. I had the biggest crush on the girls and used to write Ruthann for years after we moved. My sister Carola had a crush on Roger for a long time as well. Anyway, I'm pretty sure Roger went to KSU and is the same person in this letter. He would be about 45 years old now. I'd sure like to know if it is him. Is there a way to maybe forward this message to him from me in hopes of finding out if he is the same Roger Aeschliman I knew? I'd sure like to find out.

Thanks! Alex Lankhorst
**

Hello all – I think this is the Roger we all know too. How many Aeschliman's could there be – in Kansas – and from KSU? What a great writer too – even sounds like him. I don't know if anyone remembers but he and I even went to a formal at the Brookville Hotel when he was at KSU – this was when it was still in Brookville. The crush was just as real then as it was when I was a kid – let me tell you. He is a great guy and a real gentlemen too. Tom – do you know this Roger, or are you forwarding something from a friend? Anyway – please keep me on your cc's. I'd like to know if this is our mutual friend.

Carola
**

Greetings old and new friends!

I hope this finds everyone well. I must confess to being the old Grantville Roger Aeschliman and apologize for being such a terrible friend, out of touch for these long years. It is very nice to hear from you now and it brings back many pleasant memories.

Hot summer nights at the little league baseball diamond with your parents in lawn chairs cheering for which ever gaggle of sprouts was playing; giving the Lankhorst family members rides on the little blue mini-bike; being tormented and teased by Carola unmercifully until I finally whacked her with my baseball glove (forgetting I had a baseball inside it) and then running away in terror as she went screaming and crying home. I think I did about two months of extra farm work as punishment...

How old then? 13, 14?

I'm afraid there may be evidence still out there of underage drinking on the part of Carola and me at the Brookville Hotel. At one time I had a party photo of the two of us and a number of equally lit up partygoers all leaning on each other for mutual support. I'm sure I would have fallen down otherwise. Goodness, how did we ever survive those years? And it scares the beejeebeez out of me to know my own children 12 and 14 will be doing the same sorts of things in a few years.

From the several e-mails I cannot tell who knows whom exactly but I do remember Karen from one or two visits at KSU to see her brothers in my fraternity; and Tom, while we have not met, I am a brother in arms in the financial industry, serving as a trust officer at Commerce Bank and Trust in Topeka. I still have a number of college friends in Salina, Dennis and Cindy Egan, Steve Blackwell, Kelly Thomas, and others I'm sure. If you know any of them please send them a howdy from the great hot desert.

So, thank you all for your inquiries and please let me know if I may ever assist any of you in any manner. Feel free to contact me back at this address, but please do not pass it on to others as the military email system limits my traffic and cannot handle large "junk mail" type files.

Most truly your old friend, rog

Howdy everyone, 20 August 2006

Mid-August 2005 I began writing these weekly reports to home. It's a pretty small group that has been reading from the beginning. Certainly fewer than 100. Now I'm sure it must be in the several thousands. I regularly hear from friends saying "I forward it to 20-30 people and I know they send it on." I also hear from people saying "you don't know me but I'm a friend of so-and-so who sends me your letter," but I don't even know who so-and-so is. It has been a great joy to connect with old friends as well. Just this week I corresponded with childhood pals (the Lankhorst family now in Salina) and with fraternity brothers in Wisconsin (Dawdy), Arizona (Vanier), Texas (Morris) and Uganda (Malone, whose own son in heading over here soon). I can only wonder how many forwardings this weekly report goes through. Please know I enjoy writing it and I hope it has been informative and worth reading.

While the JVB Captain, the four lieutenants, the medics and I all fly across Iraq frequently, most of our soldiers do not. Our soldiers get up at 0400 or 0500 hours to eat, get the vehicles ready, then drive to the Baghdad International Airport to greet a dignitary. They roll in an armored Suburban convoy, usually with a small bus as well. Typically they only assist the dignitaries in moving from the fixed wing aircraft to the rotary wing for movement by air. If that's the deal then they are pretty much done for the day and have a chance for maintenance, exercise, laundry, training. They are expected to be back on duty again late in the evening to assist with the transfer of the dignitaries back from the rotary wing to the fixed wing in order to leave the country. So, a typical day for them is four or five hours of work, getting up early and staying up late with a huge gap in the middle. The other typical mission is when they pick up the "package" in the limos and drive them to meetings somewhere in the Victory Base/BIAP Complex, most often the spectacular Al Faw Palace where all the senior Generals work. In these cases they run the motorcade and security until the dignitary flies away to somewhere else. A third type of mission sends them down the highway in our armored gun trucks into the International Zone where they will provide escort and convoy duty once the dignitary arrives by helicopter. Said differently: One team takes me and the medic to the airport where we greet the dignitaries at the airplane, put them in limos and drive to the palace for briefings. Then the same team puts us on helicopters to fly away leaving that team on the ground. We are greeted by a second team in the IZ with the limos and gun trucks to drive us around to meetings and briefings with US Embassy and Iraqi Government dignitaries. Then we fly away leaving that team for other meetings elsewhere in Iraq where we are greeted by still more teams for convoy and security. Then we return by helicopter to BIAP where the first team handles the final transfer back to the airplane. We all get to bed at midnight or 0100. So, long, hot days for these young guys.

Sometimes we will take several riflemen with us when we fly so they get to see the countryside. Of the 130,000 military in Iraq probably less than 30 percent ever get out of their fort, camp or forward operating base (FOB). Everyone else is in support of those front-line troops. That's historically normal.

This week I had missions with a group of Congressional staff members and then a group of Congressmen that included the Secretary of Veterans' Affairs. He told groups of soldiers: "My Department provides benefits on injury, illness or death. So between us and the IRS we're the only two agencies in federal government I can positively guarantee you're gonna deal with sooner or later."

That mission had a couple of interesting things: First, there is a group of scroungers who fly the Medevac helicopters and have created a fully furnished coffee bar where you can sit in comfy sofas, play games, read books, watch DVDs and enjoy hot and cold coffee drinks. I had an icy cold fruit blended thing that I would not be caught dead with back in the USA (house coffee, black!) and realized it was the first truly cold thing I have had in a year. I actually had a brain freeze! The pilots indicated they traded a little of this and a little of that and voila' a coffee bar. They promised they still had all their helicopters and narcotics but I'm danged if I can see how they managed it.

Second, this was the first time in JVB history where the airplane actually flew away without the dignitaries. At the end of the mission our guests were having a light meal and cool down break. I was in commo with the airfield crews and watching the C-130 taxiing towards us. Suddenly it turned down the runway and took off! We quickly contacted them through air traffic control and got them back on the ground but it could have been a career defining moment. As it was it turned into a ten-minute delay and a good laugh between the Congressmen and Secretary.

A few facts learned in this week's meetings: The Iraq-wide average power supply is 10 hours a day. This exceeds the pre-war power supply. The difference is that the pre-war supply was hoarded by Saddam for his friends and cohorts for 24-hour-a-day electricity, and much of the country was without power at all. Now the pain is spread. I did see the big electricity plant in Baghdad with three smokestacks burning out of four. It's the first time I have ever seen more than one running. Also, the oil production is back to pre-war levels and is projected to increase about 20% over the next year.

Baghdad lacks storm sewers or drainage planning at all for that matter. US forces are working with Iraqi officials to begin this huge logistical improvement.

More and more Iraqis are replacing third country workers on contracts all over Iraq. This creates security risks for us soldiers here but it is putting Iraqis to work and that will make all the difference in the future.

Cards and letters from Pop x 4 (and monthly magazine shipment), Mom, Gary Shofner, Gerry Browning, Roy Browning, Debbie Heiniger, Tam Engler, Sarah Beyer, Linda Tuller (who we young'uns in the Masters program called "mom" with true affection), Charles Jeffress, Joan Crouse, Phil Coolidge, Chris and Deb Russo, Paul Fink, Dick Spingler, Joanie Lewerenz, Connie Pitman, Asel Mukova, Kirk Johnson, Susan Anderson, and goodies from John and Mary Van Dyke.

Makasib boxes from Corey Neill x 2, Mom and Pop x 5, Karen Ebert x 3, Rick and Sarah Beyer x 2, Mike Lamone, Linda Hubbard, Robert Caplinger, Diane Aeschliman, Jean Nickell, Beth Tormey, Mark and Greg and the gang at the Federal Home Loan Bank x 5, Nancy Lonergan, Phil Coolidge x 2, Mike Morris.

American by birth. Soldier by choice. Volunteer by God!

Roger T. Aeschliman
Major, Armor
Deputy Commander, First Kansas Volunteers

US Troops nearly all live in climate-controlled trailers, with heat, air and electricity for their X-Boxes and a short walk to the showers and latrines. Cool bat-house too!

From: Mary Alice Avery
To: raeschliman
Sent: Monday, August 21, 2006 3:17 PM
Subject: RE: Fw: Fw: Mary Alice Avery

Roger,

My son is currently in Kuwait and should arrive in Iraq in the next couple of weeks. He will be at Camp Summerall with a FOB of Camp Anaconda. Is there any other information I can send you that could help you tell me "the no bull" assessment of the risks he faces. Thanks so much and THANK YOU for all you do and for the email and pictures to send out to all of us here in the states.

Mary Alice
**

Good afternoon from Baghdad!

FOB Summerall is one of the smaller bases near the enormous LSA Anaconda (both near the city of Balad; when I refer to Balad I am usually talking about Anaconda). Summerall is a very secure camp with little concern about enemy attacking it or shooting rockets into it. It is the base for the units that actually go out into the Iraq lands nearby to patrol the roads, escort convoys and help the people try to improve their lives and communities. When they go on those missions they are usually well received and appreciated by the Iraqis. But the area is not totally pacified and sometimes patrols get shot at (not often because Iraqis actually shooting at a USA armored vehicle means the Iraqi will pretty likely get killed). The larger risk comes from the roadside bombs of all types ranging for tiny to big. This risk is all over Iraq. Summerall is not better or worse than the rest of the area.

No Americans travel outside of any Forward Operating Base (FOB) without being inside a heavily armored vehicle. The armored Humvees we drive are very impressive and resistant to bombs. They are designed with a highly protected "cabin" that will survive even if the engine, wheels, etc are completely blown off. There are also a number of special vehicles that regularly patrol routes looking for these bombs to destroy them. There are many other protective measures of secret nature that enhance the survivability of the US Soldier on patrol.

About one half of all bombs are found and destroyed rather than attacking us. Of the one half that surprise us about nine out of ten cause little or no damage. Of the one out of twenty bombs that causes damage, only two or three of those injure soldiers. Of the typical injured soldiers, about 9 out of ten are treated for minor wounds are returned to duty with a day or two. Of those with more severe wounds 9 out of ten are still returned to duty within two-three weeks.

I wish I could tell you your son will be completely safe but IF he is a soldier that will be leaving the FOB on patrols then there are risks, but his area is not especially dangerous and the safeguards are remarkable. If he is a mechanic or clerk or some other specialty soldier then the odds are good he will never leave the FOB.

Also, I believe Summerall is one of the FOBs scheduled to be closed in the coming months and the area turned over to the Iraq Army and Police for control. When that happens your son will be reassigned somewhere else.

I know your son is not a statistic (and neither am I), but I am very logical and the statistics help me keep a reality check in place. So, there have been nearly 1 million individual US soldiers in Iraq since the war began. Of that one million, about 2,600 have been killed and about 20,000 wounded. That means only 1/4 of one percent fatalities and two percent wounded. Those numbers are so small historically that most soldiers don't think about it. Those numbers fall in the range of random or just bad luck. In WWII on D-Day 5,000 were killed the first day. At Iwo Jima, 25,000 were killed in a month. At Antietam in the Civil War, 20,000 were killed in one day. I don't know if any of that helps you or whether it makes you angry at me for downplaying things, but the risk is so low overall and we are (and you son will be) so busy that we just don't think or worry about it.

I wish you peace and comfort in knowing that your man will do his job whatever it is and generally will not be at high risk as a constant state of being.

Finally, my personal advice to you if you want to be truly helpful to him, write to him every damn day. Even if it's only a few lines about what you had for breakfast, who you talked to at work, where you went shopping . . . all the little things at home that are normal. That will make him feel good and he'll be the envy of all his mates.

I hope some of this is helpful to you. With kindest regards, rog

From: Pat VanHooser
Date: Monday, August 21, 2006 3:28 am
Subject: (no subject)

Hi Roger,

The world got even more dangerous since the last time we communicated. I'm incredibly disappointed in Israel. I never expected to see them fold so easily and bow to the U.N. I've come to expect that from the United States-unfortunately. Bush #1 had the chance to finish the job in Iraq and didn't - thanks to those idiots in N. Y. I honestly believe that's why you have to be there now. I blame them and the cowards in our own government. Hell, I'm in the pest control business and I know it...I'd like to think the people in Washington are smarter than me. Maybe not.

And crazy President Imanutjob of Iran seems determined to blow up the whole freakin world. Brother.

Anyhow, back in the USA, I bought tickets online to Eric Clapton this morning. I love the Internet. Think about how wars for the soldiers have changed. My dad was in the Navy and met my mother in Australia on shore leaved during WW2. They became engaged and my dad shipped out. They wrote to each other for 2 years. When my mother didn't get a letter from him for more than 6 months she just gave up. The war ended and she didn't hear anything, so she wrote him and said just forget it. A few weeks later he showed up on her door step ready to get married. Three months after that a sack full of mail came from my dad...he had been writing all along...the mail just wasn't getting through. They had been married for quite a while when my dad got the letter telling him the engagement was off! Now at least the military can stay in touch with email and web cams and calling cards. How much worse would it be for you and Robyn without technology! I'm still amazed that my parents ever got married...and stayed married...they only knew each other through letters... sporadic at that! It really was a different time.

We have been hearing a rumor that Hillary Clinton will be coming over to see you. I'd be interested to know how that goes. I'm sure she will get polite treatment but I'd love to know if there is a different feeling towards her....or do all the politicians seem the same after awhile?

Great photo of you in front of the homesick wall. What a super idea. I am delighted to see all the boxes stacked up. I was hoping you would get a great response from your appeal. There are so many of us who want to support all of you. Please continue to make known what you need...

After you called me I told Mike you are like my personal rock star. No kidding, I'm going to love to see Clapton, but you are my hero. Playing guitar is one thing defending freedom is quite another. As always, thank you.

Take care my friend. Pat
**

Dear Pat,

What a great story on your parents. How different times are now.

Iran = irrelevant. Don't fret on that hole. The 60% of the population there under age 25 will take over the country one of these days. They watch our TV and our internet and they want to be like us, not burka-wearing pariahs of the world. All we have to do is keep the pressure on and be prepared to blow up a few nuke facilities at the right time. Or let the Israelis do it...

Hillary and the Governor of California are always on our rumor list but never on the missions. We'll see. If Kerry can come here and be treated decently then anyone can. For us it is easy to engage the DVs and equally easy to ignore them. She would likely be swarmed by soldiers who through ignorance don't understand her brand of evil. They would just respond to her celebrity. Sad isn't it?

And yes, Congress is just like the US population as a whole. Some bright, some dumb. The only difference is there are way more lawyers in Congress than the general population. That would be bad except that most of them never even tried to practice. The law degree is the "required" degree for a political career track. Sad, sad, sad. History would be much better but most lawyers can't read very well so that's out. rog

PS - I'm no hero. Just a guy that was too stupid to stay home with his wife and kids, career and community when he had the chance.

August 23, 2006

Hi Roger,

Have been getting your updates from friends and Rotary. Good to hear that you have the opportunity to give the real news from Iraq. I hear soldiers are doing a great job there, and even though the cult thugs (shites and sunnis) are culling out each other (which is probably good news), most of the providences are doing quite well, including economic recovery.

We utilize the email route to get the real news out. We just can't count on the liberal news media to do anything right anymore.

Walter Cronkite and Dan Rather were two of the most liberal biased assholes during my tour of Viet Nam. When I got home we only had 3 networks that carried the news. They were all baised, but NBC would give good coverage in 1 out of 10 broadcasts, which was the best we could hope for. There was no other means of spreading the news in a meaningful way. So I was always frustrated and carried a chip on my shoulder. I did some things over at KU while pursuing my civil engineering degree that offset some of the bad publicity, including some macho stuff during the aftermath of the Kent slayings. The flag remained up one day at the military ROTC building. I sent one "renowned expert on Cambodia" scampering one day just seconds after he started his propaganda speech, brushing aside his long greasy hair. I preached every time I got a chance. We even formed a vigilante group after the computer building front was blown up, putting out a girl's eye. We never mobilized though, which was probably a blessing. If you ever get bored, read "The Viet Nam War, a Necessary War" I believe is the name. I gave mine to someone and have regretted it since. It particularly explains the settlement of America and how the various political beliefs took root.

Keep up the good work and keep your head down.

Mike Welch
**

Dear Mike,

Thanks for the great note. As a country we have completely failed to learn the true lessons of Vietnam the most critical of which is the national media is lazy, ignorant and biased, and second, that it is nearly impossible to fight a war when the national media is so fundamentally opposed to your entire existence as a President.

The war here was won a long time ago. We just must have the patience to persevere in building governmental systems and the rule of law. It is happening. It just takes time.

I truly hope we are not turning into a nation of pussies, afraid of everything and afraid of offending the world. The world will be better when it is more like the USA and not the USA more like the rest of the world.

Most kindly and with great respect for your incredible service to our country in a time of war and our city and state in your civilian career. rog

Howdy everyone, 27 August 2006

I fought August and August won. Another nine-mission month with 22 flying days About 1,700 sweaty miles. Though the days are beginning to shorten it remains in the 120 degree range and has yet to dip below 90 at night. That's six weeks above 90 degrees.

Doc Sims and I had a brief respite early in the week when we flew with Congressmen all the way to Sulaymaniyah near the Iran border. This is the hometown of President Wilfred Brimley…I mean Talabani, part of the Kurdish heartland. It is over two smallish mountain ranges and at higher elevation than most of Iraq thus cooler. It was positively brisk to skim over the peaks and feel the 70 degree air rushing into the helicopter. The airport there is modern and functional with jets from Jordan and Europe on the tarmac. The city is still mostly Arabic looking but had business streets like any in America including a McDonald's look-alike and a mall. All the signs were in Kurdish and English. Lots of traffic on pretty decent streets. No explosions or gunfire anywhere. This northeastern quarter of Iraq was carved off and protected by the USA after the first Gulf War. Thus the overwhelmingly Kurdish population has had time to rebuild and establish the fundamentals of democracy and free enterprise. It's not perfect but it's a great example of how this country can look and act given enough time to learn.

My young medic friend Doc Shawn Sims said it this way: "Iraq with democracy is like a ten-year-old with a car. He's seen mom and dad drive and he has a rough idea where the grocery store is. But only a lunatic would give him the keys and tell him to drive to the store, to obey all the traffic laws, don't crash, don't run out of gas and don't make any wrong turns. You have to teach him to drive and let him have the experience with oversight, and when the time comes for him to drive on his own you have to accept that he'll probably make wrong turns and bend a few fenders." That's a pretty smart 22-year-old medic…

The mountains between Kirkuk and Sulay appear to be layers of red sandstone with intermittent layers of a denser gray capstone. Pretty.

I put the Congressmen on a plane at Sulay and waited for them to fly away. After 30 minutes I ran back out to see why the propellers weren't spinning and was told by the pilots that instead of flying to Jordan as planned the delegation wanted to go instead to Beirut. That required approval from Syria to fly over, from Lebanon to arrive and the US Embassy to greet and protect – none of it my responsibility. I don't know if they ever got approval, but after an hour sitting in the C-130 in the 110 degree heat I'm sure they regretted trying to change their plans.

When they finally flew away I was irritated but not surprised to learn our scheduled helicopter ride home aborted due to dust/sand and thunderstorms in the mountains. We instead drove nearly two hours through the mountains to Kirkuk, a route known for IEDs and snipers. I wish I could tell you it was exciting and interesting but I was so tired I slept most of the way. We arrived unscathed, spent the night at the Kirkuk Regional Embassy Office then caught a C-12 twin prop back to Baghdad to get ready for the General Abizaid mission the next day.

One mission took us to a private residence in the International Zone for a meeting. There was a tiny back yard that was green and blooming, looking very much like my California parent's house in Torrance, complete with postage stamp lawn, lime and lemon trees.

You can eat the dates right off the trees now but they are better if you wash off the dust.

My personal call sign is "Lucky." I am not the commander so I can't be "6" as most commanders are known and I'm not the executive officer so I can't be "5" as most XOs are known. I'm not officially part of the JVB Company run by a Captain so I'm not a "Bandit" as they are known. So I just self-named after General George Patton's famous 3rd Army from World War II, code named Lucky. So far so good.

General Abizaid's trip was normal meaning it was frenetic with 20 meetings in two and half days and changes throughout. Three interesting things: 1 – he made a personal ground move all through the "worst" neighborhoods in Baghdad touring, visiting soldiers, the Iraq Army and the Baghdad man on the street. It was uneventful and a great example of how well the current operation to reduce Baghdad violence is working. It was a powerful statement from the most wanted man in Iraq with an Al Qaeda bounty on his head. Did that make the nightly news? 2 – The second day was insane with a total agenda rewrite that we had to execute on the fly. We did it, but only after many Cheetah flips by us and by the planner. On the third day I called the planner, and told her we were completely canceling day three and needed to instead go to the three major Kurdish cities, needed to meet with the Kurdish Prime Minister, needed to refuel the C-17 at an airport without a refueling contract, and needed meals planned at all stops. She yelled at me for a whole minute after I told her I was only kidding and the day three agenda was fine . . . and 3 – do you remember hearing about the water bottling plan explained to Abizaid in December? Well, this trip he heard all seven plants are now up and running removing 8,400 trucks a month from the highways and saving $54 million a year.

Cards and letters from Pop x 5, Dan Busby (through Shawn Tipping), Adriel Class at TBC, Betty Cazier, Becky Evans, Marilyn Rees, Betty Beeler, and Lucky DeFries.

Makasib boxes from Cindi Yingling Mitchell (secret and unrequited 14-year-old love), Max Halley, M.D. (Rotarian), Charlotte Adair (Rotarian), Kandy Reed (5 of 6!), Jack and Marilyn Rees, Ed Haug (Fiji brother once hailing from Manhattan Kansas where the cow is king, the sow is queen and every night is a Saturday night!).

American by birth. Soldier by choice. Volunteer by God!

Roger T. Aeschliman
Major, Armor
Deputy Commander, First Kansas Volunteers

PS – Pop, at the end of August (almost) 18,010 miles in the air and 863 running.

Dear Ed, Becky, young'uns, 30 AUGUST 2006

Thanks for another great letter Ed! Brightens my day every time.

Please, please do send another box of Goldfish grahams (if they are still in your stock)!

Makes my commander very happy to get his daily late afternoon carb load...I may not have mentioned ever that he is an adult onset diabetic and I was terribly worried about him even coming over here. My whole existence over here is to work, work, work on mission after mission that he (the Lieutenant Colonel) historically went on (last three tours before us). With all the combat operations down at Camp Slayer my boss just doesn't have the time to do what his predecessors did. So I am doing all the historical work of the Major and the LTC at the JVB. Anyway, he doesn't travel at all, never overnights anywhere but his "home" and always has at least two people with him at all times including a true giant of a soldier, about 6'6" and 300 pounds. He has good meds, had a high tech monitor/calculator attached to his thigh/belt and rests as necessary. It's been reassuring to me to see him both working so hard but also taking care of himself so he can keep taking care of the men. So, the point is that at 1700 every day when we have our briefing for him, he snacks out of my munchie drawer and it is now empty so please send ASAP!

Very scary...Ryan, Katherine, and Billy Bloomquist all on the roads soon. How fast that happened and (curiously) how eager Robyn and I are to get him driving safely to relieve the burden of the early and post-school activities. Maybe the days of the one-room schoolhouse on the corner a ½ mile away wasn't such a bad idea. Just stake the pony out in the grass until time to go home like my dad did...

Regan reports that she, Lea and K are enjoying each other's company in their spare time. That's three really good kids...I hope they will be able to maintain a friendship over time. I asked Regan if they called any boys on their last overnight at your place and she just said "ewwwehhh."

Great luck with the store placement and wheeling and dealing. I admire your entrepreneurial skills and spirit. The secret is to always spend someone else's money, right?

Happy birthday to both you and Eddie. I'm closing on 46 myself. Time flies.

Thanks to all for of you for your friendship and concern for my family. I know Robyn and the kids have found it much easier with all your support and family activities.

Most gratefully and with love. rog

Dear Dave and Joyce, 30 AUGUST 2006

Thanks for another nice note. Sure does brighten the day over here. I now have a couple of your cards posted on the homesick wall (which is in itself a day brightener for the soldiers here; I often walk in to find a young troop looking at all the photos and cards).

Wish you had good news for me on the chemo and on your arm/shoulder therapy. You are both in my daily prayers and I know that the prayer chain ripples far and wide for you two.

Football is one of the things I really miss about home. Although there is the Armed Forces Network available we don't watch it during the work day and the work days are long. When I could watch it that means going to some nearby morale support building and watching with a bunch of strangers in a loud room where others are playing pool, video games or dancing. When we do occasionally watch in our own command post it means the Chiefs or whatever is showing usually two or three days after the actual game and I already read about it on the Internet. Not the same. So, looking forward to getting home for that reason high among others. Wishing you a good season of watching the young'uns play the greatest game.

Thanks for being such good friends to my parents. I know it has been mutual support over all the years but I know how much they both cherish you two and I thank you for that.

I hope that God has more in mind for you Dave and that you'll come through this one. But more than that I know God has a plan for you and I truly wish you the peace and contentment that you've earned for a good life devoted to others.

With much love, rog

"Greetings All,

"No photos this week. Roger's been out on a mission and didn't have the time to do photos. For those of you who keep asking when he will be home, it looks like sometime n November. So barring any glitches Roger should be able to enjoy Thanksgiving' turkey here this year. Yeah!! No specific dates right now but the general timeline is replacement troops arrive in October, two-week transition, back to Ft. Sill for a week or two then home. Of course, I always keep in the back of my mind that the Army likes to change dates and time at the last minute. Enjoy this week's report.

"Robyn"
**

Howdy everyone, 03 September 2006

I'm writing this on Thursday (heading out the door pronto for two missions over five days) so Robyn will have something to send out on Sunday. The only interesting thing so far this week is that I woke up this morning to 84 degrees! YAHOOOOOOOO!!!!!! September is supposed to be about 10 degrees cooler than August so perhaps we are out of the woods now on the weather. About two months left, but who's counting?

Otherwise all quiet so I'll answer a couple of questions from home.

1 – From sisters Ronna and Karen: How dangerous is it?

Not really for me and the Kansas gang. First, we all live inside a totally walled and gated camp with 24-hours guards in towers. While the enemy could invade the camp here it would be strictly a PR move for them like the Vietnam Tet offensive, doomed to failure. The only risks here are random mortars or rockets. Not one of the 20,000 people here has been injured by rockets or mortars in the 10 months we've been on duty. Further there are many, many tools and processes in place to keep us healthy and alive. All of these things can be found on the Internet so I'm not telling you any secrets. Every vehicle that leaves the FOB is armored and has the ability to return overwhelming firepower. The armor is greater than that of the first tanks of World War I and if a blast strikes they are designed to disperse the explosion around the crew compartment. Highly survivable. Most also have a tracking system that allows higher commands to see where we are on the roads and highways and allows the crew to track its own progress. Much better than the old maps (although we still carry them). There are numerous devices of various names designed to disrupt the enemy's roadside bombs. Some set the bombs off early, others jam them so they can't explode until we pass. These devices are both in our convoys and can fly over. There are regular patrols of IED engineers with several special vehicles designed to find, remove or destroy IEDs. They are also highly survivable and I have seen pictures of one that blew off the wheels, engine and every external part but left the cabin intact on the ground. There are robots that can disarm or blow up IEDs from 100s of yards away, operated by someone through video camera eyes. These look a lot like Johnny 5 from the movie "Short Circuit." We have blimps in the sky with more cameras and sensors than you can imagine with the ability to see clearly day or night and even through significant dust. The enemy acts, we see and respond. There is a giant vehicle called the Rhino that is an armored bus to carry people comfortably through dangerous areas (most vehicles have run flat tires and many have reinflation devices). The Rhino looks a lot like the Urban Assault Vehicle from the movie "Stripes." There are continuous flights of Apache helicopters over Baghdad as well as a pair of F-16s on station, loaded to the teeth. All helicopters and airplanes have flare dispensers to interfere with the possibility of ground to air attack. I think I've mentioned that these go off regularly and scare the bujeebers out of our dignitaries. If we like them we warn them in advance that this will happen. If they are jerks then we just let them wet themselves.

2 – Mom – I think – asks if all soldiers have the same access to the things I do. Yes and no. We are truly lucky here at the JVB. Because we have commercial internet and Armed Forces Network TV available for our guests our hooch's can piggyback on those. Everyone on camp has AFN wired into their trailers and can purchase reasonably-priced Internet access. We have laundry in the hotel for hotel linens. A couple of old machines wore out/burned up but our talented maintenance man scrounged parts and rebuilt them so the JVB guys can do laundry on our own. Elsewhere laundry service is free but you turn your bag in and get it back in three days. We have a bank of low-cost phones available for guests that can be used by our soldiers, as well as the Defense Services Network (the military's own phone system) that can be used to make a call back home. These same things are available everywhere on the camp and across the country but ours is more convenient. So the shorter answer is we have it good with resources right at hand but we don't have anything more or better than anyone else. If you have a loved one over here that isn't calling, e-mailing, or webcaming regularly they are probably being lazy, not wanting to walk the ¼ mile to the phone/Internet trailer, or cheap (thrifty?), not wanting to pay for service in their own quarters.

Best stupid joke currently going around: What's ugly and smells funny? YOU!

Jogging early this week one of the Ugandan contractor security guards stopped me and asked in his heavily accented central African patois "hey running man. Where have you been? We were worried about you." Seems a number of the guards set their clocks on my exercise schedule and missed me over a nine-day mission/flying span. I reassured them I was fine. He asked me my name, shook his head at the difficult pronunciation and said "we'll just call you the running man." That's ok with me as long as it references the Arnold Schwarzenegger movie of the same name as he survives in the end. In the original Stephen King (writing under the non de plume Bruce Bachmann) novelette the protagonist wins but dies...

3 – Someone e-mailed how did I think of the homesick wall? I stuck up the Christmas cards as a part of the holiday season and it brightened the room up so much I just kept adding. Many times I have come in to find some young soldier or other staring at the cards, notes and photos perhaps trying to cheer himself up. It sure is colorful but I have to use a ladder now.

Cards and letters from Pop x 1, Ed Linquist, Don and Marie Boaz, Joyce and Dave Phillippi, Betty Beeler.

Makasib boxes from Joe McFarland (Rotarian), Kandy Reed (#6 of 6!), Lezlee Heryford, for a current total of 59.

American by birth. Soldier by choice. Volunteer by God!

Roger T. Aeschliman
Major, Armor
Deputy Commander, First Kansas Volunteers

Howdy everyone, 10 September 2006

I had a way cool mission with James Baker, Lee Hamilton, Leon Panetta, Ed Meese, Robert Gates, William Perry, and Chuck Robb. Amazing living history with a bit of excitement out in the red zone. But first...

Another end-of-tour portent: Please don't send me any mail after September 15. Not that it won't arrive before we leave the country in late October, but because of the surge of rotational units into the country there is an overlap meaning we actually lose our official unit "mailbox" to our replacements. So, it's a good sign.

Second, I thought about this then rejected it as melodramatic. But all my sisters, mother, Robyn and several correspondents think it is a good idea. If you are reading this will you please send me a postcard with your name, city, state and (in some cases) country written on it? The original 50 or 60 readers must be in the several hundreds now and I am curious about the diversity and reach of the distribution. A postcard will allow me to count them and easily sort them by state and city as they come in and is easy for you too. You don't have to write anything, just annotate where you are. You may be thinking "he doesn't mean me because we've never met," but I especially mean you. Would all of you do it as a favor for me? Thanks, it will be interesting. But do it before September 15 please. (If a postcard is hard instead of easy, then just send an empty envelope with a return address that I can count and sort). Mail to:

MAJ Roger T. Aeschliman
B Co 2-137 INF
APO AE 09342-1400

Third, so far received 69 boxes for Makasib. I put it at more than 500 pounds of medical, health and hygiene supplies and a large number of toys. Thanks to everyone. But the same for these boxes. If you intend to send one please do it this week and beat the September 15 mailing deadline. This is NOT an appeal for more (everyone has already far exceeded my expectations) it is just a notice of a new deadline.

Back to the first paragraph: If your eyes were open in the 80s and 90s you know that Baker, Meese, Gates, Panetta, Hamilton, Robb and Perry were WORLD-CLASS players in international relations and the daily operations of our great nation. I expected to meet the typical mix of visitors and political hacks – some bright, some dim. Instead I was totally impressed with the powerful intellect and class of each of these gentlemen. Bright, nice and desirous of doing a good job. That job? They are all members of the congressionally chartered Iraq Study Group, a BI- (I perceive it more as NON) partisan group tasked to develop recommendations for success and completion in Iraq. They are not looking back at why, how, or who to blame for anything, strictly forward. How do we get to the end from here?

Very rough four-day schedule. We made every possible stop with every possible faction, interest, leader and office. And these guys are getting some years on them too. 78, 77, 76, 83, etc. They wore me out. (But they went into air conditioned meetings and sat down- I stood guard outside in the sun so I don't feel too badly). Over four days I had nice (short) visits with all of them and chatted about mutual friends dating back to a youngish Bob Dole and a couple who knew Governor Sebelius's father back in Ohio. Robert Gates (former Director of the CIA, native of Wichita and current President of Texas A&M) visited about distant acquaintances in Kansas. Baker told me a few short stories about my hero Ronald Reagan. I was perhaps most impressed with Leon Panetta as I expected him to be a Clintonista type. He was smart, very nice and had a great sense of humor and ready laugh. He talked about his neighbor Clint Eastwood. All in all very much fun and an honor to serve them.

The trip did include a red zone move taking former Senator Chuck Robb into the Baghdad neighborhood of Dora – until recently a hotbed of sectarian violence. The Iraqi-Coalition Operation Together Forward has made a difference there and the killings dropped from several hundred over six months down to a handful in August. We drove around and got out to visit with locals on the street. Very edgy for me as I was the assigned bullet sponge for Robb but quiescent and uneventful.

My naked eye amateur astronomy has observed Jupiter dancing all around Libra for the past three months. I'm not into astrology but even a skeptic can hearten from seeing such a powerful planet (Holst called Jupiter the Bringer of Jollity) seemingly refusing to leave my birth sign (balanced, stable and always seeking solutions and justice).

Cards and letters from Pop x 5, Mom, Robyn (with first day of school photos!), oldest younger sister Ronna (in Costa Rica!), Susan Henry, the fun table at Rotary (Eldon Sloan, Rick Dalton, Gary Shofner, Paul Fink, Joe and Betty Casper, Joe McFarland, and Breta Bloomberg), Lezlee Heryford, Alaska Governor Frank Murkowski, Scouter Jeff Moe, Grandmother Dorothy, the

May family (formerly neighbors now sadly displaced Minnesotans), Sandy Pambechy, and a goody box from Linquist family pals.

Makasib boxes from Joe McFarland (Rotarian) x 3, Maria Russo Wilson x 2, Betty and Nolan Williams (Texas readers), Carolyn Keegan, Dultmeier (no first name...in Topeka I even searched the Internet and couldn't find you), Virginia Schwartz, Chief Justice Robert Miller (Rotary), Barbara Long (Rotarian sponsor back at the beginning).

American by birth. Soldier by choice. Volunteer by God!

Roger T. Aeschliman
Major, Armor
Deputy Commander, First Kansas Volunteers

At the very end of the mission I asked James Baker if I could take a shot of the whole group (I never asked dignitaries to pose...). He grabbed me, called the gang together and had an aide take this photo. I respected each of these men.

Howdy everyone, 17 September 2006

Our battalion commander, Colonel (he got promoted! ☺) Jim Trafton has officially declared it time to count the days. Even through the specific time frame is flexible most of the men are figuring the end of October as our "date" to leave Iraq. 44 days...

Recent interesting things:

1 – Temperatures have dropped into the high 70s at night a couple of times and are low 100s during the day. It's like God flipped a switch to our great relief.

2 – As the weather improves Iraqis move outdoors into the pleasant evenings. This includes the elected leaders and I was at a recent garden party with President Wilford Briml...Talabani as he entertained some Congressmen. I was still sweaty but was allowed to sit at the kiddie table with security guards and agents and we supped on stuffed cucumbers, onions, grape leaves and squash, roasted rabbit, and rice dishes.

3 – Talabani gives large chess/backgammon sets, small carpets and ornate boxes of dates and baklava as gifts to visiting dignitaries. When they come in groups of 10 then we have this enormous pile to haul around the rest of the trip and hump onto and off of helicopters. I have suggested that our Ambassador suggest that no gifts or only token gifts might be appropriate and was told the President is going to do what he wants to do. I suggested it couldn't hurt to ask and that perhaps the president might find it a relief and cost effective not to do a gift exchange all the time and was told to butt out.

4 – The state department kind of lives in a different world. They work mostly 8-5 and typically take Friday and Saturday (the Muslim weekend) off (and sometimes Sunday too). They operate on MCI cell phones exclusively. They have numerous going away parties and have no prohibitions on alcohol, physical relationships and eating and shopping on the local economy. They live in their own self-contained walled city and have 600 private security guards as well as 100 Marines to protect the compound. In the Army we work 24/7/365. There are no days off. There are limited Iraqna network cell phones in the JVB and with other critical personnel but most of the military is not on any cell phone network so we cannot easily contact department of state folks. There are never going away parties. One day a co-worker is there and the next they are redeployed. You already know General Order No.1 prohibits everything that anyone could consider fun. We at the JVB just kind of giggle at the 20-30

contractor guards that swarm all over the dignitaries INSIDE the embassy then disappear completely when the dignitaries leave the state department compound and we Army folks take over with four. (The contractors also drive like maniacs INSIDE the safe areas; we are aggressive but not insane...). I guess it's no wonder that the Departments of Defense and State have different world views. Kind of reality and kind of *Wolkenkuckucksheim* - cloud cuckoo land.

5 – We had a three US Senator visit and one made several poor choices. He and his staff drove the entire agenda to the detriment of the other two. Specifically he spent most of the two days trying to find several of his own state and Washington D.C. staff - mobilized Guard or Reservists here in Iraq. The agenda kind of focused on seeing them. Day 2 was scheduled to fly all three senators 150 miles to Tikrit to see troops from all their home states. The lead guy decided he didn't want to go there and instead wanted to see his deployed aide in Balad. Balad is on the way to Tikrit so we were able to stop and let him off (after many last minute coordination efforts) before going on to Tikrit with the others. The bottom line was that the two Senators going to Tikrit had about 30 minutes with a handful of their own state soldiers while the 300 soldiers from the other Senator's state were left standing in the blowing sand wondering why he never showed up. It was a very hard day of major changes and coordination and long movements for very little positive effect. I hope it was worth it to the one Senator.

6 – Admiral "Hi, I'm Ed" Giambastiani is the Vice Chairman of the Joint Chiefs and thus the number three guy in the US military (after Rumsfeld and General Pace, the Chairman). He is one of the smartest and nicest people I've ever met. We did three days of Improvised Explosive Devices review, both what the bad guys are doing and how we are countering them. He gave out more challenge coins than anyone else ever. Hundreds of these souvenirs over three days. Have I written about challenge coins before? If not then next week...

7 – A protocol officer in another unit kind of freaked out on the Giambastiani mission and called me an asshole and an idiot. While I have the proven capacity to be an asshole I most certainly was not on this occasion and I am confident I have never been an idiot. She just has issues of power and control. All the JVB men understand this and call her "Skeletor" and her command post "Snake Mountain." This is really, really funny if you grew up with the 1980s cartoon "He-Man!" in which Skeletor, the evil villain, is a skeletal figure (of whom she is a clone) and the evil fortress is Snake Mountain. Well, we have now added her to the official list of people we don't like which includes one trip planner,

two US based officers who come over with Congressional dignitaries and two Congressional staff members who also abuse us regularly. Five isn't too bad for 10 months, two weeks, and two days (but who's counting?).

8 – This weeks' photos include the Ziggurat at Aqar Quf (ancient capital of the Cassites in the northeast suburbs of Baghdad) dating back 4,000 years and built in honor of the Babylonian god Enlil. It is made from of reed mats and reed bundles layered with bricks and mud. The part that still looks good is newer reconstruction. I have seen this towering ruin from miles away many times, but this week was the first time we flew over in photo range. If you are interested there is a lot of info on the Internet.

Cards and letters from Pop x 5 (and monthly magazines), sis Ronna, magazines from Auntie Nancy (Tenn.), Betty Beeler, Jean Crouse, Evelyn Damron, giant snack box of Goldfish Grahams from Taco John's magnate Ed Linquist for the troops.

A Makasib box from childhood piano teacher and friend Don Hemme totals 70!

American by birth. Soldier by choice. Volunteer by God!

Roger T. Aeschliman
Major, Armor
Deputy Commander, First Kansas Volunteers

P.S. After completing this report the first postcards arrived: 10! Also arriving: a large banner from my beloved Topeka Rotary Clubs, putting the crown on the homesick wall. See photo.

Dear Troy (especially) and guys, 17 September 2006

I want to thank you for the gift of Undaunted Courage - the Lewis and Clark history bestseller. It was a truly remarkable read; once we got past Meriwether Lewis's silver-spoon childhood it was fascinating. Junior High would have been a lot more interesting had our teachers told us that Lewis was shot in the ass by one of his own men, that he encouraged sex with the Indians as a way to release stress and keep the men happy (and then treated them all for VD), and that he rapidly cratered into a sad, manic-depressive drunk who tried to blow his brains out but failed so settled for shooting himself in the chest, lingering for six hours.

I devoured it!

If any of you want to dust off your latent reading skills, and stimulate some unused synapses this is a very well written book and explains clearly how important this expedition was to the future of our small, young nation, and intuits that the mission may have been the causal factor of the War of 1812.

Oh Yes, how about them 'Cats? 3-0! And improving every week.

Much love, rog

From: roger.aeschliman
To: Maria Russo Wilson
Subject: Thanks to everyone
Date: Mon, 18 Sep 2006 17:22:20 +0400

Dear Maria,

Would you please pass on to the joint Rotary Clubs (and especially Kip Slattery and Brad Stauffer) my kindest thanks for the wonderful Rotary banner you all signed and sent? By now I hope most people have seen the photo of it hanging on the wall in our command post. It really brightens up the place! Everyone who comes in comments how cool it is and how many people I have who care about me.

Most appreciatively, rog
**

Roger - You bet I'll pass on your thanks. Brad was definitely the one who came up with the idea and pulled it together. Kip was very generous in making the banner.

I hope that you will someday see that you, being you, have created two very significant "pebble in a pond" chain reactions. As we have already discussed, I do believe that asking service organizations for help will become a very viable way for Iraqi people to receive help. That came about because you are someone whom people want to help. You asked - people responded. Wow.

Secondly, this banner. When Brad first asked me about it, I thought it was a pretty cool idea. I was attending a Rotary district meeting, and I stood at a table explaining who and what the banner was for and asking people to sign. It was amazing how many people said things like, "I know someone else who would really appreciate something like this," or "We know someone preparing to be deployed, we could do this for him," or "What a great way to tell someone we care. We can do this for the soldiers in our community." Because of this community's love for you, other people will feel the hug and warmth of their communities. If even only 10% of the people who commented actually do something similar for others, there will be an amazing amount of love and positive support sent to the far corners of the world.

You being you has caused a wonderful, positive, loving ripple through the universe. I get chills thinking about it!

Hugs to you!!
Maria

From: John Heinley
Date: Wednesday, September 20, 2006 9:25 am
Subject: Ad in National Review

Just wanted to let you know that someone noticed your ad in the classifieds. I'm not much of an entrepreneur, nor an angel, though am a bit creative myself. Good luck with finding someone to work with you on projects. If you need a civil engineer, let me know.

Oh, and while you're over there, don't 'offend' any locals. ;-)

Well, maybe that's a bit much to ask. Just do your best, don't find yourself in the front-leaning rest, and have a hoo-ah day.

Say, In WWII we had Jerry and Charlie, Korea, 5-o'clock Charlie (M*A*S*H), Vietnam / Charlie or other words, and of course Ivan, I wonder what we have in Iraq? Abdul? Or, maybe there's no particular name.

I suppose there's bound to be a few locals who might be like some of the British at one time, "There's three things wrong with you Yanks, you're over-paid, over-sexed, and over here." I hope that most realize in some way that things could be a lot worse if we weren't there until a victory is secured (Iraqis and Americans).

Former Light-Wheel Vehicle Mechanic / Civil Affairs.

John C. Heinley, P.E.
**

Dear John,

Thank you for your very nice letter AND for your service to our great country - both military and in your civilian career. As a Rotarian in Topeka I have several club member friends who are civil engineers and always enjoy their lunchtime discussions about current projects (especially the current demolition and reconstruction of a WPA bridge over the Kansas River in the heart of our fair city).

What I really need most of all is a publisher or agent for several children's books (already written over here as a way to stay connected to my own children at home over these past many months) and for the memoirs of this year (also mostly written). If you have any such connection I would welcome any exploratory contact. I also have some ideas for games and inventions but nothing tangible...

The bad guy over here is named "Hajji." While I believe that is an Indian name, that is what they are called. Something poorly made is "hajji-built" and the vehicles they drive are "hajji-mobiles" with "hajji-armor." These are the most common uses. There is nothing respectful about it. They are also known as "booger-eaters," and due to their propensity to engage in very casual man on man sex they also have earned other unprintable nicknames.

Most Iraqis welcome the American presence and our largess. The actual number of illegal combatants engaging in this terrorist violence against fellow Muslims is tiny. But they are fanatics who want to be in power and are thus dangerous. Like the Viet Cong they will kill anyone who gets in their way and most of the deaths you read or hear about are just one bad guy faction killing another bad guy faction. It's the marketplace IEDs that are most terrible for these poor people. Random evil...

Thanks again for your nice note. You are the first response to my ad (which I threw in as a lark after my daughter told me the last book was so good that it just had to be in print...)

Most sincerely yours through our beloved National Review,

MAJ Roger T. Aeschliman
Deputy Commander, 2-137 INF

From: Kirk Johnson
To: Roger Aeschliman
Date: September 20, 2006

Hi Roger: Like our Rotary friends, the folks at CB&T really got behind the idea of sending things to help the folks in Iraq. I've attached a couple of pictures of the boxes before they were shipped last week. I'd expect quite a bit from Topeka, as the Rotary groups really got into it. I think the bank picked up the postage on the stuff that was sent from here.
Good things are happening here in the new business department and the bank as a whole. I'm anxious for you to be back on this job.
See ya soon.
Kirk
**

Dear Kirk,

Thanks for the update. What a pile! I look forward to receiving and passing on. There was a meeting this morning with the Makasib "elders" about how best to distribute these things and I have not heard the answer back yet but will let you know and hope to get some photos to send back home too. Getting photos seems to be harder than it should be but I don't go out there myself (yet...but I may have to) and rely on others to take and forward to me.

Tell everyone hello and thanks. Especially Duane and whole family for the postage costs. That had to be quite a bit and is very generous.

By the time you read this I will be out the door once again on a multi-day mission. Busy and time flies.

Most affectionately, rog

From: Ronna von Knorring
Sent: Tuesday, September 19, 2006 7:28 PM
To: Aeschliman Roger T MAJ MNF-I JVB Deputy Commander
Subject: Wondering...

I was wondering if you have to have any kind of debriefing when you get back. If so, can you share about THAT in your update? Do you plan to send a few updates to folks AFTER you return. I think it would be interesting for ALL to hear your stories of "adjustment" to life in Kansas again. Do soldiers get any special aid in helping them readjust??? Especially those that have seen combat??

Also was wondering when you plan to, have to, report back to work? I didn't know if you would get a nice amount of R & R after you are home, or if you are expected to return ASAP?? Just thoughts I had.

Mom wrote from a truck stop that they made it into Colorado in time to find a hotel where dad could watch the Chiefs play. hee hee

Carol Lauffer wrote that she got to talk to you the other morning and reported that you sounded "really good". Who does she work for that you would call her office? I forgot!

LOVED the last update and the picture of you with such a big smile!!!!!

Hope your days are going by quickly!!! As busy as you are, I know that helps! Hope you are getting some good night's sleep though! Thinking of you!
Love, Ronna
**

Howdy sis,

Yes, we will have lots of stuff and some has already started. We have already had briefings about reunion "letdown," that life back at home might not be as great as we remember it or have been idealizing; on suicide prevention and awareness; on family reintegration; yadda, yadda, yadda. We will have lots more at Fort Sill during that week or 10 days there then even more back at home for the first couple of months instead of normal training drills. I'm already sick of it but I suppose that many people will need it and more.

I hope I have been clear to everyone that things really just aren't that bad around here in our work. It's noisy and our sleep gets interrupted sometimes but other than that it's not much of a war. There is tons of assistance of all types for people who really need it and historically since the civil war the number of people affected by "malaise," "shell shock," "combat fatigue," or "Post-traumatic stress syndrome," or whatever they want to call it has been the same, between 10 and 20 percent get mentally wounded from minor to major (most very minor, treated and recovered). So far I show no signs of such a wounding and don't expect too. Our guys overall seem fine.

I'd like to go back to work in January. We'll see if the bank and our finances can support that six-seven weeks off.

I hadn't thought about continuing for any period of time; was sort of planning on a "well I'm home and here's my final thoughts" piece and be done.

Carol's boss is an attorney and lobbyist I have known for a long time and also a General in the Kansas National Guard and I was calling on Army business but it always nice to visit with Carol when I call there or go visit. You and she have kept in great shape for "old girls." Compared to the rest of your classmates and age group you are both total hotties (right after Robyn!)

Love you too and thanks for the concern and support but I think I'm coming back pretty much the same jerk as I was when I left. rog

Howdy everyone, 24 September 2006

Today is the beginning of Ramadan, the most holy of the multitude of holy days, weeks, months and locations of Islam. Yes, that's a tad cynical but the multitudes who practice this religion do so just like the practitioners of all other religions all around the world – in a multitude of ways from ultra-pious, devout and strict-text adherents all the way to complete failure to adhere to even the most basic tenets of the faith while still proclaiming it. Ramadan is the closest thing Muslims have to our wonderful Christmas holiday season with nightly celebrations, social visits with neighbors, feasting and gift giving. In western civilization Christmas historically has led to truces and even cross-no-man's-land visits between warring factions. The history here is contrary. In Islamic countries Ramadan has been marked by attacks, broken truces and surges of violence. We expect more of the same in Iraq over the next month despite the voices of the Iraqi government and coalition forces calling for a slowdown and reduction of violence.

Ramadan celebrates Archangel Gabriel's recitation of the Koran to Muhammad in 610 as well as the birth and death of several of the 12 Imams who followed Muhammad. During this lunar month (28 days) Muslims are required to fast during the daylight hours including no fluids, and no smoking. They feast every night after dark and stay up late celebrating. So, throughout this month they become ever more bedraggled and crankier during the day. It is a terribly unproductive month. It is hard to imagine nations in this region ever becoming globally competitive when they yield 1/13th of the work year right off the bat.

Anyhow, we are all notified here violence will probably get worse in the short term (as it has during Ramadan each of the previous three years). Then things start to improve and calm down in the cooler months (as it has each of the previous three years because the Iraqis sense 50 degree days and 40 degree nights as frigid and they don't go out).

This week I had General McKiernan, the senior US military official in Europe. He came to visit soldiers and units traditionally under his command in Europe but now deployed in Iraq. We hopped to Ramadi where the General and his top advisers went into the increasingly pacified city (the medic and I sat on our tails, left behind at the base, pleasing Robyn). In the past month we have seen a major change in trip planning – we now kind of expect to take military leaders and even some civilian leaders into the combat zones. This is a huge shift from the "never take them off the base (except helicopter movements)" planning that has ruled since last November. The understanding we have is that the senior leaders of this theater believe it is important to show everyone that things are improving on the streets and that it is generally safe to move around Baghdad. It's powerful statement of progress.

Well, I understand and concur, but it doesn't control for random. If you put enough dignitaries on the streets for enough hours sooner or later one of them will run into an IED and that will be a major PR coup for the bad guys. We do what we are told and look out for the package and each other. 37 more days.

Per last week: challenge coins came into existence in the mid-late 80s, as a way for senior military leaders to provide on the spot, informal recognition short of an official award of a ribbon or medal. At the Col. Trafton level he is authorized a fairly small supply and hands them out most often to our own junior soldiers (he gave me one 18 months ago but I in turn gave it to a young troop). At the higher levels Generals have bags of these things and some throw them around like penny candy. Admiral Giambastani from last week was one of those. Others are very stingy with coins. At the JVB we've all received dozens of coins from our dignitaries. At first it was very cool but after 50 or 60 they start to look like dust-collectors and lose the glitter. I've gotten hundreds of coins (often 8-10 at a time to pass around to all the troops on a mission) and have given nearly all of them away as there is always a cook, a mechanic, a hotel clerk that doesn't get them and deserves a pat on the head. There is a collectors market for these things now and there are thousands available on E-bay. See photo for a few examples.

My youngest, little sister Karen sent me a large box of toys last Christmas. They have mostly self-destructed but a number of balls from her and various sources are still in circulation. These are all Nerf-type balls of different sizes and shapes and they regularly fly around the command post, bonking the unwitting on the head. Once in a while you catch a guy in the face and feel a little bad but sooner or later you get yours right back. Two coffee pots have died over the year but they were both leaking so due for replacement anyway.

At our daily battle update briefing we always have a slide with a joke, cartoon or a comedy clip. Recently this joke-of-the-day has turned into a doctored photograph placing an unlikely soldier into a bizarre situation. See attached photo for one example; this was titled "CPT Denney's leave in Scotland."

Cards and letters from Pop, Jeff Wagaman. Shelly Huey, Betty Beeler. There are probably others still mixed in with the incoming post cards! Magazines and Claritin from Robyn (the last box from home!).

Makasib box from Kirk Johnson (my boss and Rotarian), James Price (Auburn, WA), cousin Susan Durando, Mary Lou McPhail x 2 (Rotarian), Sharon Caplinger (mother of Jess Caplinger, one of my best soldiers), Ellsworth County Cares x 11 (they are connected through hometown boy Doug Brownback, another one of my best soldiers), and Commerce Bank & Trust, Topeka, a whopping 18 extra-large boxes (I don't know exactly what the number is at which something starts to whop but this pile surely does)! As of today 107 boxes for Makasib and at least 1,000 pounds of first aid, health care and hygiene supplies, and toys.

American by birth. Soldier by choice. Volunteer by God!

Roger T. Aeschliman
Major, Armor
Deputy Commander, First Kansas Volunteers

"Greetings All,

"Roger's update this week includes information about the Makasib project. He talks about this quite a bit on the phone with me and he is thankful and humbled by the response to his request for help. It really is amazing the outpouring of support – many, many boxes. You have helped make the end of this deployment much more bearable for him by supporting this project.

"Thanks, Robyn"
**

Howdy everyone, 01 October 2006

Several times this year everything canceled right out from underneath us. Such too this week. There were significant missions scheduled and we looked to be nearly maxed out. Then one by one they all disappeared. We never know beforehand why these lulls occur but afterwards sometimes learn. Once was when Zarqawi got whacked; once when all the senior commanders demanded some relief from visitors so they could fight the war; another time was the seating of the new government ministers. Wonder what this one will turn out to be?

For the nonce, very slow for me and most of the JVB, though as predicted last week, Muslims are killing Muslims more now during their holy Ramadan than prior.

Much of my spare time this week was absorbed by the mission planning and delivery of all your boxes of health, hygiene and first aid supplies, as well as toys and soccer balls, to the town of Makasib (my desk area is tidy again after about a month of piled up boxes).

Charlie Company, one of our Wichita-based units, owns the territory outside of Camp Slayer, including the town of Makasib. I coordinated with Captain Rob Stone to insert our armored utility truck into one of his combat patrols into the town. Here at the JVB we loaded all the boxes Wednesday evening, early Thursday picked up an Army Public Affairs Reporter, then headed to the Royal Palace Complex to meet CPT Stone. Broke fast in yet another wonderful mess hall in yet another impressive palace, then received the patrol briefing and rolled out of the gates into the farmlands south of the Baghdad International Airport.

The convoy was four M-1114 gun trucks (formerly known as Hummers, now heavily armored and armed) and the armored truck (replacing all the old 2 ½ ton trucks that served the army since World War II). We wheeled by the farms and occasionally the .50 caliber machine gunners would throw a soccer ball to the children that magically cluster along the roadways. There must be some kind of ESP linking all these kids as they popped up out of nowhere to line the way ahead of us. The roads ranged from a few decent blacktops down to narrow, rutted, dike-top footpaths and we wove back and forth over an unpredictable route. This area is very calm, mostly poor Sunni farmers and not the site of any sectarian violence. Nevertheless Charlie Company troops discovered roadside bombs over past months, had a few blow up near patrols and encountered random small arms fire. This trip was blissfully uneventful other than kids fighting over soccer balls.

We made it unscathed to Makasib rolling straight into the middle of town, stopping right in front of the clinic. We dismounted just in time to see the local butcher cut the head off a living goat. By the time we were all done the goat was skinned, quartered and hanging on hooks for sale.

As foreshadowed by CPT Stone we were immediately surrounded by children – truly hundreds. They all wanted something: "hey mister. Gimme ..." a pen, rank insignia, a lighter, money, whatever. Tugging at sleeves and trousers. You can't let them swarm you as they will pick your pockets. So smile, smile, tousle hair, pat cheeks and say "La! La!" No, No.

The village headman (not actually a tribal sheik or the official mayor but nevertheless accepted as in charge by the locals) met us at the clinic and we chatted and toured. There are a dozen rooms in the building and half of them are empty. The rest have some hodge-podge of castoff furnishings and nothing else. A male and a female doctor were on hand to receive the boxes. After further discussion we allowed the headman and the doctors to decide what to do with the whole shebang. Their decision? Store everything in the clinic where it would be safe from pilfering. The people would have extra incentive to go to the clinic where they could leave with some item of health or hygiene after a checkup or treatment. The docs would also have toys to give away to their frightened young patients. The headman retains the right to distribute things amongst the populace as he sees fit.

This is a win/win/win outcome for us. Your Kansas soldiers (AND YOU!) got credit for bringing necessary and helpful things they could not otherwise afford, the clinic and the ministry of health get credit for being effective and the headman gets to exercise leadership and largess bolstering his position and maintaining tribal norms.

We talked at length about Topeka and that these gifts were from real people who care, not a governmental program. We tried to explain Rotary but the translator gave up saying that the idea of a large group of people sitting down together to do good works for others without desire for recognition or reward was incomprehensible in this culture. I found that fascinating yet hope he is wrong.

They know we will be back in a few weeks to bring the 62 boxes of medical clinic supplies and equipment collected by Topeka's four Rotary Clubs, spearheaded by my dear friend Maria Wilson. And they are grateful. Yet they also have a sense of doubt about our motives. Why would these people from Topeka and Texas and Washington State (some of whom I don't even know) care about Makasib? In Islam giving to the poor is *required* in order to go to heaven. You MUST do it; it is a fundamental pillar of the faith. So giving is not a choice made selflessly; there is a quid pro quo. This is a cultural difference that must be overcome by them as they seek to develop a civil society rather than the hunker down and avoid pain dictatorship society they have known for 3,000 years.

So far I've received 102 postcards (or envelopes) representing 236 readers. I suspect this experiment has failed as that number barely covers my own Downtown Topeka Rotary Club. Thanks to all who sent one (lots from unmet Texas readers).

Makasib boxes from Rotarians Joe McFarland x 3, Anita Wolgast, and Frank Memmo (and Sandra). 112 boxes for Makasib. That's probably it except for the 62 full of clinic supplies coming from Rotary and the many donors throughout Topeka. Thanks!

American by birth. Soldier by choice. Volunteer by God!

Roger T. Aeschliman
Major, Armor
Deputy Commander, First Kansas Volunteers

Pop, end of September count is 18,630 miles in the air and 999 running.

The Miracle in Makasib resulted in tons of health, hygiene, first aid and durable medical goods delivered to this town of 5,000 near the Baghdad Airport. Kansans, Texans and Washington Staters help equip the town's looted clinic.

My Dear Cathy, 01 OCT 2006

I believe in fair play and because I wrote such a nasty note those months ago I can only apologize for it now and offer my most hearty thanks. I just received the replacement boots as well as the socks and caps. What incredible service! I know you had to try repeatedly to make this happen and I had given up any thought of ever seeing them.

For the record 5.11 has GREAT customer service and will be first on my list of suppliers for boots and gear from now on.

You, personally, ROCK!!! and I order you to share this note with your superiors. Please tell everyone how impressed I am and place me in the "Totally Satisfied" column.

Most gratefully,

MAJ Roger T. Aeschliman
Deputy Commander, 2-137 INF
Baghdad, Iraq

From: Neil Gibson
Date: Wednesday, October 4, 2006 10:51 pm
Subject: Need an Update

Roger,

We have been hearing a lot about 4 to 8 month extensions on Sand Pile tours. What is your read on how that may hit you and your troops? It has to be a bear for morale over there to have the finish line moved so often. How would you like to be the field grade re-up officer over there?

I have been reluctant to send anymore boxes due to your impending DEROS. If that has changed or if there is still time to send one let me know. It sounds as if you have enough stuff for the little guys and I am more worried about field grade officers without a LURP or two in their cargo pocket if the flight gets delayed.

Was glad to hear that some of the commanders over there had the cajones to tell the stateside glory seekers to stay the hell home and quit mucking up the area. When you run for Governor of Kansas you will have a much better appreciation of what that rare bird - a good politician - does to help his constituents. My great uncle, Hodges, was the Kansas governor in about 1914 or so. His older brother called the shots when Hodges was in office and gave Dems a bad name out there then. And so richly deserved.

Our elected officials back here are so polarized that nothing gets done - which actually may not be a bad thing. We don't need any more 7 trillion dollar Medicare additions that you and I will have to pay for. The off year elections don't look good for the conservatives thanks to so many stupid blunders on their parts. On the good side, we are now in the Major League Baseball Divisional playoffs and that is finally uniting the country on one issue - - its hatred of the Yankees. The Twins made the playoffs with a payroll of less than 65 million compared to the 212 million payroll of the Yankees. But this may be the Yankee's year. All eight starting position players have been multiple year all-stars. The best team that money can buy.

All I know about your theatre over there is that the militias are all killing each other and we don't have the manpower or leadership guts to stop it. Does it sound like Korea, Nam or Iraq I to you? Where the hell is George Patton when you need him? I am afraid that the rag heads will do a major bad on us within a couple of years and then, just maybe, we will suck it up and do the job the way it needs to be done.

I am trying to get some of my old Ranger group together in Atlanta after the first of the year. Can't get enough interest to have a full fledged re-union so about 10 of us are going to stay at the airport hotel, lie about our successes, conceal our shortcomings and have a good time for a couple of days. Have tried to reach Colin Powell to see if he wants to come but it sounds like he doesn't appear anywhere unless his speech fee is paid. We will suffer through without him. We all remember in '58 how he used to throw up with anxiety each day before we went into the "Pit" for our hour's daily fist fight. Smart guy and a brother Ranger but not much on getting it on.

Roger, it should be a source of the best kind of personal pride for you to see all the good things that are coming from your personal efforts on behalf of those poor bastards over there. My guess is that, a few years from now, some of those ragged kids you helped will be adults and hold a good memory of the results of your efforts and what America did for them. And who knows where that kind of spirit might lead? I have never even met you and I am proud of you.

Hang tough.

Neil Gibson
**

Dear Neil,

Thanks for the notes and best attempts to send video content. The military is very tight on security and on limited bandwidth for this network. Don't bother trying again. They kill almost everything that is not jpg or doc.

Not much chance of our Kansas National Guard Battalion being extended. Extending Guard units instantly unites all 50 governors against the Sec Def and President as if you do it to one you could then do it to all in the future. Not saying that pressure is the best answer for the USA but it is a reality. Extending the Guard means WAR! both politically and in terms of "this global conflict is the real, true deal."

No more boxes please. You have been so generous and kind to continue your correspondence. Every time brightens my day. It is nice not to have to try to convince you that things are going well over here or to reassure my wife and others that I am reasonably safe (not controlling for random). We are pretty much out of time to get any future mail and I am already getting hollered at because those Makasib boxes and the postcards are still coming in. I am hoarding nine cans of tuna in my ruck so am good for two days of emergency rats!

I have a good friend that says the 1st Amendment to the Constitution is the only one we need and it should be shortened down to "Congress shall make no law." As time passes I agree with him more and more. I would like to see a Constitutional Amendment saying that "No program shall be created and implemented unless approved by majority vote of the people." And "No program shall be created until an old program of equal or greater cost is abolished." I have another friend who is writing a book called "The Next Amendment" and that would be to say that congress shall be prohibited from spending money on anything other than the basic operations of federal government. Good bye to bridges to no where, the Lawrence Welk tourist trap and the enormous subsidies to business, farmers, welfare queens, and everyone else we all pay to not be productive. I think he is a genius. I am ccing him.

Damn Yankees!

This war, like all wars, is a totally new experience. It is such a low intensity environment and is so hard to explain in the absence of people understanding Arab, Islamic, and 10,000 year old culture. I think that it can only be won in two ways: 1- Exactly the way we are doing it, patiently and calmly, accepting these very low casualties over two or three more years in order to create a decent culture and society here thus setting the stage for continuing and eventually winning the global war on terror, or 2 - Do it the tyrannical way, bring over four more divisions, kill everything that moves and level Baghdad block by block, returning them to an agrarian society with our friends the Kurds in the north eventually taking over the whole thing. There is no third option for winning; there are only other options for getting out. People don't read anything anymore. Diplomacy, conciliation and appeasement have never worked and have always led to disaster.

I feel good about my service over here, my outreach to Iraqis at a personal level and my limited ability to influence the 150 Congressional officials who have been here this year. I appreciate YOUR expression of pride in me as the highest badge of honor and I will wear it proudly.

Your friend, rog

"Greetings All,

"The update is a day early since Roger is out on a mission this weekend and I'm off to a conference on Sunday. Enjoy!

"Robyn"
**

Howdy everyone, 08 October 2006

I could tell you about our missions with Senators Warner (Va., of Elizabeth Taylor marriage note – now getting quite long in the tooth but mentally crisp), Sessions, Levin and Pryor (sounds like a law firm doesn't it?), and with Senate Majority Leader Bill Frist and Mel Martinez (Fla.), but they were typical missions with typical meetings and typical problems (late helicopters, rearranged airplanes, schedule changes). Other than just wearing me out yet once more the work was just work. I'll add that there were no dolts among these six and all were pleasant. But I have a lot of orts that are interesting.

There is a giant snake living in the lakes and canals surrounding the JVB. Some of the Iraqis that clean the lakes and the contractors working around here are missing. There is a photo taken from a helicopter that shows a huge, submerged snake-like object. All rumor of course or is it a cover-up? Must be the Republicans again...

I have personally seen a brilliant green and orange, iridescent kingfisher-esque bird streaking by. It is incredibly beautiful. Can't find it on the Internet. Additionally have seen green-footed, white egrets as I jog and had a large bluish heron (probably 5-feet-tall with neck extended) land about ten feet away as I sat watching the sunset. He didn't want to watch with me and flew away on pressing business.

A few ducks are back as the air and water temps cool. So are the dragonflies and the actual flies they dragon upon.

The canals are choked with giant reeds, reaching 20 feet into the air. Iraqi farmers use these to weave corrals, fences, screens, roofing material and even sturdy walls for primitive housing.

The bougainvillea and locust flowered again hither and yon. This rebloom provided both enticing sights and smells in this otherwise beige and odiferous environment.

I have added 5.11 Tactical to my list of good guys. These are the folks I bought my high speed boots from in February that immediately ripped a seam. I wrote to complain and they mailed three times fighting the US postal service to get my replacement boots over here this week. Great customer service.

On the Frist mission it was overcast on the second day and 99 degrees. The windshield of the armored van was speckled with rain drops though I felt none.

I enjoyed a quiet 46th birthday with a few well-wishing e-mails, a few greetings from co-workers, and the anticipation of cookies coming from Mom. Also visited with two classes of freshmen at Shawnee Heights High School (where I was school board president a few years back) via webcam. Great young people. Good questions.

All mail services to us are now cutoff in order to facilitate our replacements' mail. Anything already in the pipeline has a good chance of being delivered. Anything else, especially boxes, will incur the wrath of higher, so please, thanks to everyone for everything, but no more letters, magazines or boxes.

Makasib (Project Roger; Miracle in Iraq) resulted in a total of 112 boxes with 1,500 pounds of supplies (and I know as I lifted every one of them off the back of that truck). Additionally I've received 58 of 62 boxes of specific medical supplies from the four Topeka Rotary Clubs to equip the Makasib clinic and also another smaller clinic operated by our own troops nearby. I put it at another 1,000 pounds. That's a lot of love from you to people you don't even know and a tremendous amount of goodwill earned for your Kansas soldiers. And it will carry over for our replacements, giving them a leg up that we did not have. This project was written up in the Victory Base newsletter and has generated favorable comments from higher levels. Thanks for everything, but as above, no more Makasib boxes please.

Summoned to a hastily called ceremony with six other senior officers of the battalion, we received our end-of-tour medals. I was awarded the Bronze Star for meritorious service (not valor as I have had no opportunity to perform valorously) as did the other officers. Nice to be appreciated and even nicer knowing the ceremony foreshadows departure.

A couple of weeks ago I saw General Casey (the head guy in Iraq) in his tennis gear and I told him his legs were almost as nice as mine. He snarled back: "Aeschliman! You're extended!" So far there's no official paperwork...

Does anyone have a contact in the publishing world or know an agent? This book is nearly written ...

Cards and letters from Pop x 4, Grandma Dorothy, mom's pal Marjorie Hagerman, Anita Wolgast, Admiral Giambastani (thank you note!), and daughter Regan sent me the first leaf of fall, a lovely variegated maple, all reds and greens, now stuck to the homesick wall.

American by birth. Soldier by choice. Volunteer by God!

Roger T. Aeschliman
Major, Armor
Deputy Commander, First Kansas Volunteers

From: Maria Wilson
Date: Saturday, October 7, 2006 10:29 pm
Subject: project update - no need to respond

Roger - I know you are busy so just enjoy this message. I am not expecting a response.

This week I was feeling a little discouraged about all of this. I felt like I was in over my head and didn't know where I was going. I talk about this project as putting good karma out into the universe. I have no idea how or when or where or by whom this will all be used, but it is all being done from the heart - from many hearts. This is more than sending medical supplies. It is giving soldiers a positive distraction. It is giving soldiers one more way to be the hero there. Maybe cleaning a wound will save an arm or a leg. Maybe, in some obscure way, it is saving a soldier's life.

Mike talks about the book, "The Five People You Meet in Heaven," by Mitch Albom. Have you read it? It's about a man who dies and sees the pieces of his life in a very different way. Mike sees this project as one of those pieces of my life that, at this point, no one knows what the impact will be or where or when, but it will have an impact. It's a good analogy. Even though, all along, I've believed in the value of this project, this week had a few rough moments. But here's what's been happening. This project has given my parents something to talk about with their new neighbors. Apparently one of their neighbors is a Rotarian (Judge Miller?) You don't know how much I've worried that my parents were isolating themselves. This has given my mom something to break the ice with. That is a relief for me.

Then I get an email from Gary Lucas, the South club treasurer. A check was sent to our club for the project - $500!!! How cool! I don't know yet from whom. I'll let you know when I know. Then two friends of mine give me checks - another $50. Way cool.

Then today I take 53 boxes to the post office. I thought they were open until 12:30. Nope, only 12:00. I walked in at 5 minutes to 12. I asked for a cart because I had 53 boxes to bring in. The station manager commented that I had to wait until the last minute to get them there - in a not so warm and welcoming, how can I help you, tone. Fortunately for me, I ran into Lisa Stubbs there. She helped me unload the car and get the boxes sorted.

As we are unloading, another woman there is asking what we are doing. She was quite impressed that this was strictly a humanitarian project. Maybe this will prompt her to do something good for someone today.

As I was the last customer, I had all three of the clerks working on this mailing. One of them, James, has a son in Baghdad with the National Guard who is coming home soon. So James was talking about his son. Apparently James has also seen a few of your weekly messages. The three clerks all recognized your name. All three of the clerks know who you are without knowing you. They were commenting on how many boxes they have processed to you!

They were all quite friendly about getting the 53 boxes into the system today, since Monday is a holiday. They were great. As we finished and I was telling them how much I appreciated their good-spirited nature to get this done, they all thanked me. As James unlocked the door so I could leave, he said to me, "Thank you for letting us be a part of this. It was fun."

Holy cow! That blew me away. Roger, to you also... thank you for letting me be a part of this. I'm having fun!

Maria
**

Dear Maria;

How could I NOT respond to this warm and inspiring message? Once again you totally Rock!

The whole "It's a Wonderful Life" motif is greatly appreciated. As time passes and we get a bit older it is good to review and take stock once in a while. If we can look back and say "I made a difference there with him/her" then we are doing what human beings should do. I think from your career and mine so far we can both feel a touch of pride that there are people living healthier, happier lives because we were able to nudge them in some way.

This "web of life" connectedness became clear to me when I left the department of human resources. A young man came up to me after eight years and was kind of teary-eyed and said thanks for putting his life on track. For the life of me I had no clue what I had done. He reminded me that when I began there I had seen him sitting at the switchboard reading a book and I pretty much said "I don't mind you reading. I understand the job is what it is and there are times the phone doesn't ring. But if you have empty time why don't you either A) use it to improve yourself through Internet courses and learning how to use all the Microsoft products, or studying state rules and regs and department laws and processes, or B) tell your supervisor you are bored and want to do more work and volunteer. Over the next eight years he zoomed up the ranks. He said he would have been content reading had not I challenged him without upbraiding him. Another example, same going away reception, a woman grabbed me and just sobbed her gratitude because I had said to screw the rules and let her have a day off from work with pay in order to work on adoption issues for her grandchild. It was a nothing thing but she perceived it as someone caring enough to let her save her family.

So, are you doing incredible work? Yes! Will it make a difference in Topeka, Kansas, USA and Makasib, Iraq? Yes, absolutely. There will be peace here someday and you, Rotary and Topeka will have laid a brick in that wall. Love you my dear friend, rog

Howdy everyone, 15 October 2006

Our replacements are pouring in, curiously peering over our shoulders, listening intently, crowding our mess hall, wide-eyed in shock and awe at the volume of techniques, tactics and procedures they must learn in the next two weeks. Were we so stunned a year ago? I truly can't remember.

They are a fine looking group of Kentucky National Guard Infantrymen and I'm grinning just thinking about it. Their arrival means many things. I am moving today (Sunday) out of my trailer/hooch and back into the villa I occupied briefly last November. The plumbing still stinks there but I do get the King-sized bed. All our meetings and briefings will be jam-packed as everyone tries to absorb everything. The team room looks like a flea market as our soldiers attempt to sell off the televisions, video games, DVDs, stereos, fans and other gear they bought over here but prefer not to ship home. The newcomers will get a good deal if they buy used now rather than new later. I have no dog this fight as I purchased little over here. I'm leaving cleaning supplies, a camp chair, a reading lamp and a few other odds and ends for my replacement.

Training these men is the sine qua non for going home. Until they are certified as ready to assume the mission we cannot leave. So we will teach them to drive heavy armored Hummers and Suburbans, to operate the variety of jammers and force protection equipment in those vehicles, to react to threats, protect the dignitary and especially to navigate all over the Victory Base Complex (where we and all the senior military officials work), the International Zone (where all the Iraqi government leaders live and work), and key bases and camps all over Iraq. We'll try to get their escort officers and medics to Mosul, Tikrit, Fallujah, Ramadi, Al Asad, Taji, Talill, Erbil, Sulaymaniyah, and other key sites. We will teach them the six different places a helicopter can land at Balad (and it better be the right one every time), show them the secret locations where the spooky warriors work and the protocols for getting dignitaries in, and train them to find the coffee pot in every building in Iraq.

Thus we are swamped with our quotidian work and the nearly daily duties required to exit – briefings on legal affairs (you can't ship a jackal or a machine gun home), reunion expectations and suicide prevention; packing, inspecting, repacking and loading footlockers and duffle bags into connexes for the slow boat home; medical updating and record-keeping to validate any Iraq-caused injury, illness or disease (I, for one, have lost some hearing over here; not terribly so but I have continuous ringing caused by nearly daily exposure to helicopter noise and despite religious use of earplugs).

So, not only must we conduct the normal mission (and the operational tempo is pretty high right now), we must train everyone on everything and do all the extra work to leave. 'Twill be a blur.

The week began with Senator Jack Reed (R.I.) who generally opposes the war here but is a reasonable and thoughtful man, and Senate Minority Leader Dick Durbin whom I was prepared to hate but he said so little and was pleasant enough that I couldn't work myself up over him. Uneventful except we went to a little tiny Iraqi Army base on the Tigris near Tikrit where a sniper is working, so edgy. Also, upon arrival there the Iraqi soldiers slit the throat of a sheep and sawed its head off as a greeting of high honor for the Senators. Apparently it's a Ramadan tradition to eat EXTREMELY fresh meat nightly after the day-time fast.

The week ended with our final General Abizaid mission. He's a gentleman, scholar and warrior. He wrote a note to my parents about me, Mom wrote back and he brought her note over here to show me. Abizaid landed Friday the 13th at Tikrit and we were unable to join him there as the whole country was socked in by a terrible, early season storm. The medic and I tried for 36 hours to get to him but we never flew. We finally linked up in Baghdad on mission Day Two and heard how their Friday the 13th had been jinxed with missed flights, broken helicopters and confused meetings. I joked with his top aide saying: "well, that's what happens when the Kansas JVB isn't there." And he nearly came out of his seat in agreement and praise. Perhaps we have done a few things right over the year. I hope General Abizaid will be a candidate for the Joint Chiefs of Staff. He is truly remarkable. And I don't impress easily.

That storm was really something. It was dark and we'd just arrived at the airport when the dust blew in, instantly reducing visibility to zero. The wind jumped to 50 miles per hour. That lasted a few minutes before the rain came down in sheets for five minutes, pouring mud from the sky. Lightening for a half hour then all was well. Portapotties blew over everywhere along with trees. The date palms will be green for a short while now until the dust settles again.

You read how FOB Falcon blew up when a stray mortar round hit the ammo dump. That was six miles from here and was the loudest explosion I've heard in my hooch. It is a credit to Army rules, regulations and leadership enforcement that the ammo holding area was designed, built and maintained correctly to send all that energy up into the sky rather than out into soldier housing and offices.

Throughout this tour I've handed out hundreds of buffalo nickels to Iraqi guards and children. This allowed me to say in terrible Arabic that I am "Ash," then draw a map to show I'm from Kansas where the buffalo roam. I run into Iraqis I don't remember who shout out "Ash!" and then show me their nickel. Maybe a small good thing . . .

Cards and letters from Pop, Grandma Dorothy, and the final, absolute last Makasib box from the wonderful Linquist family. 52 boxes of medical supplies from the Topeka and Holton Rotary Clubs. Don't send anything! I was nearly executed when these arrived.

American by birth. Soldier by choice. Volunteer by God!

Roger T. Aeschliman
Major, Armor
Deputy Commander, First Kansas Volunteers

Greetings to all from Baghdad. 15 Oct 2006

This e-mail is to link everyone regarding the Makasib medical products project and to explain where I think we stand right now.

1 - 112 boxes of health, hygiene and first aid products (as well as toys and candy) from my friends were delivered to Makasib two weeks ago.

2 - 115 boxes of mostly medical products from the Topeka Rotary Clubs are in my office. They will be sorted today (some items pulled out for use in the Royal Palace Complex mini-clinic for civilians) and the vast majority shipped out to Makasib later this week.

3 - There may yet be some small number of small boxes yet to be mailed. Kirk, will you provide Maria with a new mailing address so those boxes can be received in Iraq through the US Postal Service? Your address would maintain the Kansas uniqueness of this project. The Kentucky unit replacing us will be briefed and willing to deliver those boxes when the time comes. If an address is problematic for you for any reason let me know and I'll get an address for the Kentucky unit.

4 - There are some 11 or so pallets of "hospital in a box" medical supplies from the 190th Air Refueling Group in Topeka that are expired shelf life and have been DXed. They are gifted to this project and are ready to ship. This is the magic issue. To my knowledge the following options are being explored:

A - Contractor donation of cash to pay shipping costs. The key contacts for this have left the country. I believe this option is dead.

B - 190th refueling wing flies the pallets to Baghdad. BG Jon Small (in Kansas Assistant Adjutant General) is aware of this idea. I do not know if it has any traction. Sir, any update?

C - MAJ Kirk Pederson (Kansas National Guard, here in Iraq, the POC after I leave), is researching some sort of federally authorized shipping program for humanitarian supplies. Any update Kirk?

D - Maria Wilson, Topeka great human being, is the ramrod for collecting and preparing for shipment. She indicates that Richard Barbuto and Prisco Hernandez (two gentlemen at Ft. Leavenworth - forgive me for not knowing who you are or what you do) are aware of some method for moving products like these. They are asking where should these products come to? I say right into Baghdad International Airport on the military side where they can be unloaded right onto trucks and driven the ten miles right to Makasib by our Kentucky replacements. The signer for this shipment could be Kirk Pederson or a player to be named from Kentucky.

That's what I know. I am humbled and honored that this simple request to stop getting Twinkies in the mail turned into currently two tons and $100,000 of supplies, with the possibility of another five tons and hundreds of thousands of dollars of medical support for this little town.

Please correspond with each other and me as we try to close the loop on these pallets within the next two weeks.

Most Sincerely,

MAJ Roger T. Aeschliman
Chief, Joint Visitors Bureau
(Trust Officer, Commerce Bank & Trust, Topeka/Rotarian)

October 18, 2006

MAJ Aeschliman,
I am considering you as a replacement for LTC Dittamo as the TCTF S3. If you are interested, let me know. Additionally, you should contact LTC Hester, LTC Dittamo, and CSM Haworth to get a sense of what I expect from the S3 and a sense of how I conduct my command.

COL Braden
**

Sir;

I am keenly interested in the possibility of working for you in this capacity. Thank you for considering me.

CSM Haworth, LTC Dittamo, and LTC Hester;

Per the Colonel's suggestion I welcome your comments and advice about this position and COL Braden's command expectations and environment. If you would please e-mail me a phone number where I can reach you between 0800 and 1200 hours Kansas time I would be delighted to call each of you and discuss this opportunity.

Most Sincerely,

MAJ Roger T. Aeschliman
Deputy Commander, 2-137 INF

From: Kevin Longstreet @nationalreview.com
Date: Tuesday, October 17, 2006 5:49 pm
Subject: Classified ad

Dear Sir:

I hope you are well and have arrived safely back home. I wanted you to know that I continued to run your ad at no cost in the pages of National Review and thank you for all of your efforts in defending this country. If at anytime you wanted to run another ad please let me know. It was a pleasure speaking to you a couple of months ago and I do hope that the ad generated some responses and of course, good things.

All the best.

Kevin Longstreet
**

My dear Kevin,

Thank you so very much for your generosity and kindness. I took out the ad as a lark with very low expectations and can say that I was not pleasantly surprised by the response. I did hear from one very nice subscriber - an engineer in Washington State - who wrote just to say hello and to make sure that I got at least one response. National Review readers are wonderful.

I also add that I was incredibly pleasantly surprised by your initial decision to run it twice and now your subsequent continuance. I guess I should have expected it from the greatest magazine ever.

At this time I have a "Year in Iraq" book ready to go from the we're winning the war point of view, two children's books (written over here as a way to keep in touch with my own children - and they are harsh critics ...), a game that will become a classic huge seller at the Chess and Checkers level, and a few other odds and ends. Perhaps someone will yet step up...

We are still in Iraq but are now training our replacements. I will be safely home in Kansas in time for Thanksgiving feasting but probably not in time for the first day of pheasant and quail hunting. We take the good with the bad.

With deepest regards and kinship in the journalism world (formerly newspaper man in Topeka),

MAJ Roger T. Aeschliman Chief, Joint Visitors Bureau and Deputy Commander, 2-137 INF, Kansas Army National Guard
(and in another month, laying down the sword and picking up the plowshare, Trust Officer, Commerce Bank & Trust, Topeka)

October 20, 2006
Hey Babe,

Glad to know delivery was uneventful. Today's paper has several articles about how bad things are right now and 11 more soldiers were killed. While I know that these articles are not entire story it still makes your heart clutch. I'm glad to know once again that you are well. Let's keep it that way for the next few weeks.

I think this last month is almost harder for me than the initial deployment. I can't believe how stressed I've been - back to not sleeping all night, headaches (minor migraine, I think, this week), snappy with the kids, etc.... I know it's silly but for whatever reason I'm more concerned now than before. Maybe it's a case of "we've made it this far...what if something happens now?" And there is probably some angst about having you back home and absorbing you into our schedule. You're going to hate the morning routine and all the driving around in the evening. Honestly, I really think we won't have too many difficulties re-adjusting. Our communication has been really good while you have been gone and you know everything that is going on around here. And frankly, I really am looking forward to some cuddle time. We need a football game on Sunday afternoon, a fire, and the big chair. Can hardly wait.

Regan's orchestra concert is tonight. My mom is driving in and will spend the night. Your folks aren't able to attend after all - Dave's visitation is tonight. Dad called to tell me of the conflict and I told him it was more important for him to go to the visitation; there will be other orchestra concerts. He also told me one of his birthday buddies has died. Don't know which one. Bad week for Dad. I picked a couple of cards for him - one a congrats for the Ottawa thing, and the other a thinking of you card for loss of old friends. Poor guy. I'm sure he's taking this all pretty hard.

I'm sure there's more but I need to get going on the day - have about 7 loads of laundry to get through. Eck.

Love you.
Robyn
XXXOOO

"Greetings All,

"About one more week left in Baghdad then a week or two of travel and "debriefing" state-wide. Getting closer. Yeah! We get another new vocabulary word in this week's update. Be sure to look it up. ☺

"Robyn"
**

Howdy everyone, 22 October 2006

Another week and we'll be leaving Iraq.

My own replacement is here. We've spent two days on mission together. He'll do fine.

About 20 of our men are home. All were medics called to duty from across the USA out of the Individual Ready Reserve. Most left the active army with the intention of transitioning to civilian life but were notified to report. They did a great job and because they were called up before us we are glad to see them head home early.

Most of our visitors zip in for two days and zip out. They get back to the USA and spout off about Iraq. These Congressmen, news reporters and talking heads do a great disservice to our country when they speak from such a limited background. How long does it really take to learn the conditions here? The splits in the population? The dramatic cultural differences? The dynamics of war fighting on such a limited scale? What Iraqis think about us? The region's tyrants? The tens of thousands of small successes? The dramatic year-long improvement over here in everything (except the senseless vengeance-driven violence)? How long to see things pellucidly?

Our soldiers here have a full year on the gates with daily Iraqi civilian contact. Their view of Iraq is yet a narrow one reflecting the neighborhood outside their "window." They know only a tiny fragment of what I have learned from trips, tours, briefings and discussions all over the country. I've heard Presidents talk to Presidents and Prime Ministers talk to Prime Ministers. I've listened to Sunnis complaining about Shia, Shia complaining about Sunnis, and the Kurds complaining about both in Kirkuk. Everyone has a different perspective of this place – some broad, some narrow. I can only assure you that spending two jet-lagged days here is just long enough for the unique Iraq allergens to kick in, to smell the sewage and have lunch with some soldiers. I think someone arriving well-read, historically and geographically informed, and open-minded could begin to get at the vastness of this country and her issues in 100 days of meetings and site visits.

So, when these opinionated pinheads attempt to tell you how to think remember that my guys in the towers know more than they do. Everyone is entitled to an opinion but trying to speak with authority from a position of ignorance is folly.

We continue to incrementally transition work to our replacements. Now we are in the "left-seat ride" where we "drive" while they sit in the "passenger" seat watching what we do. By the time I write next week we will be finishing the "right-seat ride" where they "drive" and we sit in the passenger seat monitoring, coaching and critiquing. Left-seat/right seat applies to all our work: guards, escorts, limo drivers, mission planners, truck mechanics and mess hall staff. It includes our hotel and maintenance team as well and I am as proud of those guys as anyone. Our folks are leaving this "hotel" palace in much better shape than we received it. Brent Long is a civilian general contractor from the Wichita area and as our "super" over here he has done more than anyone to keep the electricity on, the water flowing and the sewers clear. The place looks and smells better and is much safer in terms of electricity and tripping hazards. When we arrived power went out every day. Now we it's stable and backed up with a big generator that actually generates when needed. The place is well-lit with decorative lamps Sergeant Long installed, sidewalks instead of mud, the drainage is improved and the small grass plot and rose bushes are thriving. Our motor pool is much tidier with a place for every vehicle and every vehicle in its place, and two lovely maintenance tents replacing a haphazard Hajji tarp. The Kentucky boys are far ahead of the game.

Related: my much broken and highly sensitive nose smelled foulness this morning where t'was never foul before. I followed my nose right to a cracked sewage pipe. Repairs are underway.

Early this week at the US Ambassador's residence one of the gardeners was tending a flowering bush I recognized from Kansas. He was mighty proud, called it a "Moonflower," and pointed out the large tubes that blossom at night and furl in the daylight. I laughed out loud recognizing it as the jimson (locoweed) that I ruthlessly exterminated from Bob and Betty Beeler's soybean fields and pastures as a youth. I guess the difference between a weed and a flower is at least partly what will grow and what will not (and partly what will kill the cows if they eat it).

Had missions – blah, blah, blah. A general here, a general there. No runs, no hits, no errors: a perfect game.

We initiate many of our protocol type "partners" and those who make our work easier into "The Royal Order of the Flaming Hoop," typically naming them a "most Noble Coachman," or "Squire of the Realm." We give them a nice color certificate and tell them goodbye after a year of teamwork.

Made another great (IED-less, unsnipered) delivery to Makasib handing over 115 boxes of medical supplies from the wonderful Topeka (and Holton) Rotary Clubs. Thanks gang! The Medical Miracle in Makasib is mission complete for me, with follow-on work to be done by another great Kansas unit, the 130th Field Artillery Brigade Headquarters.

Pastor buddy Jim Congdon reported he could not see the snake in the photo. Now granted, while he is a little slow like that, the rest of you understand it is just a Baghdad urban legend. Stop looking.

Got a nice note from Kandy Reed, Minneapolis, Kansas, where my children clambered over the accretions of "Rock City" as tots a few years back.

Congrats to Eldon "Ash" Aeschliman (Pop!) on his induction into the Ottawa University Athletic Hall of Fame Saturday. Go Braves! Sympathy to my parents and their dear friend Joyce Phillippi on the news of the death of Joyce's husband Dave of cancer. A good man and true friend.

American by birth. Soldier by choice. Volunteer by God!

Roger T. Aeschliman
Major, Armor
Deputy Commander, First Kansas Volunteers

27 October 2006

To My Dear Friends, Old and New;

By the time you receive this I should be safely back in the good old, USA, perhaps even back in my very own house in Topeka. I cannot say thank you enough for your support throughout this tour of duty in Iraq, especially for your donation of supplies to the people of Makasib.

I probably can never explain clearly enough the energy of the town when we pulled in and the mobs of children all around us. Your support raised health and medical care standards in this small town dramatically and helped improve relations between your own American soldiers and the people of this area. Further, some of the supplies were separated out for the Army-run civilian medical clinic in the Radwaniya area – the Royal Palace Complex – where some of our soldiers worked for a year with the farmers and rural citizens there to provide them the only medical care they receive. The impact of this giving will ripple and be felt for years to come.

Who knows what the result with be? Perhaps a man who might be leaning toward terrorism for the money to feed his family will instead choose peace. Perhaps a teenager who was ready to shoot up one of our Kansas convoys will just chuck rocks into a canal instead. Perhaps a child who would have died at birth will grow up to be the Prime Minister of a free and democratic Iraq. The web of life is unknowable in this way. We can only pause to consider that our actions now do matter in the future and to be mindful of our own choices.

Thank you again. I am grateful and humbled.

MAJ ROGER T. AESCHLIMAN
Chief Joint Visitors Bureau (and perhaps, as you read this, once again)
Trust Officer, Commerce Bank & Trust, Topeka
Husband
Father
And Your Friend

From: Regnery Web
Sent: Thursday, October 26, 2006 12:26 AM
To: Aeschliman Roger T MAJ MNF-I JVB Deputy Commander
Subject: RE: Greetings from Iraq

Dear Major Aeschliman,

Thank you for contacting us regarding your book idea based upon the material and correspondence in your possession. Our acquisitions committee has reviewed your proposal, and although it doesn't fit into our current book publishing schedule, we feel that it could be an interesting and intriguing series of articles for Human Events Online, the website of our sister company, Human Events, the national conservative weekly newspaper. If you are interested in pursuing this possibility, please write to editor@humaneventsonline.com and mention that you were referred by me.

We greatly appreciate your thinking of Regnery Publishing and wish you every success with your proposal.

Sincerely,
Karen Woodard
Acquisitions Editor
Regnery Publishing, Inc
**

From: Aeschliman Roger T MAJ MNF-I JVB Deputy Commander
Sent: Thursday, October 26, 2006 2:37 AM
To: Regnery Web
Subject: RE: Greetings from Iraq

Dear Karen (that's my youngest sister's name)

Thank you for taking the time to review the brief proposal and for your kind response. I know you are swamped with wanna-bees so your time is appreciated.

Most cordially,

Maj Roger T. Aeschliman
Soon to be home in Topeka
**

Dear Major Aeschliman,

It was my pleasure – not only because the proposal, itself, was interesting and deserving of attention, but also because you deserve to be given a good turn by any American who has the opportunity to extend one to you as a gesture of gratitude in whatever way they're able to do so.

Welcome home when you get here, and my best wishes to you and your family as you enjoy a happy and beautiful Thanksgiving together once again.

Sincerely,
Karen Woodard
Acquisitions Editor Regnery Publishing, Inc.

"Greetings All,

"Here is the final weekly update from Baghdad...more next week but from the USA. Yeah!

"Robyn"

Howdy everyone, 29 October 2006

As you read this on Monday or later I am the very last First Kansas Volunteer out on the very last mission, on what appears to be the very last day for us in Iraq. I am writing on Saturday as I will be on mission Sunday and Monday. It's a typical DV visit with a few helicopter flights and meetings at all the places we typically have meetings. I would not be going at all except that my replacement has had limited training opportunities and he deserves the coaching and oversight as he conducts his first mission.

Joint Visitors Bureau-wide everyone else from Kansas is done. The Kentucky guys are doing the missions completely with minor monitoring from us. We have taught them to drive, move, communicate, escort, house, feed and tend to the hygiene and grooming of the dignitaries. All of us are now frantically packing a final time and busy mailing footlockers and boxes home to meet the airline weight limits for hauling gear.

Our replacements are going to be fine. We worry that they are a bit slow, that they are tentative and not high speed. The reality is that neither were we and the Texans worried about us as they left. I did have an important meeting with our higher level brass about our critical partners the Visitors Operations Bureau – the trip planners that send us the work to execute. The VOB turned over six months ago and the quality of the planning and clarity of the agenda diminished. The company commander here – CPT Steve Denney – and I coached and trained, counseled and advised and over time saw no real improvements out of the VOB. We had hoped to bring them around but the bottom-line is that for the last six months our JVB staff sergeants and escort officers have fixed agenda after agenda and prevented problems based on our experience and knowledge here. But our proficiency sets the Kentucky men up for failure so this week CPT Denney and I in separate meetings rectified that by making our concerns clear up the chain. Those who heard us indicated they would force the higher quality work required and thanked us for being honest. It still feels a bit like knifing the VOB in the back as they are all nice people but the mission comes first and if the planning does not improve quickly things will break when we leave.

The most senior Command Sergeant Major in Iraq and the Lt. General in charge of developing the Iraq Police and Military both came by to say thanks for a job well done. They awarded coins to some of our soldiers and said the extra efforts are the ones that really count. They mentioned things like a clean and neatly arranged motor pool, the hand-made power car wash that saves eight man-hours a day, and the physical appearance of our soldiers as they drive and guard.

The CSM also praised the small plot of grass and the roses. While he said it was a nice touch for the hotel and our guests he also pointed out that that kind of luxury in most cases is a waste of energy. He said there were soldiers trying to grow whole lawns in front of command posts when there were still tents sitting in wet low ground and buildings without sandbag protection against mortars. Keeping your priorities straight over here is essential.

Guard soldiers like to make the extra effort, such as the charitable medical work at Makasib. Guard soldiers are doing this kind of thing all over Iraq. Does it make a difference? We wonder ourselves when we see the Iraqi peoples seemingly squandering this wonderful gift of freedom they have been given. They often seem so unappreciative of both the big and small pictures. I think it is an actualization of Maslow's Hierarchy of Needs and as long as they can't feed their families and don't feel safe in their homes the desire and ability to build a better society for the mutual benefit of all remains repressed in favor of getting what they can for family and clan.

Still, the improvement over the past year is remarkable. I see it in little things. When we arrived all soldiers on guard duty here INSIDE the base still wore full battle rattle. Now those interior guards wear caps and carry an unloaded weapon. When we arrived mortars and rockets poured down on bases and camps all over Iraq. They trickle in now, most often failing to explode due to old ammo and poor training. When we arrived IEDs were three, four or five 155 millimeter artillery shells chained together. Now they often include illumination rounds which don't explode (they burn, if they go off at all), or homemade explosives of fertilizer and fuel. When we arrived the US military ran the entire country. Now more than 70% of the Iraq landmass is under direct Iraqi government control and the Iraqi Army or Police run security operations in all those areas. When we arrived the Iraq Army and Police were just standing up. Now they are highly effective in most cases. Schisms remain and corruption exists but there have been mass firings and house-cleaning by the Iraqi government itself. When we arrived we would actually seize a meeting place (including the Prime Minister's and President of Iraq's offices) ensure it was clear, post guards on the doors and then standby all day in full hero gear, sweating. Now the Iraqis don't even want US uniforms around at all. We are barred at the door by Iraqis providing their own security. We often park the gear all day while inside the International Zone and on most Forward Operating Bases. More schools are open, more hospitals are running, more electricity is available, more oil is flowing.

If you believe your news reporters we have failed and nothing good is happening here. This is a great dishonor to us all and to the Iraqi elected officials who risk their lives every day to improve this land. This is not Vietnam but there is one clear parallel: the Islamo-fundamentalist thugs who want to rule the entire world are murdering bastards killing teachers, doctors and elected leaders at all levels. This is exactly what the Viet Cong did 40 years ago and what both communist and fascist insurgents do historically. The people shouldering leadership in Iraq are brave heroes and will be recognized one day as the fathers of their country.

Well enough of that. This week we faced early season thunderstorms and it rained mud. See the photo for proof. I tore down the homesick wall and mailed all the cards and letters home. I cleaned out my desk and downloaded everything off my computer so my replacement could settle in. Otherwise I was mostly lazy, sleeping in, exercising, and daily training of the new Major and his junior officers.

The remontant bloom of a few weeks ago resulted in seed pods on the fragrant locust trees and a massive resurgence of flies to pollinate the bougainvillea. The flies were followed by mosquitoes as the weather has cooled into the 80s during the day and 60s and night. Other than the bugs this is the best time to be here and tourism in the future will surge this time of year.

Three Makasib boxes from First Baptist Church of Winfield, Kan. Those absolutely, final, no more ever, ultimate boxes totals 230 bundles of love for the people of this small, poor town. I'm guessing nearly two tons and several hundred thousand dollars of health and medical supplies. Kirk Pederson, a fine Kansas Major on duty here now, will coordinate the final delivery of any stray boxes that arrive and also the large number pallets of medical supplies still pending shipment from the Topeka and Holton Rotary Clubs. Thanks once again to everyone for your generosity and kindness.

American by birth. Soldier by choice. Volunteer by God!

Roger T. Aeschliman
Major, Armor
Deputy Commander, First Kansas Volunteers

PS - The final count: 20,350 miles flying over Iraq (including this current mission) and 1,090 running (and I gave my shoes away to Masi, the burly and genial Iraqi who calls me "Ash" and pumps the crap out of the latrines twice a day as he only had sandals and winter is coming).

PSS – The next report will be from some Army Post in the USA!

The last hour for my "homesick wall," covered with a year of love and prayers.

Friday, November 3, 2006

"Greetings All,

"I received a phone call in the middle of class this afternoon…it was Roger calling from Maine! He's back in the States. Yeah! I chatted with him for a few minutes – the connection wasn't very good and my students thought I was nuts until hey realized who I was talking to. Then their grins were probably as big as mine.

"We are in the planning stages of a welcome home party. For now, mark your calendars for Friday, November 17.

"On a more somber note, friends of ours from church lost their teenage son to a care accident on Wednesday night. As you say a prayer for Roger's safe return, also say one for Andy, his parents (Greg and Amy) and is younger sister (Kristen). My emotions have been very conflicted this week with celebratory thoughts of Roger coming home, and heartfelt sadness for he McLaren family. May God bless us all.

"Robyn"

"Hey All,

"The update just arrived. Enjoy. Robyn"
**

Hello darling,

Three days and a wake up! Photos of the flag over the JVB just before we left and some of the guys on the plane home. Now what kind of idiot would put that coffee cup on the sleeping head of SPC Adams? Love you, rog

PS – The medical results show me all fine with a statistically real hearing loss but still at the low end of "normal." I guess I won't have any excuses for not listening to you . . .

Greetings from Wisconsin! 04 November 2006

It is refreshingly cold and invigorating here at Camp McCoy - a regional mobilization center for National Guard units. Arriving less than 24 hours ago we've already turned in our individual rifles and pistols and have completed a number of administrative and medical process tasks. Right now it looks like return flight to Topeka and a welcome home ceremony on Thursday, the 9th at the Expocentre. We'll see if that holds.

Backing up now I'll start over by saying my very last mission was canceled due to weather and we simply couldn't fly. The Kentucky Major and I tried for several hours to get a helicopter ride to Balad in order to link up with Congressional Staff members but were grounded. My replacement suggested we call it a night and I explained to him that an agenda is an official order for the Joint Visitors Bureau. We have no authority to cancel an order so we kept on trying for helicopters from three different sources, C-130s from two locations, C-12s from two locations, Sherpa short haul airplanes, and even the US Ambassador's private helicopters. Nothing was flying. Finally the mission planners sent a new agenda (at our request) showing the cancellation. So, my mission was complete about 2200 last Sunday. Subtracting the 140 miles I did not fly, the final totals are still more than 20,000 miles over Iraq, more than 70 missions and nearly 200 mission days. I'm pooped.

Our return efforts began Monday as we were ordered out of the stinky villa and into transient tents so the new JVB could house some lousy general or other. It was a one night stay during which our departure flight changed three times, it poured into the leaky tents during a monster rain squall, and much of my gear got soaked. I finally fell asleep planning on getting up at 0600 for a 0945 bus-loading and was instead tapped awake at 0545 by the First Sergeant telling me I had 15 minutes to pack and get on the bus as the time had changed again. I made it but had to shave later.

We waited around the Baghdad Airport military passenger terminal (fancy name for a concrete slab and a steel canopy) six hours then flew to Kuwait where we hunkered down at the transient Camp Virginia (in slightly better rigid tents but on cots) for 24-hours before staging at Camp Ali Al Saleem for final briefings, customs inspections, baggage check-in and lockdown prior to flying home. After 12 hours locked down there we caught buses to Kuwait City International, boarded a charter wide-body something or other and left the Middle East. There were a few minor cheers upon wheels up leaving Baghdad, and fewer leaving Kuwait, but a positive roar and not a few tears when the pilot announced we had entered American airspace off of Maine.

Stopped enroute at Leipzig (and Leipzig is driving me crazy as I know there was a famous composer or artist born there but I can't remember and have no references right now) and had to deplane for fuel. Escorted into a GI holding pen we were allowed Class Six purchases and I was among the many having a cold German beer. It was a Pils, hinting at sweet but very hoppy. It was a typical small town German beer, not internationally known but wonderful. We also refueled and deplaned at Bangor Maine where I walked out of the airport into the next door hotel lobby to use a toilet that didn't stink and (after washing my hands) drank ice cold tap water! Bangor is a contracted provider of military R&R and deployment services and treated us incredibly well. Similar to Dallas back in March we were greeted by Veterans and other volunteers, given cell phones to use for free and called heroes to cheers and hugs. Maine gets it too.

Our final hop from Bangor to Volk Field, Wisconsin, was just long enough to watch Talladega Nights, a very funny race car movie and moving story of redemption and forgiveness, then we landed in the evening twilight to shake hands with our higher level commander, Colonel Vic Braden and some of his fine team from Topeka there to pave our way. COL Braden took the top five leaders of the First Kansas Volunteers right out the door to dinner at a quaint German restaurant and treated. I repaid him by suffering intestinal problems and spent much of the time in the latrine. I suspect he noticed so this is my official thanks and apology.

Many of our men are twisted up right now. After a year over there, living on a certain diet and atmospherics, to shift so quickly to a more traditional American diet and weather has knocked a number of us off our feed. It will pass quickly (I didn't intend that as a pun but it is pretty funny in sophomoric kind of way).

From the move out of the villa to arrival here I was pretty much awake for 110 hours. Coffee! I had solid six hours sleep last night and will be in bed before 9 p.m. tonight so should be raring to go tomorrow as we continue medical, financial, legal, veterans affairs and mental health briefings. Many of us will get dental, vision and more detailed medical check ups. I really want to get a baseline on my hearing especially.

Leaving Baghdad it was about 80 degrees and wet. Arriving it Kuwait it was nearly 100 and bone dry. The only interesting thing in Kuwait was COL Trafton awarding a number of combat badges to soldiers engaged by or engaging the enemy. As a tanker I can not qualify for the historically significant Combat Infantryman's Badge, but I was awarded the recently created Combat Action Badge for non-grunts. It was for getting shot at in the helicopter some months back and for being too close to a rocket that blew up near General Abizaid almost a year ago. It was a great honor to stand in the same formation with our brave young soldiers as they received their CIBs. Napoleon said it is amazing what a man will do for a bit of colored ribbon. I'm sure it lost something in translation as Napoleon was a good enough leader to know that men don't do it for the ribbon, they do it for the acceptance of their fellow soldiers and a bit of recognition from highers. Most of the men are coming home with four or five medals, ribbons or badges. Some would call that excessive; I say it only scratches the surface of what these men are due.

It is beautiful here and it's great to be home.

American by birth. Soldier by choice. Volunteer by God!

Roger T. Aeschliman
Major, Armor
Deputy Commander, First Kansas Volunteers

"Greetings All,

"Here's this week's installment. Sorry it's so late. Roger finished it about 15 minutes ago – right before he left to pick up the kids at church. I am so happy to turn over some of the cab driver duties to him. :)

"Roger indicates in his update that he wants to do one last letter next week. Probably to report on the drunken happenings at the party Friday night. Seriously, I'm happy to have him do one more as I'm sure many of you are. I've heard from a number of people that they are going to miss these weekly emails. So...until next week.

"Robyn"
**

Howdy from Topeka! 12 November 2006

I'm sitting in my big leather chair, wireless computer in my lap, watching HGTV with my wife and nibbling on Smarties left over from the Aeschliman family Halloween. The children are at church this evening for their normal choir and bells practice. I'll go get them in a couple of hours relieving Robyn of chauffeur duties for the first time in 16 months. A drank a Bud Light this afternoon while watching the Kansas City Chiefs lose ugly to Miami. I drank a better German lager last night while watching the Kansas State University Wildcats squeak by Texas. My family appears to be happy and healthy and I appear to be fitting right back in at home. It is truly wonderful to be here in this typical Kansas fall weather – hot, then cold, then windy, now still and cooling.

Your First Kansas Volunteers finished up processing at Fort McCoy in ordinary fashion. A few soldiers volunteered for extended duty to train deploying troops about Iraq survival skills. A small number left for their homes in other states directly from McCoy rather than returning to Kansas. All in all McCoy was a fine little Army post with a small PX, a nice little library, a good gym and a nifty new club that we were allowed in one time for Monday Night Football as a special morale event. Otherwise it was early to bed and early to rise to complete the medical screening, to turn in the 15-pound, bullet-stopping ceramic plates we all wore all year, and to repack yet once again before shoving bags onto cargo trailers for shipping back to the several Kansas armories.

Bags and gear I believe are yet problematic. I left Kansas with two duffle bags, a ruck sack and a computer bag. At this time I believe I have two bags of gear stored at Fort Sill (or back in Kansas now in some nondescript connex), four bags of gear at sea, and two on the trailer from McCoy. On the bus back I carried a ruck sack, a large briefcase, a computer bag and my JVB all purpose backpack (I can only suppose that every time I left my room the bags had an orgy and reproduced). The accountability of all these things (gear I started with, gear issued in Kansas, gear issued at Fort Sill, gear issued at Fort Irwin, gear issued in Baghdad) is going to be a challenge. Things are going to be missing when soldiers and bags all come back together in January or February and how can you hold a soldier responsible for items out of his control for as long as 14 months? More importantly to me is how quickly I will be allowed to turn most of this stuff back in. There is no room in this abode for a cubic meter of military equipment and clothing.

My hearing checked out with clear losses in both sides, still at the low end of normal, with ringing in both sides that the audiologist said should lessen over time. It seems more dramatic to me but that just may be from heightened awareness that we tankers have drilled into us from the first day of basic training. My reading vision proved degraded and I am expecting two pair of Army issue reading spectacles in the mail any day now.

Fort McCoy is not very big and drifts out into Wisconsin farmland. I went for a jog one lovely afternoon skirting clear of the live fire areas and headed steeply uphill to run along a wooded ridgeline. At the very top, gasping and heaving I heard a scrabbling in the forest and peeked downhill to see the cause of the commotion. Not thirty yards out was a large buck bolting away with a cougar right behind. I don't know exactly what I exclaimed but it was along the lines of "HOLY SHIT!" and it stopped the cougar on a dime. It whipped around to glare at me with bright golden eyes as big as teacups. It stared at me, its tail snaking back and forth like an F-1 tornado. Without thinking I reached down, picked up fallen branches, raised them overhead and began screaming "booga, booga, booga!" while dancing the tarantella. The puma screamed back at me and then was gone. It took me three-quarters of an hour to climb that first three miles. I ran the return downhill three in about two minutes and fifteen seconds hearing paw pads behind me all the way.

We left Fort McCoy about 0230 hours Thursday on nine charter buses. They were new, clean and spacious. Very nearly hit a deer right off the bat then we all just slept until breakfast in Des Moines at the Italian American Friendship Center where we had a 0800 pasta meal (don't ask me why; the Army works in mysterious ways). Drove though beautiful late fall farmland and watched a movie on the overhead screens. The miles and scenery passed quickly. At the Lawrence turnpike rest stop we connected with Post 400 of the Patriot Guard – about 50 motorcycle riders who escorted us the rest of the way. The Topeka Police motorcycle squad (old friends Jeff and Jaime among them) brought us in the last few miles, blocking traffic along the way.

We pulled bags off of the buses at the Topeka Expocentre, formed up a final time and marched in. The place was about half full and roared as the ranks tromped in. It was impossible to see your loved ones in the stands and nearly impossible for them to see us (the uniforms all look alike) but the ceremony was blissfully short with Governor Sebelius, Adjutant General Tod Bunting, and our own Colonel Trafton making very brief remarks. At "DISMISSED" the place roared again and it looked like the fans pouring onto the field to tear down the goalposts. I stood alone invisibly for a while before co-workers Tim Dreiling and Laura Bond and boss Kirk Johnson found me, then Tim wandered off to find my family. He did and I confess to weepy eyes at the sight of Robyn dashing into my arms, then Regan and Ryan, Mom and Pop, brother Rick, sisters Ronna and Karen and niece little Ronna with whom I talked about puppies and bunnies.

Since then I've been to Ryan's performance as Knight No. 3 in "Once Upon A Mattress," been taken shopping for trousers by Robyn, to church this morning and been agonizingly unpacking, unpacking, unpacking.

It is surreal to wear a uniform, carry a weapon and live one paradigm and in a blink to be upended, disarmed and at ease in a totally different world. Guess I'll get used to it.

Well, it's nice to be in a place where a broken down vehicle is not presumed to be a bomb and where a car coming up fast behind you is just teenagers. In my own back yard the viburnams still have ruby red leaves and the burning bushes are still burning. Somewhere across the river is a doe with my name on it that Pop and I will turn into burger and jerky by January.

With your indulgence I'll plan on one more letter next week to wrap it all up.

American by birth. Soldier by choice. Volunteer by God!

Roger T. Aeschliman
Major, Armor
Deputy Commander, First Kansas Volunteers

One of 500 joyous reunions at the Kansas Expocentre in Topeka.

Greetings All,

"Here's the final installment. Sorry it's late. Roger didn't write it until last night. Thank you to each and everyone of you for your support and encouragement over the past year. We couldn't have done it without you. We are slowly settling into a routine here at home and I can't tell you how good it is to have to readjust the routine for Roger. And finally, a reminder that while Roger is home there are many other soldiers serving around the world – please keep them in your prayers so that they may have a home coming as joyful as Roger's.

"God Bless,
"Robyn"
**

Dear friends and friendly readers; 20 November 2006

There are so many important things to say but I don't want to take advantage of you or bore you. I'll try to do neither and begin by saying THANK YOU! Perhaps you wrote or sent an e-mail. Perhaps you sent a goodie box or contributed in some way to the Makasib project. Perhaps you sent a post card to be counted or were one of the hundreds wrapping me in prayer armor and surrounding me with angels every day. Perhaps you are just an anonymous reader many, many forwardings removed who only thinks a little more kindly now about our US military. Regardless, thank you. My life over there was very easy with your support.

Second, just to be clear. I am no hero and I hope I have not painted myself as such. I never raised a weapon in anger or defense. No one ever looked at me with the intention of killing me specifically. The random rounds and projectiles never got too close. I am a very ordinary guy doing what Uncle Sam asked me to do. There are true heroes over there, living and dead. We honor them by not blowing our comparatively small discomforts and inconveniences out of proportion.

Third, we live in the greatest nation in the history of the world. If you have read, if you have studied, if you have discussed and debated, you know this to be true. This is due to the vastness of the American land mass, the tremendous percentage of arable land, the available water and other natural and mineral resources, the growing and vibrant population, the high level of literacy, numeracy and true appreciation for the blessings of education, the inculcation of the European work ethic, the understanding of deferred gratification, the unprecedented level of true individual freedom and liberty, all wrapped in the most amazing Constitutional, representative government ever and surrounded by shared and thriving religious values and lessons. There may be other reasons why the United States of America is great but these reasons are certainly on everyone's top 20 list. There has never been another nation like us before and it is unlikely there will be again.

What we with do with it all is the real question. Are we passing this appreciation on and preparing the coming generations to sustain it or have we already reared a couple generations of hopeless, whining crybabies? Or is it – most likely – both, just like it has always been when the next generation prepares to assume leadership roles in society?

Time in Iraq (or Kosovo, Bosnia, most of Africa, South America, etc., etc.) quickly enlightens one. For those wankers who doubt the magnificence, splendor and glory of this nation and the fundamental decency and goodness of her people please, please, please take a trip to any of these other wonderlands and get grounded again. Our nation is great on a scale unprecedented in history and we must first appreciate and believe that in order to best seek our role and mission in the world now and for the next 100 years.

Fourth, serving in Iraq was an adventure and opportunity I greatly enjoyed in many ways, but one not to be repeated anytime soon. How many get a year-long, all expenses paid, tax-free vacation in the cradle of civilization? Thanks for the chance to see it all.

Fifth, we are engaged by an enemy that wants to extinguish our way of life and to rule the world. They have told us so. We must believe them. I personally think this 30-40 year long war against non-state, Islamist, Wahhabists, terrorists is overdue by 20 years but it probably couldn't truly be fought until the Cold War was won. It will burn hot and cold over 40 years. There are nations we will have to break like Iraq and then other places where a few bombs or covert assassinations will serve. But we cannot ignore it or they will bring it back here once again. I don't care what you think about the reasons given for the war in Iraq or whether you hate George Bush. All that matters right now is that Iraq is the front-line of this 40-year war. The terrorists are converging there to fight the war and I'd rather the fight be there than Topeka, London, or Sydney (or grudgingly even Paris but only because our forefathers already saved Paris twice and I'd hate to have to do it yet a third time). Factions of terrorists fighting other sub-factions of terrorists in Baghdad is much better than nail-bombs going off at the Little League game in Lenexa or the soccer sub-state in Salina.

Sixth, we brought 499 Kansans home alive. Our one soldier killed died on mission doing his job. Our dozen wounded had relatively minor injuries – no amputations, blindness or deafness. We are grateful. And those numbers describe how it is going all over Iraq. Very low casualty levels. While not for one second denigrating the truly devastating loss to the families and friends, this war in Iraq is scarcely a war historically. At Iwo Jima there were more US men killed in two days and more wounded in 30 than in the entire four years in Iraq. In the three years of the Korean War more than 50,000 US men were killed compared to the fewer than 3,000 in Iraq in four. There were 32 MILLION civilians killed in World War II compared to some 50,000 in Iraq. There are unending such examples. Is it worth fighting or not? If not - if our national will has failed us and if our sense of perspective is irreparably lost - then we must get out right now. To stay facing inevitable retreat will only waste lives. Leave now and let the Iraqis pound it out. But if the big war is worth fighting then Iraq is where it's at. Let's grit our teeth and accept that warriors will die. That's what happens in a war.

Seventh, your military is doing far, far more than you know. The national media gives you one percent of the story of Iraq – the bloody one percent. You don't know that US soldiers are training Iraqis how to be mayors and governors, showing them how to build roads, bridges, sewers, water treatments plants, electrical generating stations, helping them open new hospitals and schools and teaching them how to teach something more than only the Koran. You don't hear about the blossoming of a free media, a banking system, a stock market and creation of a civil society where one has never existed, the ordering of courts and a judicial system, the developments in farming and animal husbandry and the redevelopment of lost irrigation skills. Yes, people are fighting and dying. Yes, there is some fraud and corruption, but the nation is alive and Iraqis are just getting on with it. All they need to turn into an open, ordered and productive society is time. Will we give it to them or is our vision so clouded by fear and ignorance that we will yield this battlefield to the dozens of divergent insurgency groups, and Iran, Syria and the Saudi money/terrorist vending machine? I hope we will stick it out because:

Eighth, if we leave too soon, the Iraqis will fall back into the normal Arab/Persian pattern of chewing each other to bits. Given no other motivation the Arab/Muslim/Iraqi will fend first for his nuclear family, then his larger familial group, then tribal clan, then a region or province of similar tribal backgrounds, then and only then the notion of a nation. Muslims have battled amongst themselves for 1,200 years over the Sunni/Shia split and in the absence of any other reason to get along, they won't. I believe that if we leave too soon the Iraqi state will crumble into 40 separate tribal zones with a half dozen major players, variously supported by Iran, Syria, the Saudis, the French, the Russians, etc. We will be left with no choice but to throw in with the Kurds in the north and pray they can avoid war with Turkey and Iran (or even between their own three major sub-groups) AND can keep the oil flowing.

Well, that's a bit longer than normal. Please forgive me.

I'll conclude by saying that it was an honor to serve this great nation and to begin to repay the great debt I owe her for citizenship. With the exception of a few butt-chewing's and adrenaline-rush moments it went quickly. Sitting here now in peace and quiet, with crisp, clean air and drinkable tap water, it hardly seems real. Was I really there at all and gone from here for 16 months or was it as Edgar Allen Poe penned: "Where all that we see or seem is but a dream within a dream?"

Wishing everyone a truly thankful Thanksgiving, a Merry and Joyous Christmas, a Happy New Year and for the last time...

American by birth. Soldier by choice. Volunteer by God!

Roger T. Aeschliman
Major, Armor
Deputy Commander, First Kansas Volunteers

PS – Since returning home 18 miles - twice around Lake Shawnee ☺ zero in the air.

November 21, 2006

Roger and Robyn:

You have no idea of the positive influence your conduct during the deployment has meant to those who have read and digested the weekly updates.

Robyn, your calm and candid thoughts reflect your character and unwavering support for Roger during what was surely a difficult and trying time for you and your children. I am awestruck by your patriotism, moral strength and dedication to the overall American effort. An effort that some in our country do not understand. Please accept my heartfelt THANK YOU for the sacrifices you endured over the last 18 months. Our military cannot do what it does without the kind of home-front support that you have consistently displayed.

Roger, I don't care what you think or say; You are a True American Hero. You have voluntarily dedicated a large portion of your adult life to serving your Country. When the call came, you accepted the mission without question. Isaiah 6:8. Heroes are not limited to those who engage in direct combat. They are the ones who serve, without complaint, to facilitate the successful completion of their mission; be it combat patrols, maintaining vehicles, taking care of supply requirements, and, yes -- even escorting elected officials and others who make the higher level decisions about the conflict. While you may view your mission as mundane and not a "mainstream combat" assignment, it was extremely important to the overall effort in Iraq.

I could go on and on about why I think you and your family are heroes. I won't. Hopefully, you understand that you, and your family, have just completed one of the most important events of your life. You risked everything to serve your Country in a noble effort.

That is the stuff of which Heroes are made. I'm gonna miss your weekly emails, but I am happy the reason for them no longer exists. I am extremely proud of the Aeschliman family. Have a great Thanksgiving and a Joyous Christmas.

God Bless!
Lyn Smith
**

Robyn,

Roger is a hero in my eyes, as is any soldier who serves our country. The letter was truly moving and a confirmation of what a friend of mine who serves in the military told me as well. The media paints a very different picture of things than the soldiers do.

I was glad to see him at the handball blind doubles.

God Bless,

Stephen D. Johnson
Director of Quality Improvement
Licensure & Certification
Kansas Department on Aging
**

Dear Roger and Robyn;

Thank you for the final installment. I cannot tell you how much I looked forward to them. And Roger, THANK YOU for taking the time with this Mom to tell me facts when my son was headed that direction. I truly appreciated it then and now. My prayers will remain with you and with the other men/women who also defend our nation. I will forward this email on to others as I have done before but will also save it as I thought it said so many things that need to me said.

May you and your family have a joyous Thanksgiving together.

God Bless, Mary Alice Avery (Junction City, KS)
**

Roger,

Thanks so much for your service, and for your insightful writings about the situation in Iraq. Reading what you have reported certainly gives one a different perspective and a much better feeling about what the US is doing in that country. I know that your reports have been circulated around the nation, and I hope that the entire population can be exposed to your assessments - just to have some kind of balance and thus a more informed opinion. Will you write a book?

Mike

From: Paul Hughes
Date: Tuesday, November 28, 2006 9:19 am
Subject: Belated Greetings and Thanks

Roger -- I am still digging out from the ISG paperwork following our visit last Sept to Baghdad that you so capably managed. Hope all is well with you and your team. We are very grateful for all you did for the ISG. If there is anything I can do for you, please let me know.

VBR,
Paul Hughes

Paul D. Hughes, Colonel, USA (Retired)
Iraq Senior Program Officer, Peace & Stability Operations
U.S. Institute of Peace
1200 17th Street, N.W.
Washington, DC 20036-3011

The United States Institute of Peace is an independent nonpartisan national institution established and funded by Congress. Our mission is to help prevent, manage, and resolve violent conflicts by empowering others with knowledge, skills, and resources, as well as by our direct involvement in peace building efforts.
**

Dear Paul,

Thanks for the nice note. Glad we were able to help meet your goals. I and the entire team are redeployed and all back home now. It is very interesting now to watch the news and to see the result of the work appearing on TV before our eyes.

Please let me know if I may assist you in any manner and wishing you and yours a merry Christmas and Happy New Year!

rog

"Greetings All,

"It seems strange to sit down and send you an update on Sunday afternoon after weeks of not doing so. Roger and our family have adjusted well to having him back home though I tell people that we are all still fighting over bathrooms in the morning. But...that may be due to the fact that we have two teenagers in the house. Roger has had a hard time this past month with the dreadfully cold temperatures we've experienced. He thinks the house is far too cold but I have the thermostat set at the recommended temps for day and night time use. He wants it set at around 75 night and day. That isn't going to happen....so he bought a pair of really ugly flannel pjs. I figure by next winter he'll be totally adjusted and the summer months will feel quite mild to him. :) I ramble...Roger asked me to forward all of you the attached note about his promotion. So for those of you who have expressed a continued interest in Roger's activities.....

"Robyn"
**

Hello everyone, 13 FEB 2007

I am very sorry to report to you all that the United States' Army made a terrible mistake and promoted me to Lieutenant Colonel. Please be assured that despite this error your US Army is otherwise a sound and efficient military machine of which you can be proud...☺

Many of you will remember that I was selected for promotion in Kansas in early 2005 and asked to be removed from the list in order to go to Iraq with my soldiers. The promotion system did finally catch up and the federal government cut the orders last week so it is official. I have transferred out of the First Kansas Volunteers and am now the planning, training and operations officer (S-3) for the 69th Troop Command Task Force, the Kansas higher headquarters for training and mobilizing up to 3,000 Kansas Army National Guardsmen. It is a great assignment and weighty. It comes with a lot of extra duty and love time but is important work and needs to be done. So, with Robyn's blessing and the support of family and Commerce Bank & Trust we'll just keep getting it on and doing the best we can to support these great American warriors.

If anyone is interested you are welcome to attend my pinning ceremony at 4 p.m. Thursday, February 15, at the Topeka Armory, 27th and Topeka Blvd. It will be a brief (5 minutes and hand-shaking) and unimpressive event so don't feel any pressure to attend. This is just a friendly FYI and thank you for all your previous support, well-wishes and prayers.

Hope this finds you all in great spirits and filled with the joy that comes from knowing we live in the greatest most remarkably free country in the world (and knowing that spring is just around the corner).

MISSION READY! (Our new motto at the 69th TCTF)

LTC Roger T. Aeschliman (that kind of rolls nicely, doesn't it....)

KEYNOTE REMARKS TO 2007 KANSAS MODEL UNITED NATIONS
March 5, 2007
What's Taking So Long In Iraq?

What kind of moron asks such a stupid question?

Never before in all human history has such dramatic and impressive change and reform happened with such blazing speed. Overthrow of a tyrant and defeat of an aggressive state? Creation of a new state with a functioning multi-level government? Creation of an operational military and police structure from nothing? All in the blink of an eye, historically!

Comparing this lightning development in Iraq to historical precedence in the United States of America may prove illustrative.

The American revolt against tyranny began roughly in 1765 over the Stamp Act. It was cold and hot for a decade before boiling over into open warfare April 19, 1775. The combat generally ended at Yorktown in 1781 but it was two more years before the Treaty of Paris ended the war in 1783. Sporadic insurgency and terrorist acts between Tory holdouts and the revolutionaries continued for 20 years with lynching's, house and farm burnings and 100,000 Tories fleeing the new country for Canada and England.

Compare this to the war to end tyranny in Iraq. We first focused on Iraq in January 2002, attacked in March 2003 and ended heavy mechanized war operations in May. The terrorists and anti-government holdouts continue their efforts currently, October 2006.

We could add detail upon detail to these timelines but the broad-brush stroke is clear: USA overthrow of tyranny was nearly 40 years in the final making; Iraq is at four years and counting.

Compare the creation of our national constitutions. In wartime USA the hastily drawn Articles of Confederacy provided limited government from 1777 until their failure was broadly recognized in the mid-1780s. The Constitutional Convention lasted from May-September 1787 resulting in our base document. Delaware was the first state to approve the document in December 1787 and Rhode Island was the last in May 1790. The first ten amendments – the Bill of Rights – were not a part of the initial Constitution. The amendments were not approved by the states until December 1791.

In Iraq the interim government was given authority in June 2004. A transitional assembly was elected in January 2005. The Constitution was drafted between April and September and approved by national referendum in October 2005. The first permanent government was elected in December 2005.

USA constitutional creation took 14 years (or generously, from the end of the war, eight years). The Iraqis did it in 18 months.

The creation of a functioning national governmental system in the United States, from local units to the federal systems, took an incredible length of time. In fact, our first 80 years of national elections were all about defining and refining the type of nation we were going to become. From George Washington's and John Adams' creation of departments of the federal government to Andrew Jackson's declaration of "To the Victor Go the Spoils!" the face and form of our own governmental system evolved and changed. I would argue that the ultimate face of the United States government was not finally set until the conclusion of the Civil War in 1865 when it was decided once and for all that our nation would be a strong central government executed at the state level, rather than independent states loosely guided by the federal government. Ponder that. Our own country fought a civil war about governmental structure 100 years after the first efforts against tyranny. 100 Years!

In Iraq the governmental systems are rapidly falling into place. Towns, cities and provinces are developing working governments today, less than a year after the December national elections. A federal government is in place with two dozen functioning ministries. All these governmental systems are feeling their way and learning about sharing power. The December election was overwhelmingly run by Iraqis all over the country and there is much effective policing and Iraqi Army presence running 70% of the Iraq national landmass today. While the current agonies are sad and the threat of a total Iraqi civil war can be wargamed with a variety of triggers and a number of outcomes, the overall direction of the national government is set. No one can logically suggest that an Iraq civil war of governance will be fought 97 years from now.

Creation of the ultimate governing systems: USA 100 years; Iraq three, to remarkable success, and counting.

In the United States we have an ongoing love/hate relationship with our military. The national debate over a standing Army continued with little result until the Civil War. As that war began the Army numbered only 16,000 men. Until that time the nation relied on the militia to provide manpower. At the onset of World War I the Army numbered fewer than 100,000. It was not until the outbreak of the Second World War that the US Army in peacetime exceeded 200,000 men out of a national population of 138 million. And this nearly 200 years after the first efforts to throw off tyranny.

In Iraq there is a viable military of 200,000 today, armed, trained and in charge of its own battle space. There is an additional police force of 130,000-plus, all in a country of 26 million.

USA: 200 years to exceed 200,000 man standing army. Iraq, two years.

Just how long does it take to completely reform a governmental system? From historical precedent we can logically suggest that it is three generations – perhaps 40 years – the defeated generation, their children who saw it, and the grandchildren who have totally moved on from that "ancient history." Victory in World War II, with unconditional surrender of the enemy, left it to the US and her allies to govern the defeated nations of Germany and Japan. In both cases constitutions created by the USA and other allies were essentially forced onto the populations within a few years of surrender. Although both countries were granted limited autonomy to go with the new constitutions, occupational armies retained true control of both nations for an extended period, perhaps 5-8 years, until the Korean War took center stage of US foreign policy. US military protection, rebuilding and largesse resulted in renewed economies that led to increasing self-governance. Certainly the US remained an informal occupational force in both countries until the late 1970s. Many would argue that we are only now finally calling it a success in Germany (a country that after 60 years is only now standing up to the US in matters of policy), and we still have 41,000 military personnel in Japan at 91 facilities.

40 years? 50 years? 60 years? How long is too long to put into weaning a reborn nation-state? In terms of economic development that benefits the entire world and in terms of ensuring the bloom of liberty and freedom, were not these two fabulous world partners worth the effort? Are four short years in Iraq too much time now?

Throughout Africa and the southern swath of Asia we can see the result of abandoned efforts. Regardless of failures and successes, colonialism proved to be unsustainable in the face of indigenous opposition and nationalist movements. But the premature abandonment of colonies to the rule of tyrants is now seen in the numerous failed states in both regions. Had colonial efforts continued for only another five years, or ten years, might many of these states have turned the corner toward real democracy and true economic liberty? Taking another decade to teach the principles of the rule of law, to inculcate the understanding that rules apply equally to everyone, would have been worth the effort and the human and financial cost. If France, Germany, England, Belgium, the Netherlands and Spain had stayed the course another decade might not many of these terrorism incubators have grown in a different and better direction? Perhaps.

Indeed, in the biggest picture, how long does it take to move from a culture of being individually dominated and controlled in every facet of your daily existence to being a free and independent human being of self-worth, able to make individual decisions about right and wrong, for better or worse? How long?

The Code of Hammurabi, written more than 4,000 years ago in Iraq, is the earliest recorded effort by man to create rules that would apply to all. Before then (and for most of recorded history since) humans have survived under the iron and usually terrible rule of "Power." One powerful person, usually a man, ruled all at his whim. If you were "in" you were going to do just fine. If you were out, you were probably going to be destitute, enslaved or dead.

Even the Greeks and Romans, long praised for their innovations in democracy, had kings, Caesars or dictators. Even in their enlightened states the man in charge had the power to throw down competitors, give away their lands and estates, enslave or kill them. History is often an ugly thing.

This pattern was world-wide, across all cultures. A chief may have had counselors but the bottom-line was absolute power held in the hands of the few over the many.

While there were many wars and conflicts over the millennium they were almost never about liberty or freedom and almost always were about power – those without seeking it from those with or those with inflicting it on those without. No serious challenge to the rule of "power" was seen until the development of Christianity as a revolutionary idea of individual freedom and responsibility. Not until the Magna Charta in 1215 did the higher ranking subordinates of kings first throw off some of the shackles. Not until 1314 at Bannockburn did we see the Scots rise up in a limited sense of freedom based on nationalism (but even they were internecine squabblers based on formal clans). Not until the Reformation in 1517 did religious leaders begin a serious examination of their doctrines leading to an examined faith. Not until the English Civil War in 1642 did the ideas of real democracy begin to root in Western Civilization. This war set into motion the American Revolution, the French Revolution, and all the wars of liberation since. The US Civil War is an example of revolution against what might at least be called "perceived" tyranny.

There have been many revolutions over the past 200 years that simply exchanged one dictator for another. They are not the point.

The point is that after 10,000 years of recorded human history it is only in the last 400 years that the world began to move away from the "power" rule of the one, or the clan, or the tribe; the rule of the "them" over all the rest of "us." Only in the last 400 years have we begun to see the rule of law over the rule of caprice. It is really only in the last 50 years that we have seen true leaps of personal responsibility and liberty over the control of the "power."

I believe that history will record the time from 1700 to 2100 as the Great War for Freedom, of which this current effort against fundamentalist, Wahhabist, Baathist, Muslim, non-state terrorists in Iraq is just another Theater of that War. We are naïve if we think the current combat is somehow individually special. The Great War, that War to End all Wars, is already forgotten and World War II is fading rapidly from human awareness and into remote history.

If this current war is only about 9/11 or Saddam or Osama, then it is only revenge and the strong beating up on the weak. Fortunately I believe this current war is important in the greater sense as a part of man's ongoing struggle for liberty.

Because men and women have fought and died for freedom, especially in the last 400 years, the world has moved systemically away from the mercurial whims of the powerful at the expense of the weak. It is still happening today, hopefully accelerated by the advance of telecommunications. The youth of the world will see life in the USA and will want our lifestyle. They will demand freedom. I believe Iran is the best example of this. That country is boiling now and the children will take it over soon from the mullahs. It was indeed the children who did this once already in the late 1970s, deposing the Shah.

Those who would oppose this global tide will be swept into the ash heap of history as Reagan said. Time is against them.

Finally, our opponent at this time was often in history the most powerful force on the planet – often to great good. The Sumerians, the Assyrians, the Caliphates, the Ottomans. Their early developments in the arts, sciences and reason were incredible. But something happened 1,200 to 1,400 years ago and despite their military reach their culture froze in time. They have never had a renaissance or a reformation. They live an unexamined faith, an unquestioned faith, an obedient faith. Islam needs a reformation and reconciliation.

It took nearly 1,000 years for Western Civilization to adapt and shape into its present form, to move from being individually controlled to becoming prepared for individual liberty, democracy and free enterprise. In Iraq that adaptation and shaping has been underway now for three years. We mustn't be short-sighted as we fight now for an extension of these noble principles. They are probably the only things worth fighting for.

And what about that fighting? What about the human cost? Soldiers are dying. People are dying. We are at war, at least on a historically limited scale. Is it worth it?

In a last look at history we see the American toll was about 4,400 deaths in the Revolutionary War and about 200,000 in the Civil War. There were 54,000 in World War I, 290,000 deaths in World War II, about 33,000 in the Korean War, and about 47,000 in the Vietnam War – the war that shaped this current revulsion toward battle losses. Additionally, as an example only, in World War II there were an estimated 50 million civilian deaths, 30 million in China alone.

In Iraq the US death toll is nearing over 3,000 with another 20,000 wounded. Civilian losses are estimated at about 60,000. Every loss is a terrible blow to the families, friends and communities. In modern times these are considered horrific, tragic numbers. But historically, and in terms of the anticipated result, the numbers are small and the cause infinitely just.

By any measurement – including this most terrible one – the progress in Iraq is breathtakingly fast, low cost in human life and is setting new standards for future historians.

So, what's taking so long in Iraq? Nothing. Nothing at all.

Appendix 1

Mike,

I've had so little time to read here in Iraq; that's one thing I really miss. Each month I've read through the following magazines sent by Robyn, Pop and Aunt Nancy (Tennessee):

ARMY
National Guard
LEGION
JOURNEYS
The ROTARIAN
SCOUTING
KANSAS Wildlife and Parks
Readers Digest
American Hunter
ARMOR
National Review
National Geographic
The Bottom Line
Military History
Smithsonian
Country

I read the following books:

The Bitter Woods by John Eisenhower – History, Battle of the Bulge (good! Best Battle of Bulge book I've read)

History of the Arab Peoples by Albert Hourani – scholarly overview of Arab history (Boring and dry; very hard to get through)

The Complete Idiot's Guide to Middle East Conflict by Mitchell G. Bard – exactly what it says. (history lite and easy to read)

7 Dick Francis novels – English mystery writer (highly recommend any of the 50 books he's written - mysteries that revolve around horse racing; he was a jockey long ago).

Goldwyn: A Biography by A. Scott Berg – biography of Samuel Goldwyn, movie maker. (Picked it up for free out of the throwaway bin at the Fort Sill Library. Not a topic I would normally care about but it was a really interesting look at a different slice of history. I sent it home to pop).

A General's Life an Autobiography of Omar Bradley – Pretty good and easy to read. (It was published in 1984 and Bradley was the last survivor of the WWII superstars so he gets the last word in after reading all the other biographies. Not much nice to say about Ike, Patton or Montgomery, but liked Truman and Marshall), sent to me by buddy Mark Harris.

The Night The Bear Ate Goombaw by Patrick McManus – Outdoor humorist (very witty and light reading)

Angels and Demons by Dan Brown (Da Vinci Code) – Really well written thriller also on religious theme. Sure to irritate Catholics everywhere (remember...it's FICTION!)

Finally finished reading Caesar and Christ, the third volume of Will and Arial Durant's 11 volume History Of Civilization (three feet of books and 11,000 pages). It is terribly hard reading (about five-10 pages at a bite is all the brain can handle) but very good stuff.

The Broker by John Grisham, another international thriller by the churn-em-out Grisham.

Amazing But True Sports Stories by Steve Riach – compilation of interesting sports trivia. A gift from someone out there...thanks!

Rebels : The Irish Rising of 1916 by Peter De Rosa – tragic and dramatic account of the hapless Irish revolt in the middle of World War I that set a century of Ireland terrorism into motion. Interesting and sad to read. A gift from Jerry Lonergan (failed Irishman).

12 Louis L'amour books. Greatest western writer ever. Wonderful traditional tales of good versus evil, sacrifice and just getting on with it in the face of adversity.

Seabiscuit – An American Legend by Laura Hillenbrand – Tremendously well written and highly readable history of this depression-era race horse. One of the best things I've read in a long, long time.

The Great Train Robbery by Michael Crichton – fictional account of an actual London gold heist in 1855. Early work of very good thriller writer.

Presidential Wit by Bob Dole – Dole's rating of the presidents from funniest to not at all. Only coincidentally I was reading this when Elizabeth Dole was here.

Deception Point by Dan Brown – earlier work by the Da Vinci Code author. Page-turner techno-thriller.

Prince of Fire by Daniel Silva – spy thriller unique in that Palestinians are the unmitigated bad guys!

Another Fine Myth and Myth Conceptions by Robert Asprin – two fantasy spoofs. Fun!

Living Beyond the Limits by Franklin Graham – Revival meeting in soft cover.

House by Frank Peretti and Ted Dekker – run of the mill horror. Not recommended.

The Mask of Atreus by A.J. Hartley – run of the mill thriller. Slow pace but nice twist at the end.

Undaunted Courage by Stephen Ambrose – bestseller biography of Meriwether Lewis. Remarkable story and details of the legend we all thought we knew. Read this!

Military Commanders, The 100 Greatest Throughout History by Nigel Cawthorne – don't bother with these error riddled, factually flawed, personal opinions of an Anglophone.

Beyond Band of Brothers by MAJ Dick Winters – quick and easy WWII years autobiography of noted 101 Airborne Leader.

Digital Fortress by Dan Brown – His first book. A good thriller and page-turner. I hope he will write more rather than retire on his bazillions earned from The Da Vinci Code.

Cold Service by Robert B. Parker – Another terrific Spenser (detective genre) novel. Wonderful dialogue and characters set in Boston. One of my favorite authors.

The Secret Of Chimneys by Agatha Christie – 80-year-old standard by inventor of the modern mystery. Another favorite author.

1776 by David McCullough – Wonderful and award-winning history of this most trying and dramatic year in the rebellion. Pretty good writing for a true historian.

Napoleon's Glands by Arno Karlen – Older pop non-fiction introduction to Biohistory with a flavor of 70s activism.